I0796409

WAR PLAN TAIWAN

WAR PLAN TAIWAN

OPLAN 5077 AND THE U.S. STRUGGLE FOR THE PACIFIC

ROWAN ALLPORT

NAVAL INSTITUTE PRESS
Annapolis, Maryland

Naval Institute Press
291 Wood Road
Annapolis, MD 21402

ISBN: 978-1-68247-808-0 (hardcover)
ISBN: 978-1-68247-814-1 (eBook)

Library of Congress Cataloging-in-Publication Data is available.

♾ Print editions meet the requirements of ANSI/NISO z39.48-1992 (Permanence of Paper).
Printed in the United States of America.

34 33 32 31 30 29 28 27 26 9 8 7 6 5 4 3 2 1
First printing

All maps created by Chris Robinson

With the exception of an unredacted version of the RAND Corporation report *The 1958 Taiwan Strait Crisis: A Documented History* (1966), which was released to the public without authorization in 2017, all previously classified materials that appear in this book have been formally declassified by the U.S. government.

To my family—both born into and found

CONTENTS

ILLUSTRATIONS

MAPS

PHOTOS

FOREWORD

As Supreme Allied Commander Europe for NATO and Commander of United States European Command from 2009 to 2013, I faced the challenge of addressing some of the central defense and security matters of the time, including in Europe, the Middle East, the Mediterranean, and Central Asia. Today, I am concerned about the potential for war between the United States and the People's Republic of China (PRC) over the fate of the Republic of China (ROC), or Taiwan. It may represent the most pressing threat of military confrontation. In *War Plan Taiwan: OPLAN 5077 and the U.S. Struggle for the Pacific,* Rowan Allport has successfully taken on the task of weaving a narrative covering a century of military planning and conflict; United States–ROC relations; evolving technology, strategy, and doctrine; and the sobering potential reality of near-future great power conflict featuring an attempted invasion of Taiwan by the PRC. This book invites us to consider the central aspects of one of the defining security issues of our era and represents a major contribution to its study.

It is important to note that the operation plan (OPLAN) discussed here is part of a larger set of concerns in the Pacific. In two of my earlier books, I address the potential for great power war in the region. My 2021 novel, *2034: A Novel of the Next World War,* tells the story of the United States and China stumbling into a massive global war that begins in the South China Sea. And my most recent book, the novel *The Restless Wave,* is historical fiction that studies the last great power war in the Pacific, World War II. I have been seized with the challenges of this vast region for much of the decade after relinquishing command of NATO and U.S. European Command in 2013.

Taiwan in particular has long been a feature of U.S. Indo-Pacific strategy. While largely operationally sidelined by the Allies during the World War II advance to Japan, the decision to transfer Formosa, as it was then styled, from the colonial rule of Tokyo to the de facto control of the ROC triggered a chain of events that has inextricably drawn the United States into involvement in the island's fate. With the withdrawal of the ROC's rulers to Taiwan in 1949, the territory represented a last stand of defiance against the communist-controlled mainland. While the population was subjected to the incompetence, brutality, and corruption of Chiang Kai-shek's government, sound developmental policies adopted with U.S. support and the later democratization of the ROC have produced a nation whose importance has grown exponentially. Today, despite U.S. derecognition of the ROC in 1979, Washington and Taipei enjoy relations that reflect both the realpolitik of great power competition and their shared liberal values. Taiwan now is a thriving democracy of 23 million people, with an economy that as a standalone entity is in the top thirty in the world—an impressive accomplishment.

My own experience of high-level planning began with my participation as a junior officer in the drafting of the U.S. Maritime Strategy of the 1980s, and I am pleased to see it featured in this book as one of the sources of lessons for the current era of international relations in the Pacific. One of the strengths of *War Plan Taiwan* is that it successfully identifies historical case studies of planning and—where necessary—execution. Some, including those of the Pacific Campaign of World War II (which I thoroughly explore in *The Restless Wave*), are well known. Others, including Cold War examples, have a far lower profile. In both instances the author draws out their relevance to a potential twenty-first-century Taiwan contingency involving the United States. Importantly, this book does not shy away from instances of miscalculation and failure. This was the central theme of my own *2034*. For some of these mistakes, the United States and its allies have paid a high price. In other instances the possible involvement of nuclear weapons meant that human civilization itself was endangered. Recent conflicts have reminded us of the challenge of ending wars on favorable terms, and the centrality of this puzzle is never more critical than when opponents possess the ability to inflict mutually assured destruction.

Planning is, of course, not a one-way street—our opponents get a vote on how events proceed. As this book outlines, we know what a Chinese attack on Taiwan, aiming to remove the democratically elected government and replace it with direct rule from Beijing, would broadly look like. The author analyzes not only the strategy and capabilities of the People's Liberation Army (PLA) in these areas but also provides an incisive examination of how the United States has sought to address the initially largely theoretical threat from China during the post–Cold War "unipolar moment," which has since transformed into the reality of today. This book also outlines the recent reforms of Taiwan's approach to defense and military strategy in pursuit of sustaining its autonomy.

As discussed in *2034*, I am familiar with the challenge of portraying a convincing hypothetical conflict between the United States and China. The final chapter of *War Plan Taiwan* uses contemporary U.S. planning approaches to provide a compelling account of the trajectory of just such an event. The reality portrayed is stark and compels the reader to ask difficult questions as to what such a conflict would mean for the United States and the wider world.

I urge readers of *War Plan Taiwan* to consider the subject matters addressed in the context of both the fate of the Taiwanese people and the national interest of the United States. Today, the ROC stands as a beacon of liberal governance to those who seek an alternative to the authoritarianism of Beijing and its allies. A central lesson I learned during my service has been that the strength of the United States and other democracies around the world is ultimately rooted in the freedoms their citizens enjoy, including free elections, free press, and free speech. I have visited Taiwan on many occasions and have met with the ROC's leaders. I do not doubt that they would fight to preserve their liberties in even the most trying circumstances. Yet as this book illustrates, the ROC would ultimately be dependent on American-led assistance to have a hope of prevailing. Today, the United States sits at a crossroads in its engagement with the world. Despite these challenging headwinds, it is more vital than ever that we aid free people who are facing off against our greatest rival.

Admiral James Stavridis, USN (Ret.)
Former Supreme Allied Commander of NATO

ACKNOWLEDGMENTS

This book would not have been possible without the support of many people. I would like first and foremost to thank my late parents Christine and Derek Allport, my late grandparents, and my brother Laurie. I am also indebted to my friends Meghann Jones, Rhiannon Sanders, Frances Powrie, Sabrina Huck, and Carl Thomson for their encouragement.

It was a privilege to have the Naval Institute Press agree to publish my book. I am grateful to Senior Acquisitions Editor Padraic (Pat) Carlin for giving me both the opportunity and advice along the way. I also extend my appreciation to the book's expert reviewers for their guidance. Adm. James G. Stavridis, USN (Ret.), graciously agreed to provide the foreword to this book. Credit goes to Chris Robinson for the maps. My thanks to Emily Hegranes of the USNI for her help with the archive photographs, to Matthew Simmons for the cover design, Brennan Knight for the production editing, and to Kevin Brock for the copyediting.

I would also like to thank my colleagues at the Human Security Centre, most notably Dwayne Ryan Menezes and Simon Schofield.

My gratitude additionally goes to the people—there are too many to name—who have made the declassified material, official histories, and other papers relevant to this and similar work accessible to myself and others; without them, projects such as this would be impossible. Finally, I extend my thanks to all those along the way who opened doors for me, especially when they did not have to.

ABBREVIATIONS

A2/AD	anti-access and area denial
AAA	antiaircraft artillery
AARGM-ER	advanced anti-radiation guided missile–extended range
ABM	anti–ballistic missile
ACE	agile combat employment
AEW	airborne early warning
AEW&C	airborne early warning and control
AIM	air-intercept missile
ALCM	air-launched cruise missile
ANZUS	Australia, New Zealand, and United States Security Treaty
AOR	area of responsibility
ARA	Armada de la República Argentina
ASB	Air-Sea Battle
ASBM	antiship ballistic missile
ASM	antiship missile
ASuW	antisurface warfare
ASW	antisubmarine warfare
ATACMS	Army Tactical Missile System
AUKUS	Australia, the United Kingdom, and the United States
BMD	ballistic-missile defense
BPLAN	base plan
C2	command and control
C4ISR	command, control, communications, computers, intelligence, surveillance, and reconnaissance
CA	coordinating authority
CATOBAR	Catapult Assisted Take-Off But Arrested Recovery
CCDR	combatant commander
CCMD	combatant command
CCNAA	Coordination Council for North American Affairs

CCP	Chinese Communist Party *or* CCDR campaign plans
CFC	combined forces command
CIA	Central Intelligence Agency
CIC	combat information center
CIMSEC	Center for International Maritime Security
CINC	commander in chief
CINCPAC	Commander in Chief Pacific Fleet
CIWS	close-in weapon system
CJCS	Chairman of the Joint Chiefs of Staff
CMC	Central Military Commission
CNAS	Center for a New American Security
CNO	Chief of Naval Operations
COFA	Compact of Free Association
CONOPS	concept of operations
CONPLAN	concept plan
CONSOL	consolidated cargo replenishment
CP	contingency planning
CPG	contingency planning guidance
CSBA	Center for Strategic and Budgetary Assessments
CSIS	Center for Strategic and International Studies
CTC	combat theater command
DARPA	Defense Advanced Research Projects Agency
DMO	distributed maritime operations
DNA	Defense Nuclear Agency
DOD	Department of Defense
DPG	defense planning guidance
DPP	Democratic Progressive Party
DPRK	Democratic People's Republic of Korea (North Korea)
DSG	defense strategic guidance
DSR	defense strategy review
EABO	expeditionary advanced-base operations
ECM	electronic countermeasures
EDCA	Enhanced Defense Cooperation Agreement
ELINT	electronic intelligence
FAS	Federation of American Scientists
FEOP	Far East Outline Plan

FAA	Fuerza Aérea Argentina
FRUS	*Foreign Relations of the United States*
GCP	global campaign plan
GDP	gross domestic product
GFMAP	global force management allocation plan
GFMIG	global force management implementation guidance
GLCM	ground-launched cruise missile
GOM	global operating model
ICBM	intercontinental ballistic missile
ICP	integrated contingency plan
IDF	Indigenous Defense Fighter
IISS	International Institute for Strategic Studies
IJA	Imperial Japanese Army
IJN	Imperial Japanese Navy
IRBM	intermediate-range ballistic missile
ISR	intelligence, surveillance, and reconnaissance
ISTAR	intelligence, surveillance, target acquisition, and reconnaissance
JAAC	joint anti–air raid campaign
JAM-GC	joint concept for access and maneuver in the global commons
JASDF	Japan Air Self-Defense Forces
JASSM-ER	joint air-to-surface standoff missile–extended range
JBC	joint blockade campaign
JCS	Joint Chiefs of Staff
JFSC	joint firepower strike campaign
JGSDF	Japan Ground Self-Defense Force
JILC	joint island landing campaign
JLSF	Joint Logistics Support Force
JMSDF	Japan Maritime Self-Defense Force
JOAC	joint operational-access concept
JSCP	joint strategic campaign plan
JSDF	Japan Self-Defense Force
JSPS	Joint Strategic Planning System
JWPC	Joint War Plans Committee
KMT	Kuomintang

KTO	Kuwaiti Theater of Operations
LCAC	landing craft air cushion
LHA	landing helicopter assault
LOCE	littoral operations in a contested environment
LPD	landing platform dock
LRASM	long-range antiship missile
LRSP	Long-Range Shipbuilding Program
LSL	landing ship logistic
LST	landing ship tank
MAAG	Military Assistance Advisory Group
MCM	mine countermeasures
MDO	multidomain operations
MDTF	multidomain task force
MND	Ministry for National Defense
MSC	Military Sealift Command *or* minesweeper coastal
MSG	military strategic guidelines
MTW	major theater war
NDAA	National Defense Authorization Act
NDRF	National Defense Reserve Fleet
NDS	national defense strategy
NMS	national military strategy
NSC	National Security Council
NSM	Naval Strike Missile
NSS	national security strategy
ODC	overall defense concept
ONA	Office of Net Assessment
OOTH	Office of the Historian
OPLAN	operation plan
OTH	over the horizon
PACAF	Pacific Air Forces
PLA	People's Liberation Army
PLAAF	People's Liberation Army Air Force
PLAGF	People's Liberation Army Ground Force
PLAN	People's Liberation Army Navy
PLANAF	People's Liberation Army Navy Air Force
PLANMC	People's Liberation Army Navy Marine Corps

PLARF	People's Liberation Army Rocket Force
PLASSF	People's Liberation Army Strategic Support Force
PRC	People's Republic of China
QDR	quadrennial defence review
PrSM	precision strike missile
RF	Russian Federation
RFA	Royal Fleet Auxiliary
ROC	Republic of China
ROK	Republic of Korea (South Korea)
RRF	Ready Reserve Force
SAC	Strategic Air Command
SAM	surface-to-air missile
SAMDT	Sino-American Mutual Defense Treaty
SEAD	suppression of enemy air defenses
SIGINT	signals intelligence
SIG-T	Senior Integration Group for Taiwan
SIOP	Single Integrated Operational Plan
SLBM	submarine-launched ballistic missile
SLOC	sea lines of communication
SOF	special operations forces
SPF	strategic planning framework
SSBN	nuclear-powered ballistic missile submarine
SSGN	nuclear-powered guided-missile submarine
SSK	conventionally-powered attack submarine
SSN	nuclear-powered attack submarine
STOBAR	short takeoff but arrested recovery
STUFT	ships taken up from trade
S/VTOL	short/vertical takeoff and landing
TECRO	Taipei Economic and Cultural Representative Office
TEL	transporter erector launcher
TLAM	Tomahawk land-attack missile
TPFDD	time-phased force and deployment data
TPFDL	time-phased force and deployment list
TRA	Taiwan Relations Act
UAV	uncrewed aerial vehicle
UCAV	uncrewed combat aerial vehicle

UCP	Unified Command Plan
USCENTCOM	U.S. Central Command
USINDOPACOM	U.S. Indo-Pacific Command
USMC	U.S. Marine Corps
USPACOM	U.S. Pacific Command
USSF	U.S. Space Force
USSR	Union of Soviet Socialist Republics
USSTRATCOM	U.S. Strategic Command
USTRANSCOM	U.S. Transportation Command
USTDC	U.S. Taiwan Defense Command
USV	uncrewed surface vessel
UUV	uncrewed undersea vessel

The Republic of China

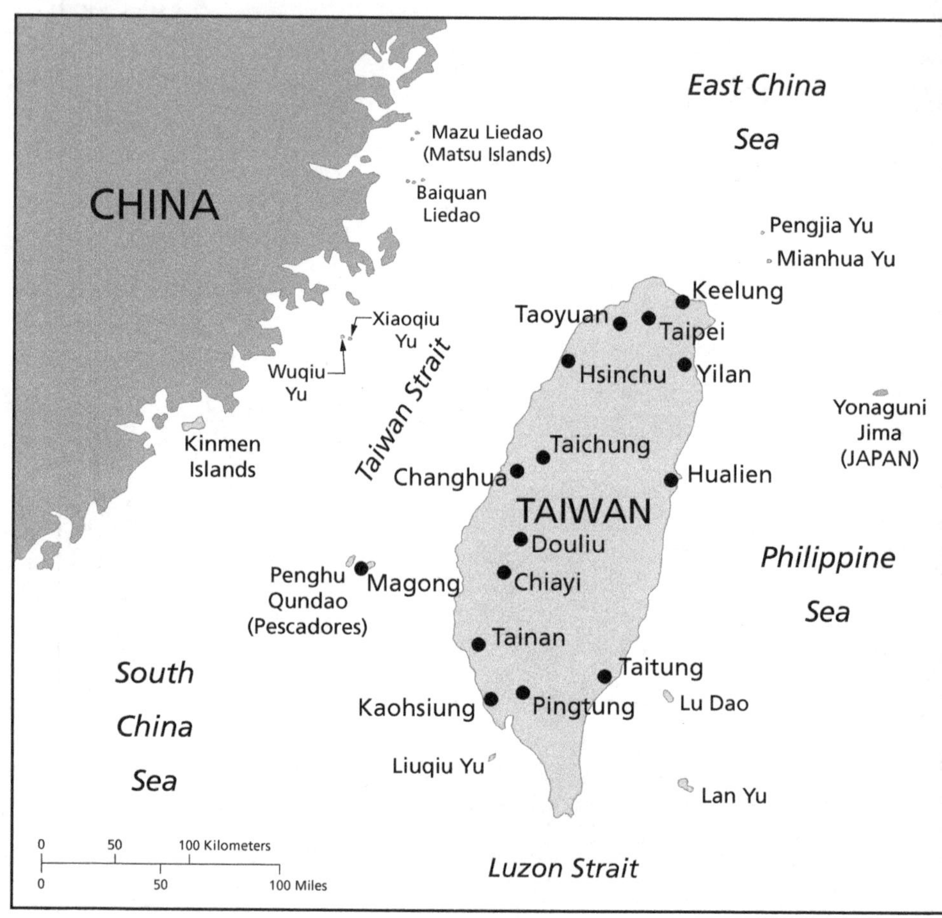

The Western Pacific Region

INTRODUCTION

The standard talking points on the imminent threat China poses to Taiwan and the associated risk of a conflict between the United States and the People's Republic of China (PRC) hardly need reciting. Headlines warning of the PRC preparing to invade the Republic of China (ROC) in the near future have become almost clichés.[1] Even the U.S. Navy's 2024 *Navigation Plan* from the Chief of Naval Operations (CNO) has 2027 set as the deadline to be ready for war.[2] More broadly, the United States has designated China its defense "pacing challenge," stating that "a Taiwan contingency is the pacing scenario."[3] The U.S. government has claimed that the People's Liberation Army (PLA) is developing a capability to invade Taiwan by 2027 but has not asserted that there is an intent by China's leadership to execute such an operation at that point. For its part, Beijing has continued to accelerate its defense-modernization efforts and exert increasing military pressure on the ROC while denying having an invasion timetable.

Since its founding, the United States has prepared for conflicts with a range of state actors. The War Plan Orange model for the Japanese Empire became the standard-bearer contingency after World War I, with many of the lessons derived from the planning process absorbed into the Pacific component of the global Rainbow 5 plan, whose execution ended with the unconditional surrender of Imperial Japan in Tokyo Bay in September 1945. Planning for war with the USSR evolved from envisioning something akin to a World War II–type model to a one-sided atomic emaciation of the communist world, then to mutual destruction, and finally to a more adaptable approach that preserved hope of avoiding global nuclear catastrophe. From the fall of the Berlin Wall to the mid-2010s, contingency planning focused on lesser regional challenges, with the liberation of Kuwait in 1991 being the high point of this model.

The position of China in the U.S. threat matrix has oscillated since the 1949 communist victory in the Chinese Civil War, but until recently it was only secondary at best, being overshadowed by the USSR during the Cold War and the rogue states and terrorism that dominated the international narrative afterward. While wars in Korea (1950–53) and Indochina (1955–75) were transient low points in relations between Washington and Beijing, the continued existence of the ROC has been the most persistent irritant, with the period between President Harry S. Truman's decision to "neutralize" the Taiwan Strait in June 1950 and 2025 exceeding the average human lifespan and approaching double the length of the Cold War. The First and Third Taiwan Strait Crises (1954–55, 1995–96) alone were separated by over forty years.

For its part, the post-1949 ROC has transformed itself from the last bastion of Chiang Kai-shek's corrupt and authoritarian government that once held sway across most of mainland China to an economically advanced liberal democracy. During the early Cold War, the United States was willing to go to war with China to defend Taiwan, with the use of nuclear weapons codified as part of the plan, even if that risked triggering Soviet intervention and a global war. The subsequent U.S. derecognition of the ROC came not out of distaste for the regime but because of the value of a partnership with the PRC in the confrontation with the USSR—dealignment with Taiwan was part of the price Beijing required paid. After the Soviet Union's fall in the late 1980s, Taiwan's democratization and China's rising power and human rights abuses gave new incentives for the United States to support the island.

The geographical separation provided by the Atlantic and Pacific Oceans to the United States from the threats it faces has resulted in a maritime emphasis on its defense engagement with the world. Most major U.S. land and air campaigns from the world wars to the early twenty-first century took place on the Eurasian periphery, frequently requiring American forces to secure supply lines from the homeland and establish themselves in the relevant region. Nazi Germany, Imperial Japan, and the USSR all presented some degree of what is today termed anti-access and area denial (A2/AD) challenge. The former component, "anti-access," is officially defined as "action, activity, or capability, usually long-range, designed to prevent an advancing enemy force from entering an operational area," while the latter, "area denial," is "action, activity, or capability, usually short-range, designed to limit an enemy force's freedom of action within an operational area."[4] Many lesser opponents have paid a price for their inability to prevent the United States from entering the theater of operations. While "A2/AD" as a concept encountered criticism, countering what it describes encapsulates a major part of the central challenges the United States would face in a modern conflict over Taiwan.

Following the Gulf War (1990–91), American analysts anticipated adversaries adopting advanced A2/AD systems to combat the United States. Beijing mirrored this by concluding that the PRC required such a capability from its observations of both Iraq's defeat and the Third Taiwan Strait Crisis, when it had no credible conventional options to counter deployed U.S. forces. In Washington it was also clear to many that the U.S. hegemonic moment of the 1990s and the early twenty-first century would be transient, with China, rapidly developing economically, high on the list of potential future peer competitors.

The United States has long prepared for a conflict with the PRC. From the defense of the ROC's territories, to China's incorporation into a general nuclear war between the United States and the "Sino-Soviet bloc," to downgraded regional contingencies later in the Cold War, the notion of a threat from Beijing never dissipated entirely. Even when the last U.S. forces departed Taiwan after derecognition by Washington in 1979, it appears that some plans remained in place to support the island. More detailed revised plans—initially at least centered upon the regionally focused operation plan (OPLAN) 5077—were reportedly put in place in the twenty-first century's first decade. Since then, contingencies have further evolved as the PRC's military potential has grown, with war plans to counter Beijing now likely led by a globe-spanning integrated contingency plan (ICP).

Literature exists that examines individual components of the above. Ian Easton's *The Chinese Invasion Threat: Taiwan's Defense and American Strategy in Asia* (2017) provides an account of China's war plans and Taiwan's defensive approach. Volumes that provide histories of U.S. relations with the ROC include John W. Garver's *The Sino-American Alliance: Nationalist China and American Cold War Strategy in Asia* (1997) and Nancy Bernkopf Tucker's *Strait Talk: United States–Taiwan Relations and the Crisis with China* (2009). Sam Tangredi's *Anti-Access Warfare: Countering A2/AD Strategies* (2013) gives an overview of the history of A2/AD warfare using select case studies and provides examples of near-future regional contingencies that will require the United States to defeat its opponent's anti-access capabilities, including those of the PLA in East Asia. Other books, as well as reports from think tanks such as the CSBA and the RAND Corporation, explore the potential timing and course of a conflict between the United States, Taiwan, and China. *War Plan Taiwan* builds on these works and develops and integrates the matters they address within the wider context of U.S. war planning to provide the reader with an understanding of how—while of course, we cannot know the detailed plans for a conflict with China—it is possible to identify the nature, hazards, and form of such a war.

This book has four central arguments. First, war planning, both historically and in the current era of great power competition, is both important and perilous. The U.S. record of planning for conflict over the last century has seen common themes, with the identification of threats frequently proving a national strength, while the nature of the contingency plans to counter them falling vulnerable to excessive optimism and failure of imagination. Learning lessons from such historical tendencies can inform planning for conflict with the PRC—including on how to end a war on favorable terms.

Second, the A2/AD challenge that now faces the United States in the context of a conflict with China is more familiar than it may appear. The Pacific War against Japan is the most well-known instance of the United States having to overcome such defenses. But important to study are the plans for wars that did not take place—most notably against the USSR during the Cold War—and those fought by others, with the Falklands War (1982) being the most cogent post–World War II case study.

Third, it is important to have strong allies in the region in which the conflict is taking place. Attempts by the United States to project power and enforce its will have been least successful where allies have been absent, passive, or "Potemkin" in nature. In this context *War Plan Taiwan* will examine the relationship between the United States and the ROC from shortly after the end of World War II to the present day. Washington has swung between times of support and cooperation with Taipei and periods when favoring Beijing was perceived as being politically expedient. Only by fully realizing Taiwan's potential strength can the resilience of American regional interests be optimally supported. If the United States is serious about countering China's malign influence, abandoning the ROC is not a credible policy position.

Fourth, the threat the United States faces from China is more profound than any in living memory. Unlike Nazi Germany, Imperial Japan, and the Soviet Union—each of which fell short as to be comprehensive peer competitors—the PRC increasingly poses a credible challenge to the United States across the spectrum. This should not prompt a counsel of despair: there are measures that can and in many cases are being taken to deter and, if necessary, to combat the threat. Yet it is important not to lose sight of the magnitude of the task at hand or the amount of work still ahead.

Chapter 1 explores U.S. planning between the world wars for a conflict in the Pacific with Imperial Japan, with War Plan Orange and its successors as the primary framing mechanism, alongside an examination of Tokyo's preparations. The evolution of these plans before the outbreak of war and then during the conflict provides a case study into how contingency provisions must evolve to reflect the reality of the situation faced, along with the risks of failing to do so. It also delves into operational concepts and enablers behind Imperial Japan's A2/AD strategy and American countermeasures, including prewar military buildups. Case studies, including those of U.S. Navy fleet air-defense provisions, the bombardment and blockade of Japan, and U.S. logistics in the Pacific, also feature. The chapter concludes with an overview of Operation Causeway, the abandoned plans by the United States to invade Formosa—then the commonly used name for the main island of Taiwan but later falling out of favor—as part of the advance toward Japan.

Chapter 2 then provides a historical account of the situation in Taiwan in the immediate aftermath of its transfer from Imperial Japan's rule to the de facto control of the ROC in 1945. Initially, the island appeared doomed after the 1949 communist victory on the mainland, but events intervened to allow for the shoring up of Formosa's defenses with U.S. support. Areas of focus include the debate in the United States as to Taiwan's fate and Mao Tse-tung's attempts to capture the remaining ROC-controlled islands.

Moving into the early Cold War, chapter 3 examines select U.S. planning efforts, which were initially centered on the USSR but, after the triumph of communist forces in China and the outbreak of the Korean War, expanded to countering what became known as the Sino-Soviet bloc. With Imperial Japan defeated, a limited maritime anti-access challenge, and ownership of forward bases, the U.S. Navy pivoted to a strategy of transoceanic warfare and forward defense. The enablers for this approach came in the form of both advancing conventional technology and nuclear weapons development. The "New Look" strategy pivoted toward a high dependence on the latter in what became retrospectively known as the "First Offset." But the Second Taiwan Strait Crisis (1958) highlighted the folly of such an approach. More broadly, initial U.S. plans to conclude a great power war with the Soviet Union's devastation became unworkable as Moscow developed its own nuclear weapons.

An account of the development of the alliance between the United States and the ROC following the outbreak of the Korean War is provided by chapter 4. Initial U.S. reluctance gave way to close cooperation, culminating in the signing of the Sino-American Mutual Defense Treaty (SAMDT) in December 1954 and the establishment of joint contingency plans for the defense of the ROC, with the United States providing it substantial military aid. The First Taiwan Strait Crisis and the Second Taiwan Strait Crisis saw both sides working together—not always harmoniously—to counter the PRC threat.

Chapter 5 gives an account of how the ultimately unsustainable status quo of the United States recognizing the Taipei government as the legitimate representative of China in its entirety came unstuck under the pressure of realpolitik. While Washington ultimately derecognized the ROC in January 1979, officials put provisions in place to facilitate a limited relationship with the ROC, including through the Taiwan Relations Act (TRA).

The focus of chapter 6 is the evolution of U.S. Cold War strategy away from a near-total reliance on nuclear weapons. The "Flexible Response" approach instigated in the 1960s matured during the 1970s and 1980s through the "Second Offset," which emphasized fielding precision weapons, sensors, and network systems, and doctrinal initiatives such as AirLand Battle to overcome Soviet ground-force numerical superiority. The 1970s was a low point for the U.S. Navy, as the Soviets increasingly fielded A2/AD systems in the air and at sea, but the 1980s Maritime Strategy saw planners present new options, including for war termination on favorable terms as opposed to a nuclear apocalypse.

Chapter 7 presents two major modern case studies of relevance to a Taiwan scenario to illustrate the challenges faced by planners in the modern era. The first is the Falklands War, an example of a conflict with an A2/AD component. The central role of aircraft carriers, nuclear submarines, antiship missiles (ASMs), and merchant shipping, together with the immense logistics required, make it the most relevant modern conflict, despite its limited scale, to the challenges facing the United States today. The second case study is the

U.S. involvement in Southwest Asia from the late 1970s to the present day. The contingency plan for conflict with Iraq evolved from what were widely considered unworkable plans to counter a Soviet incursion into the Persian Gulf region. Nevertheless, while the 1990–91 hostilities provide an outstanding contemporary planning case study, the lessons the war itself provided were limited. It also failed to facilitate sustainable war termination.

Chapter 8 provides an account of U.S.–ROC relations from the end of the Cold War in the late 1980s to the present day. The USSR's collapse, the Tiananmen Square Massacre (1989), and Taiwan's democratization removed significant barriers to the redevelopment of links with Washington. The Third Taiwan Strait Crisis of 1996 helped lead to increased arms sales to and closer official and unofficial links with the ROC and contributed to the redevelopment of U.S. contingency plans to support the defense of the territory.

The PRC's approach to securing control of Taiwan is the focus of chapter 9, along with the potential form of such an operation. The PLA has restructured and reequipped into a force with a major focus on combatting Taiwanese independence and countering attempts at outside intervention. PLA joint campaign plans are designed to blockade, bombard, and invade Taiwan while denying U.S. forces access to the theater and preventing the operations of those already locally based, providing the foundation of a model for conquest.

Chapter 10 examines the ROC's provisions for its own defense. Taipei's advantage in military force quality has eroded at the same time Beijing has moved to modernize its armed forces. This has resulted in an uneven pivot by Taiwan toward an asymmetric strategy to counter China's advantages using nonequivalent capabilities and tactics. Funding cuts and failed attempts to fully professionalize the armed forces have hindered the military's ability to offer sustained resistance to an attack by the PRC. Nevertheless, the ROC Armed Forces are undergoing a period of reform and reequipping in the mid-2020s.

After the fall of the Berlin Wall in 1989, the United States enjoyed a "unipolar moment," the focus of chapter 11. While dominated by wars against rogue states and counterterrorism operations, many U.S. analysts understood that the era of American dominance would not last indefinitely. They identified A2/AD methods as a key challenge, with China resourced and motivated to adopt them. Moves to counter this, with Taiwan's defense in mind, accelerated during the early twenty-first century. Yet this did not prevent ongoing cuts to military capabilities required to counter a peer competitor.

Chapter 12 continues the overview of the evolution of U.S. strategy forward to 2025. The 2010s witnessed a steady shift toward countering major regional and global competitors. AirSea Battle and later initiatives led attempts to counter the A2/AD challenge. The "great power competition" concept shifted into high gear after 2016, along with initiatives to modify war planning and operating concepts and to provide suitable equipment.

The book's final chapter provides an outline of a potential conflict between a U.S.-led coalition and China over Taiwan in 2029. Such speculative analysis of future conflict can provide important insights for the modern world. A notable early example of this is Hector Charles Bywater's *Sea Power in the Pacific: A Study of the American-Japanese Naval Problem,* which was published in 1921. Bywater focused on the tensions and the military balance between Imperial Japan and the United States, with a penultimate chapter outlining the course of a potential conflict. His later novel *The Great Pacific War* (1925) centered on this matter entirely. Similarly, chapter 13 provides a set of plausible assumptions of the nature of the conflict that would be fought, the centers of gravity of the participating parties, a possible U.S. approach, and a study of the question of how the conflict may be terminated once initiated. It then provides an overview of a multiphase campaign.

To be clear, this is not a call for conflict: a war between China and a U.S.-led coalition would be a catastrophe and represent the greatest setback for humanity since World War II. This book will hopefully become as much a historical curiosity as have the Cold War studies of potential conflicts over West Berlin or the Fulda Gap.

PLANNING FOR WAR

This book is not intended to provide a meticulous explanation of the contemporary (mid-2020s) U.S. war-planning process. Those wishing to fully immerse themselves in this can find detailed official material online.[5] Nevertheless, a simplified explanation is helpful for context.

Strategic policy, direction, and guidance for U.S. commanders and planners are chiefly supplied by written documents. Three central examples are the national security strategy (NSS), national defense strategy (NDS), and the national military strategy (NMS). The president's NSS outlines the broad national security priorities of the executive and the approaches to addressing them using all aspects of national power, including that available through the Department of Defense (DOD) and the integrated and unified military capabilities of the United States across all service branches, often referred to as the joint force. The secretary of defense's NDS builds on this by outlining how the DOD intends to implement the NSS through outlining the vital U.S. national interests, defense priorities, threats faced, and the DOD's approach to countering them. The final component of this trilogy is the NMS from the Chairman of the Joint Chiefs of Staff (CJCS), which spells out the national military objectives (ends), the capabilities (means) required, and the resultant necessary military output (ways) to accomplish them.[6]

There is additional written and nonwritten input from relevant individuals as well as departments and agencies. Written material includes the Unified Command Plan (UCP), which codifies the existence of and allocates responsibilities to combatant commands (CCMDs) that hold auspice over specific geographical areas or functions of U.S. military activity, including the mission, planning, and operational tasks of these combatant commander (CCDR)–led organizations. It is at the CCMD level of planning that the classified OPLAN 5077 reportedly once led in the context of a Taiwan contingency. Contingency planning guidance (CPG) provides direction on the creation of campaign and contingency plans. Defense planning guidance (DPG) supplies direction on issues such as force development and prioritization.[7]

Planners also must be aware of the process by which forces are to be allocated to tasks and the forces likely to be available for executing campaign and contingency plans. Information in this sphere is chiefly provided through the Global Force Management Implementation Guidance (GFMIG) and Global Force Management Allocation Plan (GFMAP).[8]

The Joint Strategic Planning System (JSPS) is the formal process by which the CJCS supports the president, secretary of defense, and others in achieving national policy by providing advice and options for the employment of the joint force in partnership with other departments and agencies. This is accomplished by facilitating strategic direction to the armed forces, campaign and contingency planning, global force management, and integration and evaluation, among other tasks.[9]

Global military integration under CJCS auspices rather than a CCDR-led regional focus during competition and crisis—the situation that persisted from the end of the Cold War to the mid-2010s—is critical. The new era of great power competition has necessitated a return to an approach more akin to the globe-spanning Rainbow series of plans of World War II and the worldwide elements of contingencies for conflict with the Soviet Union that could not be confined to one geographical space or to particular domains.[10] The CJCS acts as the "global integrator," whose duties "with respect to planning include developing strategic frameworks, preparing strategic plans, providing for the preparation and review of contingency plans, and advising the SecDef [secretary of defense] on allocation and transfer of forces among geographic and functional CCMDs to address transregional, all domain, and multifunctional threats."[11] Should OPLAN 5077 of the U.S. Indo-Pacific Command (USINDOPACOM) still be in place—war plans are subject to constant evolution beyond the public gaze—it would be a regional contingency component of a global ICP for a Taiwan scenario rather than the entire plan.

Planning itself is split into two broad and interlinked streams. The first is preparing for campaigning, which seeks to identify the ongoing activities required to implement national policy and is embodied in the joint strategic campaign plan (JSCP). In this context it is essential to note that "campaigning" refers to all joint forces activity campaigning across the "competition continuum" to achieve given objectives on a day-to-day basis and continues even without military action.[12] For the major challenges identified by the U.S. national leadership—recently China, Russia, Iran, North Korea, and violent extremist organizations—global campaign plans (GCPs) integrate campaigning activities across the geographical and functional boundaries of CCMDs.[13] The CCDR with the greatest degree of responsibility for the threat in question (for Taiwan, the USINDOPACOM commander) is generally assigned as the coordinating authority (CA) for the GCP by the CJCS.[14] The CCDR campaign plans (CCP) facilitates the day-to-day implementation of strategic guidance in the form of campaign and contingency plans within the CCDR's geographic or functional area of responsibility.[15] Regional campaign plans (RCP) address matters that require coordination across CCMD boundaries, while functional campaign plans (FCP) address nongeographical threats also requiring this coordination.

OPLAN 5077 is an example of a second type of planning: contingency planning (CP). Contingency plans are branch plans from or sequel plans to a campaign plan and are designed to address developments beyond regular operations.[16] The development of OPLANs and other contingency plans can be the result of either deliberate planning or crisis-action planning. Deliberate plans are assembled to support foreseen scenarios considered critical to the United States and require detailed planning, for which a conflict over Taiwan qualifies. Directed by the JSCP and led by the appropriate CCDR—in OPLAN 5077's case, the USINDOPACOM CCDR—these are often referred to as "war plans" and are informed by the perceived intent and capability of a potential opponent, the desired end state, and the resources available.[17]

In contrast, crisis planning is used to deal with an event in progress. Such plans can be either derived from modified existing plans or drafted from scratch using CJCS guidance.[18] Indeed, precrisis plans are rarely the final incarnation of the plan executed if a foreseen contingency occurs—the specifics required in terms of the threat, national policy decisions, and available resources only become apparent as a crisis develops, and predrafted material can provide the basis for more developed plans. Importantly, contingency plans are resource constrained, designed—as Donald Rumsfeld put it when referring to another matter—for "going to war with the army you have, not the army you might want or wish to have at a later time."[19] When activated, contingency plans are subsumed into the relevant campaign plan.[20] ICPs allow for multiple CCMDs to coordinate their activities in response to a threat. As with GCPs, a CA is assigned to lead this effort.[21] They are facilitated by the centrally drafted strategic planning frameworks (SPFs), which serve to facilitate and shape the creation of integrated plans to deal with priority challenges.[22] Instead of a regionally integrated view of contingency planning and crisis response, they require CCDRs to provide a global perspective across multiple geographic and functional domains to allow for a full view of the likely demands on the joint force.

CCDR contingency plans come in four formats with escalating levels of detail: commander's estimates, base plans (BPLANs), concept plans, (CONPLANs), and OPLANs.[23] The last, defined as "a complete and detailed plan containing a full description of the concept of operations, all annexes applicable to the plan, and a time-phased force and deployment list," are the most developed.[24] OPLANs are first and foremost deployment plans. As with all joint plans, they seek to identify how (the ways) to accomplish goals (ends) using military forces (means) with an acceptable level of risk. CCDR planning focuses on supporting the accomplishing of national strategic goals via acting at the operational level, with the latter defined by the DOD as that level at "which campaigns and major operations are planned, conducted, and sustained to achieve strategic objectives within theaters or other operational areas."[25]

OPLANs exist to meet various contingencies. In May 2006 U.S. journalist William Arkin revealed the existence of OPLAN 5077-04 (the last two numbers denoting the year of its approval) in a *Washington Post* blog.[26] His article outlined how the preexisting CONPLAN 5077 was upgraded to an OPLAN in 2001, including with details of forces to be deployed and additional annexes. It was subsequently revised with a new "strategic concept" that was implemented in 2004. The last public acknowledgment of the plan's existence—although it has never been openly confirmed by the DOD as relating to Taiwan—was in December 2017.[27] The pivot to planning with global scope means that it is unclear whether 5077 remains an active contingency plan.

The format of an OPLAN is written to a template.[28] The main body of the plan includes a summary of the situation and a description of the area of operations, as well as a Concept of Operations (CONOPS) that outlines, among other elements, the commander's intent, operational objectives supporting the broader national strategy, the overarching approach to mission accomplishment, key assumptions, major friendly forces and capabilities, lines of effort, the desired end state, and a phased framework indicating the sequence of major actions required to reach it. The main body also provides a summary of matters including enemy and friendly centers of gravity and critical vulnerabilities.[29] Added to this is a long set of annexes providing details, a time-phased force and deployment list (TPFDL), and "transportation feasible" time-phased force and deployment data (TPFDD).[30]

In a hypothetical OPLAN 5077 for a near-future (2029) conflict, which the final chapter of this book describes, the opening pages are likely to resemble the following.[31]

Secret/ORCON
HEADQUARTERS, U.S. INDO-PACIFIC COMMAND
CAMP H. M. SMITH, HI 558-64176
23 September 2029

USINDOPACOM OPLAN 5077-28

(a) Theater Contingency Plan

(b) CJCS Planning order 86797Y August 28

1. *Situation*
   a. *General. See Annex B (Intelligence)*
      (1) This is a Combined Forces Commander (CFC) Operation Plan (OPLAN) for combat operations in the Taiwan (TW) Theater of Operations (TTO). It should be read in the context of the Global Campaign Plan (GCP) for China and if necessary, implemented in concert with the associated material under the relevant Integrated Contingency Plan (ICP).
      (2) *Policy goals.* Maintain ROC as an autonomous political entity with a representative government and sustainable economy; defend U.S. allies and partners; deny the PRC regional hegemony.
   b. *Area of Concern*
      (1) *Joint Operations Area.* This is defined as the entire USINDOPACOM AOR, which extends from the U.S. West Coast to the Pakistan border and encompasses thirty-six nations, including the PRC, JPN (Japan), PHL (Philippines), AUS (Australia), IND (India), IDN (Indonesia), ROC, ROK, the DPRK, NZL (New Zealand), the majority of the Pacific Ocean and Indian Ocean. The wider ICP covers the operating area worldwide.
      (2) *Area of Interest.* The USINDOPACOM's area of interest is worldwide owing to the global reach of the state and substate actors resident in the AOR. This requires extensive coordination between combatant commands, allies and partners, interagency actors, and international agencies.
   c. *Deterrence Options.* Anticipated early warning of major adversary action provides a window of opportunity to telegraph deterrence through increased readiness, deployment of additional forces into the theater, political signaling, and public diplomacy.

d. *Risk*

(1) *Strategic.* The primary strategic risks are the severe degrading of present USINDOPACOM regional influence to the benefit of the PRC and other malign regional actors; major harm to U.S. global economic, political, and security interests; "detaching" of regional treaty allies; and the use of nuclear weapons.

(2) *Military.* The primary military risk is joint force losses that critically undermine the U.S. ability to project power globally and provide for homeland defense; and the severe degrading or loss of regional bases.

e. *Adversary Forces*

(1) *Adversary Centers of Gravity*

(a) *Strategic.* The PRC's strategic center of gravity is Chinese Communist Party (CCP) control of the state, the loyalty of the military (which serves as the CCP's military component and is only the de facto state armed forces), and security service elements that facilitate its continued rule. The legitimacy of CCP rule among the population is important for its long-term sustainability.

(b) *Operational.* The PLA's operational center of gravity is its ability to project power across the Taiwan Strait by air and sea to compel an end to the autonomy currently exercised by the ROC. Also critical is PLA's ability to project power to prevent friendly access and freedom of operations within the Joint Operations Area.

(2) *Adversary Critical Factors*

(a) *Strategic.* The central strategic critical factor is the unity of purpose of CCP leadership, PLA, and the population to sustain hostilities. Maintaining this requires sustained confidence in the likelihood of strategic success and personal survival and prosperity within civilian and military leadership. A critical vulnerability is the erosion of this unity.

(b) *Operational.* Operationally, the central critical capability is the availability of full-spectrum armed forces with high qualitative and quantitative capabilities and with adequate power projection capabilities. Requirements for sustaining this includes the protection of crucial staging areas and forces in transit. A critical vulnerability is the limited resilience of key enablers.

(3) *Adversary Courses of Action*

(a) *General.* The PRC's primary goal in the projected scenario is to take control over the territory currently governed as the ROC.

(b) *Adversary's Political Intentions & End States.* The political goal and desired end state is the irreversible assimilation of the current ROC-controlled territory into the auspice of the CCP with sufficient global legitimacy to allow for the continued development of the PRC's economy and international influence.

(c) *Adversary's Strategic Objectives.* The PRC seeks the termination of ROC autonomy in favor of its control by Beijing, together with the undermining of the U.S.-led system of regional alliances in a manner that allows for PRC regional hegemony.

(d) *Adversary's Operational Objectives.* The PRC seeks to destroy or force the capitulation of the ROC government and armed forces, secure ROC territory, and deter or degrade U.S.-led coalition forces to the extent required for favorable war termination.

(e) *Adversary Concepts of Operations (CONOPS). See Annex B (Intelligence).* Broadly, the PRC seeks to secure air and sea superiority over ROC territory and adjacent areas sufficient to land a ground force by sea and air on the main island to terminate armed resistance to CCP rule. Open-source literature lists several CONOPS, the most relevant of which are as follows. *Joint Firepower Strike Campaign*: Adversary operations are likely to commence with a massive strike utilizing ballistic and cruise missiles, UAVs, conventional aviation, and cyber capabilities against key military and civilian targets, chiefly in ROC-controlled territory. *Joint Blockade Campaign*: The implementation of an air and sea blockade enforced by PLAAF combat aircraft, PLAN ships and submarines, minelaying and electronic measures, and cyber and kinetic attacks. *Joint Island Landing Campaign*: A ground invasion would likely open with air and amphibious landings on the Pescadores Islands and then proceed to the main island at select locations, with the intent to rapidly secure port facilities suitable for use by requisitioned civilian transport vessels as well as securing airfields. Land operations would seek to secure key population centers before pacification efforts and the establishment of a CCP-led administration. *Joint Anti–Air Raid Campaign*: To counter U.S. intervention, offensive strikes would be executed against U.S. air and naval assets and bases in the region, while a joint air defense and antimissile effort would be executed to both secure the Chinese mainland and ensure the completion of the TW operation.

(f) *External Sources of Support.* It is likely that the PRC will be granted airspace access and political and intelligence support from DPRK, and political, intelligence, and economic support from RUS. Political support will also be received from states hostile to the U.S. and select nonaligned states.

(4) *Adversary Logistics and Sustainment.* The PRC has at its disposal a robust military logistics system with a high degree of redundancy and the option for civilian augmentation.

(5) *Other Adversary Forces/Capabilities.* The PRC will likely utilize kinetic and nonkinetic capabilities on a global scale when possible and judged to be beneficial.

(6) *Adversary Reserve Mobilization.* Regular PLA forces will be augmented by reserve and militia forces.

f. *Friendly Forces. See Annex B (Intelligence)*

(1) *Friendly Centers of Gravity*

(a) *Strategic.* Friendly strategic centers of gravity are the policy preferences of the senior leadership, public opinion, the mobilization of its innovation and manufacturing capability, and the network of allies.

(b) *Operational.* Friendly operational centers of gravity include the forces fielded around and transiting to the PRC's periphery for the purposes of interdiction and to suppress and defend against attacking PLA forces.

CCDR-level OPLANs are quite general and are primarily focused on deployments, with many implementation details left to the commands below the regional CCMD. For example, while OPLAN 1003V was the overall U.S.

Central Command (USCENTCOM) plan for the invasion of Iraq, the primary implementation plan was Cobra II, the land component of the invasion developed by Coalition Forces Land Component Command.[32]

Additionally, while CPs are themselves branch plans of campaign plans, they will themselves have branch plans to manage developments that deviate from the primary plan but are nevertheless possible—for example, if a particular OPLAN assumption turns out to be untrue—and sequel plans to manage the follow-up operation required once the OPLAN is completed. An example of the latter is Eclipse II, the land-force command's plan for stabilizing Iraq following the initial 2003 invasion.[33]

CHAPTER 1

FROM ORANGE TO RAINBOW

> The war with Japan had been reenacted in the game room here [at the Naval War College] by so many people in so many different ways that nothing that happened during the war was a surprise—absolutely nothing except the kamikaze tactics toward the end of the war; we had not visualized those.
>
> —*Adm. Chester W. Nimitz, 1960*

The United States became a true Pacific power in the nineteenth century, with the 1867 annexation of Midway Island, the purchase of Alaska from Russia the same year, and the capture of Guam and the Philippines from Spain during the 1898 Spanish-American War. Hawaii was also annexed in 1898, and Wake Island followed in 1899.

Formosa—the common name for the island of Taiwan at the time—was present among these developments. After evaluating it during his 1854–55 expedition to Japan, Commodore Matthew C. Perry believed that the territory—then part of Imperial China—should be brought under U.S. control for use as a coaling station, a concept echoed by U.S. Commissioner to China Peter Parker.[1] This suggestion came to nothing but reflected the imperial drive of the era. In 1895 Formosa became part of the Japanese Empire after being ceded by the fraying Qing dynasty in the aftermath of the First Sino-Japanese War (1894–95).

Despite its expansion in the region, the United States had broader concerns than the Pacific, with the European powers perceived as a significant threat to the Western Hemisphere. These challenges (as well as issues within Latin America) were felt to be real enough to spur the development of a series of color-coded war plans. Most important from a Pacific perspective was War

Plan Orange. This envisaged a conflict with Japan resulting from Tokyo's expansionary goals, which would lead them to attempt to seize control of U.S. territory in the western Pacific. The Joint Army and Navy Board (formed in 1903, a precursor to the JCS, and joined by the subordinate Joint Planning Committee in 1919) acted as the central point of coordination between the two services to assemble the joint plan, with service-specific plans drafted by the General Board for the U.S. Navy and the Army Board for the U.S. Army, which in turn prompted the development of regional plans by local fleet and ground-force commanders.[2] The Naval War College and the Army War College also had significant supporting roles in these efforts.[3]

ORANGE AND BEYOND

In the early years of developing War Plan Orange, serious consideration was given to the wartime deployment of a U.S. fleet to the western Pacific via the Mediterranean Sea or the Cape of Good Hope and the Indian Ocean. But the 1914 opening of the Panama Canal vastly reduced the difficulty of transferring assets to or from the West Coast and Pacific Ocean. With the naval threat from Germany eliminated following Berlin's defeat in World War I, in 1919–22 most of the Atlantic-based elements of the U.S. Navy were relocated to the U.S. Pacific coast to form the Battle Fleet.[4]

At this stage a wartime advance west across the Pacific became the primary focus of the U.S. effort to defend the Philippines and Guam—or at least eventually free them from any future Japanese occupation. This focus shaped multiple strategies over two decades, including the first full edition of War Plan Orange in 1924. A critical development affecting how the transpacific deployment would be accomplished occurred during and immediately after World War I when Japan, as one of the Allies, seized the islands that formed part of German New Guinea in 1914. These territories—the Mariana, Marshall, and Caroline Islands—were formally awarded to Tokyo in 1919 as the South Seas Mandate. These islands sat astride the most viable route of advance from the United States to the western Pacific. The threat they posed was somewhat reduced by the February 1922 Washington Naval Treaty, which, as well as limiting warship construction and possession, forbade the further development of fortifications on territory held by the United States, Japan, or the United Kingdom in the Pacific region, in theory lessoning the challenge the unfortified Mandates could pose. Yet this treaty also prohibited the fortification of the Philippines and Guam until 1937, thus limiting American defensive options.[5]

U.S. strategy debates focused on whether and how to defend the Philippines and Guam. Some envisioned a rapid drive across the Pacific to counter a Japanese attack before it could secure victory. Yet the U.S. Navy did not have overwhelming superiority over the Imperial Japanese Navy (IJN). Until the mid-1930s, Congress resisted building the Navy to its treaty-authorized size, and treaty restrictions negated the notion of preemptively constructing a "great western base." Additionally, the United States correctly deduced that Japan planned to use a strategy of attrition, using smaller units, including cruisers, destroyers, submarines, and aircraft—many of which could operate from the Mandates—to wear down the U.S. Navy as it steamed west, with the aim that the main body of Japan's fleet could defeat the survivors in a climactic battle.[6]

The main point of contention for the United States was whether to advance rapidly across the Mandates, stopping only for refueling, or to move steadily and construct support facilities along the way. Then-recent history warned against the rapid advance: following the outbreak of the Russo-Japanese War (1904–5), the Russian Baltic Fleet was rushed to the Pacific only to arrive in poor condition and be defeated by the IJN at the Battle of Tsushima (May 27–28, 1905). The debate between what Edward S. Miller referred to as "thrusters" and "cautionaries" oscillated over the decades before finally settling on the steady-advance model, with the United States intending to systematically capture key islands and establish basing facilities on them to support the fleet. After the Washington Naval Treaty expired at the end of 1936, officials made a late push to fortify the Philippines and Guam, but support was weak. Yet the steady-advance approach left little hope for the defense of these U.S. territories. Such was the controversy around the exact fate of the Philippines that the Navy decided in 1934 not to propose a detailed course of action beyond securing forward bases in the Mandates (although officially plans simply remained unchanged from earlier plan drafts), with further steps to be decided as the situation dictated.[7] The cautionary model was technically complex and time consuming, but it would exploit the U.S. workforce and industrial-production advantage. But the time issue would cut both ways—on the downside was the risk that the American public would not tolerate a long war.[8]

The natural follow-up issue at this point was how to conclude the war. Initial assumptions of forcing full Japanese capitulation occasionally gave way to thoughts of a more limited war to simply roll back Tokyo's territorial gains. Despite these deliberations, as hostilities approached, most thoughts remained focused on a "blockade and bombardment" of the Japanese home islands leading to a victory.[9]

Formosa was listed as a potential objective on the road to Japan, foreshadowing the debate that was to come during the course of World War II. A 1928 Joint Planning Committee version of Orange foresaw bypassing Japanese-occupied Luzon, conquering the Pescadores Islands—also known as the Penghu Islands—in the Taiwan Strait, and then invading northern Formosa, all as part of an advance north to the Ryukyu Islands, including Okinawa, which was considered central to securing Japan's capitulation.[10] But other Orange drafts looked to bypass both Luzon and Taiwan, the latter owing to the challenges and resources necessary to capture it as well as its limited utility as a naval base.[11]

Around a year prior to the outbreak of war, the final incarnation of Orange before its replacement was divided into three phases:

- Phase I—Japanese advance with likely capture of U.S. possessions, chiefly the Philippines and Guam, as part of a wider effort to establish regional hegemony
- Phase II—The U.S. advances west across the Central Pacific in the face of a Japanese campaign to inflict attrition, building forward bases to support the advance while interdicting Japanese sea lines of communication (SLOC): A decisive battle between the United States and Imperial Japanese Navies would occur during either Phase II or III at a time and place of Japan's choice
- Phase III—U.S. advances north up along a "ladder" of islands to lay siege to Japan and blockade and bombard it into acquiescence[12]

By this point, however, it was clear that the binary Blue-Orange war—in plans, the United States was always the former color—was unlikely to manifest in reality. While the Army War College had undertaken work on a series of plans that involved coalitions of allies and opponents based on real-world developments, these had not yet been translated into official plans.[13] The closest official drafts had come were the Red-Orange plans to fight Britain and Japan simultaneously.

The Rainbow series of plans was initiated to rectify this. Rainbow 5, in its original incarnation, assumed a United States allied with the United Kingdom and France to defeat Germany; the German conquest of mainland Europe before 1941 made the work done on it obsolete.[14] In the Plan Dog memo of November 1940, CNO Adm. H. R. Stark assessed that should the United States become embroiled in a war, only a "Europe First" strategy would make sense. If Japan entered the war, the Pacific should initially be a mostly defensive effort.[15] This approach was approved by the Joint Navy and Army Board in December 1940. After initial approval of the Rainbow 5 concept in May 1941, the plan was developed into Joint Army and Navy Basic War Plan Rainbow No. 5 and signed off in time for the outbreak of the war.[16]

To accomplish its part of Rainbow 5, the U.S. Navy developed Navy Basic War Plan Rainbow No. 5, or WPL-46.[17] The Pacific subplan was U.S. Pacific Fleet Operation Plan Rainbow 5 (Navy Plan O-1 Rainbow 5), or WPPac-46, approved by the CNO on September 9, 1941.[18] This (and its counterparts for other parts of the world) is the closest U.S. document to be found at the opening of World War II to a contemporary U.S. regional OPLAN. WPPac-46 contained details of the theater of operations, command arrangements, an overview of the general assumptions on which the plan was based, likely enemy courses of action, deployment arrangements, a list of key tasks, and the phases of planned operations. It assumed that Japan would be seeking to capture Malaya (along with the Philippines) and Hong Kong as a primary offensive effort, with the capture of Guam and other outlying islands and the disruption of allied SLOC as secondary efforts. Planners also assumed that Tokyo's defensive focus would be on destroying opposition naval forces; holding or denying locations that could be used by the enemy for advanced bases, including through denying U.S. access to the Marshall-Caroline-Mariana area and the use of fixed defenses, aircraft, and light naval forces to inflict attrition on the U.S. Navy in addition to carrying out "raids or stronger attacks" on Wake, Midway, and other islands; and a broader effort to hold national and captured territory.[19] WPL-46 listed the assigned tasks of the U.S. Pacific Fleet as

a. Support the forces of the associated powers in the Far East by diverting enemy strength away from the Malay Barrier through the denial and capture of positions in the Marshalls, and raids on enemy sea communications and positions;
b. Prepare to capture and establish control over the Caroline and Marshall Island[s] area, and to establish an advanced fleet base in Truk;

c. Destroy Axis sea communications by capturing or destroying vessels trading directly or indirectly with the enemy;
d. Support British naval forces in the area south of the equator as far west as longitude 155 east;
e. Defend Samoa in category "D" [may be subject to major attack, but not immediate invasion];
f. Defend Guam in category "F" [destroy facilities of use to enemy, capture expected];
g. Protect the sea communications of the associated powers by escorting, covering, and patrolling as required by circumstances, and by destroying enemy raiding forces;
h. Protect the territory of the associated powers in the Pacific area and prevent the extension of enemy military power into the Western Hemisphere by destroying hostile expeditions and by supporting land and air forces in denying the enemy the use of land positions in that hemisphere;
i. Cover the operations of the naval coastal frontier forces;
j. Establish fleet control zones, defining their limits from time to time as circumstances require;
k. Route shipping of associated powers within the fleet control zones.[20]

WPPac-46's phased model from the opening of hostilities to the establishment of a forward fleet base in the Mandates can be summarized as:

- Phase I—*Initial tasks—Japan not in the war.* These involved preparing for mobilization and operations; transferring Atlantic and South Pacific reinforcements (if ordered); deploying patrol aircraft and tenders to the South Pacific (if ordered); protecting communications and territory of associated powers by light force and air patrol and by the actions of the striking group; establishing defensive submarine patrols at Wake and Midway; using submarines to observe possible raider bases in the Mandates if authorized; establishing and defending subsidiary bases at Midway, Johnson, Samoa, Guam, Wake, and Canton (if authorized); and guarding against surprise attack by Japan.
- Phase IA—*Initial tasks—Japan in the war.* These involved an initial sweep against Japanese shipping in the North Pacific; reconnaissance and raids in force on the Marshall Islands; if possible and advisable,

cruiser raids against Japanese shipping near homeland offshore islands; the use of submarines to interdict shipping near Japanese home islands; escorting shipping between Hawaii and the West Coast; continue the protection of territory and lines of communication of the associated powers; and an order to "prepare to capture and establish control of the Marshall Islands area."

- Phase II and Subsequent Phases—*Succeeding tasks*. These involved capturing and establishing a protected anchorage in the Marshall Islands area, conducting raids on Japanese land objectives and SLOC, and capturing and establishing a fleet base at Truk.[21]

The Marshall Reconnaissance and Raiding Plan would sit at the center of the tentative operation plans designed to facilitate phase IA. It aimed at "diverting Japanese strength away from the MALAY BARRIER through the denial and capture of positions in the MARSHALLS." This operation was intended to begin about five days after Japan attacked.[22]

WPPac-46 noted that the local naval element of the defense of the Philippines would be led by the small and elderly Asiatic Fleet—the surface element of which was led by one heavy cruiser, one light cruiser, and thirteen destroyers—"so long as that defense continues."[23] But it was not planned that it would receive any reinforcements from the Pacific Fleet.

The U.S. Army had its own top-level Rainbow 5 plan, *War Department Operations Plan Rainbow No. 5*, or WDOP-R5. The Army Chief of Staff approved this on August 19, 1941. In the Pacific the Army's main tasks would be the ground and air defense of Hawaii and the Philippines. For the latter, the plan made clear, "no reinforcements from the United States will be sent to this frontier."[24]

At the proverbial last minute, officials made prewar attempts to deploy additional forces to the Philippines.[25] For the U.S. Navy, motor torpedo boats and additional submarines—bringing the total of the latter to 29—arrived in the territory. For the Army, this included artillery, tanks, fighters, and B-17 Flying Fortress bombers—some considered the B-17s a major game-changer, although only 35 of the planned 165 were in place by December 1941. Radar and antiaircraft weapons were scarce. Overall, preparations were not expected to be complete until March or April 1942. Despite this, Lt. Gen. Douglas MacArthur, appointed commander of U.S. Army Forces in the Far East in July 1941, believed the territory could be defended, with reinforcements mobilized, received, or en route. This optimism contributed to a broader shift to a more aggressive defense, reflected in updates to Rainbow 5's vision of the defense of the Philippines—originally similar to Orange—approved in November 1941. Notably, it now called for Japanese forces in Formosa—the invasion's expected launch point—to be targeted using B-17 bombers and a broader ground defense. Yet the bold plans clashed with reality: any U.S. relief force was likely years away.[26]

A further problem was the indigenous component of the force defending the Philippines. While the Philippines Division of the U.S. Army—a composite force of American and local troops—provided the core of the defense force, mass was reliant on hastily mobilized and poorly equipped reserve divisions of the Philippines Army.[27] Nor could the United States call on its allies for substantial assistance: the European colonial powers were consumed with the war in Europe, while their regional forces faced their own threats from the Japanese and lacked the capacity for extra duties.

OPERATIONAL CONCEPTS AND ENABLERS

Naval aviation was critical to the development of the U.S. Navy in the interwar years in the context of future war plans. The ability of carrier aircraft to deliver offensive effect was clear to many, particularly as more capable vessels entered service and proved themselves in exercises. Yet until 1934 the United States possessed only three carriers: the small USS *Langley* and the two larger *Lexington*-class vessels. These were subsequently joined before the Pearl Harbor attack by the USS *Ranger*, and three *Yorktown*-class and the USS *Wasp*, although *Langley* had been converted to a seaplane tender by this point. *Essex*-class carriers were under construction at the war's outbreak but would not reach the front line until mid-1943.

Battleships remained prominent despite wider innovation. Many World War I–era dreadnoughts were upgraded with improved protection from torpedoes, mines, and bombs as well as enhanced antiaircraft defenses and fire-control systems. Steaming range and ease of refueling was improved by the conversion of older battleships from coal to fuel-oil propulsion. Aviation also granted them opportunities: catapult-launched spotter floatplanes from the battleships provided eyes in the sky assisting naval guns to fire more accurately from beyond the horizon after turret modernizations increased gun elevation and thus range. In 1938 the USS *New York* received the first permanently installed U.S. Navy shipborne radar—technology that Japan did not field until 1942—providing early detection of incoming aircraft, allowing time for defense preparations.[28]

The development of fleet submarines by the U.S. Navy was critical to plans to inflict attrition on the IJN and implement an economic blockade of Japan. During the interwar years, the Navy developed long-range submarines, including the *Porpoise, Tambor, Gato, Balao,* and *Tench* classes, capable of two-month missions from Hawaii to Japanese waters.

The "Fleet Problems" series of exercises from 1923 to 1940 was critically important in preparing the U.S. Navy before the war's outbreak. The primary focus was a prospective war with Japan, with the problems directly or indirectly related to War Plan Orange. These exercises sought to establish how best to integrate new technology into fleet operations; tested operational concepts and tactics, including those related to carrier strikes, antisubmarine warfare (ASW), and amphibious landings; and allowed commanders to develop the skill sets required for transpacific operations. The Grand Joint Army-Navy Exercises provided interservice training opportunities.[29]

Other initiatives developed in parallel, with the Mobile Base Project identifying the methods by which forward fleet-support facilities, including floating dry docks, could be established along the path of the advance to support concepts such as those articulated in both Office of Naval Intelligence research and Maj. E. H. Ellis's 1921 publication, *Advanced Base Operations in Micronesia*. The USMC's *Tentative Landing Operations Manual* of 1934 provided the foundational doctrine for capturing territory via amphibious landings.[30]

Legislation, government planning, and industry played crucial roles in prewar preparation. World War I had been a difficult experience for the United States from a production point of view, and numerous initiatives were undertaken to ensure there was no repeat, including through the National Defense Act of 1920 and the War Department's 1930 Industrial Mobilization plan (with significant revisions to the latter in 1933, 1936, and 1939). It was not only a paper exercise, as "educational orders" were placed to give manufacturers experience producing wartime goods.[31]

Much of the success of World War II was ultimately dependent on prewar procurement decisions. The National Industrial Recovery Act of 1933 provided funding for warship construction, while the 1934 Vinson-Trammell Act aimed to build the Navy up to Washington Treaty limits. The Naval Act of 1938 raised the Navy's strength by 20 percent, greenlighting vessels including the first *Iowa*-class battleships and construction of the *Yorktown*-class carrier *Hornet.* The Two-Ocean Navy Act of 1940 ramped up fleet size by 70 percent, with orders authorized for more *Iowa*-class battleships, eight *Essex*-class carriers, and forty-three *Gato*-class submarines.[32]

Logistics was vital for transpacific operations, but by the mid-1930s, the U.S. Navy's peacetime logistic train was relatively weak, while the merchant fleet that would be mobilized in wartime was elderly. To prepare for a future crisis, the Merchant Marine Act of 1936 established the U.S. Maritime Commission and made provisions for a long-range shipbuilding program (LRSP), which sought to recapitalize the U.S. merchant fleet with five hundred subsidized vessels suitable for wartime use. These included the C2- and C3-type cargo ships. The commission also advanced the production of the T2- and T3-type tankers, examples of which all saw military service. The linked "national defense tanker" program saw merchant tankers intended to be operated by commercial companies subsidized to be built to military specifications. These included T-3 variants that subsequently served as *Cimarron*-class oilers.

THE VIEW FROM TOKYO

Both the Imperial Japanese Army (IJA) and the IJN submitted annual operation plans each year, outlining how they would fight the campaigns they envisaged and acting as a guide for peacetime activities, including procurement. IJN plans for war with the United States can be traced back to 1907, a similar time of origin to that of U.S. plans. Japan's 1937 attack on China and the wider global war led the services to the same conclusion reached by their American counterparts: a conflict against multiple opponents simultaneously was on the horizon. Detailed planning, however, was late in coming, with the Imperial Army Operation Plan for the War and the Imperial Navy Operation Plan for the War only being approved on November 5, 1941. Planning culminated on November 15 with the Japanese leadership's adoption of the "Draft Proposal for Hastening the End of the War against the U.S., Great Britain, Holland, and Chiang," which was derived from the earlier "Guidelines for the War against the U.S., Great Britain, and Holland."[33]

Rather than outright victory, Japan only aimed to deprive the United States of the will to continue the upcoming war.[34] Tokyo aimed for a short conflict that would allow them to secure their territorial goals and then deter the United States from embarking on a counteroffensive.

At the operational level, the IJN's longstanding Decisive Battle (*Kantai Kessen*) doctrine for war against the United States led to an operations model following the seizure of the Philippines and Guam divided into three phases:

- Phase I: Locate and destroy remaining locally based U.S. Navy forces (chiefly the Asiatic Fleet)
- Phase II: Attrition operations (*Zengen Sakusen*) against U.S. forces advancing across the Pacific
- Phase III: A decisive naval battle (the presumed location of which moved steadily away from Japan to eventually northwest of the Marshall Islands by 1940)[35]

The final plan was significantly modified through the plan for an opening strike on Pearl Harbor—an initiative led by Adm. Isoroku Yamamoto and brought about by the realization of the potential of massed-carrier operations, fear of the consequences of passivity, and the need to strike a psychological blow against the United States.[36]

Japan took a more aggressive approach to rearmament than the United States during the early interwar years. The Washington Naval Treaty had capped the force at 60 percent of the U.S. Navy's capital ships, while Japanese doctrine instructed that 70 percent would be required for a reasonable chance of success, considering U.S. global responsibilities and the stress of operating across the Pacific. Japan raced to hit treaty limits and exploited gaps, although the London Naval Treaty of 1930 placed restrictions on submarines, cruisers, and overall destroyer tonnage. This effort was further accelerated by a series of naval armaments supplement programs known as the "Circle" shipbuilding plans, and battleship upgrades also enhanced the fleet.[37] By 1937, when the treaties expired, Japan was ready to expand beyond previous limits, but the larger U.S. shipbuilding programs would only grant it a brief window of regional dominance.

To compensate for numerical shortcomings, the IJN focused on superior technology and training, aiming to "outrange" opponents—that is, hitting them before they could strike at all. This was epitomized by the *Yamato*-class battleships, equipped with 18.1-inch guns and requisite fire-control systems capable of reaching farther with heavier and more advanced shells than the U.S. Navy's 16-inch weapons.[38]

Less spectacular but more effective was the Type 93 "Long Lance" oxygen-fueled torpedo, a weapon fitted to IJN cruisers (importantly, as cruiser guns were treaty regulated but not torpedoes) and destroyers, which had a far-greater range and larger warhead than similar U.S. weapons and left little visible wake. It also matched or bettered the range of the guns of any U.S. battleship, further undermining the platform.[39]

The G3m "Nell" bomber with a range of over 3,800 kilometers and the similar G4M "Betty"—termed *rikujo kogeki-ki* (land-based attack aircraft)—both offered a antiship and land-attack capability with a reach beyond that of their counterparts.[40] The carrier-capable A6M "Zero" fighter had a 1,600-kilometer range. The B5N2 "Kate" acted as the IJN's carrier-based torpedo bomber, with the D3A "Val" as the fleet's dive bomber. Reconnaissance was the realm of the H6K "Mavis" and later the H8K "Emily" flying boats.[41]

The IJN submarine force had been in development for decades through a mix of indigenous efforts and imports. By 1941, many IJN submarines, including the *Kaidai* and *Junsen* types—some of the latter capable of carrying aircraft—could patrol off Hawaii or the U.S. West Coast in order to interdict shipping at the maximum distance from the Empire. Midget submarines were also developed for defensive and offensive use.[42] After the war began, the IJN built the I-400 class, which could carry up to three floatplanes.

Like the United States, Japan was dependent on its merchant fleet to support the war effort. By the beginning of World War II, its fleet was the third largest in the world after those of the United Kingdom and the United States. As in the United States, government subsidies were critical to ensure the fleet was available for wartime operations. During the conflict, many vessels were requisitioned for military transport, including the facilitation of amphibious landings.[43]

RAINBOW MEETS REALITY

It is not worthwhile to detail the attack on Pearl Harbor here. In short, the attack sank four U.S. battleships (two were later salvaged) and damaged four more; hit three light cruisers, three destroyers, and some auxiliaries; and destroyed 188 aircraft. Pearl Harbor can be seen as an anti-access operation designed to prevent U.S. reinforcements from reaching the western Pacific, although the survival of the U.S. carriers robbed it of total success.

Initial Japanese air and naval strikes against U.S. assets in the Philippines—launched hours after the Pearl Harbor raid—were primarily staged from Formosa, which Tokyo considered to be a "stationary aircraft carrier" and a "stepping stone to the south."[44] Much of the Philippines invasion force sailed from Taiwan as well.

The largest of the initial air strikes in the Philippines fell on Clark Field and nearby Iba Airfield—an area-denial operation to prevent force elements already in the theater from operating. IJA G3M and G4M bombers and IJN Zero fighters flying from Formosa destroyed dozens of aircraft on the ground, including B-17s and P-40 Warhawk fighters. American strikes against Japanese targets in Formosa were never carried out, as the mission had been repeatedly delayed despite MacArthur receiving orders to implement Rainbow 5.[45]

Raids on Cavite Naval Base two days later destroyed much of its infrastructure, including a critical stockpile of submarine torpedoes.[46] Thus, plans to stem the impending landings with submarines came to little.[47] What of the U.S. Asiatic Fleet survived the war's opening months withdrew to Australia.

Once Japanese forces landed in the Philippines—U.S. air attacks on their transports and escorts inflicted limited losses and failed to halt the buildup—it became clear that the small U.S. military force and underprepared local garrison could not execute MacArthur's ambitious defensive plan. The general decided to revert to the conservative WPO-3 model, but the stage was set for a siege with an inevitable outcome.[48]

One area in which the United States could count itself fortunate was that the IJN's submarine force performed little better than its U.S. counterpart in their anti-access missions. Early war patrols near Hawaii and the West Coast achieved little, with the exception of a torpedo attack that damaged the USS *Saratoga* on January 11, 1942, temporarily reducing the number of U.S. carriers in the Pacific to three.

STRIKING BACK

The relatively late-in-the-day shift by Tokyo to strike at Hawaii forced a change in the U.S. plans for phase I. Planned immediate offensive action—already constrained owing to the Europe First policy—was put on hold in favor of the strategic defensive and maintaining SLOC with Australia. Initially, only

American submarines went on the offensive, but limited numbers and faulty torpedoes greatly constrained their effectiveness.

Recognizing the need for a stronger offensive, the Navy conducted a series of carrier raids—the first in U.S. history—and surface-ship bombardment operations similar to those envisaged in the Marshall Reconnaissance and Raiding Plan. After several false starts, on February 1 the group centered on the carrier USS *Enterprise* struck Kwajalein, Roi, Wotje, Maloelap, and Taroa in the northern Marshalls while the *Yorktown* group hit Mili and Jaluit in the southern Marshalls and Makin in the Gilberts. The *Enterprise* group bombed and shelled Wake Island on February 24 and Marcus Island on March 4. Strikes against Lae-Salamaua by *Yorktown, Lexington,* and B-17s flying from Australia on March 10 targeted a Japanese invasion force, sinking three transport ships, but failed to halt the landings. The campaign's finale, although not an official component of it, was the Doolittle Raid on Tokyo, launched from the carrier USS *Hornet* on April 18. Collectively, the damage inflicted by these early U.S. raids was limited.[49]

The U.S. Pacific war plan needed reworking. In April 1942 a revised draft was completed that the U.S. Navy's account broadly summarizes as

- Phase I: Defend the South and Southwest Pacific and conduct raids while offensive forces are prepared and raids against exposed enemy positions
- Phase II: An amphibious air-sea offensive through the Solomons and New Guinea to retake the Bismarck Archipelago, together with raids against the Caroline and Marshall Islands to inflict attrition
- Phase III: Advance across the Central Pacific to capture the Caroline and Marshall Islands, constructing forward bases in the process
- Phase IV: Advance to the Dutch East Indies or the Philippines, with the choice dependent on the circumstances at the time[50]

THE DEFEAT OF TOKYO'S A2/AD

Japan's war termination strategy was diplomatic, with its defensive strategy designed to deter the United States from embarking on a protracted battle of attrition. Fully mobilized, the United States held an overwhelming advantage in resources—something no Japanese tactical win or advanced weapon could offset. The story of the U.S. island-hopping advance across the Central Pacific is well known (and will not be repeated here), and is fundamentally one of penetrating and systematically dismantling of an anti-access system in a mutually supporting air, sea, land, and electromagnetic campaign. For our purposes, fleet air defense, the effort to bombard and blockade Japan into surrender, and the logistics challenges faced and overcome are most relevant.

Fleet Air Defense

The early naval engagements in the Pacific War made it clear that air cover for ships at sea was mandatory, with the British battleships HMS *Prince of Wales* and HMS *Repulse* being the most prominent casualties in this regard. Carrier-versus-carrier battles took place in the Coral Sea and off Midway, the Eastern Solomons, and Santa Cruz. The Midway victory owed much to the American use of radar to provide early warning of incoming raids.[51]

By 1944, two developments had reshaped fleet air defense. First, a combination of technological developments and experience with German Fritz X and Henschel Hs 293 guided antiship bombs—the first precision-guided aerial antiship weapons deployed in combat—had spurred the need to examine the "problem of protecting a task force against guided missiles launched from enemy mother planes beyond the range of present fire controls." To this end, the United States instigated the Bumblebee program. Its initial report of February 1945 confirmed that a project to develop "a guided, jet-propelled, antiaircraft missile, preferably with supersonic speed," should proceed. Practical results were a matter for the postwar era, with a separate short-term effort that looked to produce a surface-to-air missile (SAM) for wartime use, in the form of the SAM-N-2 Lark, failing to deliver a usable weapon.[52]

The second development was the formal introduction by Japan of dedicated Kamikaze units in October 1944 during the Battle of Leyte Gulf—essentially the standoff guided missiles the United States had envisioned. The later deployed MXY-7 suicide rocket, air-launched from a bomber and with a range of over thirty kilometers, fit the profile in every way. To counter the Kamikazes, the Navy prioritized preemptive strikes on airfields, with carrier raids targeting Japan's home islands and Formosa before the invasions of Iwo Jima and Okinawa. Yet these preemptive raids had the advantage of Japanese aircraft being tied to relatively easy-to-locate airfields. In the European theater, attempts to strike V-1 or V-2 missile launch sites—most commonly small fixed footprints sites or mobile instillations, respectively—via air attack had limited success despite a significant diversion of resources from other tasks.[53] Yet the inaccuracy of the V-1 and V-2 limited their effectiveness. An MXY-7 variant, the 43B, that was planned to be hidden in caves and launched via catapult—arguably the first ground-launched antiship missile (ASM)—promised better concealment and human-guided precision but never became operational.[54]

To further counter the Kamikazes, carrier air groups shifted to a higher proportion of fighters, while radar and picket destroyers extended early warning times. Combined with preemptive strikes, these constituted the "Big Blue Blanket" concept of fleet air defense. The increasing number of 20-mm and 40-mm guns on ships and the introduction of an improved fire-control system, combat information centers (CIC), and radar-proximity-fused shells fired from improved 5-inch guns further enhanced defenses.[55]

Other initiatives would not see wartime service but like Bumblebee would set the postwar tone. Project Cadillac aimed to address the Kamikazes approaching at a low level under the radar horizon of ships by fitting a Grumman TBM Avenger with an APS-20 to provide airborne early warning (AEW). Cadillac II took the concept a step further by fitting B-17s (redesignated the PB-1W) with the same radar and using them as airborne early warning and control (AEW&C) fighter-direction aircraft.[56]

The Bombardment and Blockade of Japan

While impressive, the Doolittle Raid did not present a sustainable model for a bombardment campaign against the Japanese home islands. The B-29 Superfortress was the answer, but basing remained a challenge: limited sorties out of China under Operation Matterhorn achieved little. Bases on Saipan, Tinian, and Guam built during the Central Pacific campaigns solved the problem. Japanese attempts to counter the B-29 are of particular relevance here—with the failure of the anti-access component of Japan's strategy, they represented a case of area denial. There were attacks on the island bases, including by G4M and more modern Ki-67 "Peggy" bombers as well as Zeros operating in a ground-attack role. A commando raid took place on Okinawa on May 25, 1945, destroying or damaging dozens of U.S. aircraft (although no B-29s), but more extensive plans for such attacks under Operation Tsurugi were repeatedly delayed, leading to the mission never being carried out.[57] B-29 losses on the ground, while an irritant, were minor compared to early war raids like those on Clark Field, and they failed to disrupt U.S. operations significantly.[58]

Efforts to defend Japan directly from air attacks had only minimal success. Radar coverage of the home islands was limited, constraining the degree of early warning it could provide. Kinetic defense elements also fell short. Japanese fighters such as the twin-engine Ki-45 "Nick" and J1N1 "Irving" struggled to intercept the B-29 at its cruising altitude of over nine thousand meters, although the single-engine Ki-84 "Frank" performed better. Similarly, antiaircraft artillery (AAA) and the required shells capable of reaching the bombers were in short supply.[59]

Japan made attempts to disrupt U.S. operations and strike back. Submarine-launched shelling and an air raid on the U.S. West Coast early in the war achieved little, as did late-war Fu-Go balloon bombs carried by jet streams. More substantial were plans to disable the Panama Canal—a scenario featured in Hector Charles Bywater's better-known fictional counterpart to *Sea Power in the Pacific*, 1925's *The Great Pacific War*, and explored in multiple Fleet Problems exercises—using M6A Seiran floatplanes launched from I-400 submarines.[60] This reached the advanced planning stage before being canceled and replaced by a plan to strike U.S. Navy carriers anchored at Ulithi Atoll and posing a threat to the home islands; the war ended before it could be attempted. Japan's Project Z to develop an intercontinental bomber to strike the United States went nowhere, and a plan to unleash biological weapons on North America was canceled at the war's end.

U.S. blockade efforts eventually proved fatal to Japan. Early attempts at offensive minelaying using submarines, aircraft, and occasionally surface ships targeted its outer empire, but in March 1945 Operation Starvation brought a systematic assault to inner shipping lanes. B-29s laid mines at key chokepoints, sinking or trapping many ships.[61]

The U.S. submarine campaign underpinned the blockade. At the war's outbreak, there were only 39 modern fleet boats in the Pacific, only a third of which could be kept on station at a time due to transit, resupply, and maintenance requirements. These were the only force elements that could sustainably penetrate Japan's anti-access defenses. But growing numbers—182 were on duty at the war's end—and rectifying torpedo faults allowed for a campaign to develop that devastated Japan's naval and merchant fleets. Weak IJN antisubmarine defenses made Japan's reliance on imports and island trade a fatal vulnerability.[62]

Later in the war, there were also several further efforts against the home islands. These included carrier-aircraft raids on Tokyo and what amounted to the final destruction of the IJN during the raids on Kure in July 1945. Battleship-led groups also unleashed numerous bombardments on coastal targets.[63]

U.S. Pacific Logistics

Logistical difficulties plagued the initial phase of post–Pearl Harbor Pacific operations. Oilers—required to allow warships to operate over great distances—were in short supply, with those available only sufficient to support the carrier groups on limited operations. A combination of vessels ordered in the approach to the war under naval efforts, the LRSP, and later the emergency shipbuilding program, together with requisitioned merchant ships, ultimately provided the backbone of the logistics force. These included T1, T2, and T3 tankers; C1, C2, and C3 cargo ships; Liberty and Victory ships; and specialized vessels like tugs and landing ships.

The original WPPac-46 goal to secure islands in the Mandates as part of an advance across the Central Pacific was a long time coming. The Gilbert and Marshall Islands Campaigns—Japan had occupied these British-controlled islands on December 10, 1941—began with landings on Tarawa and Makin Islands in November 1943. The Marshall Islands Campaign proper took place in January and February 1944, with the successive capture of Majuro, Kwajalein, and Eniwetok. All became advanced bases, collectively covering the region. Truk, once a key target, was bypassed in favor of Manus Island (captured in March 1944) and Ulithi Atoll (seized without resistance on September 23, 1944). Both were developed as advanced bases—essentially completing phase III of the revised Rainbow 5 in the Pacific. For the latter part of the war, Service Squadron Ten became the backbone of mobile logistics, advancing with the offensive. Its assets included floating dry docks, repair shops, and even ice cream facilities, all supported by conventional fuel and cargo ships. At sea, other Service Force units managed oilers and supply ships, while commercial vessels moved supplies to advanced bases.[64]

OPERATION CAUSEWAY

Formosa was subjected to detailed U.S. analysis from early in the war. Extensive data was gathered to determine the island's contribution to Tokyo's war economy, identifying possible targets for bombing, and its potential as a base for the final push against Japan. Civil-affairs preparations were made for the island's wartime governance by the U.S. military.[65]

The issue of postwar control of Formosa also loomed large: the ROC—led by Chiang Kai-shek and the Kuomintang (KMT; Nationalist Party of China) since 1928—claimed the island as its own. The December 1943 Cairo Declaration issued by Roosevelt, British Prime Minister Winston Churchill, and Chiang declared, "All territories Japan has stolen from the Chinese, such as Manchuria, Formosa, and the Pescadores, shall be restored to the Republic of China." Partly, this was a gesture to keep the ROC in the war against Tokyo.[66]

On examining the need to secure the South China Sea, Allied planners judged Formosa valuable, given its position astride Japan's air and sea lines of communication and overall proximity to the home islands—bombers based there could strike them—and the Chinese coast.[67] The draft plan for the invasion of Formosa—"Island X" for planning purposes—eventually evolved into Operation Causeway.[68] The most developed variant was a two-phase initiative to capture both the southwestern portion of Formosa and a bridgehead at Xiamen Bay on the adjacent mainland. A June 1944 preliminary draft of the anticipated invasion plan outlined the sequence:

- Phase I: (D–3 days) Carrier air attacks in preparation for assault begins; (D–2) Naval Gunfire Support in preparation for assault begins; (D-day) land Army and USMC units with the intent of securing and developing the southwestern region of Formosa
- Phase II: (W-day (D+20)) Land ground forces to seize Quemoy, Wu Su, and establish a toehold on the mainland coast; (W+3) seize Little Quemoy; (W+10) seize Amoy Island; (W+20) seize areas in mainland China[69]

The ground force would require two hundred landing ships tank (LSTs) and hundreds of other landing-craft types, over two hundred cargo ships, and hundreds of amphibious assault vehicles. Estimated naval support would include eleven fleet carriers, seven light carriers, thirty-two escort carriers, eight battleships, and almost two hundred cruisers and destroyers. Opposing this armada were estimated to be 98,000 Japanese personnel, of whom 32,000 would be ground forces, with reinforcements expected to arrive before the invasion.[70]

Ultimately, logistical problems, personnel shortages, the risk of high casualties, the inherent issues in securing only a small section of the island, the loss of U.S. air bases on mainland China to IJA advances, and a belief that Formosa

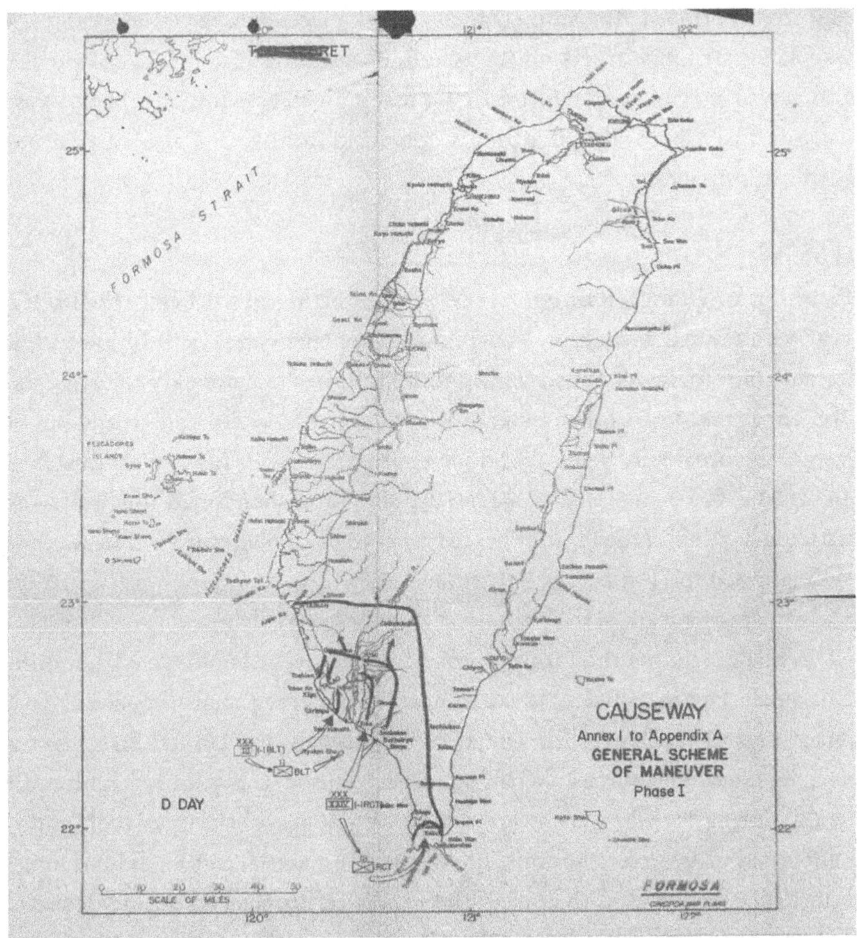

Map of Formosa component of Operation Causeway and general scheme of maneuver. *From "Causeway Joint Staff Study (Preliminary Draft for Staff Use)," June 21, 1944, Defense Technical Information Center Data, app. A, annex*

could be bypassed helped tilt the decision in favor of landing in Luzon instead on the way to Okinawa.[71]

Despite no invasion taking place, Formosa was at the center of a major air battle in October 1944. Japan anticipated an American attack and drafted a set of plans for local defense. With the U.S. fleet approach revealed by the attack on Okinawa, two plans—Sho-Ichi-Go, intended to defend the Philippines, and Sho-Ni-Go, to defend Formosa and the Ryukyu Islands—were activated. With the IJN severely depleted, both depended on land-based air power, much of it from Formosa. The air engagement took place October 12–16, with U.S. warplanes striking targets on the island, devastating IJN and IJA airpower, and rupturing a major defensive line. Most damage was inflicted by the Fast Carrier Task Force, although B-29s operating from China also carried out bombing missions.[72]

LESSONS

Planning for Orange, Rainbow 5, and the supporting efforts before the Pacific War were key to U.S. success—not because the plans were strictly followed, but because the process identified challenges and allowed for necessary adjustments. The Thrusters' desire for a rapid advance across the Pacific went in and out of fashion before finally being abandoned as unpragmatic. The gravest mistakes emerged either when well-considered policy was abandoned unwisely—as with MacArthur in the Philippines, who put in place plans for a war he was not yet equipped to fight or had a path to victory for—or failure of imagination and underestimation of the opponent, as with Pearl Harbor.

While defending the Philippines more effectively would have been difficult due to Japan's anti-access capabilities, stronger regional allies could have posed greater challenges for Tokyo. Yet ultimately, the United States had a decisive edge in resources—a fact Japan understood. U.S. planners both prior to and during the war were aware that the regional superiority of their opponent could be overcome in time, providing nonmaterial factors did not intervene. They understood that an initial loss of territory need not be decisive. Tokyo's A2/AD strategy was logical but not designed to support a protracted war; it was ultimately not resourced to counter overwhelming American military power and production. Only a U.S. political capitulation could have made Japan's strategy viable.

The Pacific War ended much as Orange had envisaged, with blockade and bombardment forcing Japan to surrender. Its creators did not foresee a requirement to invade Japan, although U.S. leaders planned such an endeavor under Operation Downfall. Ultimately, the invasion never took place, with cumulative Japanese defeats, the Soviet invasion of Manchuria, and U.S. atomic-bomb attacks, together with Allied flexibility over the fate of Emperor Hirohito, leading to Tokyo's capitulation. Ironically, the nuclear weapons that helped facilitate the total surrender of Japan were to ultimately make such a war termination policy unviable for future great power conflict.

CHAPTER 2

AFTERMATH

If when I die, I am still a dictator, I will certainly go down into the oblivion of all dictators. If, on the other hand, I succeed in establishing a truly stable foundation for a democratic government, I will live forever in every home in China.

—*Chiang Kai-shek (died a dictator)*

Despite suggestions of placing Formosa under U.S.-led military occupation or United Nations trusteeship until the final settlement with Japan was agreed, Washington was in no mood to extend its postwar responsibilities. As such, it opted for an immediate handover of the island to the KMT-controlled ROC (although with the territory's final status left unsettled), with General Order No. 1 of the JCS, following Tokyo's surrender, ordering the Japanese on Formosa to surrender to "Generalissimo Chiang Kei-Shek."[1]

After the first arrival of Nationalist troops ferried in by U.S. Navy ships on October 15, 1945, and the landing of the new KMT governor ten days later, the situation quickly took a turn for the worse. Almost immediately, ROC officials and other well-connected mainlanders began enriching themselves by seizing Japanese assets rather than establishing effective governance.[2] Matters came to a head on February 27, 1947, with the beating of a cigarette vendor by government agents and the death of a bystander who had attempted to intervene. Public demands for justice were met with more government violence the next day, sparking a wider revolt that triggered a broader armed rebellion in what became known as the "February 28 Incident." The subsequent suppression efforts—aided by thousands of additional KMT troops sent from the mainland—killed up to 28,000 people in a little over a month, with tens of thousands more imprisoned.[3] Authorities declared martial law, beginning what was to become known as the "White Terror."[4]

THE END OF THE CHINESE CIVIL WAR

After a hiatus to resist Japanese occupation, the Chinese Civil War resumed in 1946. Chiang's forces began to suffer setback after setback as the military wing of the Chinese Communist Party (CCP)—reorganized and renamed the People's Liberation Army (PLA) in 1947—advanced through battlefield success and the defection of ROC units. A CIA assessment in August 1948 warned, "Chiang's position is steadily deteriorating, and his government is in such a precarious situation that its collapse or overthrow could occur at any time."[5] On October 1, 1949, Mao Tse-tung proclaimed the establishment of the PRC.

Chiang, having resigned as ROC leader in the wake of the mainland losses but still director general of the KMT and pulling strings from behind the scenes, although not without challenge, had begun transferring gold and other portable state assets to Formosa in late 1948.[6] Ultimately, at least one million armed forces personnel and civilians moved to the island, with Chiang flying out and the national government relocating there in December 1949.[7]

THE VIEW FROM WASHINGTON

On December 1, 1948, the National Security Council (NSC)—the body that advises the U.S. president on national security and foreign policy—circulated the paper NSC 37, which featured a November 24 response from the JCS on a request for information from Secretary of State George C. Marshall on the security implications of Formosa and the Pescadores coming under the control of "an administration which is susceptible of exploitation by Kremlin-directed communists."[8] It noted: "Unless Formosa can be denied to Kremlin-directed exploitation, we must expect, in the event of war, an enemy capability of dominating to his advantage and our disadvantage the sea routes between Japan and the Malay area, together with a greatly improved enemy capability of extending his control to the Ryukyus and the Philippines, either of which could produce strategic consequences very seriously detrimental to our national security."[9] Regarding both the deteriorating situation on the mainland and the government on the territory, the Department of State judged the ROC administration to be "corrupt and incompetent," underlining a key barrier to allying with the KMT to defend the territory from the CCP.[10]

NSC 37/1 of January 19, 1949, contained draft recommendations for the U.S. policy position. As proposed by the JCS in NSC 37, the State Department supported diplomatic and economic, rather than military, means for denying Formosa to the communists.[11] NSC 37/2 of February 3 offered a finalized report on the current U.S. policy position. It recommended that the United States seek to "develop and support a local non-Communist Chinese regime" on Formosa while limiting the influx of mainlanders and keeping the option of engaging with the island's independence movement in its back pocket.[12]

A JCS memo of February 10 noted that the loss of Formosa to the communists, while serious, was not directly vital U.S. national security.[13] NSC 37/5 of March 1 contained recommendations from the same JCS response, noting, "In spite of Formosa's strategic importance, the current disparity between our military strength and our many global obligations makes it inadvisable to undertake the employment of armed force in Formosa."[14] The paper also recommended that the United States support the island's governor in developing a "viable, self-supporting economy," again on condition of reforms.[15]

A Department of State memorandum of August 4 judged that the loss of Formosa to the communists was probable absent major improvements in governance, the most significant risk being a rebellion by disaffected Nationalist troops should a Communist landing take place.[16] But in NSC 37/7 of August 22, the JCS restated their opposition to committing U.S. forces to the island's defense given other commitments.[17]

In the wake of the first Soviet atomic test on August 29, 1949, NSC 37/8 of October 6 outlined the U.S. position on Taiwan. Noting that "present U.S. policy with respect to Formosa and the Pescadores calls for efforts to deny those islands to the Chinese Communists through diplomatic and economic means," it outlined the JCS's position and highlighted the risk American military involvement would have of rallying support behind the CCP. It also flagged that it remained the estimate of the CIA that Taiwan "probably will be under Chinese Communist control by the end of 1950."[18]

The year ended with the approval by President Truman of NSC 48/2 of December 30, 1949, a wider report on overall U.S. policy in Asia, recommending that the United States should forgo military involvement on Formosa. It rejected the Pentagon's call for "modest, well-directed" military aid and urged against providing military and political support to noncommunist elements within

China unless they met a high bar of utility. Instead, it stated that the United States ought to exploit any split between the PRC and USSR.[19] This ended the JCS's pre-Korean War push to provide material assistance to the Nationalists.[20]

On January 5, 1950, President Harry S. Truman announced at a press conference that the United States would honor the Cairo Declaration, which stated an intent to assign Formosa to the ROC. As such, the country did not have "any intention of utilizing its Armed Forces to interfere in the present situation," nor would it "provide military aid or advice to Chinese forces on Formosa."[21] A week later Secretary of State Dean Acheson gave his "Perimeter Speech" in which he excluded the Republic of Korea (ROK) and Formosa from the U.S. Pacific defense line, running from the Aleutians to Japan and through the Ryukyu Islands to the Philippines.[22]

STALLED AMBITIONS

PLA preparations for the invasion of Taiwan began even before victory on the mainland. In June 1949 Mao, who saw the island's capture as critical to ending the civil war, called for a study of how to invade Taiwan and for an invasion the forthcoming winter. He later became more flexible as the challenges became apparent, with the summer of 1950 suggested as a target period.[23]

Beyond national unity, an underlying motivation was a fear that the United States sought to incorporate Taiwan into its defensive sphere. Like American officials, Mao judged the Communist path of least resistance to securing the island as obtaining the assistance of disaffected Nationalist forces already there. He was also clear on the need for thorough preparations, noting the importance of adequate transport and securing air and sea superiority before any landing attempt. Following negotiations in the summer of 1949, the Soviets agreed to sell aircraft to Beijing and support pilot training.[24]

The October 1949 operation to capture the largest of the Kinmen Islands—part of a wider effort to secure Nationalist-held offshore islands and viewed as a critical step—was to mark a major turning point in the PLA's prospective journey to Taiwan. Suitable boats and crews were in desperately short supply, forcing the landing to occur in two waves. The defending infantrymen, under-estimated in number, were supported by Nationalist ships, tanks, and aircraft. Only hours after the commencement of the landing, at daybreak on October 25, ROC airstrikes and attacks by naval vessels began, destroying many landing boats and suppressing the ferrying of reinforcements. Combined with counterattacks on the ground, this doomed the operation, which ended on October 28. Mao reportedly called it the civil war's greatest loss.[25]

On December 17 the invasion of Taiwan was postponed, with a revised plan for the operation already submitted.[26] On February 14, 1950, Mao and Josef Stalin signed the Sino-Soviet Treaty of Friendship, Alliance, and Mutual Assistance in Moscow. Among the provisions was a $300 million loan, of which half was allocated to buy naval equipment from the USSR. Secondhand ships were sourced internationally, while domestic shipyards built or converted vessels, despite Nationalist air raids targeting ships and shipyards, including in Shanghai. By January 1950, 500,000 personnel were expected to be involved in the Taiwan campaign. Beijing made requests for aircraft deliveries from the USSR, and Soviet Air Force warplanes deployed to take over the air defense of Shanghai and Xuzhou. Mao also ordered the formation of a paratrooper force.[27]

In April–May 1950 the PLA captured Hainan Island using a fleet of junks and help from local insurgents, overwhelming poorly prepared ROC defenders who had only limited air and naval support (the island was some 1,300 kilometers from bases on Taiwan)—albeit with the sting of 70,000 Nationalist troops escaping to Taiwan. The overrunning of Dongshan Island that same month led to the evacuation of 3,000 more ROC troops. To this was added 120,000 personnel withdrawn from the Zhoushan Islands. These retreats swelled Taiwan's defense force to 400,000 men and nullified the PRC's plan to inflict disabling attrition on the Nationalist forces before the main assault on the island.[28]

In early 1950 the PLA estimated that 575 ships of over 1,000 tons plus 2,000 smaller landing craft would be required just to land the first wave.[29] During planning revisions in June 1950, the number of defenders on Formosa was expected to reach 500,000 troops, and personnel and landing-craft requirements for the PLA were revised upward accordingly.[30]

Even with the rushed acquisition program, officials judged that naval quantitative and qualitative superiority could not be established against the Nationalists until the end of 1950, with qualitative air predominance attained at around the same time. In April 1950 the ROC possessed over twice the naval tonnage of the PLA Navy (PLAN). At that time the ROC Air Force outnumbered the PLA Air Force (PLAAF) four to one in combat aircraft. The extensive training required for new aircrews would mean a landing was impossible until the summer of 1951.[31]

THE U.S. PIVOT

In 1950 the United States adopted a new hard line in the Cold War. Instead of a nuanced challenge, the April NSC 68 policy paper presented Soviet communism as a monolithic threat bent on world conquest and called for a massive increase in defense spending to facilitate containment of Moscow and its allies.

On June 14 General MacArthur transmitted his classified "Memo on Formosa." In it he stated, "The front line of the Far East Command as well as the western strategic frontier of the United States rests today on the littoral islands extending from the Aleutians through the Philippine Archipelago." In contrast to then-current U.S. policy, MacArthur argued that the domination of Formosa by an unfriendly power would be a "disaster of utmost importance to the United States."[32]

Eleven days later North Korea invaded South Korea. Truman subsequently announced the "neutralization of the Straits of Formosa," with the U.S. Navy's Seventh Fleet to act to prevent any invasion of Taiwan by the PRC or any major operation by the KMT against the mainland. The president's announcement led to Beijing deciding not to invade Taiwan in 1951, then suspending plans indefinitely when many of the troops earmarked for that operation were moved to the border with Korea.

A CONFLUENCE OF INTERESTS

Washington's initial hesitation to support the remnants of the ROC was understandable. The JCS's reluctance stemmed from early U.S. plans prioritizing Europe over the Pacific and the strain of post–World War II military cutbacks. Still, Formosa's strategic importance as an A2/AD platform with the potential to disrupt U.S. access and operations in the region if it fell under hostile control was clear.

ROC forces on Taiwan represented a formidable challenge to a successful PLA invasion, but one that could be overcome with time and preparation. Capitalizing on the preexisting defensive strengths of Formosa in a way that would also support U.S. regional goals would require cooperation between the United States and the ROC.

CHAPTER 3

THE PLURAL OF APOCALYPSE

SAC B-47 squadron of 15 aircraft now ready on Guam can be made available by JCS for use if hostilities broaden to require nuclear attacks against mainland targets. This squadron has no conventional capability.

—*Telegram from Joint Chiefs of Staff to Commander in Chief, Pacific, August 25, 1958*

While many, including the JCS, believed late in World War II that the USSR was destined to be the major postwar challenge, a formal outline for conflict with the Soviet Union was not put forward until after the close of the Pacific War.[1] The initial effort, the Pincher plan, was circulated by the Joint War Plan Committee (JWPC) on March 2, 1946, as a CONOPS and then submitted a revised version on April 27, 1946, as a joint basic outline war plan.[2] Pincher envisaged that the initial U.S. component of war against the USSR would primarily be executed through homeland defense (although the threat was minimal), air bombardment launched from forward bases, destruction of the Soviet naval and merchant fleets, and naval blockade.[3] Further revisions and regional plans followed. The backdrop to this war plan and subsequent efforts was a presumed massive initial superiority of Soviet conventional land and tactical air forces in Eurasia. Yet the Pincher plan series lacked critical detail and was only approved by the JSC as the basis of further planning. As part of the preparations for this work, a U.S. Army Air Forces plan, Earshot, with an "atomic annex," took shape, from which the first Strategic Air Command (SAC) nuclear plan, OPLAN 14-47, emerged.[4] The successor plans to Pincher included Broiler, Halfmoon, Offtackle, and Dropshot.[5]

THE FORWARD DEFENSE PERIMETER AND TRANSOCEANIC WARFARE

The maritime strategy the United States adopted at the outset of the Cold War was fundamentally different from that of War Plan Orange.[6] U.S. forward basing near Eurasia and Soviet anti-access capabilities largely being limited to submarines restricted the requirement for open-ocean warfare to obtain theater access. Instead, the U.S. Navy was required to shift from being an oceanic navy that fought for control of the sea to what Samuel P. Huntington called a "transoceanic navy" that applied pressure to the enemy littoral.[7]

A fall 1945 Joint Planning Staff planning paper, JPS 1518, identified the Soviet Union as the primary threat and proposed that the United States aim to keep "a prospective enemy at the maximum possible distance, and conversely to project our own advanced bases into areas well removed from the United States" to "enlarge our strategic frontier."[8] This presented the need for a pivot from a focus on the Pacific, where the vast majority of the fleet was located in 1945, to a greater emphasis on the Atlantic and Mediterranean areas, which were critical to the defense of Europe and adjacent to the main Soviet centers of power.[9]

In his 1948 paper "The Future Employment of Naval Forces," retiring Fleet Admiral Nimitz emphasized the enduring importance of sea power despite U.S. maritime supremacy and its role against an opponent without a fleet. He noted, "Offensively, our initial plans should provide for the coordinated employment of military and naval airpower launched from land and carrier bases and of guided missiles against important enemy targets."[10] Counting against this argument was, first and foremost, the specter of nuclear weapons, including their use against maritime targets—the United States demonstrated this capability in the 1946 Crossroads nuclear tests. On the other hand, the ability of the Navy to use nuclear weapons to strike naval and air bases ashore housing submarines and aircraft threatening its vessels—an approach later known as "attack at source"—would be of great potential utility.[11]

The U.S. Navy's 1947 draft global maritime strategy envisaged that its units would "assume the offensive immediately in order to secure our own sea communications, support our forces overseas, disrupt enemy operations, and force dissipation of enemy strength," including through forward submarine operations in the northwest Pacific.[12] Nevertheless, at the onset of a conflict before the Reserve Fleet was mobilized, it assumed that all but one Pacific fleet carrier would be reallocated to the Atlantic.[13]

Prior to the end of World War II, U.S. planners anticipated the need for postwar Pacific access, with President Roosevelt approving a 1943 JCS plan for a network of bases across the region. While civilian leaders rejected annexing Japanese Mandate islands, they were placed under U.S. trusteeship.[14] The conflict ended the prolonged prewar debate over building extensive support facilities in the central and western Pacific. Construction of Guam Naval Base began following the island's liberation in 1944. North Field—what was to become Andersen Air Force Base—was also established. The 1952 Security Treaty and the subsequent 1960 Treaty of Mutual Cooperation and Security between the United States and Japan gave the former the right to maintain military bases in the latter. The 1953 Mutual Defense Treaty between the United States and the ROK also allowed U.S. bases in South Korea. Though the Philippines gained independence in 1946, a Washington-Manila agreement granted U.S. access to facilities including Clark Air Base for ninety-nine years, later reduced to twenty-five years in 1959. The United States and the Philippines also signed a mutual defense treaty in 1951. The status of the former Japanese Mandate islands as U.S. trust territories made Washington responsible for their defense affairs; this would persist through mutual agreement after the territories became independent nations.

THE THREAT

Postwar Allied testing revealed that German Type XXI U-boats, with advanced hulls and larger batteries, made many ASW tactics obsolete. The Soviets acquired several such vessels along with parts, blueprints, and German designers, using them to enhance their fleet. The Soviet *Whiskey*- (entering service in 1950), *Zulu*- (1952), and *Romeo*-class (1957) submarines were all derived from the Type XXI and assessed by the United States as major anti-access threats to SLOC. *Whiskey*-class vessels were delivered to China and subsequently built domestically by Beijing, with production of *Romeo* boats following.

The USSR also obtained the V-2 ballistic missile from Germany. It was recognized that a more capable version could deliver nuclear weapons a great distance. The Soviets fielded the SS-1 Scunner, a V-2 clone, in 1950, while the

Germans' Wasserfall SAM inspired the R-11 Scud-A, the first Soviet nuclear-armed missile. The USSR supplied the design for the SS-2 Sibling. which China manufactured as the Dongfeng 1, Beijing' first ballistic missile.

Throughout World War II, the USSR was deficient in strategic-bombing capability. Requests to obtain B-29s via Lend-Lease came to nothing, but scientists reverse-engineered the B-29 from U.S. planes that landed in Soviet territory, creating the Tu-4 Bull; ten were delivered to China in 1953. While causing the most concern as a nuclear-strike platform—potentially against naval targets—the bomber was also able to mount the first Soviet ASM, the AS-1 Kennel, although Moscow did not supply the weapon to Beijing.[15] The long-range Tu-95 Bear, first flying in 1952, and jet-powered bombers like the Tu-16 Badger (delivered to China in 1958 and later domestically produced as the H-6) would also go on to have a Soviet anti-access maritime mission through the service time of the KS-1 replacement, the AS-5 Kelt ASM.

ENABLERS

Despite objections from the now-independent U.S. Air Force (USAF), the U.S. Navy advanced its own nuclear capability. The A-2 Savage was a carrier-based bomber that first flew in 1948 and was capable of carrying early, large nuclear bombs. It was succeeded by the larger jet-powered A-3 Skywarrior, which first flew in 1952, and the A-5 Vigilante, which followed in 1958.[16] Targets for naval air missions were initially envisaged to be maritime related, including naval bases, shipyards, airfields housing aircraft that threatened seaborne targets, as well as minelaying efforts to halt submarine deployments. Plans later expanded to include targets such as transportation hubs and POL (petroleum, oil, and lubricants) facilities to slow any enemy land advance into Western Europe and the Mediterranean area.[17] Later aircraft such as the A-4 Skyhawk and A-1 Skyraider were tasked to suppress communist-bloc air defenses before the arrival of SAC bombers, with carriers stationed in the Mediterranean to target sites in Eastern Europe as part of the Rollback Campaign.[18]

Like the USSR, the United States was also developing technology derived from German systems. The V-1 was developed into the Republic-Ford JB-2, which led to the MGM-1 Matador and submarine-launched SSM-N-8A Regulus nuclear cruise missiles. The V-2 fed into the wider ballistic-missile effort. Drawing from the German Type XXI boats, the United States launched the greater underwater propulsion power (GUPPY) program to enhance wartime endurance and developed hunter-killer submarines (SSK), starting with the *Barracuda*-class, and later nuclear-powered attack submarines (SSN).

Anticipating Soviet submarine threats, the U.S. Navy modernized destroyers for ASW roles through the fleet rehabilitation and modernization (FRAM) program. Postwar, the *Norfolk*- and *Dealey*-class destroyers were conceived for such operations from the start. Many *Essex*-class carriers were also converted into ASW platforms.

Naval air-defense-missile efforts under the Bumblebee program produced the RIM-8 Talos (long range), RIM-2 Terrier (medium range), and RIM-24 Tartar (short to medium range) SAMs. Mirroring other SAMs of their era, none were particularly effective against anything but high-altitude targets on a predictable course, but they provided a modicum of protection against Soviet bombers and early ASMs. Despite the sudden cancelation of the large aircraft carrier USS *United States* in 1949, the first of the *Forrestal*-class carriers began construction in 1952. Together with the *Kitty Hawk*-class and the USS *Enterprise* of the 1960s, these were the first-generation supercarriers.

For its part, the USAF retained the lead in strategic bombing it had obtained in its USAAF guise during World War II. The B-29 and its B-50 evolved variant were succeeded by the long-range B-36 Peacemaker and medium-range bombers like the B-47 Stratojet, later replaced by the B-52 Stratofortress and B-58 Hustler. A further critical postwar development was the utilization of in-flight refueling. For the USAF, this began with converting bombers into KB-29 and KB-50 tanker aircraft before the Boeing KC-97 Stratofreighter replaced them, itself replaced by the Boeing KC-135 Stratotanker. Initially, these types were intended to give strategic bombers a global range, but their use proliferated to support other aircraft types. The U.S. Navy followed the USAF lead by converting some of its own bomber types into aerial tankers and also used "buddy" refueling packs carried by fighters and attack aircraft to extend range.

AEW&C had also matured from Project Cadillac's initial efforts. The first such aircraft, the TBM-3W Avenger, served until replaced by the Grumman E-1 Tracer. The U.S. Navy and USAF operated the larger land-based Lockheed EC-121 Warning Star.

LOOKING EAST

In April 1947 the JCS recommended that in the context of the Soviet threat, "for the proximate future, United States military strategy in the Pacific should be offensive-defensive in nature, should recognize that the area is of operational importance secondary to the European Mediterranean area."[19] Plan Moonrise, presented by the JWPC on August 29, 1947, was a regional plan covering the East Asian element of Pincher. It viewed the Pacific region would prove a distraction for both Moscow and Washington in a great power confrontation, emphasizing defense there as the main goal. A broader emergency war plan soon followed, including a more offensive Far East strategy but still ranking the Pacific a low priority.[20]

China itself became a target upon completion of the CCP's takeover of the mainland. This initially began following the PRC's intervention in the Korean War. In April 1951, B-29s and nuclear bombs were deployed to Okinawa, only to be withdrawn again in June.[21] In January 1953 Dwight D. Eisenhower was inaugurated as president, and he considered the use of nuclear weapons should an armistice in Korea not materialize.[22] But that war would end without any such action.

One of the earliest but less-discussed instances of U.S. nuclear planning against China arose over the potential resumption of the Korean War, with North Korea again supported by the PRC. The United States was unwilling to recommit conventional forces on the same scale, and a nuclear response was the obvious alternative. A November 1953 JSCP report advocated for the mass use of nuclear weapons against targets directly supporting the war in North Korea, Manchuria, and northern China as well as a broader target set across the PRC—the latter defined vaguely enough to allow for mass targeting of cities. Revised JCS plans later narrowed nuclear-weapon use, focusing on directly Korean conflict–related targets and extending the policy to any regional conflict involving the PRC. SAC already had Far East Outline Plan (FEOP) 8-54, which covered China.[23]

The JCS proposed the creation of a three-phase program for hostilities with China that foresaw a phase I with regional forces assisted where needed by SAC striking PLA assets directly supporting renewed fighting. In phase II, a broader range of the same targets would be struck. SAC would lead on phase III, with a briefing to reduce the PRC's war-making capabilities while still being "confined to military targets."[24] But SAC's revised FEOP 8-54 identified multiple military targets in cities and provided no options for conventional strikes, rendering the notion of restraint an illusion.[25]

THE FIRST OFFSET STRATEGY AND EISENHOWER'S "NEW LOOK"

Eisenhower believed the United States needed to prepare for a long-haul Cold War. As a result, its posture against the USSR needed to be financially sustainable over time rather than just a short-term effort. These approaches were embodied in NSC 162/2, which the president approved on October 30, 1953.[26] This policy set was heavily biased toward a reliance on nuclear weapons delivered by long-range bombers and (when developed) missiles as well as lower-yield tactical nuclear weapons in all but the most minor contingencies in order to offset the numerical strength of the land forces of the USSR and its allies. While hardly inexpensive in themselves, nuclear weapons were a considerably smaller burden than maintaining large conventional forces and allowed the United States to capitalize on its technological strength. Thus, the First Offset strategy and nuclear "massive retaliation" was born.[27]

1958: TAIWAN AND OPLAN 25-58

In the six years following the Korean War Armistice Agreement, two major confrontations occurred between the ROC, PRC, and United States.

The First Taiwan Strait Crisis ran from September 1954 to May 1955, at which time OPLAN 51-53, devised by the Commander in Chief Pacific (CINCPAC), was the lead defense plan.[28] While featuring the PLA invasion of the Yijiangshan Islands and the U.S.-supported KMT evacuation of the Dachen Islands, it centered upon the fate of the Kinmen and Matsu Islands, both groups being subjected to shelling and thought to be under threat of invasion. While their military value to either side was limited, their loss had political and psychological implications. In March 1955 U.S. Secretary of State John Foster Dulles assessed that PLA overall manpower and resilience meant that tactical nuclear weapons would be required to destroy the airfields and gun emplacements supporting an attack on the islands.[29]

Limited detail is available of the U.S. plans in place during the first crisis. But more is at hand for the Second Taiwan Strait Crisis, which ran from August to October 1958. The central issue—the fate of the larger offshore islands—was much the same as earlier, as were the arguments for and against intervention. The unauthorized leaking of Daniel Ellsberg of an unredacted RAND study of the crisis revealed details of OPLAN 25-58, adopted just as the second crisis began.[30] The document outlined a three-phase operation to defend Taiwan, the Penghu Islands, and select islands in the Quemoy and Matsu groups "when deemed appropriate by U.S. authorities."[31]

- Phase I, which was already in progress, involved continuous patrols and reconnaissance of the region.
- Phase II focused on defeating the attacking force.
- Phase III, which would only proceed if judged necessary, involved operations by SAC to destroy the PRC's war-making capability.[32]

A declassified USAF analysis of air operations during the crisis described the same sequence and additional operational detail.[33]

The plan assumed operations would take place in conditions of less than total war, that nuclear weapons would be authorized for release, and that permission to strike targets on the Chinese mainland would be granted.[34] It also considered that there might be an intermediate phase between I and II where the PRC stopped short of launching an all-out attack on Taiwan and its outlying islands, instead carrying out probing attacks to test the U.S. response—the OPLAN made no provision for retaliation and proposed that any action in response would be dependent on circumstances, in part because U.S. policy toward the defense of the offshore islands was still highly uncertain.[35] The supporting Pacific Air Forces (PACAF) plans for OPLAN 25-58 assumed the use of nuclear weapons from the outset of phase II without a conventional phase.[36]

At a White House meeting on August 25, two days after the main phase of PLA shelling and the blockade attempt against the Kinmens began, Eisenhower approved an order stating that only the use of conventional weapons would likely be approved initially to defend the offshore islands.[37] But five B-47 bombers based on Guam, armed with nuclear-bomb types better suited to the task of striking coastal airfields rather than alternative nuclear munitions, were incorporated into attack plans.[38] Previously, on August 24 the aircraft carrier USS *Essex* was ordered to the Pacific, with the USS *Midway* steaming from Pearl Harbor to the Taiwan Strait on August 27. Along with escorts, the U.S. Navy Seventh Fleet now boasted six carrier groups with ninety-six nuclear-capable aircraft, three heavy cruisers, forty destroyers, and a submarine group—the largest force deployed since the Korean War.[39]

U.S.-controlled Matador nuclear cruise missiles had previously been sent to Taiwan in February 1958.[40] But U-2 reconnaissance flights along the Chinese coast indicated no major force buildup for an invasion.[41]

USAF Gen. Laurence Kuter, commander of PACAF, proposed on August 26 that an escalation ladder be employed for a potential offshore-island invasion. First, the ROC Air Force would strike mainland airfields with conventional weapons. If unsuccessful, U.S. nuclear strikes would target airfields opposite Taiwan as well as the military control center at Ching Yang. Continued PRC aggression would expand nuclear attacks to targets within 644 kilometers of Taiwan, followed by the full implementation of OPLAN 25-58's phase II via attacking the remainder of the targets listed and, if necessary, phase III to destroy the war-making ability of the PRC.[42]

During discussions of U.S. options on September 2, CJCS Gen. Nathan F. Twining stated that in the event of military action, the United States would have to utilize low-yield (seven to fifteen kilotons) nuclear weapons against five local airfields opposite Taiwan. Army Chief of Staff Gen. Maxwell D. Taylor noted that the immediate use of nuclear weapons would be unnecessary but stated that they would be the only effective way to knock out the artillery batteries or counter an otherwise sustained attack. CNO Adm. Arleigh Burke stated that while the initial phase of resisting an invasion of the offshore islands could be conventional, only nuclear weapons could stop a determined effort.[43]

At a subsequent White House meeting on September 6, Eisenhower authorized the use of conventional weapons while withholding permission for nuclear use, confirming his earlier decision.[44]

The crisis carried major global risks. Most notably, if early nuclear strikes failed to halt the PLA offensive, further attacks deep into China would have to be undertaken, which might trigger Soviet nuclear strikes on Okinawa, Taiwan, and the U.S. Seventh Fleet—a development that would almost certainly result in a general nuclear war between the United States and the USSR, which at the time was closely allied with China.[45]

One of the major changes initiated to the OPLAN was the creation of Annex H, "Countering Chinese Communist Interdiction and/or Aggression against Chinmen [Quemoy]/Matsu Island Groups, Taiwan, and the Penghus without Using Nuclear Weapons." This was a new component of OPLAN 25-58 developed in response to a White House request and was issued on September 11, although the final conventional component of the plan was not complete until October 24.[46] But the United States was not well placed in theater for such operations owing to a limited number of appropriately configured aircraft and logistics pipelines.[47] Three new intermediate phases were added between the original phases I and II.

- Phase I-H, which assumed no signs of an invasion of the main offshore islands, would restrict the United States to providing material and logistics support to the ROC.
- Phase II-H envisaged a PRC attempt to invade one or more of the main offshore islands, with the U.S. supporting the Nationalists in attacking the invading force, artillery positions, and local airfields with conventional weapons.
- Phase III-H, which envisaged the PRC extending operations to Taiwan and Penghus or nearby waters, would see the United States potentially extend its conventional attacks on mainland targets to a distance of 1,287 kilometers from the main island.[48]

As of September 5, assessments held that the regional USAF units only had sufficient munitions and supplies for thirty days of conventional operations, whereas the U.S. Navy could only sustain an air effort for twenty days.[49] Conventional operations would serve as only a short-term effort to dissuade Beijing from pursuing an invasion of the offshore islands.[50] As it was, the crisis abated in the fall.

The 1958 Taiwan OPLAN had crashed into reality and been found wanting. Quite apart from being unclear on how many of the offshore islands the United States might seek to defend, authorities found the use of nuclear weapons as a first resort unappealing. Indeed, orders that nuclear weapons were not to be used from the outset were issued early in the crisis at the White House meeting of August 25.[51] Additionally, the islands the United States was willing to help defend were narrowed down as the crisis progressed, limiting the potential for hostilities.[52] The postcrisis assessment of Taiwan Defense Command, the U.S. headquarters on the island, best summarized the effect of the crisis on contingency plans: "The most significant change in planning assumptions was that concerning the possible employment of atomic weapons. Although U.S. participation never reached the shooting stage, this changed assumption radically affected the offensive capabilities of U.S. forces available for contingent employment, and required major revisions of operational planning and computation of logistics support requirements, ordnance and other."[53]

THE SIOP AND CHINA

By the end of the 1950s, the lack of coordination between service branches, conflict between regional command and general war plans, and the imminent introduction of the Polaris submarine-launched ballistic missile (SLBM) led to the commissioning of the National Strategic Target List. From this came the initial Single Integrated Operational Plan (SIOP), SIOP-62, for the targeting of nuclear weapons.[54] In support, U.S. Pacific Command (USPACOM) drafted General War Plan No. 1-61.[55]

SIOP-62 treated the entire "Sino-Soviet bloc" as a single target set that would be subjected to comprehensive attack in the event of war. Seventy-eight urban-industrial locations in the PRC were on the list.[56]

Under President Richard M. Nixon, nuclear strategy shifted toward more discriminate options. SIOPs for China and other states that could be separated from those for the USSR were in place by 1972, with the PRC allocated around six hundred warheads.[57] A requirement for a broader set of distinct attack options were codified for China in 1974 under the Ford administration.[58] Discussions to remove the PRC from the SIOP began under President Jimmy Carter, but it was not until a shift in the nuclear weapons employment policy in July 1982 and an updated SIOP-6 in October 1983 that the PRC was removed from the SIOP and became subject of a separate, more limited nuclear war plan.[59]

DEFINING VICTORY

The U.S. nuclear monopoly and the recent experience of World War II were reflected in early visions for war with the Soviet Union. Offtackle was drafted under the guidance of NSC 20/4 of November 23, 1948, with war aims including "eliminating Soviet Russian domination in areas outside the borders of any Russian state allowed to exist after the war," all "without a predetermined requirement for unconditional surrender," in the context that the USSR was judged to be "not capable of sustained and decisive direct military attack against U.S. territory."[60] To this end, Offtackle envisaged

- Phase I: D-day to D+3 months: Soviet attack, allies launch nuclear attacks on USSR—104 cities struck with 220 bombs. Western Hemisphere defended, Japan/Taiwan/Philippines/UK/Iceland defended, North African coast held, Soviet fleet and ports destroyed, Western Europe bridgehead held or forces withdrawn from continent with intent to reinvade later
- Phase II: D+3 months to D+12 months: Continued strategic air campaign, mobilization and build-up in UK and North Africa for reinvasion of Western Europe, potential secondary offensives
- Phase III: D+12 months to D+24 months: Continued strikes on USSR, two-pronged reinvasion of Europe, Soviet forces in Western Europe cut off. Liberate Europe. Invade USSR in the event of Soviet failure to capitulate[61]

Yet whatever realism this had would not survive the Soviet acquisition of an effective nuclear capability. The NSC's Net Evaluation Subcommittee (NESC) released a report in November 1963, *The Management and Termination of War with the Soviet Union,* that explored war scenarios with grim conclusions. The most extreme possibility—a "war initiated by a Soviet massive intercontinental nation-killing attack"—was seen as plausible between 1964 and 1972. In this event, it noted, "The concept of sophisticated response capability, war management to limit the total effect of the war and a negotiated termination of the war, would have very little meaning in the event of such a war." The report added, "There is not much that can be said for the bases [*sic*] for ending this kind of war, except that the objectives of both sides will start with the issue of survival." Even the scenario that began with a communist overthrow of the Italian government ended with a limited intercontinental nuclear exchange. A conflict over control of Thailand with the PRC taking place in parallel with the Italian scenario ended with a large-scale use of nuclear weapons against the PRC with the hope that this would prevent further offensive action by Beijing and facilitate the eventual overthrow of the CCP by Nationalist forces.[62]

FROM VISIONS OF VICTORY TO MUTUAL DESTRUCTION

The United States had accurately assessed even before the end of World War II that the Soviet Union would be the primary global threat to American interests. The succession of plans put in place sought to take advantage of U.S. strengths in terms of industrial power as well as the country's short-term nuclear monopoly. The USSR could not match the United States in terms of economic output or technology, and its anti-access capabilities were still in the embryonic stage and markedly inferior to those formerly possessed by Imperial Japan.

Yet U.S. regional allies were weak, as were the nonnuclear elements of American forward-deployed forces. Plans for the defense of ROC territory were perceived by many as ultimately dependent on the use of nuclear weapons. As the USSR's nuclear capability grew, it became clear that the New Look concept was increasingly unviable. New plans were required that would better leverage U.S. advantages.

CHAPTER 4

ALIGNMENT

Formosa in the hands of such a hostile power could be compared to an unsinkable aircraft carrier and submarine tender ideally located to accomplish offensive strategy and at the same time checkmate defensive or counter-offensive operations by friendly forces based on Okinawa and the Philippines.

—*Gen. Douglas MacArthur, August 1950*

Douglas MacArthur wrote a letter intended to be delivered to a Veterans of Foreign Wars convention shortly after the beginning of the Korean War.[1] Though President Truman ordered it withdrawn and the general complied, the press had already circulated it, making it public.[2] While against official policy, MacArthur's statement was in tune with NSC 68. A breach in the U.S. maritime perimeter risked cutting SLOC to Japan and the Philippines, with a communist-controlled Taiwan acting as a base for Soviet submarines and aircraft from which to strike allied targets—echoing Imperial Japan's use of the territory during World War II.[3] At the center of Truman's objections to the statement was that U.S. intervention in the Taiwan Strait, ordered on June 27, 1950, was only ever intended to be temporary.[4]

The ROC's control of about three dozen small islands near the PRC mainland added complications. The islands could host forces disrupting Beijing's trade routes, serve as launch points for attacks on the mainland, or, if captured, provide the PLA jumping-off bases for an invasion of Taiwan. To avoid entanglement in this, the United States declared it would not take part in the "defense of any coastal islands held by the Nationalist Chinese nor will they interfere with Nationalist Chinese operations from the coastal islands."[5] Initial U.S. operations in the Taiwan Strait began immediately.

What eventually became the Taiwan Patrol Force was formally instigated on August 4, 1950, supported by land-based surveillance aircraft.[6] Its key role was to provide early warning of a potential invasion of Taiwan. While U.S. forces had overwhelming conventional air and sea superiority, the PLA's use of small craft, including junks, posed a challenge due to their size, construction, and numbers. Proposed countermeasures included level bombing by patrol aircraft, napalm strikes to set fire to sails, and possibly nuclear strikes.[7] Indeed, contemporary accounts state that during discussions in August 1954, Secretary of State Dulles "said that if the Communists tried an invasion of Formosa by a fleet of junks, this might make a good target for an atomic bomb."[8]

The ROC's direct role in the Korean War was limited. For his part, Chiang—he had resumed the presidency of the ROC on March 1, 1950—offered 33,000 Nationalist troops for service in Korea. The offer was rejected to soothe the concerns of U.S. allies and out of fear of leaving Formosa exposed and triggering a wider war.[9] Nevertheless, Nationalist forces carried out numerous minor covert paramilitary and raiding operations to distract Beijing from the Korean theater.

Domestically, the Chiang regime was from the start dependent on its propaganda message of *fangong dalu* ("counterattack the mainland") and *guangfu dalu* ("recover the mainland") to secure its legitimacy in Formosa.[10] Ironically, Chiang himself was initially reluctant to launch a large-scale offensive against the PRC in support of the wider effort in Korea. He rebuffed suggestions from both his subordinates and the United States of an attempt to recapture Hainan Island in light of his weak domestic position, his appreciation of the KMT's shortcomings, and the geographical and material challenge such an operation or a major attack on the mainland would pose.[11] But as the Nationalists' situation stabilized, they adopted a more offensive posture toward the PRC without losing sight of the necessity of U.S. support. In January 1953 the new Eisenhower administration signaled a shift, and by February, it lifted some of the restrictions preventing ROC attacks across the strait against the mainland.[12]

While the Nationalist leader had extensive ambitions, reality fell short—U.S.-supported raiding operations against the PRC accomplished little. The largest effort came in July 1953, when the ROC launched a division-sized amphibious landing and air assault against Dongshan Island. Poor coordination hampered the initial attack, and the Nationalists failed to fully dislodge

Communist forces from the island, with PLA reinforcements ultimately compelling a retreat.[13]

ROC DEFENSE REFORMS

After MacArthur's brief visit to Formosa in July–August 1950, a detailed military survey led to the Fox Report, which highlighted major weaknesses in the ROC's air and naval forces and the island's reliance on the Seventh Fleet for defense.[14] To support the reform and modernization process, the United States established the Military Assistance Advisory Group (MAAG) for Taiwan, with the first commander arriving on the island on May 1, 1951.[15] The MAAG supervised an extensive reorganization, retraining, and reequipping of the ROC Armed Forces. American aid was conditional on military reforms and economic stabilization. MAAG controlled Taiwan's military budget to ensure responsible spending and operated from the same building as the ROC Ministry of National Defense (MND).[16] American resources allocated to this and broader projects reached their peak later in the Eisenhower administration due to the incorporation of Taiwan into the U.S. defense perimeter and the associated NSC 146/1 and later NSC 146/2 guidance, with MAAG staffing reaching 3,240 personnel by the end of 1954.[17] Between 1950 and 1966, Taiwan received some $2.4 billion in military aid.[18]

An early major initiative for the ROC Army was to reduce the force in organizational size from thirty-one understrength divisions in 1950 to twenty-one at-strength divisions by the autumn of 1952.[19] The ROC Army received equipment including M4 Sherman, M5 Stuart, and M24 Chaffee tanks as well as trucks and artillery.[20] MAAG claimed substantial progress, although other assessments were mixed.

The ROC Navy was also extensively retrained and reequipped, with much of the training responsibility falling on the Taiwan Patrol Force. While numerically larger than the PLAN, in September 1952, according to assessments, the ROC Navy had a limited ability to fight mobile operations and was at risk of losing its firepower advantage as the PRC's navy further developed; mid-decade analysis indicated that the Nationalists had indeed lost their superiority at sea. To address this, the United States implemented intensive training and transferred surplus warships, including landing ships, minesweepers, and destroyers, the latter starting with *Benson*- and *Gleaves*-class destroyers and followed by *Fletcher*-, *Sumner*-, and *Gearing*-class vessels in the 1960s–70s.[21]

The ROC Air Force also received substantial U.S. support via MAAG. After initial deliveries of P-47 Thunderbolts, the air branch was brought into the jet age to combat the PLAAF's Soviet-sourced MiG-15s, with the first F-84G Thunderjets arriving in June 1953, followed by F-86F Sabres, F-100 Super Sabres, and later during the 1960s F-104 Starfighters and F-5 Freedom Fighters. Transport aircraft like the Fairchild C-119 and air-defense systems, including Nike Hercules and Hawk SAMs, further bolstered the force.[22]

By December 1958, reports indicated that U.S. assistance had helped create "21 regular infantry divisions, eight air wings, a small but efficient navy and marine corps, plus various special combat and support units."[23] These forces were designed not only to defend Taiwan but also to serve as a regional reserve in a general war with the Sino-Soviet bloc. The availability of a cheap but effective U.S.-allied force was referred to as a "strategic bargain" by U.S. Ambassador to the ROC Walter S. Rankin in a 1954 embassy dispatch.[24]

THE FIRST TAIWAN STRAIT CRISIS AND THE SINO-AMERICAN MUTUAL DEFENSE TREATY

In November 1953 NSC 146/2, "United States Objectives and Courses of Action with Respect to Formosa and the Chinese National Government," declared the "maintenance of the security of Formosa, independent of communism, as an essential element within the U.S. Far East defense position." This officially incorporated Taiwan into the U.S. defense perimeter, a position to be maintained "even at grave risk of general war."[25]

The fate of the minor islands near the mainland controlled by the ROC would become the subject of much debate in Washington. Even the JCS split on its recommendations, with the chair and U.S. Navy and USAF leadership recommending the defense of the ten largest islands, including Quemoy, but the remaining members stating that these islands were "important but not essential to the defense of Formosa from a military standpoint."[26] President Eisenhower tended to side with the latter view but had concerns about the possible psychological effect of losing the islands on the ROC and other U.S. allies.[27]

For his part, Chiang had few doubts as to their value, seeing the outlying islands as Taiwan's first line of defense, stepping stones back to the mainland, staging posts to continue raiding and blockade operations, and—like Eisenhower—important psychological symbols.[28] For its part, China planned to recommence the "mopping up" of the immediate offshore islands (Mao recognized Taiwan was still out of reach), although for the larger islands the initial intent was to pressure the United States to both negotiate with the PRC and lean on Chiang to withdraw from them.[29] Such action would also disrupt the Nationalist blockade and demonstrate Beijing's independence from Moscow.[30]

PLA shelling of Quemoy began in August 1954, intensifying in September. On November 1 the PLAAF began strikes against the Dachens, with air attacks and an amphibious assault leading to the successful capture of the nearby Yijiangshan in January 1955. Renewed and intensified attacks on the Dachens the following month led to a withdrawal of the Nationalists under U.S. pressure. To support the pull out, the U.S. Navy's Operation King Kong oversaw the evacuation of approximately 15,000 civilians, 11,000 Nationalist troops, artillery, vehicles, and 12,900 tons of military equipment and ammunition. Six attack carriers and one ASW carrier provided protection.[31]

ROC officials were privately assured that the United States considered Kinmen and Matsu important to Taiwan's defense, but public ambiguity remained.[32] Amid the crisis, CINCPAC had OPLAN 51-53 at the ready to provide for the defense of Taiwan, the Pescadores, and some of the offshore islands.[33] But despite a large PLA buildup, the United States did not expect a move against Taiwan itself.

The signing of the SAMDT in December 1954 proved to be a decisive development in the U.S.-ROC relationship, stabilizing the status quo for both parties and clarifying the security status of most Nationalist-held territory. "Most" is a critical qualifier—the treaty covered both Taiwan and the Pescadores Islands but was only "applicable to such other territories as may be determined by mutual agreement." A private exchange of notes also took place, clarifying that any significant Nationalist operations against the mainland would require consultation with the United States.[34]

Congress remained concerned about the offshore islands issue. In January 1955 it passed the Formosa Resolution, authorizing President Eisenhower "to employ the Armed Forces of the United States as he deems necessary for the specific purpose of securing and protecting Formosa and the Pescadores against armed attack," granting scope for the island's defense.[35]

By the spring of 1955, the PRC began to send signals that it was willing to negotiate with the United States for a reduction of tensions in the Taiwan Strait—likely at least in part due to the USSR's tepid enthusiasm over the

ROC soldiers load ammunition onto the LST 772 (later re-named USS *Ford County*) amid the evacuation of the Dachen Islands during the First Taiwan Strait Crisis. *Official U.S. Army photo, February 1955, U.S. Naval Institute photo archive*

confrontation. The Chinese-American ambassadorial talks, which commenced due to this incident, remained the only formal contact between the United States and PRC until the 1970s.[36]

The significant operational change that resulted from the signing of the SAMDT was the formation of the U.S. Taiwan Defense Command (USTDC).[37] This command oversaw U.S. military activity on the island, including its defense. In 1955 contingency plans solidified into two options: a unilateral defensive OPLAN and the joint US-ROC OPLAN Rochester.[38] A dispatch from Ambassador Rankin in Taipei from May 1955 noted aspects of Rochester:

> In summary, the plan contains a general estimate of the military situation, including enemy capabilities and [Nationalist] Chinese-U.S. potential, a listing of U.S. forces which it is expected will be deployed

> in the event of hostilities, and an outline plan of how the U.S. and Chinese forces will coordinate their planning so that an efficient combined combat operation might be possible. Operational responsibilities are allocated, the Chinese assuming the burden of ground activity and the United States' primary tasks of air defense, naval support, and bombardment. Understandings appear to have been reached that Chinese Naval and Air Forces shall be employed under U.S. operational control in the event of a combined effort.[39]

As is generally the case with contingency plans, exercises tested their efficacy. For Rochester, this included the "Food Chain" series. A declassified exercise briefing from 1975 described the scenario that year as including a naval blockade against the ROC by the PRC, leading to a confrontation at sea, the introduction of U.S. forces, and air attacks on Taiwan.[40]

Between 1957 and 1974, U.S. nuclear weapons were also based in Taiwan: the aforementioned Matador missiles and, from 1960, free-fall nuclear bombs. Nuclear weapons were also stationed in Guam, Okinawa, the Philippines, and the ROK, providing the United States with nuclear artillery, landmines, surface-to-surface missiles, and SAMs as well as free-fall bombs for fighter-bombers.[41]

THE SECOND TAIWAN STRAIT CRISIS

The second crisis in the Taiwan Strait was briefer than the first, running from August to October 1958, and centered upon the stepped-up shelling and blockading of the Kinmen Islands, beginning on August 23, as well as air battles and naval clashes, most notably near Dongding Island.[42] In addition, a bombing raid on the main island in the Kinmen group occurred on August 24. The PLA hoped to force the Nationalists based there to surrender or withdraw. China also sought to further weaken the already limited ROC blockade, which was inflicting economic damage on the PRC, and eliminate the islands as bases for infiltration, raids, and artillery strikes.

By September, the United States was reinforcing its deployment to Taiwan with additional ships, aircraft, and air-defense systems. Additionally, new equipment was supplied to the Nationalists: ROC Air Force F-86 fighters were fitted with the then-new AIM-9 Sidewinder air-to-air missile to grant them an edge against PLA aircraft. The U.S. Navy also assisted the Nationalists in breaking the blockade of the Kinmen Islands through providing escorts in

A USAF Lockheed F-104A Starfighter of the 83rd Fighter Interceptor Squadron at Taoyuan Air Base, ROC, during the Second Taiwan Strait Crisis. *U.S. Air Force photo, September 15, 1958, National Museum of the United States Air Force*

international waters. By the close of September, officials judged that immediate supply issues on the offshore islands had been resolved.[43]

Mao was somewhat surprised at the strength of the U.S. response to the PLA's actions.[44] Beijing declared a ceasefire in October 1958, although periodic PLA shelling—on alternate days and mainly utilizing projectiles full of propaganda leaflets—continued until 1979, when the confrontation simmered down.

COLD WAR ACTIVITIES

Beyond its defense, the ROC played a supporting role in several U.S. operations in Southeast Asia. The end of the Chinese Civil War on the mainland led to surviving Nationalist forces in the country's southwest fleeing across the border into Burma.[45] But joint ROC-U.S. attempts to use them against the PRC failed to produce results.

As well as Burma, ROC forces had withdrawn into Vietnam at the end of the Chinese Civil War. While also viewed as a potential force to use against the CCP or to support the French in their local anticommunist effort, little utilization was made of the Nationalist forces for political and practical reasons.[46] They were ultimately repatriated to Taiwan following the ceasefire in Korea.[47]

In Tibet resentment from the local population regarding Beijing's attempts to impose its rule following the territory's 1950–51 annexation provided additional opportunities to the ROC and the United States.[48] As with the Burma initiative, Taipei aimed to fan the rebellion into a broader movement that would allow the Nationalists to return to the mainland.[49] For the United States, it formed part of a global anticommunist effort until Washington ended its support in 1969.

By far, the most public manifestation of the U.S.-ROC alliance was the support Taipei offered to Washington's war in Vietnam. Taiwan's role as a logistics base for U.S. forces was substantial, with the island acting as a hub for transport and in-flight refueling assets among other services.

From the mid-1950s, the CIA supported Taiwan's Bureau of State Security, and the territories held by the ROC became key bases for signals intelligence (SIGINT) work.[50] But the standout intelligence efforts were joint air-reconnaissance operations. This was the era of the 35th "Black Cat" Squadron, a U.S.-trained ROC Air Force unit that operated U-2 spy aircraft over mainland China from 1961 to 1968.[51] The 34th "Black Bat" Squadron, a CIA-sponsored air-transport, special operations, and reconnaissance unit, flew from 1952 to 1972, including in an intelligence-gathering role over and around the periphery of mainland China.[52] The 34th's focus was monitoring Beijing's air-defense radar system and nuclear program. This effort peaked with 1969's Operation Heavy Tea, the successful airdrop of a CIA sensor pod from an unmarked C-130 Hercules near the PLA's nuclear-testing facility.[53]

A TEMPORARY STATUS QUO

Joint plans for the defense of the ROC, which sat alongside U.S. unilateral plans, were an early feature for the SAMDT. These laid a foundation that persisted for over two decades. The U.S.-ROC alliance also provided Washington with a high degree of influence and de facto veto power over Taipei's actions, leverage that would help ensure stability across the Taiwan Strait.

The transformation of the ROC into a key regional U.S. ally was a far-from-smooth process. But this enabled Washington to train and equip a force that would alleviate the peacetime workload of American units and personnel in the Pacific and potentially take on more offensive tasks itself in wartime. Taiwan was now part of the U.S. Pacific containment strategy.

CHAPTER 5

DEALIGNMENT

CINCPAC OPLAN 5025, COMUSTDC OPLAN 5025,
and MND-USTDC OPLAN Rochester were
cancelled effective 1 January 1980.
"Taiwan Wrap-Up," Commander in Chief
Pacific Command History 1979

The U.S. military came up with the first detailed plan for a KMT return to the mainland in December 1950.[1] This U.S. Army plan was intended to unfold in three phases: first, securing Taiwan and setting up a U.S. military mission within six months; second, over the following six to eighteen months, focus on bolstering mainland resistance against the CCP and developing Nationalist forces, and liberate Hainan Island. The endgame was a Nationalist landing to topple the communist government. A Joint Strategic Plans Committee plan followed, but these proposals were rebuffed, as were later U.S. and domestically-generated plans to reclaim Hainan Island. Key among the obstacles was Chiang's focus on stabilizing his own domestic position.[2]

RETURNING TO THE MAINLAND

In June 1953 and now more secure in his position, Chiang presented the "Guang" plan—a group of former Imperial Japanese officers drafted it—to the United States for a Nationalist return to the mainland requiring several years of preparation and a sixty-division ground force.[3] The revised "Kai" plan was presented the following December.[4] Both were rejected by American officials, with the MAAG noting that much of the latter plan was "completely infeasible."[5]

Claims that a Nationalist landing could trigger a revolt against the CCP underpinned further proposals submitted by the KMT in 1956, but the United States again turned them down.[6] In October 1958, under U.S. pressure at the end of the Second Taiwan Strait Crisis, Chiang agreed to a communiqué renouncing the use of force to retake the mainland, although the wording only committed to peaceful methods being the "principal" rather than the exclusive means.[7]

The last series of efforts to return to the mainland commenced in 1959, when Mao's "Great Leap Forward" began to implode. Chiang's initial proposals that year were rejected by the United States because, while immense unhappiness among the PRC's population existed, there was no sign of the regime losing its grip on power.[8]

Nevertheless, these and other plans evolved into Project Guoguang ("National Glory"), which Chiang initiated in April 1961.[9] Possible catalysts for an offensive campaign included exploiting renewed conflict on the mainland, factional fighting within the CCP leadership, or some conflict on the Chinese border—although U.S. involvement would still be critical.[10] Even the opening phase of Guoguang would require a level of personnel and sealift that was beyond the ROC military, with 270,000 troops thought necessary for the landing.[11] Plans included the possibility of using mobilized merchant ships to transport the force.[12]

Formal proposals were presented to the United States in March 1962, with Chiang's plan involving a covert but large amphibious landing designed to create the appearance of a spontaneous uprising.[13] Nevertheless, Washington did not want to provoke further PRC involvement in Indochina, so the initiative was formally rejected in June 1962.[14]

Chiang's intention to launch an independent invasion in 1965 collapsed after a sharp defeat in a pair of naval battles shook the ROC's confidence that autonomous action was possible.[15] The ROC proposed making landings in Guangdong province to divert Chinese attention from supporting the North Vietnamese, but Washington turned them down.[16] A 1965 CIA assessment of the probability of the success of the proposed ROC plans was scathing, stating that such operations had "very little chance of success" without a huge amount of U.S. support.[17] Support from the United States was sought one final time in 1967 to take advantage of the chaos of the Cultural Revolution and perceived splits within the PRC, but again, the request was rejected.[18]

Ultimately, lack of U.S. support combined with the termination of American military aid to Taiwan ended the prospect of a large-scale return to the mainland, although the "Wang-Shih" plan to use special forces to incite an uprising was taken forward independently.[19] Chiang declared a "political counter-offensive" in 1969 after practical hopes of returning to the mainland ceased.[20] The Guoguang Operations Office—renamed the Operation Planning Office in 1966—closed in 1972.

THE ALLIANCE FRAYS

The rhetoric surrounding the importance of defending Taiwan featured in the 1960 U.S. presidential election. Debating then–Vice President Richard Nixon, Senator John F. Kennedy was keen to highlight that with regards to Taiwan's offshore islands, it was not in the U.S. interest to go to war should they be attacked in isolation. Nixon countered that such an attitude would invite an attack.[21]

Once in office, Kennedy's credentials as a Cold War warrior were hawkish but pragmatic during his administration (1961–63). The president and some of his advisors desired to soften the U.S. attitude toward the PRC. But this ran against Chiang's ambitions and domestic anticommunist feelings, and Kennedy demurred from any formal policy shift.[22] He did experience his own "mini" Taiwan Strait crisis in 1962, linked to the detection of a PLA buildup opposite Taiwan, but this was defused before it reached the heights of the previous crises.[23] The administration of Lyndon B. Johnson (1963–69) saw little further change toward the ROC. Nevertheless, there were splits within the administration and a general appreciation that the policy of nonrecognition of the PRC was not sustainable in the long run.[24]

Matters came to a head during the Nixon administration (1969–74). The Sino-Soviet border conflict of 1969 took the strained relations that had developed between Beijing and Moscow—chiefly the result of ideological divergence—to new levels of hostility.[25] Tipping Beijing into the U.S. camp would substantially alter the global power balance. During his time out of office, Nixon, formally a staunch ROC advocate, had concluded that Chiang's goal of returning to power on the mainland was beyond reach. In 1967 he wrote a *Foreign Affairs* article calling for the end of the PRC's "angry isolation."[26] He subsequently carried this stance into the presidency.[27]

In July 1971 U.S. National Security Advisor Henry Kissinger went to Beijing to meet with Premier Zhou Enlai. There, he pledged to begin reducing

U.S. force levels in Taiwan, despite the United States having previously given assurances to Chiang Ching-kuo, the son and heir apparent of Chiang Kai-shek, that Washington would not offer any compromises to Beijing. Additionally, the United States pledged not to adopt a "Two China" solution that would see the ROC and the PRC recognized separately. Yet Kissinger failed to secure a pledge from Beijing not to invade Taiwan even though promising not to assist Chiang Kai-shek in any attack on the mainland.[28]

For its part, the JCS argued in August 1971 that reducing U.S. forces in Taiwan or a full withdrawal would harm American local and global interests.[29] In contrast, Secretary of State William P. Rogers and Secretary of Defense Melvin R. Laird argued that B-52s and SLBMs could take up the nuclear tasking from units on Taiwan.[30]

Nixon's February 1972 visit to China led to the Shanghai Communiqué, marking a step toward U.S.-PRC diplomatic ties and introducing Washington's enduring ambiguity on Taiwan. While Beijing asserted that it ruled all of China, the United States carefully stated that it "acknowledges that all Chinese on either side of the Taiwan Strait maintain there is but one China and that Taiwan is a part of China."[31] Mao also remarked, "We can wait, maybe even a hundred years," for unification with Taiwan.[32] But on repeating this statement to Kissinger in 1975, he elaborated: "It's better for it to be in your hands. And if you were to send it back to me now, I would not want it, because it's not wantable. There are a huge bunch of counter-revolutionaries there. A hundred years hence, we will want it, and we are going to fight for it."[33]

The administration of Gerald Ford (1974–77) had little room to maneuver on this issue with an election on the horizon, despite the fact that the ROC's removal from the United Nations in favor of the PRC in 1971 had made the course of events seem ever more inevitable. Instead, the Carter administration (1977–81) marked the endpoint of the transition of U.S. relations with "China" from the ROC to the PRC, setting the political scene for the decades that followed.

In April 1976, options for the United States to supply the ROC with weapon systems were put forward in light of the reconciliation with the mainland, ranging from like-for-like replacements of existing systems while keeping quantities level to "Substantial ROC Access to New Weapons." The DOD recommended a middle path to maintain flexibility without alienating the PRC. The backdrop to this analysis was a December 1975 study that determined that China would not be able to invade Taiwan without using nuclear weapons much before 1980 but that "the PRC's advantage will continue to increase as Taiwan faces difficulties in procuring modern equipment."[34] In November 1978 the United States rejected a request from Taiwan for advanced fighters of the F-4 Phantom, F-5G (later becoming the F-20 Tigershark), F-16 Fighting Falcon, or F/A-18 Hornet type because they possessed an offensive capability, so such sales might antagonize Beijing. Instead, the United States offered additional F-5E/Fs to the ROC as well as Maverick missiles for use against shipping.[35]

The "main event" of the Carter administration occurred on December 15, 1978, with the announcement of full U.S.-PRC diplomatic ties starting January 1, 1979. This was formalized in the Second Communiqué, where the United States adjusted its One China policy to exclude Taiwan without endorsing the policy of Beijing, stating it "acknowledges the Chinese position that there is but one China and Taiwan is a part of China."

In parallel to the resumption of diplomatic relations with the PRC, on January 1, 1979, the United States withdrew diplomatic recognition from the ROC and gave the required one-year notice for the termination of the SAMDT. The last U.S. military personnel left Taiwan on May 3, 1979, and the treaty became void on January 1, 1980. Also on that latter date, CINCPAC OPLAN 5025, COMUSTDC OPLAN 5025, and MND-USTDC Rochester were canceled, although the CINCPAC plan remained on file for two years afterward.[36] At the same time, CONPLAN 5077 emerged, but details beyond its mere existence (such as a reference in the contents section of *Commander in Chief Pacific Command History 1979*) have remained redacted from official material.[37] It is likely but unconfirmed that this CONPLAN was a downgraded replacement unilateral contingency plan for the defense of Taiwan, lacking the details of a full OPLAN but still outlining a general approach.

THE TAIWAN RELATIONS ACT

To maintain ties with the ROC after derecognition, the Carter administration drafted the TRA. Congress approved a revised version of the act which was signed into law on April 10, 1979, enshrining in law U.S. support for Taiwan's security, arms sales, a legal framework for relations, and congressional oversight.[38]

Two critical passages addressed defense provisions. The first stated that "the United States will make available to Taiwan such defense articles and defense services in such quantity as may be necessary to enable Taiwan to maintain a sufficient self-defense capability." While open to interpretation, in theory it compelled the U.S. government to offer equipment sufficient to resist a PRC attack. Second was a provision that the United States "maintain the capacity of the United States to resist any resort to force or other forms of coercion that would jeopardize the security, or social or economic system, of the people on Taiwan." This committed the United States to maintain the *capacity* to defend the ROC without a specific pledge to actually do so—part of an approach which became known as "strategic ambiguity." One can speculate that CONPLAN 5077 was put in place, at least in part, to help facilitate the TRA requirement that the United States maintain the capability to defend Taiwan, as some form of contingency plan would be a prerequisite to this. The importance of the ROC's security to U.S. policy was also emphasized by the act, which stated that the United States "consider[s] any effort to determine the future of Taiwan by other than peaceful means, including by boycotts or embargoes, a threat to the peace and security of the Western Pacific area and of grave concern."

A NEW STATUS QUO

The administration of Ronald Reagan (1981–89) was a mixed blessing at best for Taipei. Rhetorically, Reagan was heavily pro-Taiwan during his 1980 election campaign, even initially pledging to re-recognize the ROC.[39] But this stance was quickly toned down after he won the election. ROC attempts to secure the advanced fighters Carter refused to supply fell on deaf ears.[40] Fears over this move were compounded when, on August 17, 1982, in the Third Communiqué between Washington and Beijing, the United States stated, in an attempt to appease China, that it "does not seek to carry out a long-term policy of arms sales to Taiwan, that its arms sales to Taiwan will not exceed, either in qualitative or in quantitative terms, the level of those supplied in recent years since the establishment of diplomatic relations between China and the United States, and that it intends gradually to reduce its sale of arms to Taiwan, leading, over a period of time, to a final resolution."[41] To address Taipei's concerns at this, Washington subsequently adopted a series of clarifications over its arms-sales policy toward the ROC, which subsequently became known as the "Six Assurances," which stated that the United States

1. Has not agreed to set a date for ending arms sales to Taiwan.
2. Has not agreed to consult with the PRC on arms sales to Taiwan.
3. Will not play a mediation role between Taipei and Beijing.
4. Has not agreed to revise the Taiwan Relations Act.
5. Has not altered its position regarding sovereignty over Taiwan.
6. Will not exert pressure on Taiwan to enter into negotiations with the PRC.[42]

Chiang Ching-kuo received further reassurances:

> Any agreement we [the United States] reach with Beijing will be predicated on a continuation of Beijing's peaceful intentions toward Taiwan. We will not be guided simply by Beijing's word in this matter. We will continue to monitor carefully, through various intelligence capabilities, Beijing's military production and deployment. We also will keep you informed, through both periodic and ad hoc Intelligence briefings, about what we learn. Any significant change in PRC actions in the direction of a more hostile stance toward Taiwan will invalidate any understanding we may reach with Beijing regarding our future arms sales to Taiwan.[43]

Officials also decided to offer assistance for continued F-5E/F coproduction and authorize the transfer of sixty-six secondhand F-104G fighters to Taiwan.[44] In support of this, Reagan also drafted a secret memorandum to clarify the Third Communiqué, with the critical section stating: "The U.S. willingness to reduce its arms sales to Taiwan is conditioned absolutely upon the continued commitment of China to the peaceful solution of the Taiwan-PRC differences. It should be clearly understood that the linkage between these two matters is a permanent imperative of U.S. foreign policy. In addition, it is essential that the quantity and quality of the arms provided to Taiwan be conditioned entirely on the threat posed by the PRC. Both in quantitative and qualitative terms, Taiwan's defense capability relative to that of the PRC will be maintained."[45] The memorandum, which remained officially classified until 2019, was essentially a commitment to maintain a military balance across the Taiwan Strait that would help ensure the ROC's survival.

Reagan's settlement set the tone for the remainder of the 1980s. Arms sales to Taiwan continued, although they were increasingly in the form of technology transfers and commercial partnerships to provide a fig-leaf argument that they were not "arms sales" as construed in the August 1982 communiqué. Notably, the ROC Air Force received support for its Indigenous Defense Fighter (IDF) program and to build domestic models of *Oliver Hazard Perry*–class frigates via U.S. companies.[46]

TAIWAN'S NUCLEAR WEAPONS PROGRAM

Given its precarious position, it is unsurprising that the ROC moved toward developing nuclear weapons as a deterrent.[47] Chiang Kai-shek's interest in nuclear weapons dated back prior to the withdrawal to Taiwan, with ROC military officials and scientists sent to witness U.S. nuclear tests and gather as much data as possible and a supporting Atomic Energy Commission established. The urgency of this effort faded as Taiwan moved under the U.S. protective umbrella, but activities continued despite a 1953 pledge by Chiang not to develop nuclear weapons.[48]

In 1962 the ROC activated its first research reactor, built through the U.S. "Atoms for Peace" initiative. Just two years later, the PRC tested its first nuclear weapon. By 1966, Chiang had secretly advanced a nuclear arms program under the guise of a civilian initiative, raising U.S. concerns about Taiwan's civilian nuclear projects. Yet in 1968 Taiwan signed the Nuclear Non-Proliferation Treaty.[49]

Efforts to acquire a latent nuclear potential (as opposed to operational weapons) were refocused by the derecognition of the ROC at the United Nations. There were two distinct episodes in which the United States moved to shut down the program. The first occurred following leaks to the press in 1976 that U.S. intelligence had detected on the island signs of nuclear fuel reprocessing required to extract plutonium. Further inspections identified additional suspicious activity, and in 1977 the United States forced the ROC into a secret agreement to end all potentially military nuclear activities.[50]

The second incident occurred in 1988. Despite its agreement with Washington, Taipei had covertly continued efforts to develop the potential to build a nuclear weapon. Colonel Chang Hsien-yi, a CIA informant and deputy director of nuclear research, defected to the United States with proof of the efforts. This triggered another strong U.S. crackdown, permanently shutting down the Taiwanese program. There has since been no sign of Taipei reviving its nuclear ambitions.[51]

As well as developing the weapons themselves, the ROC also made provisions for their delivery. A parallel ballistic missile program, the Tian Ma ("Sky Horse"), was canceled under U.S. pressure. Plans to use the IDF then in development to deliver nuclear weapons also came to nothing.[52]

THE INTERIM ENDGAME

The derecognition of the ROC by the United States in 1979 may have seemed catastrophic for Taipei, but it did not appear to halt the U.S. contingency planning process with regard to Taiwan. While limited official ties ruled out formal defense cooperation, the TRA legally required the United States to maintain the capacity to resist the PRC use of force or other forms of coercion against Taiwan, necessitating relevant plans.

Washington sought to tread a fine line between Beijing and Taipei. Certainly, the latter was not an official ally, but stability remained the goal. Yet support for the ROC exceeded what was legally required. While no longer in the U.S. camp, Taiwan was not abandoned.

Breaking ties with the ROC reopened a gap in the U.S. Pacific defense line not seen since 1950. In practice, however, it mattered little: the Sino-Soviet bloc had dissolved, China was focused on its northern borders and rivalry with the USSR, and longer-range nuclear weapons replaced those once based on Taiwan.

CHAPTER 6

APOCALYPSE LATER

My own view of defense is that the whole Japanese archipelago . . . should be like an unsinkable aircraft carrier putting up a tremendous bulwark of defense against infiltration of the [Soviet] Backfire bomber.

Japanese Prime Minister Yasuhiro Nakasone, January 19, 1983

A review of U.S. force requirements in the summer of 1960 identified that the United States, in a variety of contingencies, including the defense of Taiwan's offshore Kinmen and Matsu island groups, was in a position to fight in only a single significant regional conflict without the use of nuclear weapons, even if its forces were supported by partial mobilization. Two or more such contingencies were beyond its capability without undermining its capacity to fight a general war.[1]

It was in this context that the Kennedy administration inherited the White House in January 1961. Officials immediately set about finding a way to raise the threshold for nuclear escalation: the increasing ability of the USSR to strike the United States with nuclear weapons undermined the credibility of U.S. strategic nuclear use in all but the most extreme circumstances. The indiscriminate use of tactical nuclear weapons also carried a high risk of spiraling into Armageddon.

Critical to this was the adoption of the Flexible Response approach, which envisaged a path of gradual military escalation allowing the United States a broader choice of options than just defeat or nuclear warfare in all but the least challenging conflicts. This was easier said than done. Maintaining large conventional forces was expensive. Furthermore, the Soviets were closing the technological gap in fields including guided missiles—a reality made clear during the aftermath of the 1967 Arab-Israeli War and during the 1973 Yom Kippur War, which saw the employment of Soviet-sourced antiship missiles, SAMs, antitank missiles, and cruise and ballistic missiles against Israel. But U.S. experience in Vietnam had demonstrated the potential of precision-guided munitions, most notably laser-guided bombs and guided missiles such as the TOW and Maverick.

In 1975 the Long-Range Research and Development Planning Program, a study sponsored by the Defense Advanced Research Projects Agency (DARPA) and Defense Nuclear Agency (DNA), examined ways of using technology to provide U.S. leadership with options to respond to limited Soviet aggression with restricted or no nuclear use. The investigators noted: "Based on the analysis, it appears that non-nuclear weapons with near-zero miss may be technically feasible and militarily effective. If so, such non-nuclear weapons, under some circumstances, might satisfy the current United States and allied damage requirements that now require the use of nuclear weapons."[2]

This and other analyses in the context of Soviet nuclear parity set the stage for the "Second Offset." Precision-guided conventional weapons, including standoff munitions; intelligence, surveillance, target acquisition, and reconnaissance (ISTAR) systems; stealth technology; and space-based support capabilities were all to become major focus points for the armed forces. New ways to track targets, new munitions to engage them, and new methodologies to deploy those munitions would be developed.[3] With appropriate data links and processing, these would become what the Soviet General Staff later termed the "reconnaissance-strike complex," allowing the United States to "look deep and shoot deep."[4]

During the 1970s and 1980s, there was a steady evolution in U.S. Army doctrine.[5] The "Active Defense" approach, first outlined in the 1976 Army operations field manual, was an attempt to revitalize Western Europe's forward defense in the most effective way possible. Further study and experimentation resulted in the "Airland Battle" concept in which the Army would operate in close concert with the USAF. The Air Force already had a battlefield-support tasking, but through the new tenets of "initiative, depth, synchronization, agility," it outlined a "deep battle" approach that would see air and ground assets engage enemy forces not only on the front line but also during their transit to the front. Airland battle had itself been built in parallel with the 1978 DARPA-initiated "Assault Breaker" concept, a program of the Second

Offset that envisaged the use of advanced conventional systems to degrade Soviet forces invading Western Europe, as well as the "extended battlefield" approach, which proposed deep attack as a solution to the Soviet echelons problem.[6] NATO's counterpart to this was the Follow-On Forces Attack.[7]

THE LATE COLD WAR MARITIME STRATEGY IN THE PACIFIC

Moscow had not stood still in the face of U.S. advances. Under the leadership of Adm. Sergey Gorshkov, the Soviet Navy became a blue-water force capable of challenging the U.S. Navy globally. Meanwhile, the situation in the Pacific was becoming increasingly fragile for the United States. The already comparatively under-resourced USPACOM had a daunting list of responsibilities. In 1972, late in the Vietnam War, CINCPAC headquarters listed the following as major OPLANs:

- OPLAN 5001—General War Plan
- OPLAN 5025—Defense of Taiwan/Penghu
- OPLAN 5027—Defense of [South] Korea
- OPLAN 5041/5083—Defense of Mainland Southeast Asia
- OPLAN 5042/5045—Offensive Options to Counter Chinese Communist Intervention in Current Combat Operations in Southeast Asia[8]

Some relief came with the end of the Vietnam War and the associated OPLAN 5042/5045 requirement in 1975. The end of the U.S. alliance with the ROC also eliminated the need for OPLAN 5025, although the TRA necessitated that the United States maintain the capability to defend Taiwan. But this era also witnessed a significant Soviet Pacific military buildup.[9]

In the 1980s the USSR was deploying its first aircraft carriers (albeit models far less capable than their U.S. equivalents) in the form of the *Kiev* class, carrying a small number of Yak-38 short/vertical takeoff and landing (S/VTOL) fighters, with the most modern surface combatants including *Slava*-class cruisers, *Kirov*-class battlecruisers, *Sovremenny*- and *Udaloy*-class destroyers, and *Alpha*- and *Akula*-class SSNs and *Oscar*-class nuclear-powered guided-missile submarines (SSGNs)—with the second-generation *Oscar II* variant among the vessels carrying SS-N-19 Shipwreck ASMs with a 625-kilometer range. Soviet Naval Aviation fielded Tu-22M Backfire bombers carrying ASMs such as the AS-4 Kitchen, a weapon that could travel at over three times the speed of sound and with a range of around 600 kilometers, which were viewed as one of the

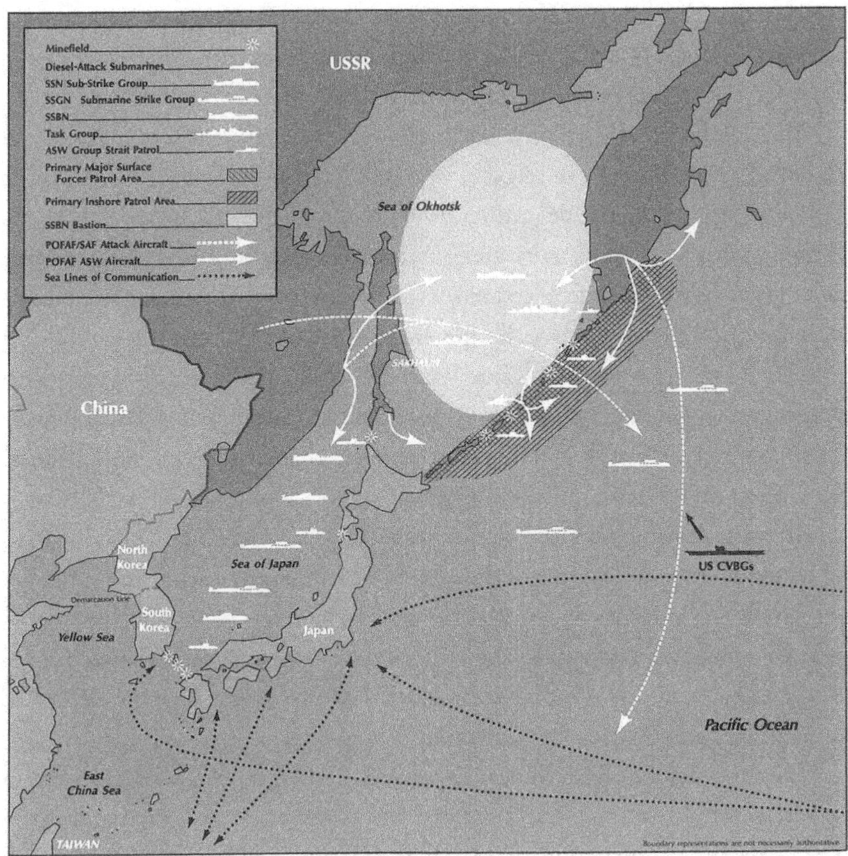

The projected Soviet maritime strategy in the event of war in the Pacific against the United States and its allies. Planners believed that the USSR would utilize an A2/AD-type strategy to defend its territory while interdicting critical SLOC as depicted on this map. *From DOD, "Soviet Military Power: Prospects for Change," August 1, 1989*

leading threats to U.S. Navy carrier groups.[10] The USSR could also call on dozens of SSKs in the region. Combined, these represented a potent A2/AD force.[11]

In the 1970s the U.S. Navy moved toward a defensive strategy that focused on the protection of SLOC. One of the Pacific Fleet's central task was to reinforce the Atlantic: a USPACOM report from 1979 indicates that three of the fleet's six carrier groups would go to Europe in the event of hostilities beginning between NATO and the Warsaw Pact.[12] Indeed, this was still the intent in the 1983 JSCP in the event of a conflict originating in Europe, even though the one from the previous year introduced a requirement for the CINCPAC and Commander in Chief Atlantic (CINCLANT) to draft supplementary OPLANs with the option of not requiring augmentation from their opposite number.[13]

The Pacific Fleet's Atlantic tasking was not new, but it was Adm. Elmo Zumwalt, CNO from 1970 to 1974, who pivoted the United States to a more defensive stance. At the beginning of his tenure, Zumwalt believed that the United States had lost its naval supremacy to the extent that, if planned force reductions beyond fiscal year 1970 went ahead, even this defensive stance would require sending naval reinforcements to NATO from the Pacific and potentially abandoning everything west of Hawaii.[14] Others disagreed with this dire assessment, but Zumwalt's successor, Adm. James L. Holloway, CNO from 1974 to 1978, stated in his memoirs that by the end of his tenure, the United States had a "one ocean navy."[15]

The turnaround from this situation partly originated in a 1976 initiative by Adm. Thomas B. Hayward, the Pacific Fleet commander at the time. He and his staff devised a scheme to strike the Soviet naval base at Petropavlovsk on the Kamchatka Peninsula, Vladivostok, and the Kuriles with conventional weapons early in any conflict with the USSR under the Prompt Offensive Action Plan, later known as "Sea Strike."[16]

Higher echelons of the military subsequently adopted Sea Strike to develop a global maritime strategy. Early assessments of Sea Strike were circulated in the Navy's Sea Plan 2000 study in 1978, which recommended an offensive posture more broadly.[17] Sea Strike was later integrated into what became known simply as the "Maritime Strategy." This global strategy was critical in clarifying the importance of the Pacific theater. As Secretary of the Navy John Lehman noted in 1985, "Our security interests in the Pacific . . . are of equal importance to our other global commitments."[18] Its requirements also justified and informed the buildup to a 600-ship U.S. Navy during the Reagan era, including a planned increase from twelve carrier groups and eighty-eight SSNs in 1982 to fifteen and one hundred, respectively.[19]

As with War Plan Orange, there were multiple iterations of the Maritime Strategy during the 1980s, although there was considerably less variation between incarnations (understandable as the Maritime Strategy was not itself a war plan). The strategy for conflict with the USSR in the 1985 version can broadly be described thus:

- Phase I: Deterrence or Transition to War—*Objective: Escalation Control*
  - Forward-deployed forces would increase readiness
  - Deploy naval forces forward, including SSNs near Soviet waters, and prepare carrier groups and wider surface forces to move forward if necessary
  - Airlift and sealift of assets into theater(s) to begin, including U.S. Army ground units and USAF tactical aircraft to defend key island territories in Europe and the Pacific
  - Begin mobilization of reservists
  - Prepare for defense of U.S. coastal regions
- Phase II: Seize the Initiative—*Objective: Establish Maritime Superiority*
  - ASW: destroy Soviet submarines as far forward as possible while maintaining barrier operations at key chokepoints
  - AAW (antiair warfare): defend carrier groups from air attack, including through "Outer Air Battle" in cooperation with land-based aircraft, and counter Soviet air attacks on land
  - ASuW (antisurface warfare): destroy Soviet out-of-area ships and those in the Mediterranean Sea and Indian Ocean, inflict attrition on those near home waters
  - Potential initial projection operations: offensive air and amphibious operations against targets outside USSR
  - Mine warfare: offensive minelaying against Soviet SSBN (nuclear-powered ballistic-missile submarine) bastions and chokepoints, countermeasures against enemy minelaying
  - Degrade and disrupt Soviet Ocean Surveillance System
  - Defend SLOC
- Phase III: Carry the Fight to the Enemy—*Objective: Favorable War Termination*
  - Strike operations: heavy strikes on flanks possibly culminating in strikes on Soviet territory
  - Amphibious operations: aiming to gain leverage for war termination, secure chokepoints and recover lost territory
  - Logistics: continue efforts to sustain force logistically, including through SLOC defense

– Mobilization: prepare for prolonged conflict if required, including by securing the international supply of critical raw materials and components[20]

In parallel to this, technology was also advancing. The ship- and submarine-launched Tomahawk cruise missile began entering service in 1983. The BGM-109A was a land-attack variant with a nuclear warhead; the RGM/UGM-109B, an antiship variant; and the BGM-109C/D designed for conventional land attack. Harpoon missiles provided shorter-range antiship capabilities.

Further critical developments included U.S. Navy efforts to reduce the vulnerability of the surface fleet. The Standard missile family, which began entering service in 1967, was an improvement over earlier generation SAMs but still inadequate in isolation against saturation attacks. After the failed Typhon system, canceled in 1963, the Navy launched the Advanced Surface Missile Systems program, later known as Aegis, in 1964. First deployed on the USS *Ticonderoga* in 1983, Aegis combined high-performance, data processing, sensors and weapons into an integrated system.

Aegis effectively acted as part of the inner-layer counterpart to what the U.S. Navy dubbed the "outer air battle." This envisaged a layered defense against Soviet aircraft carrying ASMs attempting to attack carrier groups, with the new *Nimitz*-class supercarriers entering service from 1975. The outer air battle itself would seek to "kill the archer" by shooting down aircraft such as the Tu-22M Backfire bomber—a successor to the Tu-16 in the maritime-strike role—before they were able to launch. The E-2C Hawkeye AEW aircraft would direct the F-14 Tomcat interceptor—the computer for the latter carried one of the first microprocessors in a military aircraft.[21] Armed with AIM-54 Phoenix long-range air-to-air missiles among other weapons, F-14s and other fighters would take down hostile targets. EA-6B Prowler electronic-warfare aircraft would jam the radars of the bombers.[22] Any "leakers" would be dealt with by fighters closer to the battle group, including the new F/A-18 Hornet; ship-based SAMs; the Phalanx gun-based close-in weapon system (CIWS); and electronic countermeasures (ECM).

The United States also strove to maintain its undersea advantage. The *Sturgeon*-class SSNs, which entered service from 1967, were joined by the *Los Angeles*-class from 1976. These would become the backbone of the Navy's SSN force during the second half of the Cold War. The Mark 48 torpedo and its later advanced capability (ADCAP) variant became the primary antisubmarine munition for these vessels.

Other services and allies were crucial to the plan. Army units would secure key island bases with air-defense missiles. USAF B-52s could deploy Harpoon missiles for antiship strikes and lay mines. E-3 Sentry AEW&C aircraft, with superior capabilities to carrier-based E-2C Hawkeyes, would bolster naval air operations. USAF tactical aircraft based in Japan, if available, could provide offensive and defensive support. Meanwhile, the U.S. Marine Corps (USMC) was tasked with potential land operations, such as seizing Sakhalin Island and the southern Kuriles in the Pacific.[23]

Given the terrain, the USPACOM element of a potential war against the USSR would have been heavily maritime. As such, the relevant regional late Cold War OPLANs would have closely matched the Maritime Strategy in terms of the options it would have had for conducting the war.

THE DEFENSE OF JAPAN

For much of the later Cold War, USPACOM's lead plan for war in the Pacific against the USSR was OPLAN 5000. The United States was committed to defending Japan, and Tokyo pledged to defend U.S. forces stationed there in parallel with protecting its territory. OPLAN 5051 was the U.S. contingency for defending Japan. A critical priority was sustaining Japan as a forward base for offensive and defensive operations. In the event of war, the 1985 version of the Maritime Strategy stated: "In the Far East, the Soviets would attack U.S. forces in the Pacific. They would also pressure the Japanese to deny to the U.S. the use of naval and air facilities. If they fail because of the U.S.-Japanese alliance (as the Maritime Strategy assumes), they would attack Japan, initially by air."[24]

As regards A2/AD, the Backfire threat was particularly noteworthy. The bombers would obtain targeting data from US-A Radar Ocean Reconnaissance Satellites, US-P Electronic Ocean Reconnaissance Satellites, and aircraft such as the Tu-142.[25] Surface ships and submarines could also provide tracking information. One hundred Backfire and older Tu-16 Badger bombers might also be assigned to strike a carrier group. Doctrine dictated that such attacks would be coordinated with strikes launched by submarines and surface ships.[26] Guam, Midway, and Clark Air Base in the Philippines were thought vulnerable to the Backfires.[27]

A U.S. Navy F-14A Tomcat of VFA-102 escorting a Soviet Bear surveillance aircraft. The latter aircraft would have provided targeting data for strikes on U.S. Navy carrier groups. *U.S. Navy photo by Lt. Dave Parsons, September 1, 1985, Record Group 330: Records of the Office of the Secretary of Defense Series: Combined Military Service Digital Photographic Files, National Archives*

A key task for American-led forces was to prevent Soviet SLOC interdiction and attacks on U.S. forces on sea and land. This would require ASW, blockading the four main Japanese straits, defending the airspace over Japan, and preventing amphibious landings. These aligned with the postwar focus of the Japan Maritime Self-Defense Force (JMSDF) on correcting the IJN's maritime failings. By the early 1980s, Tokyo had made a commitment to defend the sea lanes out to around 1,850 kilometers from the main islands with a focus on the Japan–Guam route and the Bashi channel between Taiwan and the Philippines. The JMSDF was proficient in ASW and mine countermeasures (MCM).[28]

A combination of the strategic bombing Japan had suffered and a popular desire to avoid an air-combat force that could be considered "offensive" led to a focus on air defense for the Japan Air Self-Defense Force (JASDF). A similar reluctance to see the Japan Ground Self-Defense Force (JGSDF) deployed abroad led to anti-invasion operations being its primary task.[29] Therefore, the most significant ground formations were stationed in the northern home island of Hokkaido. In the late 1980s, JGSDF also began operating land-based ASMs, which would aid in both countering an invasion and blocking the country's key straits to transit by Soviet surface ships.

Therefore, Japan's primary military role was to provide for its defense and act as a forward base for U.S. forces, with the Japan Self-Defense Force (JSDF) operating in a supporting role. This was the embodiment of the "shield and spear" strategy, with Japan providing the former and the United States the latter.

Nuclear warfare aside, the most extreme situation involving Japan envisaged an attempted Soviet invasion of Hokkaido, which was incorporated into the OPLAN 5051 contingency plan. Tokyo believed the initial assaults would likely occur at Wakkanai near a small airport, near the village of Sarufutsu, and somewhere between the cities of Teshio and Embetsu—all near beaches suitable for an amphibious assault supported by paratroopers and helicopter-borne assault troops. Securing the Wakkanai port would be critical for unloading merchant vessels bringing in reinforcements and supplies.[30] If successful, the Soviets would control both sides of the Soya Strait, easing access to the Pacific.

There is no proof that Moscow seriously envisaged such an operation, however, and some argue this scenario was driven by a desire to provide a mission for the JGSDF.[31] Others questioned whether the Soviets had the required air and sealift capability to achieve this. The USSR had a large fleet of merchant vessels that, in theory, could be tasked with moving heavy army units into Hokkaido via ports captured in an initial airborne and amphibious assault: in 1985 USPACOM estimated that "the Soviets had over 400 Pacific-based merchant ships that could be used for the administrative lift of 6–7 motor rifle divisions and their equipment."[32] But turning a theoretical capability into action would be a tall order.

While the JSDF held the line, U.S. forces in the area would go on the offensive. Initial targets for carrier aviation—the carriers themselves likely "screened" by the Japanese home islands and the forces they hosted—would include the naval bases in Vladivostok, Petropavlovsk, and Sovyetskaya Gavan as well as the bases supporting Soviet naval aviation.

FAVORABLE WAR TERMINATION

Phase III of the 1985 Maritime Strategy designated "Carry the Fight to the Enemy" as a methodology to achieve favorable war termination and described the types of operations for establishing the conditions to achieve this outcome. These included potential strike operations on Soviet territory and reclaiming any lost territory, including through amphibious operations. Also highlighted was inflicting attrition on Soviet SSBNs in an attempt to alter Moscow's perception of the nuclear "correlation of forces."[33] The strategy summarized the approach thus:

> The desired culmination of this strategy is *war termination on terms favorable to the U.S. and our allies.* This requires putting sufficient *conventional pressure* on the Soviets to convince them that they would have no gain in continuing aggression and that they should in fact cease hostilities, while simultaneously giving them no incentives to escalate to nuclear war. For the Navy, this means neutralization or destruction of the Soviet Navy and of ground and air forces on the Eurasian flanks; sea control; and intervention in the land battle. In this way, maritime forces provide strong leverage for the Soviet Union to accept a *negotiated termination* of the conflict.
>
> At the end of the conflict, from the Soviets' perspective, the operations envisioned by the Maritime Strategy would *defeat their strategy and amputate their global reach* by neutralizing or destroying their fleet. The Communist Party would remain in control of the Soviet Union, and the *homeland would be intact, although it would now be threatened.*[34]

The war termination mechanism presented in the Maritime Strategy was by no means the only one. Indeed, as the conflict envisaged would ultimately be decided on the Eurasian—chiefly European—mainland, Pacific operations could only ever act in support of more decisive events elsewhere. Yet the maritime focus is very much at the center of a Taiwan scenario. As such, the envisioned approach to the USSR may have more relevance to the great power competition of the early twenty-first century than to the one in progress when it was conceived.

THE SHAPE OF THINGS TO COME

Some of the more interesting "what ifs" of this era were the systems in development on both sides but abandoned either because of other priorities, politics, technological barriers, or the end of the Cold War. The USSR developed the R-27K, a submarine-launched antiship ballistic missile (ASBM) armed with a nuclear warhead and designed to destroy carrier battle groups. Targets for this weapon were to be identified using satellites and airborne reconnaissance. Terminal guidance was provided by a seeker that homed in on the targeted ship's electronic emissions.[35] The Soviets were also working on the Kh-15S, an air-launched ASBM designed to be deployed by the Backfire bomber, but it never entered full development.[36]

The U.S. projects then in train are also instructive. The AIM-152 was envisaged as a more capable replacement for the AIM-54 Phoenix but was canceled when the need for long-range engagement diminished.[37] The "forward pass" concept, intended to give the ability to fire ship-based SAMs at targets beyond the horizon using data relayed from aircraft in support of outer air battle, fed into a requirement for a new long-range SAM. This became the SM-2 Block IV program, but it was truncated with only one hundred units produced, seventy-five of those later modified to perform an anti–ballistic missile (ABM) role.[38]

A variant of the nuclear-armed Pershing II ballistic missile, the Conventional Airfield Attack Missile, was designed to aid in the suppression of Soviet airpower; it was explored but not taken forward.[39] Then in 1987 the United States signed the Intermediate Nuclear Forces (INF) Treaty, which prevented similar projects going forward. As a result, the MGM-140 Army Tactical Missile System (ATACMS), with a range of 300 kilometers, became the farthest-reaching ground-launched conventional missile in the American inventory.

Efforts to counter opponent transporter erector launchers (TELs) for ballistic missiles—these streamlined successors of the mobile V-2 launch systems of World War II rendered the missiles extremely difficult to locate and destroy on the ground—were also hampered with the end of the Cold War. One lesser-known project was the Advanced Airborne Reconnaissance System, a stealth reconnaissance uncrewed aerial vehicle (UAV) designed to loiter high over enemy territory to pinpoint TELs for destruction by B-2 Spirit bombers.[40] A similar project, Thirsty Saber, sought to develop a UAV capable of performing TEL search-and-destroy missions using precision-guided munitions.[41] The absence of such a capability would soon present a major challenge.

A WAY OUT?

An important trend of U.S. war plans during this era was toward a model that would seek to halt a superpower conflict short of a strategic nuclear exchange. Technological advantage and changes to doctrine and strategy were seen as the key components to achieve this. While the Soviet armed forces were impressive on paper, it was already clear that they were substantially behind the West in fields such as microelectronics. Moscow's wider economic weakness also became apparent as the 1980s progressed—an issue with major implications for the Soviet Union's claim to be a true U.S. peer.

In the maritime domain, rapidly advancing Soviet A2/AD capabilities were a key threat. While the ROC was largely out of the picture in the Pacific, regional allies led by Japan provided not only bases but also force elements that would be difficult for the United States to bring to bear in a meaningful timeframe. While the Reagan administration is often remembered for the U.S. military buildup, the 1980s Maritime Strategy made the critical role of U.S. allies clear.

CHAPTER 7

THE SOUTH ATLANTIC AND SOUTHWEST ASIA

Lose *Invincible* and the operation is severely jeopardised. Lose *Hermes* and the operation is over.
—*Rear Admiral Sandy Woodward, commander, Royal Navy Falklands Task Force carrier group*

While the twentieth-century contingency plans for another global war were never required, there was no shortage of conflicts that actually materialized. One was the Falklands War, a unique example of a modern air-sea-land expeditionary A2/AD fight in the guided-missile and nuclear-powered-submarine era. Unlike U.S. wars since World War II, it involved two nations that, while not equal, were at least not hopelessly mismatched in their fielded forces.

The Gulf War was another, and it showcased the large-scale use of precision-guided munitions, cruise missiles, ballistic-missile defense, and space-based assets. While far from a perfect comparison to the challenges that would be faced in a modern great power war—a huge disparity existed in the forces of Iraq and the U.S.-led coalition, with A2/AD matters rarely encountered—it marked a turning point in modern U.S. warfare and remains a key case study in war planning. The events that followed the war, most significantly the 2003 invasion of Iraq, highlighted the implications of planning failures and the challenges of conflict termination.

FALKLANDS WAR

Argentina had long claimed the British-ruled Falklands and other nearby islands, having inherited its sovereignty claim from Spain following Argentina's independence. Frustrated with slow diplomatic progress, Buenos Aires set an unofficial deadline of January 1983—the 150th anniversary of the British taking control of the islands—to reclaim them.[1]

Before the conflict, Britain grappled with how to reinforce the Falkland Islands in the event of Argentine aggression. Limited air facilities there meant that only reinforcement by sea was possible, and this would take time. A February 1976 UK assessment included harassment of shipping and the cutting off of air links from bases on the South American mainland as potential Argentine actions.[2] The potential countermeasures could not be easily enacted. Given Cold War demands, permanently stationing an SSN in the region was not a realistic option.[3] Defending against a full invasion of the islands was judged to be impractical. Liberating the islands after an invasion would require a carrier group and a brigade-level force, as well as associated logistics support and a variety of other enablers. A 1977 exercise reaffirmed these conclusions.[4]

With tensions again rising in 1981, an additional assessment occurred. A paper completed in September surveyed Argentina's options, outlined in the postwar Franks Report on the conflict as "harassment or arrest of British shipping; military occupation of one or more of the uninhabited islands; arrest of the British Antarctic Survey team on South Georgia; a small-scale military operation against the Islands; and full-scale military invasion of the Islands." Deterring an invasion, it judged, would require a carrier, escorts, supply ships, potentially an SSN, and brigade-strength ground forces. Liberating the islands postinvasion would require an even larger effort.[5] Nevertheless, detailed contingency planning was not taken forward.[6]

The Argentine Navy (Armada de la República Argentina (ARA)) began the detailed planning stage for an invasion of the Falklands in December 1981, although the official decision for that was not approved until January 12, 1982.[7] This was initially regarded as a contingency in case negotiations with Britain failed, with no intention to carry forward an operation until the second half of the year—although this was later advanced to no earlier than May 15.[8] The working group tasked with this planning defined the military end-state goal:

"Impose on Great Britain the acceptance of a military *fait accompli* which will allow the exercising of Argentinian sovereignty over the Islands of the Malvinas [the Argentine name for the Falklands], Georgias, and South Sandwich, and prevent further efforts to usurp this sovereignty, in order to attain the stated political objective."[9] The military junta then ruling Argentina was under the impression that no armed response from London would be forthcoming. As a result, no sequel or branch plans to defend the islands from a British liberation attempt were put in place despite the working group's recommendations.[10]

Invasion

The United Kingdom underestimated the threat from Argentina and overlooked signs of escalation. Until almost the end of March, intelligence assessments concluded that military action was not imminent but that this could change without progress in negotiations.[11]

The short-term trigger for the invasion of the Falklands came on March 19 in the form of the unauthorized arrival in South Georgia of an Argentine party of scrap-metal merchants. Britain's diplomatic protest over this presence failed, and on March 26 Argentina brought forward its invasion plans in part to preempt British reinforcements being sent to the South Atlantic.[12]

Sensing a deteriorating situation, London ordered two SSNs and a supply ship to the region. But even as late as March 29, UK intelligence suggested Argentine action that would stop short of a full invasion despite reports of unusual fleet movements. That an invasion was potentially imminent became apparent to the British only on March 31.[13]

Following accelerated preparation, the Argentine invasion fleet sailed on March 28, and after a delay, the invasion itself—initially codenamed Azul then later Rosario—took place on the night of April 1–2.

Countermeasures: Operation Corporate

After the invasion, the main body of the Falklands Task Force left the United Kingdom without an agreed CONOPS and only a vague plan for an air and sea blockade that might be followed up by an amphibious landing, although preexisting plans to deploy 3 Commando Brigade to Norway as part of Britain's NATO tasking would help with the latter.[14] A ninety-day timeline was set to mitigate issues such as ship mechanical failure, deteriorating weather, and the risk of falling public support.[15] On May 12 Operational Order 3/82 for Operation Sutton, the amphibious landing, formalized the mission "to repossess the Falkland Islands as quickly as possible" through a phased campaign:

- Phase I: Carrier group to continue blockade of islands
- Phase II: Carrier group to conduct Special Forces reconnaissance and direct action prior to landing
- Phase III: Amphibious group and 3 Commando Brigade to conduct main landing, including MCM operations
- Phase IV: Land Operations by 3 Commando Brigade prior to the arrival of land force HQ and 5 Infantry Brigade
- Phase V: Establishment of land force HQ on HMS *Fearless* and landing of 5 Infantry Brigade
- Phase VI: Repossession of Falkland Islands by the landing force supported by the carrier group and amphibious shipping[16]

Countering A2/AD in the South Atlantic

Argentina's A2/AD kill-chain sensor element took two primary forms: covert surveillance and airborne reconnaissance. Spy ships disguised as merchant vessels deployed in the waters around the Falklands and Ascension Island. Long-range patrol aircraft were the most visible aspect. Conventional military strikes on the United Kingdom or other bases outside the operational area were effectively impossible, although covert attacks remained an option. Naval and air force elements acted as the outer kinetic barrier, benefiting from the Falklands being only 480 kilometers from the Argentine coast rather than the almost 13,000-kilometer distance the British had to contend with.

At sea the ARA surface force possessed the carrier ARA *Veinticinco de Mayo,* the light cruiser ARA *Belgrano,* and an escort force of vintages varying from *Allen M. Sumner*–class destroyers to UK-sourced Type 42 destroyers. Most of both the older and newer escort ship types were fitted with Exocet ASMs. Below the surface, the ARA had one operational *Balao*-class submarine, the ARA *Santa Fe,* and a Type 209 vessel, the ARA *San Luis;* two other submarines were nonoperational. It also contributed an improvised shore-based Exocet launcher—this damaged a British destroyer toward the end of the war—and laid mines in the approaches to Port Stanley, the Falkland Islands capital.

Air power was led by the ARA Super Étendard (only five of fourteen ordered had arrived by the war's outbreak, together with five air-launched Exocets) that could fly from land bases supported by a pair of KC-130 tankers. These tankers could also support the A-4B/C Skyhawks of the Argentine Air Force (Fuerza Aérea Argentina (FAA)) and the ARA's A-4Qs. The FAA also possessed Mirage IIIEA fighters, Dagger attack aircraft, and Canberra bombers. A C-130 was fitted with bombs to strike supply ships. FAA IA 58 Pucará and ARA T-34 Mentor MB-339 light-attack aircraft were deployed on the Falklands themselves. During the course of the war, the British lost two destroyers, two frigates, a landing ship logistic (LSL), a landing craft, and a merchant ship to FAA and ARA aircraft flying from the mainland—one of the destroyers and the merchant ship to air-launched Exocets—and suffered damage to many more ships.

The four principal counter-A2/AD capabilities of the British were submarines, aircraft carriers, land-based expeditionary airpower, and special forces, with logistics as a critical supporting element.

Submarines

Britain's SSN force, designed to counter similar Soviet vessels, vastly outmatched Argentina's submarines and broader ASW capabilities. After the war the Argentine Chief of Naval Operations Vice Admiral Juan José Lombardo stated that one British SSN in position could have thwarted the invasion.[17] The rapid response time of the SSNs—five of which were eventually sent south—was itself insufficient to block the invasion but narrowed the window in which Argentina could send reinforcement by sea. The British announcement of a maritime exclusion zone on April 12 did not immediately halt reinforcement efforts, as permission had not been given to attack merchant shipping and desperation for supplies led to Argentine ships running the blockade. But the total exclusion zone (TEZ) imposed after April 30 along with broadened rules of engagement forced Argentina to rely on air resupply for its occupying garrison.[18]

British priority targets were Argentina's carrier and cruiser groups. While the former escaped detection, HMS *Conqueror* tracked the latter and sunk the *Belgrano* on May 2. This resulted in all significant ARA surface ships withdrawing to the country's territorial waters and taking no further part in the war.

A less glamorous task later assigned to the SSNs was that of an improvised picket vessel. With the Falklands Task Force lacking AEW aircraft, the submarines were stationed along the known Argentine flight paths approaching the islands. By detecting electronic emissions, they could provide British forces with advanced notice of air attacks.

Argentina's submarine fleet had a less than auspicious war. The *Santa Fe* was attacked and forced to beach itself following a mission to deliver reinforcements to South Georgia. *San Luis* undertook multiple attempted attacks on British vessels, but technical issues prevented success.

Aircraft Carriers

The air groups on board HMS *Hermes* and HMS *Invincible* were initially built around Sea Harrier FRS.1 warplanes and Sea King helicopters configured for ASW or transport tasks. The carriers had neither AEW nor in-flight refueling aircraft. Ship-based defenses within the Falklands Task Force included the medium-range Sea Dart and short-range Sea Wolf SAMs, with obsolete Sea Cat and Sea Slug SAMs plus cannon and machine guns in support and some basic ECM systems.

The carriers' fixed-wing air groups inflicted significant attrition on Argentine aircraft and conducted ground-attack, antiship, and reconnaissance missions. But they were constrained by a combination of short aircraft range and the requirement to keep the carrier group at a safe distance from the primary source of threat. Royal Navy assessment indicated that as long as ships remained over 1,296 kilometers from mainland Argentine bases, the aerial threat was negligible but increased significantly if moving within 556 kilometers.[19]

Argentina's carrier experience was far less positive. A planned raid on the British task force was abandoned due to low wind above the flight deck, preventing any takeoffs with a meaningful bombload, and detection of the force by the Royal Navy.[20] The sinking of the cruiser *Belgrano* only emphasized that it was too risky to keep the aircraft carrier at sea in the presence of British SSNs, and its air group was sent to land bases for further operations.

Land-Based Expeditionary Air Power

During the Falklands War, the British utilized land-based air power from both outside and within the main operational theater. The former mostly (but not entirely) focused on Ascension Island in the mid-Atlantic. The distance from Britain to Ascension was some 6,700 kilometers—considerably more than the 4,000 kilometers from the U.S. West Coast to Hawaii—although the British territory of Gibraltar was available for use along the way. The air distance from

Ascension to the Falklands was 6,360 kilometers—less than the 8,480 kilometers from Hawaii to Taiwan but more than the 2,730-kilometer distance from Guam to Taiwan.

The United Kingdom judged the threat to Ascension low. Yet attacks via ARA submarine or civilian ships carrying a raiding force were a possibility, as were a commando-type air landing or parachute drop, using either civilian or military transport aircraft on a one-way trip, or the use of an FAA C-130 to drop incendiaries on the flight line. To counter this, an air-defense radar was installed and provisions made for ground and air defense.[21]

The most high-profile aircraft on Ascension was the Vulcan B.2 bomber. Authorities decided that attacks against the Argentine mainland would be politically risky and ineffective, as the Vulcan's unguided bombs were unlikely to produce damage that justified the backlash of bringing the war to the South American mainland. Fitting the Vulcan (and Hercules) to deploy naval mines was also explored.[22] But Port Stanley Airport on the Falklands became the primary target for the bombers to deny its use as a forward base for Argentine combat aircraft or as a reception point for supplies being airlifted from the mainland. All missions against the airport required extensive in-flight refueling support.

Maritime patrol tasks were carried out by Ascension-based Nimrod MR.2 aircraft hastily modified with in-flight refueling equipment. Hercules transport aircraft were fitted with additional internal tanks and in-flight refueling systems, extending their range and allowing them to drop critical personnel and equipment to the Falklands Task Force. A mix of military and civilian aircraft sustained the air bridge from the United Kingdom to Ascension Island.

A little-known aspect of the British air campaign was the forward operating base at San Carlos. In a European conflict against the Warsaw Pact, RAF GR.3 Harriers could use their S/VTOL ability to relocate from vulnerable bases to dispersal sites in West Germany to avoid air and missile attacks.[23] The plan was to build a facility near the Falklands landing zone to support Harriers and helicopters, extending operations beyond the carriers and adding redundancy in case a carrier was lost. Initial designs for a twelve-aircraft base with a 400-meter runway were scrapped after an Exocet missile sank the MV *Atlantic Conveyor*, taking key equipment with it. Instead, forces improvised a more basic facility from material found elsewhere.[24]

A further notable forward deployment was made to the Chilean island of San Felix in the Pacific by a Nimrod R.1 and support aircraft under Operation Acme. Chile's tensions with Argentina left its leadership agreeable to providing support for British reconnaissance missions during the conflict.[25]

Argentina's expeditionary operations were less than successful. Their failure to adapt Port Stanley Airport to handle fighter jets limited them to the deployment of armed propeller-driven aircraft, light attack jets, and helicopters. All suffered badly at the hands of British air power and special forces.

Special Forces

Both sides tried using special forces for A2/AD or counter-A2/AD missions, with mixed results. Argentina's boldest effort, Operation Algeciras, aimed to sabotage British ships in Gibraltar to prevent them entering the operational theater—an anti-access action. Combat swimmers traveled to Spain on forged passports and planned to swim in and attach limpet mines, but Spanish authorities caught and detained them, stopping the mission before it began.[26]

The most successful UK effort was the raid on the Argentine airstrip on Pebble Island on May 14–15. This attack by helicopter-deployed Special Air Service (SAS) members backed by naval gunfire destroyed eleven aircraft and their support facilities, among them six Pucará ground-attack aircraft that could have sortied against the British landing a week later on area-denial missions.

The most ambitious mission envisaged by the British was a potential raid on the Argentine mainland to destroy the ARA's Super Étendard aircraft and Exocet ASMs. Operation Mikado envisaged two Hercules aircraft landing on the runway of the squadron's home air base of Rio Grande and deploying SAS personnel to destroy the aircraft and missiles and kill the pilots. After that, the raiders would fly out or run to the Chilean border. This plan was abandoned due to the failure of a preliminary reconnaissance mission (Operation Plum Duff) and the high risk involved.[27]

Logistics

The overwhelming challenge of the Falklands War for both sides was logistics, with the British bearing the more significant burden. All air sorties heading from Ascension to the Falklands area were heavily dependent on the Victor K.2 tanker aircraft, which limited such activity.

Maritime challenges were also immense, requiring fuel, stores, and repair support for the Falklands Task Force. Civilian ships were essential to this. After requisitioning, they were equipped with extra communication gear and freshwater systems and allocated with Royal Navy personnel for specialist tasks. Many were modified with the addition of helicopter decks and at-sea replenishment systems. These vessels, called "Ships Taken Up from Trade" (STUFTs), became a critical part of the operation.[28]

Notably, the Royal Navy's support arm, the Royal Fleet Auxiliary (RFA), had just fourteen oilers, of which ten went south to the Falklands. Some provision existed to augment the RFA's tanker force to support transatlantic convoys in the event of war with the USSR, and two civilian British Petroleum tankers were rapidly fitted with equipment to refuel warships. Ten more civilian tanker ships were equipped to supply RFA oilers in a consolidated cargo replenishment at sea (CONSOL) role. Two others acted as base-support tankers, and one carried fresh water.[29]

There were also a variety of specialist missions. A small cruise ship's conversion fulfilled the need for a hospital ship.[30] Two oil-rig support vessels served to carry out repairs to the fleet, and three ocean-going salvage tugs provided long-distance towing—capabilities vital if ships were disabled but remained salvageable.[31] Five trawlers were also converted to act as minesweepers.[32]

The British established three zones for rear-area operations. The Replenishment and Consolidation Area, midway between Ascension and the Falklands, served for supply transfers between requisitioned merchant and RFA vessels with a second such area, east of the TEZ, to support amphibious shipping. The Tug, Repair, and Logistics Area on the northeast edge of the TEZ supported resupply, maintenance, and repair operations. South Georgia was also utilized as an anchorage for this purpose.[33]

The Royal Navy possessed only two landing platform docks (LPDs), six LSLs, and an RFA stores ship to transport the units for the land war—inadequate for a ground force that ultimately numbered two brigades. The requisitioning of cruise ship *Canberra*, ocean liner *Queen Elizabeth II*, and eight Ro-Ro ferries provided additional personnel, equipment, and stores transport capacity.[34] Seven freighters acted in support.[35]

Argentina also faced major logistics hurdles, from sustaining offensive operations to supplying its Falklands garrison. Most combat aircraft operating from the mainland flew at maximum range, with even those equipped for in-flight refueling limited by the availability of only two KC-130 tankers. The buildup of the garrison took place almost entirely before the British sea blockade began, with only the air link to the mainland subsequently available for priority cargo and personnel. Britain's failure to fully disable Port Stanley Airport thus meant the garrison was never completely cut off.

Lessons

As in every conflict, subsequent studies looked to identify lessons for the future. One U.S. contribution to this was the Department of Navy's *Lessons from the Falklands*, a nonclassified summary of which was published in January 1983.[36] It helpfully framed the war in the context of a potential great power conflict—in this case, with the USSR. The superior training of British personnel—a professional military as opposed to the conscript-heavy Argentine forces—and intelligence were cited as major factors in the UK victory.[37]

The Falklands War was a cause of some problems for the U.S. Navy. Secretary of the Navy John Lehman stated that the Falklands War proved a hindrance to his push to expand the U.S. fleet as part of the Maritime Strategy, with some members of Congress claiming that the conflict supported claims of surface-ship vulnerability despite U.S. naval forces having AEW aircraft; long-range supersonic fighters with radar-guided missiles, including the F-14 with the AIM-54 Phoenix; capable SAMs; Phalanx CIWS; and advanced electronic-warfare systems.[38] As such, the 1983 analysis criticized the absence in the Royal Navy of such a "defense in depth."[39] The British shared this view and rapidly purchased Phalanx close-in weapon systems for many of their ships, deployed Sea King AEW aircraft, continued to increase the number of ships carrying the Sea Wolf SAM, and equipped the Sea Harrier with enlarged drop tanks, and later improved radar and AIM-120 AMRAAMs.

Regarding logistics, the U.S. report noted that while the creation of the Ready Reserve Force (RRF) had already advanced U.S. sealift potential, more work was needed to develop self-defense and other capabilities for these ships and the merchant vessels requisitioned during wartime. In addition, the report claimed that the conflict had proved that given the scale of effort required from merchant shipping and an inability to absorb losses, "Allied naval forces can only defend the sealanes by ensuring a forward offensive defense against submarines"—essentially an endorsement of the 1980s Maritime Strategy.[40] The report highlighted merchant tankers in particular as critical to compensate for a shortage of naval oilers.[41] Argentina's inability to strike UK SLOC meaningfully was an advantage the British would have suffered without.[42] Also noted was the "re-learning" of the lesson of ammunition consumption being higher than peacetime projections and a recommendation that older-model weapons be retained in stockpiles.[43]

Analysis of Chinese-language studies of the Falklands War identified it as a source of lessons for the PLA. They recognized that the conflict paralleled a Taiwan scenario in that such a war would see a need to prevent a nonregional power projecting its military into a regional territorial conflict (putting China in the position of Argentina) and that such a war would require significant amphibious operations (putting China in the position of both combatants). Lyle Goldstein, for one, has noted extensive Chinese writings on the subject.[44] Specific lessons included Argentina's failure to correctly judge the likely UK reaction to the initial invasion, the junta overestimating its own military capability, poor preparation in areas such as antiship air warfare, capability shortfalls in areas such as air-to-air refueling, and inadequate stockpiling of air-launched Exocets.[45] Like the official U.S. analysis, the Chinese noted British deficiencies in AEW and limited carrier capacity while highlighting the effectiveness of their SSNs and in-flight refueling efforts.[46] On amphibious warfare specifically, they noted that Argentina's surprise landing facilitated a rapid initial victory. At the same time, the UK operation was seen as able to credit much of its success to deception and a wise choice of landing area that was perceived as unsuitable by Argentina.[47] The British success in mobilizing civilian transport assets in support of the war was also viewed as an essential lesson.[48] Christopher D. Yung has highlighted additional Chinese writing criticizing Argentina's inability to attack supply shipping and underscoring the importance of British access to forward bases.[49]

Coda

The period following this short war saw the creation of what became known as "Fortress Falklands." Any decision by Buenos Aires to restart hostilities would have, by necessity, centered upon air attacks. To this end, in the months following the conflict, the Vulcan force trained for the contingency that should the war have reignited, they would be used to raid mainland fighter bases.[50] While the Falklands remain garrisoned to this day, Argentina's transition to a democracy in 1983 greatly reduced the immediate military threat to them.

Ultimately, domestically generated regime change, catalyzed by the loss of the war, proved central to improving the islands' security.

SOUTHWEST ASIA AND THE GULF WAR

The turbulence of the 1970s underscored the U.S. need to defend Middle Eastern oil reserves, including from Soviet encroachment. Initial planning coalesced around a global mobile force concept, which President Carter authorized on August 24, 1977, via Presidential Directive/NSC 18.[51]

Revised plans for securing the Persian Gulf region initially came in the form of 1979's OPLAN 4230, which envisaged the transportation of up to 7,000 U.S. personnel to Saudi Arabia to guard the oil fields. But it was never formally approved, not intended to cope with overt Soviet intervention, and the United States lacked the air and sealift assets to move the forces into position rapidly even before considering its basing requirements.[52]

Recognizing this, Washington set about establishing military and diplomatic arrangements to facilitate a more significant presence during a crisis under the Persian Gulf Security Framework. This included access to military bases in the region, base construction, and the sale of arms to regional states. Critical facilities would be located in Saudi Arabia, Oman, and Egypt.[53]

Beyond local issues, the geographical distances involved for the United States were vast, and everything had to be flown or shipped in to the region. The available infrastructure in theater, even after the basing program initiated by the United States, was limited, making supply lines long and exposed. In addition, the scale of the deployable force would be badly outmatched by the Soviet forces that might be involved, thought to include twenty-four to twenty-nine armored and mechanized divisions plus an airborne division and 700–1,000 combat aircraft.[54] To this would be added wider Soviet A2/AD capabilities to prevent U.S. forces entering the region and conducting operations. As in other maritime environments, Soviet aviation could strike against U.S. assets afloat, including carriers.[55] The Soviet Indian Ocean Squadron and its available local bases would have to be suppressed to enable secure shipping of heavy land forces, potentially compounding the problem of the multiweek journey by sea from the United States. To partially address this, the central Indian Ocean atoll of Diego Garcia came to host equipment and supplies for a Marine amphibious brigade in maritime prepositioning force (MPF) ships as well as U.S. Army and USAF supply ships in what became known as the afloat prepositioning force (APF).[56] Fifty new C-5B Galaxy transport aircraft and a group of fast sealift ships (FSS) also were procured. Additionally, the RRF was created in 1976 as the high-readiness component of the National Defense Reserve Fleet (NDRF), which was itself established in 1946 to provide a reserve of ships that could be mobilized in the event of a military or other emergency.[57]

The Rapid Deployment Joint Task Force was formed on March 1, 1980; its designation changed to U.S. Central Command on January 1, 1983, anchoring it in the Middle East. By this point, the primary plan for defending against Soviet aggression in the region—briefly labeled OPLAN 1001—had evolved into three variants: OPLANs 1002, 1003, and 1004; each was a variation to account for the conditions under which a regional war started and what was simultaneously happening in the wider world.[58] OPLAN 1021 was reportedly a later version.[59] OPLAN 1004, a variant designed to halt a Soviet invasion of Iran, envisaged that in the event of execution, sea control would be secured first, then troops landed at Bandar Abbas and Abadan on the Iranian coast. Forces would then advance north to form a defensive line along the Zagros Mountains.[60] Details from one version, OPLAN 1004-84, are available via David B. Crist. As is typical, it is divided into phases:

- Phase I: Pre-C Day: Set the theater
  - Activation MPF/Civil Air Reserve/Mustering Sealift requirements.
- Phase II: C-Day to C+16: Delay and Deploy
  - Air Force/Navy conduct strikes attacks [*sic*] against Soviet forces to disrupt/delay their advance.
  - Conduct clandestine insertion of SOF [special operations forces] into Iran from Turkey, Oman, and Pakistan to support air-interdiction missions against Soviet LOCs [lines of communication] and coordinate with resistance forces.
  - Deploy Army Forces from CONUS to either Saudi Arabia/GCC [Gulf Cooperation Council] or Western bases.
    - 82nd AB Div and Rangers move to Ras Banas and Thumrait.
- Phase III: D-Day (C+16 to C+36)
  - 3A: USMC/USN/Army Airborne forces seize Bandar Abbas and SOH [Strait of Hormuz] to secure the Gulf SLOCs.
  - 3B: U.S. Army would seize Bushier/Bandar Khamenei [*sic*], then Shiraz.

  - 3C. Air Force deploys to Shiraz, Bandar Abbas, and Isfahan airfields.
  - 3D: U.S. forces move forward to a defensive line running roughly from Isfahan southeast to Kerman—a distance of 375 miles.
- Phase IV: Defeat of Soviet Forces and retrograde[61]

This concept was flawed on multiple levels. Iran would likely have actively resisted U.S. attempts to enter the country, even on the premise of stopping the USSR's invasion. The odds that a Soviet operation of this nature would take place in isolation were low. Given the overextension of the U.S. armed forces just to cover the European and Pacific theaters, adding a Southwest Asian contingency to a wider global war made a difficult situation worse.[62]

Ultimately, those tasked with executing the Zagros plan were deeply unconvinced of its viability. USCENTCOM commander Gen. Norman Schwarzkopf noted in his memoirs that it was "suicidal" and that even exercises tended to terminate with ceasefires rather than to push the operation to its natural conclusion.[63] Thought was given to horizontal escalation and cost imposition through striking Soviet targets not directly related to the invasion. Still, no option was identified for imposing a cost on Moscow that exceeded the benefits of seizing Iran without triggering escalation.[64] Some analyses were more optimistic that taking advantage of Soviet weaknesses, including blocking its limited axis of advance, or that extensive warning time could allow for success.[65] Others claimed the entire contingency plan was a waste of time, as the Soviets would never attempt such an operation.[66]

In 1989 Schwarzkopf decided to push for abandoning planning for a Soviet/Iran contingency.[67] Gen. Colin Powell, the CJCS, subsequently ordered the redrafting of OPLAN 1002-88 to focus on defending the Arabian Peninsula from attack by Iraq.[68]

For the United States, the more-regional focus dovetailed smoothly with administrative and real-world developments. The Goldwater-Nichols Act of 1986 reorganized the U.S. military command structure to further empower the regional CCMD. The Gulf War would provide the template for the type of short, localized, and decisive operations the United States wished to fight to maintain the international order.

Initial efforts for what would become OPLAN 1002-90 began with the realization that the forces planned to deploy under previous iterations would be inadequate to manage the Iraqi threat.[69] The initial April 1990 outline draft under the mission "counter Iraqi intraregional threat to Kuwait/Saudi Arabia" was divided into three phases:

- Phase I: Deterrence—USAF, USMC, U.S. Navy, and SOF deploy to Saudi Arabia to deter further Iraqi aggression.
- Phase II: Defensive-counterair and interdiction—Air campaign initiated to obtain air superiority and interdict advancing enemy forces. Ground forces fight defensive action in parallel.
- Phase III: Counteroffensive—To begin when the enemy's combat power has been sufficiently reduced to tip the balance in favor of the United States, allow the liberation of lost territory, and secure conflict termination.[70]

A second draft of the plan, with no significant changes, was completed in July 1990 and tested in the Internal Look 90 exercise. The scenario involved Iraq invading Kuwait, consolidating its position, and then advancing into Saudi Arabia.[71]

At the beginning of the summer of 1990, the plan was still incomplete—lacking as it did a TPFDL. The full OPLAN was not due for completion until August 1991. But real-world events would not respect that timetable.[72]

Invasion

Iraqi planning for the invasion was confined to a small group under "Project 17."[73] Satellite imagery and other intelligence led the Americans and British to become concerned that an attack on Kuwait was imminent. But they expected its focus to be limited to seizing territory near the border rather than capturing the entire country.[74] The invasion began on August 2. Kuwait's military was undermanned, outnumbered, and not operating on a high-alert level. Despite this, there were fierce instances of resistance, with tank engagements and strikes against Iraqi forces by the Kuwaiti Air Force—some aircraft took off from highways in the south of the country. But with no prospect of short-term success, much of the surviving Kuwaiti military crossed the Saudi border to avoid destruction or capture. The initial Iraqi invasion took less than two days.[75]

Countermeasures: Operation Desert Shield and Operation Desert Storm

The initial priority was to forestall an invasion of Saudi Arabia and provide options to U.S. leadership. Following an agreement with the Saudis, the forces allocated under OPLAN 1002-90 began to deploy on August 7.[76] Units from the broader alliance, known as the Coalition—thirty-eight nations eventually provided military units—also began to deploy.[77]

An early plan for an air campaign was designated "Instant Thunder." It was designed to run independently of ground-force operations and focused on isolating the Iraqi leadership from the forces they controlled. This would form part of the "Five Rings" approach to targeting, with Iraqi leadership as the innermost of five concentric rings, the remaining four being key production, infrastructure, population, and fielded forces largely in motion. In one draft Instant Thunder would hit eighty-four strategic targets while leaving Iraqi field forces intact.[78]

In parallel to this, a separate initiative developed two defensive plans. The first, the "D-day plan" or Air Tasking Order (ATO) Bravo, would be a two-day USAF/Navy air campaign to provide counterair, interdiction, and close-air-support (CAS) efforts to halt an Iraqi invasion of Saudi Arabia before transitioning to a general offensive. The second would be a "punishment" ATO to respond to any preemptive use of chemical weapons.[79]

Instant Thunder was ultimately reworked to become the air-campaign plan for Desert Storm. The final plan came in two forms: USCENTCOM's Desert Storm OPLAN, published on December 16, 1990, and the Coalition's Combined OPLAN for Offensive Operations to Eject Iraqi Forces from Kuwait, published on January 17, 1991.

The Commander in Chief, U.S. Central Command (CINCCENT) CONOPS was[80]

- Conduct a Coordinated, Multi-National, Multi-Axis Air, Naval, and Ground Attack
- Strategic Air Campaign Focused on Enemy Centers of Gravity
  - Iraqi National Command Authority
  - NBC [Nuclear, Biological and Chemical] Capability
  - Republican Guard Force Command
- Progressively Shift Air Operation to; and Conduct Ground Operations in the KTO [Kuwaiti Theater of Operations] to:
  - Isolate KTO—Sever Iraqi Supply Lines
  - Destroy Republican Guard Forces
  - Liberate Kuwait City with Arab Forces[81]

The following sequence was envisaged:

- Phase I: Strategic Air Campaign
- Phase II: Air Supremacy in KTO
- Phase III: Battlefield Preparation
- Phase IV: Offensive Ground Campaign[82]

The first three phases, as enacted, would not be strictly sequential, and all four phases would be in parallel toward the end of the conflict, although the weight of effort would shift. The plan was activated through Operational Order 91-001, which outlined the key military objectives:

- Attack Iraqi politico-military leadership and C2;
- Gain and maintain air superiority;
- Sever Iraqi supply lines;
- Destroy known nuclear, biological, and chemical production, storage, and delivery capabilities;
- Destroy Republican Guard forces in the KTO; and
- Liberate Kuwait City.[83]

Iraq's A2/AD Capability Gap

Arguably, the primary advantage the Coalition had during the buildup to Desert Storm was the limited A2/AD capabilities of the Iraqis. Indeed, while the threat of terrorism or the intervention of a third party that was hostile to the allies (such as Libya) was recognized, what long-range strike capability Baghdad possessed was primarily limited to a small number of obsolete Tu-16 Badger (and China's licensed copy, the H-6) and Tu-22 Blinder bombers. Of the tactical aircraft available, Mirage F1s carried AS-30L laser-guided missiles, and Su-24 aircraft delivered a variety of Soviet precision-guided munitions (PGMs), providing some modicum of precision-strike capability against ground targets. Offensive antiship capability came via Exocet-armed Mirage F1EQ fighters and Super Frelon helicopters, H-6 bombers and land-based launchers with Silkworm ASMs, and fast-attack craft armed with Styx and Exocet ASMs. But these systems were overwhelmed by Coalition offensive and defensive efforts and had minimal effect. Iraqi air defenses were primarily dependent on older Soviet-sourced SA-2, SA-3, and SA-6 missiles and only designed to cope with the limited threat posed by Iran and Israel.[84]

Iraq's most novel challenge was the notional area-denial capability of its short-range ballistic missiles, which were limited to variants of the Soviet Scud missile (chiefly the "Al-Husayn" extended-range model, with a roughly 644-kilometer reach). Before the war, the Coalition considered the Scud threat militarily insignificant. Nevertheless, the fixed launch sites in the western Iraqi desert were among the first targets hit on the opening night of Desert Storm. But the airstrikes against the complexes near the Jordanian border led to a reversion to the use of TELs to fire the missiles.[85]

The subsequent "Great Scud Hunt" campaign saw constant air patrols set up ready to strike launch sites when located, mines dropped and roadways bombed to impair launcher mobility, and special forces and airborne ground-surveillance radar (in the form of the still prototype J-STARS) deployed to provide targeting information. Results were derisory: there is no solid evidence that a single TEL was destroyed during the campaign.[86]

Initiatives to address the challenge were advanced. The Cold War–era "Thirsty Saber" program, which aimed to hunt for and destroy TELs, received new impetus due to the Iraqi challenge. Plans for an operational system, "Thirsty Warrior," initially to be built upon a cruise missile—likely the stealthy AGM-129 Advanced Cruise Missile—were instigated but then dropped postwar.[87]

At the "other end" of the Scud chain, the United States deployed Patriot missile batteries to Israel and Saudi Arabia. First deployed as an antiaircraft weapon in 1984, it was subsequently adapted to add an ABM capability as part of the PAC-1 upgrade, with the PAC-2 variant in development. Rapid improvisation sped up the introduction of PAC-2 and the doubling of overall missile-production rates by January 1991.[88] The Patriot's performance proved controversial, with claims of a high interception rate revised drastically down as more data became available.[89]

Two incidents brought home the damage the Scuds could have caused had they been more accurate. The first was a near-miss: on February 16 a missile landed around a hundred and fifty meters from a pier in Al-Jubayl, Saudi Arabia, that was loaded with ammunition and had eight vessels docked against it, including a U.S. Navy landing helicopter assault (LHA) ship. The Patriot battery tasked with defending the site was offline for maintenance at the time.[90]

The second was the single worst U.S. casualty incident of the war. As a result of Patriot software problems, on February 25 a Scud hit a U.S.

Army barracks in Dhahran, Saudi Arabia, killing twenty-eight and injuring ninety-seven.[91]

The Coalition's sea control was never seriously challenged, with the Iraqi Navy a small force possessing nothing more capable than missile-armed fast-attack craft. Most of these were destroyed by Coalition air power or fled to Iran. U.S. Navy aircraft also conducted a minelaying operation to immobilize any remaining Iraqi naval vessels.[92]

Iraqi attempts to hit Coalition ships using shore-based Silkworm ASMs failed. But naval mines did damage a cruiser and, ironically, the ship leading the MCM effort. Iraq was able to lay more than 1,200 of these weapons because of a decision taken to keep Coalition forces clear of the northern reaches of the Persian Gulf during Desert Shield, preventing them from interdicting or even monitoring enemy minelaying activities.[93]

Lessons

An important postscript to the campaign was a 1992 report commissioned by the Office of Net Assessment (ONA) to study, in light of the Gulf War, if Soviet/Russian theories about a "military-technical revolution" were accurate. The report delivered a warning: "Although defense budgets are declining in most major states, as the interwar period demonstrates there are still opportunities for exploiting advanced technology, experimenting with new systems, and testing of innovative operational concepts and organizational structures. Several states of [*sic*] groups of states—the United States, Japan, and Germany/EU—have the technological base and necessary resources to participate fully in this competition. Others—like France, Russia, and China—may emerge to full competition over the next twenty years."[94] Additionally, it stated: "If we retain our Cold War era objective of being a global power, we will find that the military-technical needs of many competitors, whose ambitions are regional, are likely to be far lower than ours. Many such competitors will probably have the far less ambitious (and far less demanding) goal of information, space, sea, and air denial, as opposed to seeking control or domination."[95]

An updated version of the paper later noted the likelihood of requiring "forcible entry operations . . . initiated at extended ranges" and that forward bases would become increasingly exposed to attack by opponents with advanced missiles and aircraft. Both of these are central elements of an A2/AD challenge.[96]

There were also more-fundamental limits to the lessons of the conflict with Iraq. As the *Conduct of the Persian Gulf War: Final Report to Congress* of 1992 made clear,

> We should also remember that much of our military capability was not fully tested in Operations Desert Shield and Desert Storm. There was no submarine threat. Ships did not face significant anti-surface action. We had little fear that our forces sent from Europe or the U.S. would be attacked on their way to the region. There was no effective attack by aircraft on our troops or our port and support facilities. . . . Saddam Hussein's missiles were inaccurate. There was no interference to our space-based systems. As such, much of what was tested needs to be viewed in the context of this unique environment and the specific conflict.
>
> Even more important to remember is that potential adversaries will study the lessons of this war no less diligently than will we. Future adversaries will seek to avoid Saddam Hussein's mistakes.[97]

The Gulf War marked a significant inflection point for the PLA.[98] Key aspects of the force structure, strategy, doctrine, and tactics adopted by the Iraqi Armed Forces matched those of its Chinese counterpart, and much of the two countries' equipment was of a similar lineage and vintage. The new military strategic guidelines (MSG) adopted in 1993 centered on "local wars under high-technology conditions"—a concept that the Gulf War came to represent for the PLA.[99]

The utilization of precision air attacks across the full depth of Iraq as opposed to a linear front line had allowed the Coalition to inflict destruction and paralysis on the enemy. This enabled air power to play a central as opposed to supporting role in the campaign. This ran counter to China's then-focus on air defense. Shortfalls in Baghdad's capabilities had allowed the Coalition to target the key centers of gravity of the Iraqi military and state, rendering ineffective much of both. Countering this type of attack and enabling the PLA to inflict a similar effect on an opponent would require restructuring and equipment modernization, the latter not just the recapitalization of traditional platforms such as combat aircraft and warships but the development of new capabilities. China's leadership saw the acquisition of the necessary technology as a central priority.[100]

They also recognized that there was a need to move away from the type of positional warfare the Iraqis had adopted in the defense of occupied Kuwait and, farther to the west, their border with Saudi Arabia. The PLA had developed a similar approach to halting Soviet armored and airborne assaults, but it was now clear that this was poorly suited to modern warfare. There would be a need to emphasize the "active" element of the active defense strategy of the PLA, with information and advanced technology key factors.[101]

Joint operations had proven central to the Coalition effort. Rather than each armed forces branch fighting its own campaign, or with one leading and the others subservient, the Gulf War had demonstrated that services would have to closely coordinate efforts in pursuit of campaign goals. Beyond the traditional sea, land, and air domains, China recognized its electromagnetic and space-based capabilities (and later cyber) would have to be developed and integrated. Such coordination would have to be supported by a comprehensive command, control, communications, computers, intelligence, surveillance, and reconnaissance (C4ISR) capability that the PLA lacked.[102]

Coda

Following the end of the Gulf War, USCENTCOM developed OPLAN 1003 to counter a potential Iraqi reinvasion of Kuwait. A later draft—OPLAN 1003-98—considered potential requirements to invade Iraq should a major crisis occur, including a state collapse.[103]

OPLAN 1003-98 was tested during Exercise Desert Crossing in 1999, which sought to study the requirements for stabilizing Iraq after the regime's collapse. Even with 400,000 troops committed, the results foresaw issues, including destabilization from external sources, religious and ethnic internal fragmentation, and bloody conflict among competing groups. One assessment also stated that a democratic Iraq was likely unfeasible.[104]

In the wake of the 9/11 attacks and with an intent to disarm Iraq of the chemical and biological weapons it was believed to possess, Secretary of Defense Donald Rumsfeld was presented with a refined version of OPLAN 1003-98 that required around 385,000 personnel.[105] Rumsfeld was convinced that the mission could be accomplished with more limited numbers, and the planned personnel commitment was reduced to around 275,000.[106] This force level was to be further compromised by not having all the required personnel in place by the start of the invasion. A debate over whether to complete the necessary buildup, dubbed "Generated Start," or to begin offensive action before the full deployment ("Running Start") had resulted in a middle path, "Hybrid Option," which would see the buildup incomplete when the war began.[107] There would also be no preparatory air campaign (at least beyond intensified preinvasion strikes against air-defense systems under Operation Southern Focus), with the ground and air offensive commencing simultaneously. Only the weakness of Iraqi forces made this invasion plan realistic.

The final draft of the enacted plan was OPLAN 1003V, divided into multiple phases:

- Phase I: Preparation
- Phase II: Shape the Battlespace
- Phase III: Decisive Operations
- Phase IV: Post-hostilities[108]

The primary implementation plan, OPLAN Cobra II, was drafted by the Coalition Forces Land Component Command. Wargaming identified that the force might struggle to maintain control over the country postinvasion, so a follow-up plan for the postwar environment, OPLAN Eclipse II, was also written. Yet even this assumed some level of Iraqi government services remaining functional. Few appear to have considered that the resources required to defeat the Iraqi military might not be adequate for stabilization afterward. This contributed to the emergence of a brutal multiyear insurgency that cost far more in human life and resources than the initial invasion.[109]

The official withdrawal of American forces from Iraq in December 2011 only marked a pause in the U.S. presence there. In the first half of 2014, large parts of Iraq were overrun by the Islamic State group. This led to a return of U.S. and allied forces and a protracted battle that lasted five years until the entity's territorial collapse.

U.S. and allied forces remain in Iraq as of 2025, thirty-five years after Desert Shield began. USMC Gen. Jim Mattis commanded a Marine battalion during the Gulf War, the 1st Marine Division during the invasion of Iraq, and was secretary of defense during the latter part of the territorial battle against the Islamic State in Iraq and Syria. At that time he observed on the then-current era of U.S. wars: "No war is over until the enemy says it's over. We may think it over, we may declare it over, but in fact, the enemy gets a vote."[110]

CHAPTER 8

REALIGNMENT

> No foreign policy—no matter how ingenious—has any chance of success if it is born in the minds of a few and carried in the hearts of none.
>
> —*Henry Kissinger*

Yen Chia-kan succeeded Chiang Kai-shek following the latter's death on 5 April 1975. Yen was then replaced by Chiang's son, Chiang Ching-kuo, in 1978, although as premier from 1972 to 1978, the younger Chiang had exercised power as de facto national leader.

During the 1980s, Taiwan's political landscape shifted under internal stresses and the pressure for global legitimacy—including from pro-Taiwan elements of the U.S. Congress who wished to see the ROC improve its international standing. By 1987, the KMT still dominated the ROC, but the banned Democratic Progressive Party (DPP) made gains in the 1986 elections by fielding notionally independent candidates. The lifting of martial law in July 1987 paved the way for a free press and political organizing.[1]

Chiang Ching-kuo died the following year and was succeeded by Taiwan-born Lee Teng-hui. Lee continued the democratization process, including through the May 1991 lifting of the Temporary Provisions Effective during the Period of National Mobilization for Suppression of the Communist Rebellion, which had placed constraints on political and civil society (and whose termination served to acknowledge an end to the civil war), as well as constitutional reform.[2]

1989 AND ALL THAT

Relations between the PRC and the United States took a turn for the worse following the Tiananmen Square Massacre, with sanctions, including a ban on arms sales, imposed. China's favorability among the American public also fell. All this occurred against the backdrop of the steady collapse of the Soviet bloc, removing much of the security motivation behind the U.S. desire to create a tight relationship with the PRC.

Also in 1989, the Reagan administration gave way to that of President George H. W. Bush (1989–93). He faced internal pressure to support the recapitalization of the ROC military, particularly given reports of Beijing's potential purchasing of advanced Su-27 fighters from a cash-strapped Moscow. With France selling frigates and Mirage 2000-5 jets to Taiwan, Bush announced the sale of 150 F-16A/Bs in September 1992, partly to protect jobs in Texas. More arms deals soon followed.[3]

Tensions across the Taiwan Strait had relaxed—in no small part due to Beijing's decision to focus on the Soviet threat in alliance with the United States and prioritizing economic growth. In 1980 Deng Xiaoping replaced Maoist "we must liberate Taiwan" sloganeering with "peaceful reunification" and "one country, two systems," a concept created to facilitate unification with Hong Kong and Macau. Chiang Ching-kuo's 'Three Noes" policy—no contact, no negotiation, and no compromise—was eroded when a May 1986 aircraft hijacking forced the two governments to cooperate. This initial contact, plus the end of martial law, allowed the establishment of links, including limited postal, transport, and trade conduits, between the PRC and ROC.[4]

The supposed "1992 Consensus" between Beijing and Taipei was a term first used not in 1992, but in 2000 by then–KMT Minister of the Mainland Affairs Council of the Executive Yuan Su Chi to describe the outcome of a meeting held in Hong Kong eight years previously. This meeting had occurred in the wake of the formation of the institutions of both sides of the strait to facilitate cooperation. Both sides reportedly agreed to abide by a concept of "one China, different interpretations," which essentially meant that the PRC considered itself the true "one China," while the ROC would take the stance that it was the true incarnation of China. This would allow for the discussing of routine matters without the overarching politics of the situation intruding. But subsequent varying interpretations by the CCP, the KMT and the DPP over what was agreed and its implications has led to the supposed consensus itself becoming a point of contention.[5]

Democratization also continued in Taiwan. Among these efforts were amendments to the ROC's constitution. One of these, passed in 1992, made the president directly elected, as opposed to being appointed by the National Assembly.[6]

THE THIRD TAIWAN STRAIT CRISIS

The administration of President Bill Clinton (1993–2001) published its Taiwan Policy Review in September 1994, which marked the first major reassessment of the relationship since the passing of the TRA. Changes included renaming of the Coordination Council for North American Affairs (CCNAA) office in Washington, D.C.—the unofficial embassy of the ROC since 1979—as the Taipei Economic and Cultural Representative Office (TECRO). Others were the authorization of the mutual entry to the offices of U.S. and ROC officials (except for the White House, the Eisenhower Executive Office Building, and the State Department), as were meetings between U.S. and ROC defense officials at all but the highest ranks.[7] Arms sales in this era included E-2 Hawkeye aircraft, *Knox*-class frigates, and Stinger and TOW missiles.

Beijing did not appreciate Lee's move toward the full democratization of Taiwan and viewed it and the president's broader agenda as further evidence that the island was moving away from its grasp. Hopes for an arrangement for unification between authoritarian leaderships on both sides of the strait—seemingly feasible under the KMT's one-party rule—were now complicated by the wishes of Taiwan's population.[8]

Following lobbying efforts and pressure from Congress, Clinton granted Lee a visa to attend an event at Cornell University in June 1995. Beijing viewed this, along with increasing U.S. arms sales, as encouraging Taiwan's independence. They also distrusted Lee's personal views of independence, with a 1994 ROC White Paper steering away from rapid unification as well as attempts to join the United Nations also not helping matters.[9]

In July 1995 PLA air and naval drills occurred as well as the launching of ballistic missiles within one hundred miles of Taiwan, potentially endangering sea traffic.[10] Secretary of State Warren Christopher relayed a confidential letter to Beijing clarifying the U.S. position with respect to Taiwan as unchanged. Beijing demanded a Fourth Communiqué to codify this stance and ensure no more visits, which the United States refused.[11]

Further exercises, including amphibious landings, continued into the autumn and were accompanied by bellicose claims from Beijing that they were intended to maintain unity and resist the "splittist" activities in Taiwan.[12]

Additional PLA exercises in October and November were followed by the December Taiwan legislative election, which resulted in a KMT win, but by a narrow margin and with a stronger-than-expected showing from the anti-independence New Party. This indicated to Beijing that its policy of intimidation was succeeding.[13] On December 19 the aircraft carrier USS *Nimitz* passed through the Taiwan Strait (allegedly at the initiative of the CINCPAC, although some sources say it was a weather-related diversion)—reportedly the first carrier to do so since 1979.[14]

The main phase of the Third Taiwan Strait Crisis commenced in the run-up to the March 23, 1996 presidential elections.[15] The PRC began an additional series of missile tests, with the projectiles landing in the waters near the ROC's two most important ports. These were accompanied by air and naval amphibious-assault exercises, including a March 18–25 exercise to land troops using airborne, air assault, and amphibious methods.[16]

American officials judged an invasion—either of Taiwan proper or one of the outlying islands—or a move to carry out a blockade improbable, and China had sought to reassure Washington by diplomatic channels that it would not attack Taiwan.[17] Indeed, the PLA had a limited ability to accomplish any significant military goal. Instead, the PRC seemed to have three aims: coerce the Taiwanese leadership to halt the proindependence activity, deter the Taiwanese population from voting for antiunification candidates, and (although unnecessary) compel the United States to reject the ROC's independence outright.[18] But the United States determined that its credibility was on the line. Washington ordered the USS *Independence* carrier battle group to waters near Taiwan and the USS *Nimitz* carrier group to the Philippine Sea to be available at short notice. Lee became the ROC's first democratically elected president. Beijing's attempts at coercion had failed.

The Third Taiwan Strait Crisis proved to be a critical juncture. It provided further evidence to Beijing that bringing Taiwan into the communist fold would be very difficult to do diplomatically. It also showed how far behind the United States the PLA was in terms of capability. Additionally, what communication links there were between the ROC and the United States were proved to be broadly effective but with shortcomings. This spurred a reconfiguration of contact between the United States and ROC, notably through the Monterey Talks between relevant officials, including those from the DOD—the first such dialogue since 1979. These exchanges since have provided a forum for discussing security issues, including crisis response, and set the stage for U.S. input into ROC defense reform, including deploying American delegations and survey teams to the island.[19] Other bilateral mechanisms now include the Defense Review Talks, which discuss policy and set the agenda for cooperation, and the USINDOPACOM-led General Officers Steering Group, which focuses on addressing issues under the guidance of the Defense Review Talks and determining future military-to-military engagement.[20]

The United States did not want the 1995–96 crisis to turn into a permanent rift with the PRC. This was emphasized when, during a visit to China in 1998, President Clinton restated the established U.S. policy toward Taiwan in what became known as the American "Three Noes": no support for Taiwanese independence, no support for a solution that creates "two Chinas" or one China and one Taiwan, and no admission for the ROC to any international organization requiring statehood.[21]

Nevertheless, arms sales also continued postcrisis. One of the most notable was that of a PAVE Paws radar system capable of tracking the type of ballistic missiles China had tested during the third crisis and of observing activity deep into the mainland. Whether the ROC shares data from this radar with the United States directly is disputed.[22] Additionally, the UK handover of Hong Kong to China in 1997 reportedly led to the additional SIGINT tasks being transferred to an already established joint U.S.-ROC facility on Taiwan.[23]

THE TWENTY-FIRST CENTURY

The 2000 ROC presidential election ended with DPP candidate Chen Shuibian as victor, concluding the Nationalists' uninterrupted rule. He had previously supported independence but had moderated his views in the run-up to the election. Nevertheless, "Taiwanization," to distinguish the island's identity from that of mainland China, was a major theme of his time in office.[24] Chen also made policy moves that antagonized Beijing, including a proposal for an emergency independence referendum power. His rejection of the One China principle and insistence that the PRC and ROC should have a "one country on each side" relationship was particularly galling for Beijing.[25]

In April 2001 the new U.S. president, George W. Bush, pledged to do "whatever it took" to defend Taiwan, although a policy change was denied.[26] Republican suspicion of China helped ease the approval of a large arms package in April 2001. While the submarine component fell through, the sale of twelve P-3C aircraft, Patriot PAC-3 SAM/ABMs, and four *Kidd*-class destroyers were among the sales that proceeded. The April 1 collision between a U.S. Navy EP-3E and a PLA J-8II fighter raised U.S.-China tensions. Yet the United States was also increasingly less than supportive of Chen, as Washington viewed him as endangering the status quo for his personal benefit.[27] Despite this, Chen narrowly won a second term.

The existence of OPLAN 5077 became public knowledge in 2006 via journalist William Arkin and the *Washington Post*. As noted earlier, CONPLAN 5077 has existed since at least 1979.[28] It was reportedly upgraded to a full OPLAN in August 2001 during the early days of the Bush administration. Subsequently, a new "strategic concept" for the defense of Taiwan allegedly was produced by PACOM in December 2002, with a new OPLAN 5077 completed in July 2003 and adopted the following year. Arkin wrote: "Pacific Command OPLAN 5077-04, as it is currently known, includes air, naval, ground/amphibious, and missile defense forces and 'excursions' to defend Taiwan. Options include maritime intercept operations in the Taiwan Straits, attacks on Chinese targets on the mainland, information warfare and 'non-kinetic' options, even the potential use of American nuclear weapons."[29]

OPLAN 5077-04 (the "04" representing 2004, the year it was put in place) is the most recently known incarnation of the plan, although it is inevitable that it will have been updated multiple times since its inception. If it is still in place, it is now only an element of the U.S. plan for a Taiwan scenario. Around this time occurred the establishment of a hotline between the ROC minister of national defense and the U.S. secretary of defense.[30]

With regard to Taiwan, President Barack Obama's administration (2009–17) was granted a quiet period largely running in parallel with Ma Ying-jeou's KMT government. Ma's inauguration speech contained a pledge of "no reunification, no independence, and no war" during his time in office. He also supported a version of the 1992 consensus. New agreements with Beijing quickly followed, including direct scheduled flights, sea-cargo shipments, and postal links across the strait; restrictions eased on business investments; and education exchanges and tourism.[31]

These moves prompted widespread protests in Taiwan.[32] In July 2010 Taipei and Beijing signed the Economic Cooperation Framework Agreement, which reduced tariffs between the two countries and opened up markets.[33] The agreement was subject to heavy debate in the ROC, with the DPP rejecting it as a pathway to unification with China by stealth. Ma was reelected in 2012. A further major agreement with the mainland, the Cross-Strait Service Trade Agreement, was signed in 2013. But protests against this new deal took place in the form of the "Sunflower Student" movement, which demanded a review of the trade deal on the grounds it would allegedly harm Taiwan's economy and undermine autonomy. The agreement was never ratified.[34]

While Ma's time in office was positive for China, U.S. arms sales to Taiwan continued, with F-16A/B upgrades, UH-60M transport helicopters, AH-64E attack helicopters, and Javelin, Stinger, and Patriot PAC-3 missiles among the sales authorized. Nevertheless, the United States was still displeased with falling ROC defense spending.[35]

In January 2016 DPP candidate Tsai Ing-wen was elected Taiwan's president, with the increasing public skepticism over the KMT's agenda of economic integration with China helping her party secure a landslide. Yet while previously perceived by Beijing as an independence advocate, Tsai now affirmed her support for the status quo.[36]

On the other side of the world, President Donald J. Trump's first administration (2017–21) brought its own drama to the Pacific region. Despite an early congratulatory phone call from Tsai following his victory, Trump had held the ROC low on his list of priorities and had little faith in the ability of the United States to defend the island.[37] This did not stymie arms sales, with sixty-six F-16C/D aircraft, 108 M1A2T tanks, four hundred ground-launched Harpoon ASMs, and HIMARS surface-to-surface launchers with ATACMS and F-16-launched SLAM-ER air-launched cruise missiles (ALCMs), both capable of reaching across the strait to strike China, among the record-setting packages approved.[38]

Congress also passed the Taiwan Travel Act in February 2018, which provided for enhanced contact between U.S. and ROC officials. The Taiwan Allies International Protection and Enhancement Initiative (TAIPEI) Act of 2019 contained provisions that included advocacy for the ROC's participation in international organizations where statehood is not a requirement and as an observer of similar status where that requirement was in place. Additional measures were taken by the Trump administration toward the end of the president's first term.[39]

President Joe Biden entered office in January 2021. By this point, Tsai had won reelection, bolstered by the PRC's 2019–20 crackdown in Hong Kong—a territory notionally governed under a "One Country, Two Systems" model Beijing had proposed for Taiwan—which had soured the population on closer relations. The first major ROC-related event under the Biden administration (2021–25) was the August 2022 visit by then House Speaker Nancy Pelosi to the island, the highest-ranking U.S. visitor since 1997. China responded with military exercises so extensive that some referred to them as the Fourth Taiwan Strait Crisis and also imposed sanctions on food and other exports from the ROC to the PRC.[40]

The Biden administration proved rhetorically more supportive of the ROC. On multiple occasions the president openly stated that the United States would come to the assistance of Taiwan were China to attack, even though such comments were always subsequently clarified by his staff as not signaling a change in U.S. policy.[41] Arms-sale authorizations during this period were limited but included Volcano landmine-laying systems and loitering munitions.

It has also emerged that U.S. special forces have been training ROC units in Taiwan since at least the late 2010s.[42] In April 2023 reports stated that around two hundred U.S. instructors were in Taiwan to assess ROC defensive capabilities and provide training.[43] In August 2023, members of the Michigan National Guard went on exercises with ROC Army personnel in the United States, and in September 2023 accounts surfaced that battalion-level training of Taiwanese units was to commence in the United States.[44] In March 2024 U.S. special forces were reportedly stationed on the Kinmen and Pescadores Islands.[45]

The Taiwan Enhanced Resilience Act subsection of the 2023 U.S. National Defense Authorization Act (NDAA), signed in December 2022, authorized $2 billion in foreign military financing (FMF) a year for five years as well as the same amount in loans and loan guarantees, although the 2023 Consolidated Appropriations Act restricted the support to loans, which the ROC declined. The NDAA additionally authorized up to $1 billion in defense support in presidential drawdown authority (PDA) and $100 million in equipment stockpiling in the region. The act also approved a multitude of support measures for the ROC, including ordering the secretary of defense to "establish or expand a comprehensive training program with Taiwan" and form "a joint consultative mechanism with appropriate officials of Taiwan to develop and implement a multi-year plan to provide for the acquisition of appropriate defensive capabilities by Taiwan."[46]

The 2024 NDAA built upon its predecessor, including authorizing a defensive cybersecurity cooperation program.[47] The 2024 Further Consolidated Appropriations Act provided at least $300 million of FMF.[48] The 2024 National Security Supplemental—most notable for the support it provided to Ukraine—also delivered $2 billion in FMF for the Indo-Pacific, of which the ROC would be eligible for $1.9 billion in funding to replenish articles and services provided to Taiwan through PDA (and has reportedly been allocated $1.2 billion), and broadens the scope of wider FMF loan and loan-guarantees provisions to include the Indo-Pacific.[49] The Senior Integration Group for Taiwan (SIG-T) within the Pentagon, which was formed in late 2022, is reportedly coordinating this and wider efforts to support the ROC.[50] The 2025 NDAA contains provisions for $300 million in training and equipment for Taiwan as well as the Building Options for the Lasting Security of Taiwan (BOLSTER) Act to authorize the planning of a joint response between the United States and Europe in the event of a PRC attack on Taiwan.[51]

In the summer of 2023, the United States provided both $80 million in FMF (likely a loan) and a $345 million aid package of man-portable air defense systems and intelligence and surveillance capabilities—the first major military aid since the end of official relations.[52] This was followed by a PDA of $567 million in September 2023 and $571 million in December 2024 in aid of Taiwan.[53]

As of mid-2025, Tsai's former deputy president, Lai Ching-te, is in the early stage of his first term as president of the ROC, with his victory in 2024 marking the third presidential-election win in a row for the DPP. He is expected to attempt to maintain the status quo during his first term and is eligible to run again in January 2028. Nevertheless, the PLA still undertook an aggressive program of exercises at the time of his inauguration to signal their displeasure.[54]

In November 2024 Trump was reelected president of the United States. In an interview the previous June, he had refused to commit to the defense of Taiwan and stated, "Taiwan doesn't give us anything. Taiwan is 9,500 miles away. It's 68 miles away from China. A slight advantage, and China's a massive piece of land, they could just bombard it." Trump also asked why the United States was allowing the ROC to treat it like an insurance policy, stating that Taiwan should pay the United States for its defense.[55] Additionally, he noted after the election, with regard to whether the United States would defend Taiwan, "I never say, because I have to negotiate things, right?"[56]

On the other hand, several key positions in the second Trump administration have gone to China hawks, many of whom are vocally pro-Taiwan. In an attempt to curry favor, Taipei has raised the prospect of a large order of weapons, including additional Patriot missiles, E-2Ds, F-35s, and Aegis-equipped warships. [57] Whatever the case, the TRA will continue to stipulate that the U.S. military must maintain the capability to defend Taiwan, and the ROC retains strong bipartisan support in Congress. Ultimately, however, any decision to use force would be made by the President, in concert with Congress.

PRESENT DAY

The gradual realignment of the United States and Taiwan can retrospectively be seen as something of an inevitability. The emergence of an increasingly outward-facing and prosperous China and—as discussed in later chapters—the U.S. suspicion, now dating back three decades, that Beijing could one day become a great power rival have made this a natural development. This was reflected in the revision of U.S. contingency plans to defend the ROC. Exactly how U.S. relations with Taiwan will pan out from 2025 onward is difficult to judge, but a sharp departure from policy continuity in Washington does not seem likely.

CHAPTER 9

THE OTHER SIDE OF THE HILL

The reunification of the motherland is a historical inevitability.

—*Xi Jinping, December 31, 2023*

Predictions of the timeline, circumstances, and nature of a PRC move against Taiwan have become something of an industry. The 2024 edition of the U.S. DOD's *Military and Security Developments Involving the People's Republic of China* summarizes that the circumstances under which Beijing has mentioned the potential use of force include "formal declaration of Taiwan's independence, undefined moves toward Taiwan independence, internal unrest in Taiwan, Taiwan's acquisition of nuclear weapons, indefinite delays in the resumption of cross-strait dialogue on unification, [or] foreign military intervention in Taiwan's internal affairs."[1] The penultimate item, in particular, is open to an interpretation convenient to the PRC's leadership.

Beijing's stance on Taiwan is closely linked to China's envisaged "great rejuvenation" by 2049, the centenary of the PRC's founding.[2] The PRC's 2022 White Paper on Taiwan, *The Taiwan Question and China's Reunification in the New Era,* notes that unification is "indispensable for the realization of China's rejuvenation," the latter being the central component of Xi's "Chinese Dream."[3] The document focuses on the "one country, two systems" model, and while it fails to set a deadline for the process, it notes, "we should not allow this problem to be passed down from one generation to the next," and it explicitly rejects a renouncement of the use of force, stating that armed action would only occur under "compelling circumstances."[4]

The 2005 Anti-Secession Law provides the contemporary legal bedrock of PRC policy. While generally prompting peaceful unification, Article 8 threatens force, most notably if "possibilities for a peaceful reunification should be completely exhausted"—again, an almost entirely subjective measure.[5] The 2019 Defense White Paper notes that "to oppose and contain 'Taiwan independence'" was among the core defense missions, declaring, "The fight against separatists is becoming more acute."

The PLA is currently working toward full modernization and a "world-class" military by 2049, with 2027 and 2035 providing waypoints to that goal.[6] The 2027 benchmark aiming to, in the words of the DOD, "accelerate the integrated development of mechanization, informatization, and intelligentization" has drawn particular attention owing to the rise to prominence of both the "Davidson Window"—so named after former USINDOPACOM commander Adm. Philip S. Davidson, who in 2021 noted 2027 as the opening of a period in which the PLA may be able to carry out a successful invasion of Taiwan—and U.S. claims of Xi wanting to be ready for an invasion by 2027. For his part, Xi has reportedly denied plans for an attack, although that was not what the United States claimed.[7] He has also alleged that Washington is attempting to "bait" China into attacking Taiwan.[8]

For its part, the latest assessment of the ROC MND (August 2024) stated that China "is not yet fully possessed of the formal combat capabilities for a comprehensive invasion of Taiwan."[9] But it acknowledged that the PRC can take forward less intense options, including a blockade. As of late 2024, the United States was of the view that Chinese readiness for an invasion by 2027 was not possible.[10]

The military angle is also presenting the PRC leadership with a temporal pincer movement. Problems with the PLA modernization process—most recently highlighted by a purge of the defense and armed forces leadership and the disbanding of the PLA Strategic Support Force (PLASSF)—have been manifest. This makes readiness by 2027 a tall order at best. At the other end of the timeline, major components of U.S. preparations for a Pacific war will come to fruition in the early 2030s. Japan's recent military-investment surge is on a similar timeline in terms of producing practical results. This leaves the PLA with a potentially short window of opportunity.

Xi himself may also be on a personal timeline. While he remains an opaque character, the cult of personality he has crafted and his abolition of presidential term limits indicates a desire for a legacy to rival Mao and other Chinese leaders. Yet in 2027 he will turn seventy-four, then eighty-two in 2035.

This leaves him a constrained window of healthy years to endure the stresses of leading a great power into an unpredictable war.

It is possible to argue in the other direction. Xi may be unwilling to risk his already considerable legacy on a potentially ruinous war. Beijing may seek to delay any forced unification by decades, hoping either for ROC political capitulation or that China becomes so powerful that the United States no longer even attempts resistance. Some factors may or may not be important either way. For example, demographic pressures within the PRC may render war increasingly unviable after 2030, but developments in artificial intelligence (AI) and general-purpose robotics may make this less relevant to any decision to go to war. Ultimately, uncertainty abounds.

PLA MILITARY STRATEGY

The evolution of the PLA's strategy can be traced back to the 1920s. At its center for most of this period has been the "military strategic guidelines" (MSG) (known simply as the "strategic guidelines" until 1988).[11] The PLA has described the guidelines as containing "the principles and plans for preparing for and guiding the overall situation of war," and that the strategy will address, "With whom will we fight? Where will we fight? What is the character of the war that we will fight? How will we fight?"[12] They have not been in the form of a single, openly published document, with this ambiguity leading to differing accounts as to what was issued and when. The primary English language analysis of the MSG, M. Taylor Fravel's *Active Defense: China's Military Strategy since 1949*, highlights three major (1956, 1980, and 1993) and four minor (1960, 1988, 2004, and 2014) MSG shifts, with a shift in 1964 initiated by Mao that occurred for internal political rather than military reasons falling into neither category, and additional analysis showing a further minor change occurring around 2019.[13]

Post-1949, the MSG focused on four elements. First, the strategic opponent and operational target were identified. Second, the primary strategic direction—that is, the decisive geographic theater—was identified. Third, the basis of military struggle—the form of warfare for the envisaged conflict—was identified. Finally, it provided the basic guiding thought of how operations would be conducted.[14]

The most recent major MSG update was predated by both the collapse of the USSR and the Gulf War. To help address the shortfalls the conflict made clear, the 1993 "Winning Local Wars under High-Technology Conditions" MSG was adopted.[15] This built on the earlier 1988 pivot to local wars by moving toward new methods of fighting featuring technologically advanced and better-trained forces configured for joint operations. In 1993 there was no formal declaration of strategic direction, although then-chairman of the Central Military Commission (CMC) Jiang Zemin noted the prevention of Taiwanese independence as a "focal point of military struggle."[16] The active defense strategy was pivoted toward rapid-reaction operations orientated upon "subduing the enemy," potentially using advanced "assassin's mace" weapons.[17] From the U.S. perspective, this was an A2/AD approach designed to hinder its forces from entering the theater of operations and prevent them from operating freely within it.

Three minor revisions to the MSG have occurred in the subsequent three decades, with the primary strategic direction—Taiwan—remaining the same and the role of the United States in aiding the ROC gaining increasing prominence. The 2004 MSG, "Winning Local Wars under Informationized Conditions," emphasized the importance of information and information dominance across the spectrum of modern warfare.[18] "Joint operations" was replaced with "integrated operations," signifying that the armed forces branches would now be expected not only to work together on discreet tasks as part of a broader effort but also to be fully integrated. New weapon systems, C4ISR, sensors, and domains including cyber, space, and the "three warfares" political strategy—encompassing psychological operations, propaganda, and legal instruments—would all be critical.[19]

The doctrine of systems confrontation and systems destruction, rather than traditional engagements between various joint force components (services, military units, weapon systems, and so forth), has become a primary operating concept. In this, all-out destruction of an opponent is not necessary, simply degrading the components of a system to the point where it can no longer function adequately is sufficient. This was not an initiative of 2004 but became a major feature in Chinese writing in the late 1990s.[20]

"Winning Informationized Local Wars," 2014's MSG, was a further minor shift.[21] There were, however, modifications of note, reportedly including the expansion of the strategic direction to encompass the western Pacific, an indication of the risk of U.S. intervention in an attempt at forced unification by Beijing.[22] Another was a focus on the maritime domain and recognition of its significance in a campaign for Taiwan.[23] "Information dominance, precision strikes on strategic points, [and] joint operations to gain victory" appeared to represent the central guiding thought.[24]

The 2019 "New Era" MSG represented the most recent update but only a minor revision, retaining its predecessor's title.[25] Key elements remained the same as in 2014. Yet here was also an added emphasis on the "Xi Jinping military strategic thought" concept. This was part of a wider effort to personalize the MSG to Xi, reflecting his consolidation of power.[26]

Finally, Beijing's nuclear strategy sits separate from the MSG, remaining in the hands of the CCP political leadership.[27] China has regarded nuclear weapons as a method of ensuring its security against nuclear blackmail, of deterring a nuclear attack, and of retaliation for a nuclear strike from an enemy. Hence, the PRC holds a "no first use" doctrine and has pledged never to use or threaten to use nuclear weapons against nonnuclear states under any circumstances. Unlike the MSG, this approach has remained broadly consistent throughout the nuclear era.[28]

POST-2015 REFORMS

At the third plenum of the Eighteenth Party Congress in November 2013, Xi announced the intention to radically restructure the PLA. By 2016, the previous seven army-dominated regional commands were replaced with five joint theater commands covering China's territory: eastern, southern, western, northern, and central, all under the oversight of the CMC. These commands are designed to lead the majority of the conventional forces in their geographical area in wartime, with each service having a subordinate command in each theater and at the national level. As such, this reform has created entities similar to the geographic CCMDs of the United States, albeit based on PRC territory rather than global regions and seemingly with an additional operational service chain of command the U.S. lacks. The closest thing USINDOPACOM has to a Chinese counterpart in a Taiwan scenario is Eastern Theater Command, which is likely to provide the core of the command for an operation against the island.[29]

Alongside this was a major reform to the formerly army-dominated general departments, which saw their functions distributed between smaller units that report directly to the CMC and other branches and services. Among these are the Joint Staff Department, which links the theater commands and CMC. The PLA Ground Force (PLAGF) has also been given a separate headquarters to put it at an equal level to the other services rather than the default lead.[30]

The branches of the PLA were also restructured in 2016. The PLA Second Artillery Corps, which historically controlled China's ground-launched nuclear and nonnuclear ballistic and cruise missiles, became the PLA Rocket Force (PLARF), giving it equal status alongside the PLAGF, PLAN, and PLAAF. At the close of 2015, the PLA Strategic Support Force (PLASSF) was formed to provide critical space-, cyber-, information-, and psychological-warfare support to the joint force. Finally, in September 2016, the Joint Logistics Support Force (JLSF) was formed to provide strategic-level logistics support to the joint force.

Yet all has not gone well. In April 2024 came the announcement disbanding the PLASSF. The organization's Space Systems Department and Network Systems Department were rebadged as the Aerospace Force and Cyberspace Force, respectively, and became separate arms alongside the Information Support Force, which took up the remainder of PLASSF's responsibilities.[31] Numerous purges of senior defense officials on corruption charges also pointed to problems.

The Aerospace Force controls space-launch activities, research and development, the network linking space assets (including ground facilities), and the satellites themselves. The latter include communications; intelligence, surveillance, and reconnaissance (ISR); electronic intelligence (ELINT); signals intelligence (SIGINT); navigation; meteorology; and early warning and research satellites.[32] This space network is a vital component of the "kill chain" required to support the use of long-range weapons such as ASBMs as part of a reconnaissance-strike complex.[33] It is unclear at this time as to whether the Aerospace Force has fully taken over the antisatellite capability portfolio; its former incarnation reportedly operated in cooperation with the Network Systems Department, built around direct-ascent missiles, ground-based lasers, and electronic and cyberattack systems as well as an apparent capability to mount attacks using coorbiting satellites.[34]

Leading cyber-, psychological-, and electronic-warfare operations is the Cyberspace Force. Even during peacetime, it poses an advanced persistent threat to the United States and its allies, seeking to infiltrate computer networks, steal information, and identify vulnerabilities for potential exploitation.

Wartime taskings would include the disruption of U.S. and allied networks. There is limited available information on the force's electronic-warfare role, although the assumption is its focus is on strategic operations rather than tactical support, which remains the task of the PLA's services.[35]

The Information Support Force is intended to better facilitate joint operations and bring about the "informationized local wars" concept that is at the center of current PLA strategy. It is believed to be an evolution of PLASSF's Information and Communication Base, which controlled the PLA communications infrastructure.[36]

The Joint Logistic Force is the fourth arm and responsible for strategic- and campaign-level logistics, incorporating joint force and civilian assets. Each theater command has its own joint-logistics center, with the central base in Wuhan.[37]

Also important to note is the concept of civilian-military fusion that Beijing has adopted. This seeks to integrate the military and civil components of PRC development into the country's national strategic system and capabilities. It includes sharing dual-use technology through the civilian and defense sectors and—critically for a Taiwan contingency—integrating civilian assets into peacetime campaigning efforts and maintaining contingency plans for military operations.[38]

CONTEMPORARY FORCE MODERNIZATION

The end of the Soviet threat and the PLA's assessment of the Gulf War resulted in far more than strategy changes. At the beginning of the 1990s, the organization's equipment inventory was substandard at best, largely comprising a combination of domestic copies and evolutions of elderly Soviet designs and equally unimpressive systems of domestic origin. A major procurement effort was required.

Three developments occurred in parallel to material modernizations critical to the PLA's future. The first was force downsizing and rebalancing: an outward-facing military demanded a far greater maritime and aerospace capability than the ground-force-dominated organization could provide.

The second component was that China avoided a "mad dash" to acquire platforms such as aircraft carriers that mirrored those of the United States. Instead, a more asymmetric approach was taken, with "assassin's mace" systems designed to counter traditional U.S. platforms as part of an A2/AD-style strategy—most notably ASBMs. Many of these programs have been reportedly conducted under the 995 Project, instigated following the accidental U.S. bombing of the Chinese embassy in Belgrade in 1999.[39] Some have argued that the PRC's counterpart to A2/AD is "counterintervention," although China does not see this as a distinct strategy or campaign plan.[40]

Finally, the critical component was financial. The Stockholm International Peace Research Institute (SIPRI) had estimated that China's defense spending grew from $9.9 billion in 1990 to $296.4 billion in 2023, or 1.67 percent of GDP.[41] The International Institute for Strategic Studies (IISS) has put the figure at $319 billion for 2023.[42] The PRC claimed its "official" budget for 2024 to be $232 billion.[43] There has remained significant debate over how to calculate Chinese defense spending, primarily the result of disagreement over what should be counted, the effect of purchasing-power parity, and the degree of "off the books" spending present. A 2024 study claimed that Beijing's true expenditure was the equivalent of $471 billion compared to the $1.3 trillion by the United States under similar criteria.[44] Yet the rate of increase has now comfortably exceeded the growth rate of China's economy, with a 7.2-percent rise planned for 2024 compared to GDP growth targets of 5 percent.[45]

The following sections provide highlights of the PLA's force composition.[46]

Modernization—PLAAF

Major strides forward began with imported aircraft. In 1990 Beijing secured an agreement with the USSR to become the first export customer for the Su-27 Flanker fighter. Later, it was produced domestically as the multirole J-11 and subsequently in an enhanced form as the J-16 strike fighter. Further purchases of Flanker variants from Russia, including the Su-30 and Su-35, followed.[47]

China's aviation industry has also rapidly caught up, with the single-engine J-10 Vigorous Dragon multirole combat aircraft first flying in 1998, entering service in 2005, and as of 2025 the most numerous PLAAF combat aircraft. Like the J-16, Su-30, and Su-35, the later J-10C variant can carry a full range of air-to-air and air-to-ground munitions. In 2017 the fifth generation J-20 Mighty Dragon, the PLA's first stealth aircraft, entered service. This multirole aircraft is chiefly tasked as a long-range interceptor, a mission facilitated not only by the aircraft's stealth and long radius of action but also by long-range PL-15 and PL-17 air-to-air missiles with a reach of over two hundred kilometers and four hundred kilometers, respectively.[48] The stealth J-35 fighter also has entered service. In December 2024 a large tri-jet stealth prototype aircraft, possibly designated the J-36, made its first flight.[49]

Instead of converting its bomber force to new types, the H-6 has been the focus of further development, including the H-6K and H-6N, with turbofan engines and heavily modified airframes. These now provide the PLAAF with a long-range, standoff offensive strike and antiship capability. The latest H-6 variants are between them able to launch—among other weapons—the CJ-20 land-attack cruise missile, the supersonic air-launched variant of the CJ-100 land-attack cruise missile, the YJ-12 supersonic antiship cruise missile, and the CH-AS-X-13 and KD-21 air-launched ballistic missiles. The H-6N variant is also capable of in-flight refueling, considerably extending its range.[50]

The PLAAF is not only responsible for the fighter force element of homeland air defense but also operates the network of radars and other sensors, electronic-warfare systems, and the command-and-control (C2) network to support the system, including data sharing. The critical kinetic element of China's integrated air-defense system is the SAM network.[51] In the 1990s, the PLA began purchasing the SA-10 and SA-20 SAM systems from Russia, eventually going on to produce similar classes of missiles, the HQ-9 and HQ-15—the latter with a range of up to two hundred kilometers—as well as an SA-12-derived HQ-18.[52] Deliveries from Russia of the SA-21, with a range of up to four hundred kilometers, began in 2018.[53] The domestically developed HQ-22 supports these. The SA-21 and HQ-18 provide a degree of terminal ABM capability, and a midcourse interceptor, the HQ-19 is also available.[54] The PLAAF's operation of a layered SAM defense necessitates medium-range systems, among them the HQ-12, with a fifty-kilometer range, and the short-range HQ-6. In addition to conventional radars, the PLAAF also operates at least three extremely long-range over-the-horizon (OTH) radar systems that provide early warning and targeting data.[55]

The PLAAF's AEW&C fleet is also critical to air defense and a variety of other tasks. A small number of Il-76 transport aircraft imported from Russia were converted into KJ-2000s, which are utilized in parallel with the domestically produced KJ-200s. The KJ-500 is the latest and most numerous AEW&C in service and is set to be augmented by the Y-20-derived KJ-3000.[56]

To bolster strategic transport around two dozen specially configured Il-76s procured from Russia, which provided an interim capability. The domestic Y-20 transport aircraft came into service in 2016. These are supported by Y-7,

Y-8, and Y-9 tactical transport aircraft. PLAAF, PLAGF, and PLAN helicopters provide additional air-landing options and include the S-70-derived Z-20, Super Frelon–inspired Z-8, and Russian-sourced Mi-17. The Airborne Corps formation is centered on six combined-arms maneuver brigades and one special forces brigade, which would be critical components of a Taiwan-invasion contingency.[57]

In-flight refueling has long been a weak point for the PLAAF, with a small number of converted bombers and, more recently, Russia-sourced IL-78s providing tanker support. But the introduction of a tanker variant of the Y-20, the YY-20 (also known as the Y-20U), has provided genuine mass for the force.

The PLAAF has a long history of UAV operations and today, alongside the PLAGF, PLARF, and PLAN, operates a suite of modern systems. With regard to uncrewed combat aerial vehicles (UCAV), the stealth GJ-11 is the most well known, with the GJ-1 and GJ-2 likely tasked with operations in less contested environments. The WZ-7, WZ-9, and WZ-10 all provide similar high-altitude, long-endurance surveillance coverage to the U.S. Global Hawk, while the air-launched supersonic WZ-8 provides a high-speed, high-altitude stealth-reconnaissance capability. To these can be added one-way loitering munition UAVs being deployed across the services as a means to strike targets: recent reports indicate one million such munitions have been ordered for delivery by 2026.[58]

The final major mission is electronic warfare. Several older H-6 aircraft have been converted to provide electronic-warfare support.[59] Much of this force is based on converted Y-8 and Y-9 transport aircraft fitted with electronic-warfare and surveillance equipment. Electronic-warfare variants of tactical combat aircraft include the J-10D and J-16D.

Modernization—PLAN and Maritime Forces

As with the PLAAF, the PLAN adopted a dual-track approach to reequipment. The first focused on imports. The 1980s window of defense cooperation with the West saw only limited procurement in the naval sphere, with gas-turbine engines and torpedo systems among the items imported.[60] As with the PLAAF, large-scale imports from Russia were later resumed. The sale of the first of what eventually numbered twelve *Kilo*-class SSKs was finalized in 1994. Four *Sovremenny*-class destroyers followed this. There was also a "Russia adjacent" purchase from Ukraine of the incomplete Soviet-era aircraft carrier

Varyag, which was eventually completed in China as the Type 001 *Liaoning*. It carries the J-15, a domestic copy of a prototype Su-33 also purchased from Ukraine as a short takeoff but arrestor-recovery (STOBAR) combat aircraft. The PLAN may seek to operate the J-35 in this configuration.

Domestic naval efforts were also significant. The completion of the *Varyag* was built upon to produce an upgraded copy, the Type 002 *Shandong*. It, too, carries the J-15 as well as helicopters for ASW, AEW&C, and utility work. The conventionally powered Type 003 carrier *Fujian* is fitted for Catapult Assisted Take-Off But Arrested Recovery (CATOBAR) operations. The J-15B, a variant modified for catapult launch, will be initially embarked as the primary combat aircraft, with the stealth J-35 subsequently joining it alongside the KJ-600 AEW&C and as-yet-unspecified UCAVs. The first Type 004, a likely nuclear-powered CATOBAR carrier along the lines of the U.S. *Gerald R. Ford* class, is rumored to be planned to be in service by 2030.

Major surface combatants have also taken a significant leap forward in capability. After initially unsatisfactory results in the form of the Type 052 *Luhu* class and Type 052B *Luyang I* class, more success was found with Type 052C *Luyang II*-class and Type 052D *Luyang III*-class destroyers, with the Type 052D becoming the backbone of the surface fleet. The cruiser-sized Type 055 *Renhai* class acts in support and can launch the YJ-21 ASBM.

The frigate force has been through a similar evolution, with production settling on the Type 054 *Jiangkai* class and Type 054A *Jiangkai II* class, with the latter now the fleet mainstay. The Type 056 *Jiangdao*-class corvette and Type 22 *Houbei*-class missile boat provide robust near-shore capabilities.

The Type 039 *Song*-class SSK represented a break with old Soviet designs from the 1950s, and both they and the Type 039A/B/C *Yuan* class are equipped with air-independent propulsion (AIP), and together with the *Kilo*-class boats, now make up the PLAN's conventionally powered attack submarines. SSN developments have been slower, with the primitive Type 091 *Han* class now superseded by the Type 093 *Shang* class—including the guided-missile submarine (SSGN) Type 093B variant fitted with vertical launch cells—while the anticipated Type 095 seemingly experiencing continuous delays. A program to produce a small SSN in the form of the Type 041 remains unconfirmed, as do accounts of a vessel of this type sinking at peirside in mid-2024.[61] The Type 094 provides the PLAN's contribution to Beijing's strategic deterrent through the deployment of JL-2 and JL-3 SLBMs.[62]

Amphibious landing capabilities are critical to any Taiwan contingency, and here the picture is mixed for the PLAN. The Type 071 LPD and the Type 075 and 076 LPHs are the most modern classes. While they can support a landing operation against Taiwan, these vessels are better suited to longer-range power projection. They are supported by older, more traditional amphibious types, including the Type 72 *Yuting*-class family of LSTs, as well as a host of smaller PLAN landing ships and craft, including the Type 726 and *Zubr*-class landing craft air cushion (LCAC), primarily designed to support the PLAN Marine Corps (PLANMC).[63] In 2017 an expansion program was initiated to grow the PLANMC from two brigades to six combined-arms brigades, a special-forces brigade, and aviation and service-support brigades, with many of the requisite personnel transferred from the PLAGF.[64] Six PLAGF amphibious brigades, which are more focused on shorter-range missions such as crossing the Taiwan Strait, operate their own force of landing craft.

This landing ship force is seen by some as inadequate for any landing operations a Taiwan invasion would require. Yet dependence on merchant shipping to supplement these landing assets reflects the historical rule rather than the exception. Allied amphibious operations during World War II utilized vast numbers of specialized landing ships and craft, but these were only possible after a multiyear mobilization of industry. Analysis of PLA exercises with merchant shipping confirms that these vessels are envisaged to have a major wartime role. Since at least 2015, ro-ro-ferries are required to be constructed to technical standards suitable for meeting defense-mission standards, a role formalized by a 2016 law. Numerous ferry companies also have shadow military designations, according to reports. Exercises have been conducted to rehearse such operations, with civilian ferries fitted with ramps to deploy amphibious vehicles directly into the water.[65] In early 2025 reports emerged of PLAN trials of floating piers.[66]

Critical to any successful landing will be countering the use of naval mines by Taiwan and its allies as well as China's own use of such munitions in support of wider efforts to subdue the island. Offensive mine warfare by Beijing would focus on supporting a blockade around Taiwanese territory and limiting the ability of U.S. and other allied vessels to act in support of the ROC. As with most navies, the ability to counter enemy mine capability currently centers upon small craft, with the Type 081 *Wochi*-class MCMs and Type 082 *Wosao*-class coastal minesweepers (MSCs) supported by uncrewed surface vessels (USVs) in the lead, with civilian vessels having a role as auxiliary minesweepers.[67]

The PLAN Air Force (PLANAF) is the PLA's maritime aviation element. A recent reorganization has reportedly transferred all but one PLAN land-based fighter unit, all bomber units, and many other land-based assets, including SAMs and radar systems, to the PLAAF. Ship-based aircraft, land-based AEW&C, ASW aircraft, miscellaneous support aircraft, and UAVs remain under PLANAF control.[68] ASW helicopters include the Z-9C, Z-18F, and imported Ka-28. Z-18J and Ka-31 helicopters provide ship-based AEW, with the fixed-wing KJ-600 later joining them on the CATOBAR carriers. As already noted, J-15s and J-35s provide the fixed-wing element of carrier air groups. The PLAN also operates UAVs, including the medium-endurance BZK-005 and the ASN-209 for maritime reconnaissance and communications relay work, along with a variety of smaller ship-launched UAVs, including the WZ-6B.[69]

The Coast Guard is a component of the People's Armed Police, while the Maritime Militia supports but is not formally part of the PLA. In wartime they would provide a supporting patrol, security, surveillance, and transport roles. In an invasion of Taiwan, the Maritime Militia would provide crews and other forms of support to operate civilian vessels.[70]

Modernization—PLA Ground Forces

The shift toward brigade-based structures is the most significant PLAGF organizational reform of the current era.[71] As of 2025, thirteen army groups are split between the five established theater commands. Each group is centered upon combined-arms brigades. These can be either light (including motorized, high-mobility, air-assault, and mountain formations), medium (wheeled armored vehicles), or heavy (tracked armored vehicles). These operate alongside artillery, aviation, air-defense, special operations, engineering, chemical-defense, and support brigades. Additional nonstandardized military districts exist in Tibet and Xinjiang.[72]

Today, Type 96 and Type 99 tank variants provide a modern armored combat capability. The Type 15 light tank serves alongside them and is also utilized by the PLANMC. Critical to a Taiwan scenario is the Type 05 amphibious fighting vehicle, variants of which are deployed with both the PLAGF and PLANMC.

Modernization of the PLA's artillery forces has seen a balance shift from towed to self-propelled systems. Rocket artillery has enjoyed a major leap forward. Most relevant to supporting a Taiwan invasion is the introduction of launchers carrying heavy precision-guided rockets. This includes the PHL-16, which is capable of firing rockets and tactical ballistic missiles across the Taiwan Strait.[73]

The PLAGF lacks long-range air-defense systems but operates an array of less capable systems in common with the PLAAF. These include the medium-range HQ-16 and short-range HQ-6, HQ-7, and HQ-17 models plus a variety of AAA.

A significant aviation component exists within the PLAGF, with each of the army groups possessing an aviation brigade as well as an additional two brigades based in the Tibet and Xinjiang Military Districts. Two of these have an air-assault role with permanently attached infantry units. Z-8, Z-20, and Mil-17 are among the helicopter types to provide transport capability. Close air support is provided by Z-10 and Z-19 attack helicopters.

UAVs have a central role in PLAGF aviation. As might be expected, these platforms are predominantly focused on battlefield support. ASN-206 and ASN-207 are among the systems that can support tactical reconnaissance, particularly in detecting artillery strikes, electronic warfare, and communication relays.[74]

As already noted, the PLAGF includes six amphibious brigades that would play a central role in the invasion of Taiwan. These are distributed among the army groups in coastal regions. The 72nd Group Army and 73rd Group Army, both part of the Eastern Theater Command opposite Taiwan, each have two amphibious brigades. The remaining two are allocated to the 74th Army Group, which is part of Southern Theater Command.[75]

The PLA operates special forces across its branches, but the majority reside within the PLAGF. Each of the thirteen group armies reportedly possesses a special-forces brigade, and the PLANMC, PLARF, and PLAAF also each have such a brigade. Missions include reconnaissance and targeting, strikes and raids, and psychological warfare.[76]

Modernization—PLA Rocket Force

Established as the fourth branch of the PLA in December 2015, the PLARF functionally replaced the PLA Second Artillery Corps.[77] Despite being an advancement, the introduction of the first models of the DF-11 and DF-15 short-range ballistic missiles (SRBMs) and the DF-21 medium-range ballistic missile (MRBM) in the early 1990s failed to provide a weapon of major nonnuclear utility. But subsequent guidance upgrades to these models gave them a conventional precision-strike capability. These missiles have been joined by the DF-12 (which may be PLAGF rather than PLARF operated) and DF-16 SRBMs, DF-17 MRBM (capable of carrying the DF-ZF hypersonic glide vehicle [HGV] with a possible antiship capability), and DF-26 and DF-27 intermediate-range ballistic missiles (IRBMs); the latter with an HGV. These MRBMs and IRBMs can all carry nuclear weapons—similar capabilities with the SRBMs are disputed.[78]

The PLA can launch conventionally armed ballistic missiles not only at land targets but also at ships.[79] These ASBMs were also, in part, a product of the Third Taiwan Strait Crisis, when the PLA realized it had no viable method to counter the pair of U.S. carriers deployed to the region. Initial targeting data and updates after launch are provided by satellites, OTH radar, and maritime (including undersea) and airborne sensors before a terminal guidance system aboard the maneuverable reentry vehicle takes over for the final approach. The DF-21D is thought to be able to strike vessels over fifteen hundred kilometers away, the DF-26B three thousand to four thousand kilometers, and the DF-27 five thousand to eight thousand kilometers, with the latter two missiles having interchangeable payloads allowing them to also be used for nuclear or conventional land attacks.[80] Notably, the DF-21D reportedly has an air-launched variant compatible with H-6N bombers. The PLAN is equipped with the ship-launched YJ-21.[81] Efforts to integrate a HGV along the lines of the DF-ZF carried by the DF-17 missile and capable of offering a more robust ability to evade defensive systems when striking ships are also apparent.

In addition to ballistic missiles, the PLARF also controls a force of ground-launched cruise missiles (GLCMs), with the CJ-10 subsonic weapon, which has a range of over fifteen hundred kilometers, being the primary system.[82]

The most critical mission of the PLARF is the provision of the land-based arm of the PRC's nuclear deterrent. The intercontinental ballistic missile (ICBM) force leads this. It is believed that of the liquid-fueled, silo-based DF-5A/B/C can carry multiple independently targetable reentry vehicles

(MIRVs). The solid-fueled DF-31/A/AG missiles are road mobile, with the AG models fitted with MIRV warheads. The most modern ICBM, the DF-41, can be silo based or road mobile. These missiles are supported by nuclear-armed MRBMs (DF-21A/E) and IRBMs (DF-26), which provide a nuclear-strike capability for regional contingencies.[83]

Analysis indicates that the PLARF is adding around 250 additional missile silos to the 20 silos for DF-5 missiles it already possesses.[84] This would tie in with estimates that the PLA is expanding its nuclear warhead stockpile (including those delivered via bombers and SLBMs) from an operational stockpile of weapons to perhaps one thousand warheads by 2030, with up to six hundred available as of 2024.[85]

CONTEMPORARY PLA WAR PLANS

The focus of this book is not on limited military options but on military action through which Beijing seeks to terminate the ROC's de facto independence by force. Notably, there has been speculation that Beijing may seek to seize one or more of the small islands controlled by Taipei in a quest for leverage. Yet there would be little value to the PRC in capturing any of these outlying islands in isolation, a point a number of Chinese sources agree with.[86] Another option might be a full or partial blockade, but it is difficult to see this resulting in Taiwan's capitulation. Furthermore, the ROC's near-inevitable attempt to break any blockade would trigger escalation to full-scale war.[87] As such, the focus here will be on the most extreme option.

PLA military planning is directed by the MSG and is shaped by its doctrine.[88] Insights into this classified information are visible in periodic publications such as the *Science of Military Strategy* (of which there are two versions, one published by the PLA Academy of Military Science and the other by the PLA National Defense University), the *Science of Campaigns,* and the *Campaign Theory Study Guide.*[89]

For a Taiwan contingency, the Eastern Theater Command's Joint Operations Command Center would lead on planning and execution in close collaboration with China's high command in Beijing.[90] PLA writing indicates that plans are split into an activity plan and a support plan, the former covering areas including the CONOPS, the leadership's intent and phasing; and the latter covering areas such as transport and intelligence, with an overall product similar to a U.S. OPLAN.[91] Each PLA armed-service branch also has its campaign plans for particular contingencies.[92] Yet in a Taiwan scenario, the most critical elements are the overarching joint campaign plans that combine the strengths of the branches.[93] For the PLA, there are four such plans:

- Joint Blockade Campaign (JBC)[94]
- Joint Firepower Strike Campaign (JFSC)[95]
- Joint Island-Landing Campaign (JILC)[96]
- Joint Anti–Air Raid Campaign (JAAC)[97]

In theory, these campaigns could be run separately.[98] But many elements overlap, and some would not be practical to run in isolation. For example, the JILC executed against Taiwan would require all three of the others to be undertaken in support in order to succeed. Nevertheless, it is helpful to examine them separately.

Joint Blockade Campaign

A blockade operation would aim to exert material deprivation and psychological pressure on Taipei to compel compliance with China's wishes. This would extend beyond the maritime to include air and information interdiction. A JBC could take a partial approach such as through the use of random and disruptive inspections and selective communications jamming (such a "coercive quarantine" has been modeled.)[99] Any blockade would be proceeded by a psychological, public opinion, and legal campaign to frame the action as justified and forestall outside intervention. Nonkinetic measures such as electronic attacks, including radar jamming, could form part of prehostilities intimidation and preparation.[100]

If China enforces a blockade, PLAAF and PLAN air patrols would see fighter aircraft looking to intercept and divert civilian aircraft traveling to and from Taiwan. The PLAN, supported by the Maritime Militia and Coast Guard, would intercept vessels traveling to or departing from the ROC. Offshore islands under Taipei's jurisdiction may also be seized. An offensive kinetic element would likely accompany the blockade, with PLARF ballistic and cruise missiles and PLAAF air strikes launched against Taiwan from the mainland, augmented by missile attacks from the PLAN and long-range artillery from the PLAGF. Cyber and electronic attacks would be conducted as well, while sea mines would block ports. Undersea cables and satellites providing links to the island would be targeted to ensure information isolation.

The destruction of the ROC's Navy, Air Force, and air-defense system would be an early priority to counter attempts to break the blockade.[101]

Joint Firepower Strike Campaign

The JFSC is designed to destroy critical targets in Taiwan and more broadly to provide an offensive-firepower element to support the other three campaigns examined here. While in theory such an operation could be limited to a "punishment" attack responding to perceived slight, the reality is that a punitive operation would accomplish little of material value while rallying global support for Taiwan and increasing domestic will to resist. As a result, it is likely to be executed as a comprehensive campaign. From the PLA's perspective, such attacks would seek to compel Taipei to surrender to Beijing's demands by degrading Taiwan's material and psychological ability to resist.[102]

PLA literature states kinetic and nonkinetic strikes would begin by targeting C2 nodes. Attacks would then move on to target air-defense systems, including aircraft on the ground, their support facilities, and SAM sites. Military logistics sites and any naval vessels in port would also be struck. Broader infrastructure would be hit, including power stations, oil-storage sites, and bridges. PLA special forces on the ground would act in a supporting role, including by identifying targets and conducting attacks in their own right.[103]

Joint Island-Landing Campaign

The JILC covers the invasion option, with a primary focus, we assume here, on Taiwan itself, with landings on smaller islands as supporting actions. This would aim to penetrate the ROC's littoral defenses and secure footholds on the island, including critical access points such as ports and airfields, in order to prepare for subsequent operations inland. The later inland battle, while not formally part of the JILC, would aim to eliminate Taiwan's ability to militarily and politically resist unification by destroying the ROC Armed Forces and government to secure territorial control and pacify the population.[104]

Operations would be integrated closely with the JBC and JFSC. Additionally, the PLA's forces would be most vulnerable during loading, transit, and landing phases, necessitating the JAAC (outlined below) for protection—including from foreign intervention.

The Pescadores Islands in the Taiwan Strait would likely be a critical early objective. PLA literature highlights how critical the islands are to the wider operations. Images leaked—intentionally or unintentionally—from a PLA exercise in 2020 depict a map showing landings on Kinmen and Penghu, followed by an invasion of the south of Taiwan.[105]

During the main landing, PLA special operations forces would provide support through reconnaissance and obstacle clearance, target designation, strike and raiding operations, sabotage, psychological warfare, and key-point seizures. These would aim to disrupt the enemy's defensive operations against the main invading force.[106]

Airborne deployments would be conducted by parachute drop, fixed-wing aircraft landing onto captured runways, or helicopter assault. These troops would conduct sabotage and similar operations prior to the main landing and during the landing itself, then, aiding the main landing force by resisting Taiwanese attempts to counterattack and by attacking and seizing critical objectives. The PLAAF's Airborne Corps would be the largest contributor.[107]

While chiefly focused on out-of-area expeditionary operations, the recent expansion of the PLANMC now allows it to fulfill a JILC role. While details are unclear, it would likely be allocated secondary landing areas owing to its limited level of armor and firepower, focusing on advanced-party operations before the main landing, with tasks including reconnaissance and raids, mine and obstacle clearance, as well as diversionary landings and flanking operations in support of the main force, aiming to complicate the task of the defenders.[108]

The PLAGF would be the primary land force of the invasion. The first wave would center on the six amphibious combined-arms brigades, each equipped with a greater mechanized-warfare capability than their Airborne Corps and PLANMC counterparts but lighter than standard heavy combined-arms brigades. Units of their parent group army on the mainland would provide support to the initial landing echelon, including through rocket artillery strikes and helicopter lift. After the landing areas and ports were secure, the nonamphibious combined-arms brigades and other units from the mainland would reinforce the effort.[109]

As noted, the PLA's dedicated amphibious ships are inadequate to land the full force required to capture Taiwan. This is often highlighted by pointing to the limited number of suitable craft available, including LSTs. But China possesses the world's largest merchant fleet by gross tonnage, including a growing ro-ro ferry force that could support second-echelon landings.

The geographical challenges of an amphibious landing on Taiwan are well understood. Estimates count only fourteen suitable beaches, concentrated near Taipei in the north and in the island's southwest.[110] These areas have been fortified for over seventy-five years, and detailed contingencies have been made to fend off an assault. Success would likely hinge on capturing nearby airfields and ports to maintain reinforcements and logistics. Still, no beach perfectly combines proximity, light defenses, and accessibility.[111]

Once a landing area was consolidated, the push inland would begin and inevitably require transiting through heavily defended terrain and key chokepoints, including bridges and tunnels, that had either been subject to PLA bombardment or sabotaged by local forces to slow the communist advance. The culmination of the move inland would be urban battles for Taiwan's key population centers, including Taipei itself. This would require a battle in a large, modern metropolis unprecedented in history.[112]

Joint Anti–Air Raid Campaign

The priority the PLA places on the threat of aerospace attack makes the JAAC a key component of a war over Taiwan. This campaign would chiefly seek to prevent U.S.-led intervention during an attack on the ROC. At its most basic, it would act as a traditional defense, with a focus on protecting PLA assets from U.S.-led air and missile attacks. This includes ensuring incoming threat detection and engagement using PLAAF and PLAN fighters supported by AEW&C aircraft; an array of land, sea, and space-based sensors; and land- and sea-launched air-defense and missile-defense systems, electronic countermeasures, passive-defense methods such as concealment, and poststrike recovery. The PLA's active defense doctrine recognizes the importance of offensive operations as part of a wider defensive strategy. A JAAC can, therefore, be expected to encompass offensive kinetic and nonkinetic attacks targeting U.S. and allied sensors, computer networks and C2, lines of communication, regional military bases, and military platforms themselves.[113]

From a broader A2/AD perspective, the PLA would have two missions. The anti-access component of the PLA effort would aim to prevent reinforcements from reaching the theater. ASBM, submarines, and potentially long-range bombers could reach beyond the second island chain—running from Japan to the Bonin Islands to the Marianas (including Guam), the Caroline Islands (including Palau), and New Guinea—to target ships and aircraft approaching the theater of operations in an effort not too far removed from Imperial Japan's *Zengen Sakusen* attrition strategy. A significant unknown is whether such strikes could extend as far as Hawaii, Australia, and the U.S. mainland. Certainly, such operations would be more challenging and carry a major risk—an attack on the CONUS may bring NATO into the conflict by route of the alliance's Article 5 provisions. Yet the potential fielding by the PLA of conventionally armed ICBMs and submarine-launched land-attack cruise missiles—to say nothing of asymmetric options such as the use of merchant ships to launch missiles and UCAVs and to lay mines—make such action possible. Potential U.S. mainland targets would include ships at pier side in locations such as Naval Base San Diego and USAF strategic bombers at unhardened bases. As with Imperial Japan, the PRC could see disrupting Panama Canal operations as an option.

The area-denial effort would target U.S. and allied forces based within theater in peacetime or deployed immediately prior to hostilities. This would likely include U.S. assets based in Japan, including those at Kadena Air Base on Okinawa, Misawa Air Base, and naval bases at Yokosuka and Sasebo. Any deployed U.S. forces in the Philippines would be vulnerable as well. Strikes could extend to JSDF facilities, and even Guam may be subjected to heavy bombardment. The C4ISR systems facilitating the operations of forward-deployed assets would also be targeted, including those based in space.

RACING TO THE STARTING BLOCK?

Major elements of the PRC's contemporary intention with regard to the ROC are unclear. Yet to a significant extent, this public ambiguity acts to provide flexibility to the leadership in Beijing. While the PLA's strategic and operational planning has marched in advance of its practical capabilities, this is increasingly no longer the case. Nevertheless, the development of the PLA remains a work in progress and is marked by ongoing difficulties.

From a historical perspective, it is clear that the PRC lacks many of the weaknesses of previous U.S. rivals. The resources available to China in both military and civilian terms mean that it does not suffer from the fragility of Imperial Japan or even the Soviet Union. It is also clear that while the United States planned for potentially unrealistic scenarios in which the USSR attempted an invasion of Iran or Japan, the reality of both capability and intent—at least in terms of the grand vision of unification—is present in the case of China's designs on Taiwan.

CHAPTER 10

ISLAND DEFENSE

Nobody will help those who are not
intending to defend themselves.
—*Former ROC Chief of the General Staff*
Adm. Lee Hsi-ming, March 2024

Taipei has little prospect of long-term success alone against an invasion but will control the primary local defensive force at the outset of hostilities. Although this may seem an overwhelming burden, Taiwan has some advantages. Power projection—potentially the great weakness of the United States in a mature anti-access environment—is not an issue for the ROC, as everything from equipment to supplies to reservists is already within the theater of operations. Indeed, with appropriate planning, Taiwan is potentially able to bring its entire national power to bear for the defense of its territory. The ROC also has the advantage of singular focus and preparation time.

TAIWAN'S EVOLVING STRATEGY

From the 1949 ROC government withdrawal to Taiwan until the second half of the 1960s, Taipei's military strategy centered on "offensive defense"—protecting the ROC's remaining territory through an offensive-leaning posture, embodied in the heavy forward presence of the military on the coastal islands and coastal raiding.[1] Chiang Kai-shek's impractical plans for an invasion of the mainland finally gave way to the "forward defense" concept, which remained in place from 1966 to 1979 and retained a heavy military presence on the offshore islands without actively attempting to engage the PLA. With derecognition and the termination of the SAMDT a year later, by the end of

1979, the ROC Armed Forces became exclusively responsible for Taiwan's defense and reconfigured to a defense-in-depth posture, maintaining this until 2000. For much of this latter period, the "decisive campaign at the water's edge" concept led the way. This envisaged a layered defense targeting PLA forces during embarkation and transit (while avoiding full commitment of the ROC Air Force and ROC Navy to a battle of attrition), but with the primary engagement led by the ROC Army once PLA forces landed.[2]

By the end of the 1990s, it was apparent that such a linear and reactive stance would be inadequate. The election of a DPP administration in 2000 and its willingness to take a stance that Beijing would find more provocative gave room for the development of a genuine defense-in-depth approach. Sometimes referred to as Taiwan's version of "active defense"—it prioritized contesting command of the sea and air surrounding Taiwan, therefore "fighting the decisive military campaign beyond the border," or "decisive battle offshore." This strategy, termed "effective deterrence and resolute defense," emphasized defeating the PLA before it reached the main island, including through striking at the mainland. But this approach was derided by many as unrealistic.[3]

By 2008, it was clear the PLA's modernization made any attempt to achieve air and sea superiority offshore untenable. With a KMT president elected that year, this reality, combined with a desire to reconcile with Beijing, led to the at least theoretical adoption of the "Hard ROC" approach. This modified Taiwan's defensive stance to "resolute defense and credible deterrence." While a subtle shift in wording, this represented a rebalancing toward a less forward-leaning approach that recognized a need to fortify territory against the PLA's growing power.[4] Emphasizing asymmetry in weapons and tactics, Taiwan's *Quadrennial Defense Review* (*QDR*) *2009* noted: "Asymmetrical warfighting capabilities tailored against the enemy's operational center of gravity (COG) and critical vulnerabilities should be developed. When conducting defense operations, advantages in time and space to paralyze or block enemy offensives and rout invading forces should be utilized."[5]

With the DPP's return to power in 2016, a new path began to solidify. Traditional air and sea battles around Taiwan with conventional platforms had largely been recognized as unwinnable, a defense focused on the landing beaches inadequate, and asymmetry ambitions under Hard ROC unfulfilled. Understanding these limitations, a new approach providing for in-depth operations while recognizing the centrality of preventing successful landings was adopted. The *2021 QDR* introduced "resolute defense, multi-domain deterrence" as the contemporary military strategy.[6]

"Resolute defense, multi-domain deterrence" is retained in the *2025 QDR*. The guiding principal is framed as "multi-domain denial and resilient defense" as part of an effort to establish a survivable, layered defense-in-depth capability. An emphasis is placed on "whole-of-society defense resilience" to reflect the need to disrupt PRC efforts using all available resources across the spectrum in peacetime and war.[7]

THE OVERALL DEFENSE CONCEPT

The most significant and contentious ROC defense strategy innovation of the last decade has been the overall defense concept (ODC), first introduced in 2017. This came about after intense discussion on how Taiwan could counter PLA qualitative improvements catching up to their preexisting quantitative advantage and the failure of the original attempt at asymmetry under Hard ROC. Analysts in both Taipei and abroad agreed that an asymmetric approach—often referred to as the "porcupine strategy"—was Taiwan's best bet.[8]

Introduced by former Chief of the ROC General Staff Adm. Lee Hsi-min (2017–19), the ODC redefined "winning" a war with China from the destruction of an enemy force to preventing the enemy from occupying Taiwan.[9] The strategy has two key components: force buildup and operational concepts.[10] Force buildup emphasizes developing force preservation and symmetrical and asymmetric capabilities. Preservation efforts include concealment, camouflage, base hardening, rapid repair, and deception capabilities. Recent initiatives include rehearsing for urban combat with military vehicles disguised as commercial vehicles, constructing a new generation of hardened aircraft shelters, and procuring mobile C2 equipment from the United States.[11]

The ODC maintains traditional weapon systems in numbers adequate to perform peacetime deterrence duties, complicate PLA calculations, and boost morale while addressing gray-zone aggression: for example, a PLAN destroyer approaching Taiwan could be met by a similar ROC vessel. Key recent acquisitions such as the F-16C/D Block 70 and M1A2T Abrams main battle tank preserve conventional combat capabilities. Additionally, traditional systems can be used asymmetrically—for example, ROC Army Cobra and Apache attack helicopters possess limited air-to-air capability.

But the focus is on asymmetric capabilities that require a "large number of small things."[12] To this end, Stinger SAMs, Javelin antitank missiles, Volcano antitank-mine dispersal systems, land-based Harpoon ASMs, NASAMS, and HIMARS launchers have been procured from the United States. Domestic production of SAMs, portable antiarmor weapons such as the Kestrel, ASMs, UAVs, uncrewed surface vessels (USVs), and loitering munitions has increased, and the *Min Jiang*–class naval minelayer has entered service.[13] UAVs are also being imported, with Switchblade 300 and ALTIUS 600M loitering munitions ordered from the United States.[14]

The ODC has suffered from serious difficulties in its implementation.[15] Alarmingly for the concept's supporters, it goes unmentioned in the *2021 QDR*, the first published following Adm. Lee Hsi-min's departure from his post, and the *2025 QDR*. It is also not referred to by name in the *2021 National Defense Report* (*NDR*) or the *2023 NDR*, although the need for asymmetry is prominently addressed. There remains a bias toward procuring large, expensive, and prestigious traditional platforms over those that could reasonably be considered asymmetric—often justified by a focus on operations short of countering an invasion. For its part, the United States has recently sought to deter acquisition of "gold-plated" platforms, with the Biden administration denying Taiwan's requests to buy the MH-60R Seahawk ASW helicopter and E-2D AEW&C platforms, both of which would have cost billions of dollars and—while useful in situations other than war—would be extremely vulnerable to PLA attack.[16] Yet some have suggested that events in Ukraine have reignited enthusiasm for the ODC.

Recent criticism of ROC procurement policy is valid, as some projects clash with the anti-invasion priority. For example, the *Yushan*-class LPD would be highly vulnerable in an all-out conflict. Similarly, acquiring ALCMs in the form of the U.S. AGM-84H SLAM-ER and the domestic Wan Chien reflect an ROC Air Force ambition to strike the mainland, but the survivability of the fighters tasked to carry them is doubtful.

Some traditional systems being replaced are justifiable, as they are nearing the end of their operational lives, and removing them entirely from the anti-invasion ROC order of battle would simplify the PLA's wartime tasks. Certain platforms blur the line between traditional and asymmetric. For example, the new *Hai Kun*–class submarines will be neither cheap nor numerous and are vulnerable in port, but they do pose a meaningful threat to dissimilar assets of the PLAN and PRC merchant ships when deployed. The Patriot SAM/ABM systems are expensive and have restricted mobility, but they remain more survivable than fixed-wing aircraft. The *2021* and *2025 QDRs*' highlighting of the ROC Armed Forces's long-range precision strike capability is also not necessarily against the ODC grain: while aircraft-deployed missiles may be vulnerable, mobile ground-launched systems such as the domestic Hsiung Feng IIE and Yun Feng and the U.S. ATACMS force the PLA to take defensive and offensive measures that add friction to an invasion attempt.

CONTEMPORARY FORCE MODERNIZATION

The ROC's post–Cold War defense modernization was seen as necessitating a pivot away from a force dependent on conscription-based quantity—particularly in the army—and toward what the *1993–1994 NDR* referred to as a "lean but effective force."[17] This evolved into a push toward a smaller, all-volunteer professional force. Following initial postdemocratization cutbacks, information from 2023 suggests that the ROC's regular forces are around 180,000 strong, with an end goal of 210,000 personnel.[18] IISS figures from 2024 give a total of 169,000 active regular personnel: 94,000 ROC Army, 40,000 ROC Navy, 35,000 ROC Air Force, and 11,800 paramilitary.[19] Data from 2024 states that the ROC Armed Forces are only at 80 percent of authorized strength.[20] Nevertheless, defense spending is now increasing after decades of reductions. The ROC's 2025 planned budget takes it to around $20.2 billion, or 2.45 percent of GDP, with a government pledge to raise it to 3 percent of GDP.[21]

By 2017, mandatory military service had been reduced to four months, having initially fallen from two years to one year. The drastically shortened conscription period—referred to as "military training"—effectively made it impossible to train personnel for emergency mobilization.[22]

In December 2022 officials formally announced that conscription would be officially restored in the ROC and extended to one year from January 2024. But this will take time to ramp up, with only around 9,100 of 78,600 conscripts expected to do the full year in 2024, rising to 53,600 by 2029.[23] To support these changes, both professionals and conscripts are benefiting from substantial pay raises and improvements in facilities. The annual Han Kuang anti-invasion exercise has been revamped from something at times criticized as being a media spectacle to a practical drill, incorporating scenarios such as losing contact with central command.[24]

Additionally, the ROC Armed Forces have been restructured to best use the professional, conscript, and reserve components as part of the "All-Out Defense System." The force now consists of

- Active Force (Main Battle Troop): Primarily the professional ROC Armed Forces members who would lead frontline fighting
- Garrison Troop: Primarily conscripts led by a cadre of regular personnel who would focus on infrastructure and territorial defense
- Civil Service System: Personnel undertaking "alternative service" integrated into broader civil-defense and military-support efforts, including in cooperation with the private sector
- Reserve System (and Reserve Force): The Reserve System will coordinate the supply of retired reservists to reinforce the Main Battle Troop and former conscripts to reinforce the Garrison Troop as well as the Reserve Force for local defense [25]

The following section presents highlights of the composition of the ROC Armed Forces.[26]

The ROC Air Force

Taiwan's first line of air and missile defense is its early warning capability. The military operates a network of surveillance radars to monitor local airspace as well as a AN/FPS-115 PAVE PAWS radar also capable of tracking ballistic missiles at extended range. These are augmented by five E-2T AEW&C aircraft. All this data, plus that from ROC Navy and ROC Army radar systems as well as civilian radar, is integrated to provide a comprehensive air picture. The Joint Air Operations Center, which operates within a hardened facility inside Toad Mountain, acts as the central command hub, with three known regional operations control centers as well as backup sites acting in support.[27]

Various aircraft make up the air fleet. The IDF, or F-CK1 Ching-kuo, is a partially domestic fighter aircraft and remains in service in the form of the upgraded F-CK-1 C/D. In addition to its air-defense role, it also possesses a ground-attack capability, including through the use of Wan Chien ALCMs, and in the future potentially an antiship capability with an air-launched variant of the Hsiung Feng III ASM.[28] The Mirage 2000, purchased from France in 1992, serves as a fighter in its direct combat role, carrying Magic II infrared and MICA RF active radar-guided missiles. It also possesses an ELINT-gathering capability.[29] The ROC Air Force F-16 fleet forms the backbone of the fighter force. Entering service in 1997, the surviving aircraft have since been upgraded to the F-16A/B midlife update (often referred to as F-16V) standard. Its air-to-air ordnance includes the Sidewinder, Sparrow, and AMRAAM missiles. Air-to-ground munitions include laser-guided bombs, Maverick missiles, Harpoon ASMs, HARM antiradar missiles, JSOW glide bombs, and SLAM-ER cruise missiles.[30] The aircraft also has a reconnaissance role. In 2019, after almost two decades of rebuffing ROC requests, the United States agreed to sell Taiwan a further sixty-six F-16C/D Block 70s (similar to the F-16V) with various enhancements, including conformal fuel tanks.[31]

The ROC Air Force also controls the majority of Taiwan's ground-based air defenses through its Air Defense and Artillery Command (ADAC). As with combat aircraft, this is a mixed force of foreign and domestic systems. Patriot PAC-2 and PAC-3 missiles procured from the United States from the 1990s onward provide air defense and ABM capability. Alongside these serve indigenous Tien Kung II and Tien Kung III SAM batteries, the latter type with an ABM capability. The Skyguard System, a mixture of RIM-7 Sparrow missile launchers and 35-mm cannons, provides short-range defense. Alongside these is the Antelope air-defense system, which fires Tien Chien I missiles.[32] These are augmented by U.S.-supplied NASAMS.[33]

Base hardening, aircraft dispersal, and concealment are all important elements of the ROC Air Force's survival strategy. While combat bases have their own hardened aircraft shelters, the centerpieces of such efforts can be found in vast underground hangars at Chiashan Air Force Base and Chihhang Air Base. There is also a capability to rapidly clear and repair damaged runways, and at least five highway strips have a wartime role of operating dispersed aircraft.[34]

Beyond tactical combat aircraft, the ROC Air Force also operates a variety of platforms in support roles. The UAV fleet is led by the SeaGuardian variant of the U.S.-built MQ-9B Reaper and the similar-in-appearance but domestically developed Teng Yun. The Chien Hsing antiradiation loitering munition can hit PLA coastal radar sites.[35]

The ROC Air Force ADAC also reportedly has responsibility for Taiwan's ground-launched land-attack missiles.[36] The Hsiung Feng IIE is a subsonic cruise missile: the original model has a range of around 600 kilometers, while the extended-range variant can travel up to 1,200 kilometers. Yun

Feng is a supersonic weapon: the initial variant can travel up to 1,200 kilometers and 2,000 kilometers in extended-range form, potentially giving it the ability to reach Beijing. These are reportedly supported by a few dozen 120-kilometer-range Tien Chi SRBMs forward based on ROC-controlled islands near the mainland.[37]

The ROC Navy

The *Cheng Kung*–class frigate, derived from the U.S. *Oliver Hazard Perry* class, is the ROC Navy's most numerous major surface combatant, and these are augmented by two ex–U.S. Navy vessels of the parent class imported from the United States. The ROC has imported warships from beyond the United States as well, with a pair of *Hai Lung*–class SSKs purchased from the Netherlands and entering service in 1987. *Kang Ding*–class frigates from France arrived in the 1990s. That decade also saw surplus *Knox*-class frigates leased and later sold by the United States to Taiwan. In 2003 the ROC bought four *Kidd*-class destroyers which entered service as the *Kee Lung*-class.

While foreign types of frigates and destroyers remain the backbone of the ROC Navy, other vessels are domestically designed and built. Thirty *Kuang Hua VI*–class missile boats and twelve *Tuo Chiang*–class corvettes lead the lighter element of the surface combat force. The latter can be augmented by twelve *Anping*-class offshore patrol vessels of the Coast Guard Administration, which are similar in design and can be armed with Hsiung Feng II and Hsiung Feng III missiles in a crisis.[38] Ten *Min Jiang*–class minelayers provide anti-invasion support as part of a wider asymmetric approach. Their MCM counterparts are U.S.- and Germany-sourced vessels. A new class of light frigate to replace the *Knox*-class vessels is entering service in the late 2020s.[39]

The single-most-expensive and high-profile procurement effort of the ROC Navy is the Indigenous Defense Submarine (IDS) program, also known as the *Hai Kun*-class.[40] This is an effort to introduce eight new SSKs into service, the first of which was launched in September 2023.

The ROC Navy's greatest contribution to asymmetric warfare likely comes from its land-based ASM squadrons. These comprise the Hsiung Feng II and Hsiung Feng III and U.S.-sourced truck-launched Harpoon ASMs controlled by the Littoral Combat Command.[41] During a crisis, these units are deployed from their bases, concealed, and regularly moved to avoid detection and destruction.

Operating as part of the Navy, the ROC Marine Corps comprises two brigades and a collection of smaller units. It is primarily tasked with amphibious operations and counterlanding missions on Taiwan and the ROC's outlying islands. In the latter role, the marines can deploy using *Yushan*-class LPDs, *Chung He*–class LSTs, landing craft, or aircraft.[42]

The ROC Navy also has an aviation component, including S- 70C and elderly MD 500 helicopters which provide a shipborne ASW capability. However, the P- 3Cs serving in a maritime patrol role are operated by the ROC Air Force.

The ROC Army

Changing circumstances led to a renewal of directly purchasing big-ticket items during the 1990s, with M60A3 tanks, M109 self-propelled artillery, AH-1W Super Cobra attack helicopters, OH-58 Kiowa and Chinook transport helicopters, and Stinger (including the vehicle-mounted Avenger system), TOW, and Hellfire missiles all authorized for sale. Javelin antitank missiles, AH-64E Apaches, and UH-60M Blackhawks followed post-2000. Sales of M1A2T tanks and HIMARS launchers, including the three-hundred-kilometer-range ATACM, were approved in 2020; the systems are now in service.

The second portion of the ROC Army's inventory comprises relatively modern domestic systems. These include the CM-32 armored vehicle, which comes in multiple variants, including APC and IFVs, with the older domestically produced CM-21 (a version of the M113) operating in support. Indigenous artillery is led by Thunderbolt-2000 rocket launchers. The medium-range Tien Chien II is the ROC Army's primary SAM, supported by the Antelope and Stinger short-range SAMs as well as AAA.

A number of Cold War legacy systems are also in service. The M1 240-mm howitzers stationed in Kinmen remain at least notionally operational (although they are largely tourist attractions), while the imported and domestically built M114 155-mm and M101 105-mm howitzers are the most numerous towed-artillery types, with M110 203-mm self-propelled guns operating alongside the M109. The CM-11 Brave Tiger tank, a domestically assembled hybrid of the U.S. M48 and M60, is the most numerous such vehicle in service.

Structurally, since 2022 the professional element of the ROC Army has been divided between five combat theater commands (CTCs), which are responsible for both the army and other ROC forces in their respective regions. The main combat elements include:

- First CTC: responsible for Penghu Islands (incorporating Army Penghu Defense Command)
- Second CTC: responsible for the east of Taiwan (incorporating Army Huadong Defense Command)
- Third CTC: responsible for northern Taiwan (incorporating Army Sixth Corps)—includes two armored brigades (542nd and 584th) and one mechanized-infantry brigade (269th) plus mechanized and armored units in the Guandu Area Command and Lanyang Area Command
- Fourth CTC: responsible for southern Taiwan (incorporating Army Eighth Corps)—includes one armored (564th) and one mechanized-infantry (333rd) brigade
- Fifth CTC: responsible for central Taiwan (incorporating Army Tenth Corps)—includes one armored (586th) and one mechanized-infantry (234th) brigade[43]

Kinmen Defense Command, Matsu Defense Command, and Dongyin Area Command also provide defense for their respective island groups. Under the Aviation and Special Forces Command sit two combat-aviation brigades, and the equivalent of a special-forces brigade. The combined-arms brigades operate alongside Artillery Commands and the standard support units, including engineers, logistics, and signals formations. Together, these units possess around 94,000 professional troops of the ROC Army Main Force.[44]

The ROC Reserves

Taiwan's reserve efforts—both military and civilian—are coordinated by the All-Out Defense Mobilization Agency, which operates under the MND. In wartime or during a natural disaster, the agency coordinates military and civilian resource mobilization to counter the threat faced.[45]

All service branches have reserve components, but by far the largest and most important is that of the ROC Army. The reserve system's highest-priority task is providing former conscripts to augment the conscript-heavy Garrison Force, which is centered upon infantry brigades. As part of the reforms, one source indicates that there will be twelve Type A infantry brigades tasked with peacetime training: in wartime all of these units would be augmented with reservists and tasked with defense against landings. In addition to this, ten Type B infantry brigades will be staffed by personnel from military schools and academies. Finally, there will be twenty-five regional infantry brigades, again dependent on mobilized reserves.[46] Yet as of 2024, IISS credits the force with just twenty-seven reserve brigades in total.

The reserve system would also coordinate the supply of retired regular-force personnel to the Active Force to ensure full unit strength and allow for casualty replacements. Beyond augmentation, the Reserves would take on broader urban- and rural-warfare tasks.[47]

But the Reserves' theoretical strength does not currently translate into reality. Estimates in 2022 observed that as few as 300,000 reservists were combat ready—this number is likely optimistic—but they still would require significant mobilization time, potentially an impossible task given the PLA's anticipated disruption of Taiwan's C2 system.[48] To help remedy this, periodic reserve recall training is transitioning from five days to seven days to two weeks annually, with more emphasis on combat skills and field operations, including at the locations specific personnel would be tasked to defend.[49]

Information, Communication, and Electronic Force Command

Launched in June 2017 and sometimes referred to as the fourth branch of the ROC Armed Forces, the Information, Communication, and Electronic Force Command (ICEFC) is within the MND and is the lead ROC organization for cyber and communications warfare.[50] This body sits as part of the "cybersecurity triangle" alongside the National Security Council's National Information and Communications Security Office and the Executive Yuan's Department of Cyber Security. The ICEFC's chief role is to defend the nation's military, state institutions, and critical infrastructure from the full array of cyberthreats, including those emanating from the PLA and the PRC's Ministry of State Security. The command also has an offensive and espionage role.[51]

CONTEMPORARY ROC WAR PLANNING

The overall OPLAN for the ROC in the event of a conflict with the PRC is reportedly known as Gu'an (solid and secure), with the invasion threat as the focus. Within the OPLAN are branch plans to manage the defense of offshore islands (Yingyuan), the dispersal of air assets (Tienchu), and the defense of ROC territory in the South China Sea (Weichiang). Gu'an is evaluated through exercises, most notably the annual Han Kuang command-post and field exercise. Gu'an does not assume successful U.S. support beyond ISR.[52]

The *2021 QDR* referred to a four-phase approach of "resist the enemy on the opposite shore, attack it at sea, destroy it in the littoral area, and annihilate it on the beachhead" as the concept of operations for countering an invasion.[53] To these, *2025 QDR* added two phases at the beginning to account for routine operations and combat preparation, gathering the initial three phases of the 2021 model into a single "joint anti-landing" phase, with the final two phases covering inland fighting that had reportedly been part of the ROC Armed Forces internal plans but not previously featured in QDRs or NDRs.[54] This resulted in the current six-phase model:

- Phase 1: Routine crisis management
- Phase 2: Combat readiness deployment
- Phase 3: Joint anti-landing
- Phase 4: Littoral and coastal combat
- Phase 5: Defense in depth
- Phase 6: Protracted operations[55]

Per *2025 QDR*, ROC Armed Forces are to "employ striking, garrison, and reserve forces to vigorously delay, disrupt and deny enemy intents in all offensive phases, including Transit, Foothold, Formation, Penetration, Consolidation, and Force Buildup."[56] The QDR reportedly has a limited influence on practical operational planning, so this phase model should not be taken as fully authoritative; still, the evolution is notable.

Routine crisis management refers to Taiwan's ability to handle ongoing, low-intensity threats and gray-zone activities such as military incursions, economic coercion, and psychological and political pressure. While critical, it is not our area of focus.

Combat-readiness deployment encompasses a variety of war-preparation measures, some of which we have already examined. It is important to note that "resolute defense, multi-domain deterrence" relies on a robust surveillance and early warning network providing advanced notice of any potentially hostile action by Beijing prior to the outbreak of conflict and a resilient C2ISR system. Protection of military assets would also be critical. Fixed sites and the assets tied to them can enhance their survivability through underground facilities or reinforced structures. Key examples include the aforementioned underground facilities at Chiashan Air Force Base and Chihhang Air Base, which between them can reportedly host the majority of the ROC Air Force's combat aircraft, complete with maintenance facilities, fuel, munitions storage, and C2 capabilities. The major air bases themselves have hardened aircraft shelters and revetments as well. There is also an ongoing effort to construct superhardened aircraft shelters to resist missile strikes.[57]

The offshore islands, including the Kinmen, Matsu, and Pescadores groups, have long been on the PLA's likely invasion route and are equipped with underground structures to provide shelter for personnel, vehicles, and stores; they also could potentially serve as offensive bases for strikes against targets on or near the mainland. On Taiwan itself, underground facilities are in place to protect ground forces and to provide storage for the fuel, food, munitions, and communications systems a prolonged defense would require.[58]

Yet no hardening measure is guaranteed to fully succeed, and it is not practical to protect the entire force from air attacks. The *2023 NDR* noted the importance of "enhanced mobility, dispersion, concealment, [and] redundant and decentralized command" as part of a military strategy still emphasizing asymmetric defense.[59] With the exception of those that are silo based, all of the ROC's SAM and ABM systems are road mobile. Most land-based ASMs and land-attack missiles are truck launched and can be concealed in urban or mountainous landscapes. Combat aircraft can be dispersed to civilian airfields and roadway operating sites, while naval vessels can use civilian port facilities and coastal inlets to complicate Beijing's targeting. Decoy aircraft, vehicles, and electronic jamming can further mislead adversaries. Damage control is best illustrated by the airfield-repair teams tasked with restoring operations following PLA strikes.[60]

Should conflict erupt, the most aggressive approach the ROC Armed Forces could take to countering the opening blows—most likely delivered in the form of a PLA JFSC—would be to employ assets such as fighters and SAMs/ABMs to intercept incoming aircraft and missiles. Yet this would inevitably lead to heavy losses, including ROC Air Force aircraft shot down by PLA aircraft and SAMs. Similarly, the early heavy use of SAM/ABM systems would risk their rapid destruction, given the focused PLA efforts on suppression of enemy air defenses (SEAD) as well as the exhaustion of munitions. Preserving these assets for use at the critical moment to defeat an invasion rather than engage in a war of attrition the ROC could not hope to win would be the most productive use of limited resources.

If full hostilities broke out, Taiwan's geography would be exploited by its defenders as a key advantage. Long-range precision-guided weapons, including GLCMs and ALCMs, would likely be launched against PLA bases and embarkation points on the mainland as part of the opening effort to counter the PLA's JILC. These strikes would be supported by antiradar loitering munitions, cyberattacks, and electronic jamming to suppress China's air defenses. Special forces may also have an offensive role in this. But the number of munitions that could be employed would be far smaller than the PLA's opening volley, and Chinese air- and missile-defense systems would limit their effectiveness. Key targets would include supply dumps, helicopter dispersal sites, amphibious and civilian transport ships in port, and C2 centers.

The ROC Armed Forces would launch a full-scale engagement through the joint anti-landing phase and subsequently the littoral and coastal combat phase only after the PLA's crossing of the Taiwan Strait began. Chinese forces would require a window of air and maritime superiority to safeguard their invasion force during passage and while securing the initial lodgment. To deny them this, Taiwanese assets that survived the initial bombardment would engage the approaching enemy with ship-, air- (although few surface vessels and aircraft would likely remain operational), ground-, and submarine-launched ASMs as well as uncrewed air and sea systems while surviving fighters and SAM units engaged incoming aircraft. The PLAN would also face the daunting task of clearing naval minefields under fire.

If the PLA managed to put forces on the main island at significant scale, fighting at the beach and other landing areas would be necessary. Artillery and antitank missiles would target forces as they approached and disembarked. Landmines, beach obstacles, and fortifications would obstruct sea landings, with the invaders engaged by presighted weapons. ROC garrison forces would defend beaches and other locations. Once the main direction of attack was identified, regular forces previously concealed to ride out the initial bombardment would engage and, if possible, contain and overwhelm the Chinese spearhead. There would also be defenses immediately beyond the beaches as part of the defense-in-depth phase.[61]

Should the PLA secure a lodgment and move progressively inland, the battle would shift into protracted operations, forcing the Chinese into a difficult campaign of forest, mountain, and urban warfare in which a combination of terrain and the mass of mobilized ROC reservists may compensate for the military's vulnerability to the PLA's firepower. Should Taiwan remain isolated from the outside world via the PLA's JBC, such an effort would be entirely reliant on the resources the ROC controlled on the island.[62]

Given that defeat is a possibility, an occupation could ensue. For this part of the operation, the People's Armed Police may take the lead, working in cooperation with the PLA and intelligence services to liquidate remaining pockets of resistance, round up dissidents, and establish a surveillance apparatus to maintain control over the surviving population. Citizens would also be put through an aggressive "reeducation" program designed to condition them for life under Beijing's rule.[63]

A WORK IN PROGRESS

The ROC Armed Forces reforms are proceeding at an uneven pace. It is certainly not the case that they exhibit shortfalls comparable to those of the local Philippine forces in the early 1940s prior to the Japanese invasion, but issues including a reliance on a mobilized reserve of unclear capability should raise alarm. Yet the reservists' role in a Taiwan scenario remains critical and thus impossible for the United States or its allies to replace.

CHAPTER 11

PRIMACY

If you want to look at serious forces designed to keep the U.S. out of part of the world, look at what the Russians did in the '70s—dozens of submarines, hundreds of long-range bombers, dozens of satellites, lots of practice. . . . Nobody in Asia is even close to that.

—*Adm. Dennis C. Blair, USPACOM commander, 2001*

By the end of the 1980s, it was clear that even if the Soviet Union was to survive, the security situation that had prevailed in Europe since 1945 was drastically changing. U.S. strategy pivoted from preparing for global war in multiple theaters toward managing regional threats. This was formally outlined in *Defense Strategy for the 1990s: The Regional Defense Strategy,* released in January 1993 at the close of the George H. W. Bush administration. Echoing post–Gulf War assessments, the document warned that regional powers would likely adopt conventional weapons, including integrated air-defense systems, advanced submarines, and stealthy cruise missiles. It also emphasized the need to be able to reconstitute the U.S. Armed Forces to be able to counter any emerging global threat, albeit over a multiyear timeframe—the anticipated global challenge was unlikely to emerge from Eurasia "for at least the balance of this decade."[1]

Nevertheless, force cuts in the aftermath of the Cold War were inevitable. The "Base Force" review resulted in a 25-percent reduction in the joint force structure.[2] While it was not actually formally codified as a benchmark until the Clinton era, the Base Force came to be associated with a requirement to fight two major theater wars (MTWs) at the same time as the benchmark that dominated planning—the most-often-cited example being a simultaneous war with Iraq and countering a North Korean invasion of South Korea.[3] Reports in 1992 indicated that additional specific scenarios had been assessed, including a Russian-Belarus attack on Poland and the Baltic States, the emergence of an unnamed global opponent, and other lesser scenarios.[4]

The Clinton administration formalized the two MTWs approach. Still, despite the model adopted—again predominantly with the DPRK and Iraq as envisaged opponents—further drastic cuts to the armed forces were made via the 1993 Bottom-Up Review.[5]

The first DOD *QDR* was published in 1997. It considered unlikely that the United States would face a "global peer competitor" until at least 2015 and asserted that no regional power or coalition would be able to defeat the United States over the next ten to fifteen years. Beyond that, however, it was possible that Russia or China could become a great regional power or even a global peer competitor that could threaten the United States, with the PRC identified as having "the potential to become a major military power in Asia."[6]

QDR 1997 did not mention A2/AD. Nevertheless, the increasing power-projection challenges were highlighted in the parallel 1997 National Defense Panel report, *Transforming Defense: National Security in the 21st Century*, which sought to envisage the challenges of 2020 and how to address them. This included an emphasis on the "Asymmetric Threat" and opponent's countering the U.S. ability to project power, including through strikes on forward bases, denial of access to said bases, and SLOC interdiction. Interestingly, given the trends that were to emerge in the late 2010s, it made note of the need for forward land forces to be "dispersed," maritime forces to be "distributed," and in-flight refueling and "austere bases" be made available to land-based air elements operating from outside the theater of operations.[7]

As well as regional and minor threats, the 1997 *QDR* also examined a "wild card" scenario of the possibility of a war against a regional great power in 2014 that would make a greater demand on available forces than an MTW, given that the envisaged opponent would be more powerful than Iraq or North Korea, with such a possibility being studied to inform modernization plans.[8] This may have been inspired in part by the Third Taiwan Strait Crisis of 1996. While this would not have been the moment CONPLAN 5077 first emerged—as noted earlier, records of it go back to at least 1979—this is likely the point at which preparation for a Taiwan contingency intensified.

In 1999 Standing Joint Task Force 519 (JTF-519) was formed, giving USPACOM a deployable headquarters capable of making and executing contingency plans, including with regard to the defense of Taiwan.[9] In 2006 JTF-519 was mobilized to exercise Valiant Shield, which saw the largest deployment of military power to the Pacific since the Vietnam War and included three carrier groups, USAF and USMC assets based in both the western Pacific and the continental United States, and U.S. Coast Guard participation.[10] JTF-519 was disbanded in 2013.[11]

U.S. concerns about the PRC's nuclear capabilities were evident in a January 1992 report highlighting the continued growth in China's nuclear forces and the risk that Beijing might pivot to a more aggressive stance over Taiwan. Further nuclear scenarios analysis involving strike options against China was undertaken by U.S. Strategic Command (USSTRATCOM) and completed in February 1994. In November 1997 new presidential guidance ordered a broadening of nuclear targeting in China, anticipating a future threat from a stronger PRC rather than addressing its then current capabilities. China returned to the SIOP in the SIOP-99 plan of October 1998. This was redesignated OPLAN 8044 in March 2003 and later changed to OPLAN 8010.[12]

MARITIME STRATEGY AND BEYOND

With the Soviet threat fading, no nation could challenge U.S. sea control. As after World War II, the U.S. Navy was forced to pivot to an emphasis on the littoral and projecting power ashore.[13] The need to replace the 1980s Maritime Strategy was publicly expressed in 1991 in a U.S. Naval Institute *Proceedings* article "The Way Ahead," coauthored by the then Secretary of the Navy, CNO, and USMC commandant. It articulated for a greater focus on areas including, crisis response, forward presence, peacekeeping, and fighting expeditionary regional wars, with the U.S. Navy and USMC centering on the littoral and supporting operations ashore to retain its relevance while still sustaining the Department of the Navy's arm of the nuclear deterrent. The article also noted that while the threat of a rival superpower was evaporating, the Maritime Strategy would remain "on the shelf" ready for a potential resurgent Soviet or other global threat. It was noted that even if this did not happen, advanced technology was proliferating to developing states.[14]

This approach was further evolved (although with an acceptance that the USSR had now gone for good) and formalized in September 1992's *From the Sea: Preparing the Naval Service for the 21st Century* white paper and 1994's *Forward . . . from the Sea.*[15] Both placed an emphasis on carrier groups delivering air power ashore—essentially a return to Nimitz's 1947 argument regarding the U.S. Navy's role early in the Cold War—and reduced emphasis on open-ocean capabilities such as ASW, long-range strikes, and fleet air defense. In his November 1997 *Proceedings* article "Anytime, Anywhere: A Navy for the 21st Century," then-CNO Adm. Jay Johnson followed a similar script but leaned back toward the importance of sea control and noted the increasing threat opponents could pose to U.S. power projection as well as area-denial threats to forward-deployed forces.[16]

The shift in strategy came amid significant cuts. Between 1989 and 1999, carrier numbers were reduced from fifteen to twelve, SSNs from ninety-six to fifty-nine, cruisers from forty to twenty-seven, destroyers from sixty-eight to fifty-two, and frigates from one hundred to thirty-seven.[17] Among the Navy's air fleet, the A-6 Intruder bomber was retired without a direct replacement after the A-12 Avenger II stealth bomber was canceled, as was the KA-6D tanker, with its tasks passed on to nondedicated aircraft. The S-3 Viking, which provided carrier groups with long-range ASW capabilities, was relegated to supporting tasks, leaving a dependence on short-range helicopters for carrier-based submarine hunting. The F-14 was replaced by the F/A-18E/F multirole aircraft rather than a dedicated replacement like the USAF F-22A (the Naval Advanced Tactical Fighter program was canceled in 1991), reflecting both the budgetary environment and the perceived threat at sea. But the success of the Tomahawk missile in the Gulf War helped it become ubiquitous among U.S. Navy cruisers, destroyers, and attack submarines. The threat of regional powers acquiring theater ballistic missiles also spurred developing the ballistic-missile-defense (BMD) capability of the Aegis system.

"Sea Power 21," published in 2002 in the aftermath of the 9/11 attacks, built off its predecessors. The article, however, also emphasized more conventional challenges, including sea control. Writing in *Proceedings* in October 2002, then-CNO Adm. Vernon E. Clark noted, "Future enemies will attempt to deny U.S.

access to critical areas of the world, threaten vital friends and interests overseas, and even try to conduct further attacks against the American homeland."[18] The July 2003 fleet response plan saw a requirement for the U.S. Navy to be able to "surge" six of the then twelve carriers within 30 days, with a further pair available within ninety days, including in support of the two-war model.[19]

A Cooperative Strategy for 21st Century Sea Power of 2007 was the decade's last major U.S. maritime policy publication and the first formal maritime strategy in twenty years. The spectrum of threats outlined included a renewed reference to a major power war and a "multi-polar world." No state adversaries were directly named.[20]

The first decade of the twenty-first century saw single-service proposals to counter anti-access threats.[21] The U.S. Navy and USMC advanced the "assured access" concept, later including this through the "sea basing," "sea shield," and "sea strike" approach as part of the "Sea Power 21" transformation plan.[22] The USAF proposed its "global strike task force" initiative to deploy force packages capable of dismantling such capabilities as their "kick-down-the-door force" via information systems, space-based capabilities, stealth, and long-range precision strikes.[23] The Army proposed the "objective force" concept as a lighter and more rapidly deployable model.[24]

Nevertheless, by 2007, fleet numbers had fallen further, with only eleven carriers, twenty-two cruisers, fifty-two destroyers, and fifty-three SSNs on strength. While thirty frigates also remained, these were all to be retired without direct replacements by 2015.[25]

The George W. Bush administration rapidly moved to publish an updated *QDR* in 2001. The vast majority was complete before the September 11 attacks.[26] It noted: "Moving to a capabilities-based force also requires the United States to focus on emerging opportunities that certain capabilities, including advanced remote sensing, long-range precision strike, transformed maneuver and expeditionary forces and systems, to overcome anti-access and area denial threats, can confer on the U.S. military over time."[27]

With regard to Asia, the risk that "a military competitor with a formidable resource base will emerge in the region" was also raised. The *QDR* also placed an emphasis on homeland defense, although the original focus of this was on countering ballistic missiles. The two-war model was modified slightly in terms of what it demanded, with the intention of defeating aggression in major overlapping conflicts but only accomplishing a decisive victory in one. There was also a recognized need to study the problem of "projecting and sustaining U.S. forces in distant anti-access environments."[28]

Despite the later focus on Afghanistan and Iraq, the Bush administration undertook the early phase of the reorientation to the Asia-Pacific. The classified *Defense Strategy Review* (*DSR*) in the opening months of the administration identified trends that might weaken the favorable conditions the United States then enjoyed, including A2/AD technology. China was an important concern, as was the underlying theme of a "long-term shift in focus" to Asia.[29]

Secretary of Defense Rumsfeld sent a memo early on the morning of September 11, 2001, requesting an unclassified version of the *DSR*. The idea fell by the wayside for obvious reasons, although aspects of the review, including the "dissuasion" and A2/AD elements, made it into the 2001 *QDR*.[30]

The early pivot to Asia was implemented with little fanfare and overshadowed by the war on terror. The 2004 *Global Posture Review* (*GPR*) proposed the development of the main USAF base on Guam to support the deployment of a USAF GSTF, including tactical combat, bomber, surveillance, and support aircraft. The Navy rebalanced its submarine fleet, stationing 60 percent of SSNs in the Pacific and upgrading Guam Naval Station to accommodate more vessels. Later, in 2007, officials decided to move an additional carrier to the Pacific Fleet. The *GPR* also proposed an enhanced military presence in Alaska and Hawaii.[31]

The second *QDR* of the Bush administration, published in 2006, reflected the wider shift in security priorities since the 9/11 attacks. Its first section, "Fighting the Long War," underlined the emphasis on countering unconventional threats. China was named as the state most likely to be able to compete with the U.S. Armed Forces, including through anti-access technology.[32]

Meanwhile, in May 2003 the Center for Strategic and Budgetary Assessments (CSBA) published *Meeting the Anti-Access and Area-Denial Challenge*. While the report restated many established points, one of its central laments was a lack of a joint strategy to overcome A2/AD threats, with each service "pursuing its own solution, for its own institutional purposes, within the boundaries of its traditional warfighting roles and domain."[33] Addressing this was to become a major area of focus.

THE INTERMISSION

The United States followed up its accurate assessment of the limitations of the Gulf War experience by correctly identifying emerging challenges, including A2/AD. Assessments were also accurate in predicting that it would likely not face a near-peer competitor until the 2010s. Yet significant policy decisions—not least on platform retention and procurement—failed to match this insight. Due to the events of September 11, 2001, we will never know if an early course correction could have been possible.

CHAPTER 12

GREAT POWER COMPETITION

You judge yourselves against the pitiful adversaries
you've encountered so far—the Romulans, the Klingons.
They're nothing compared to what's waiting.
—*Q*, Star Trek: The Next Generation

The Obama administration's 2010 *QDR* prioritized "Prevail in Today's Wars" while focusing on conflict prevention and deterrence, preparation for a full range of future contingencies, and force preservation and enhancement.[1] The review was reportedly initially based on eleven terms-of-reference scenarios, including continued operations in Iraq and Afghanistan, a potential major war with China over Taiwan, contingencies envisaging the collapse of North Korea, Russian intimidation of the Baltic States, and Pakistan's loss of control of its nuclear weapons—this set was subsequently broadened and modified.[2] The ability to deter and counter anti-access systems was identified as needing enhancement, with the paper noting, "Prudence demands that the Department prepare for possible future adversaries likely to possess and employ some degree of anti-access capability."[3] China was identified as developing an advanced military capability, including cruise and ballistic missiles, advanced submarines, and new air-defense systems, but remaining opaque about its intentions.[4]

In the fall of 2011, the United States commenced the next phase of the "Pacific Pivot." In 2012, Washington announced that 60 percent of the U.S. Navy would be deployed to the Pacific. The January 2012 defense strategic guidance (DSG), *Sustaining U.S. Global Leadership*, underlined the shift toward the Pacific region and investment in countering A2/AD capabilities.[5]

In parallel to these developments, tensions in the region between the United States and China were underlined by two incidents. In March 2009 the U.S. ocean surveillance ship USNS *Impeccable* was aggressively intercepted by Chinese vessels and aircraft in the South China Sea. In the second incident, in December 2013, the cruiser USS *Cowpen* narrowly avoided a collision PLAN units were forcing it into.

AIR-SEA BATTLE

The 2010 *QDR* stated, "The Air Force and Navy together are developing a new joint air-sea battle concept for defeating adversaries across the range of military operations, including adversaries equipped with sophisticated anti-access and area denial capabilities."[6] But this initiative was far from out of the blue: China's focus on acquiring A2/AD capabilities and the need to "secure U.S. strategic access and retain freedom of action" had featured prominently in the June 2008 NDS, which also noted, "It is likely that China will continue to expand its conventional military capabilities, emphasizing anti-access and area denial assets."[7]

The October 2008 PACAF war game Pacific Vision, financially supported by the Pentagon's Office of Net Assessment (ONA), evaluated the challenges that would be faced in a war in the Asia-Pacific, with an unnamed "Red Team" standing in for China as the lead threat. One of the first public references to the exercise can be found in the January 2009 edition of *Air Force Magazine,* which described the exercise as having "the intent of deterring any Chinese, North Korean, or Russian military aggression in Asia and the Pacific."[8] Force dispersion, force protection, base hardening, and damage repair were all identified as areas needing improvement.[9] In September 2009 the U.S. Navy and USAF leadership authorized the development of the Air-Sea Battle (ASB) concept; the ASB office opened in August 2011.[10]

Independent institutes, unconstrained by the politics of the time that demanded DOD public plans not antagonize the PRC, could develop a CONOPS for real-world use. The 2010 CSBA study *Why AirSea Battle?* outlined the threat the approach was intended to address. It identified the anti-access challenges from China and Iran, noting that the post-1945 era that had seen the United States utilize forward sanctuary bases and rapid reinforcement was under threat from the development by opponents of systems capable of interdicting U.S. power projection. It also gave an overview of China's A2/AD capabilities, including an ability to strike forward U.S. bases and potentially mobile targets such as ships out to the second island chain.[11]

The "why" was later developed into a "how" in the CSBA's May 2010 report *AirSea Battle: A Point of Operational Concept*.[12] Distinct from the public overview of the DOD's ASB, which avoided identifying opponents, the CSBA study focused on China, outlining the need for an approach to overcome PLA A2/AD capabilities. The modeled conflict assumed that China would instigate hostilities; that nuclear weapons would not be used; that there would be limited advance warning; that Japan and Australia would be "active U.S. allies"; that PRC and U.S. territory would be subjected to attack, as would assets in space; and that it would be the United States that would benefit from a prolonged conflict.[13]

CSBA's *AirSea Battle* proposed a two-stage campaign. Stage one and its lines of operations would seek to adequately suppress the PLA's A2/AD capabilities. The initial step in this process would be to survive the opening assault via establishing adequate early warning systems and using passive (such as the construction of reinforced concrete shelters and the use of deception, dispersal, and rapid repair) and active (such as air and missile defense) measures to limit damage to regional forces. Local forces would be placed in advantageous postures for survival and subsequent operations. These would be aided by the deployment of reinforcements to the western Pacific, with the defense of Japan as the initial priority. Early offensive actions would target the PLA's kill chain with a "blinding campaign" to disrupt the ISR element on which most of its A2/AD capabilities depend, including targets such as OTH radars, long-range ISR platforms, seabed sensors, and space and cyber assets, as well as denying them the use of the electromagnetic spectrum. Mirroring this effort would be a campaign to sustain U.S. ISR systems. Operations against PLA offensive platforms such as missile-carrying ships, submarines, and land-based surface-to-surface missile systems, including TELs, would run in parallel. A SEAD campaign would support strikes against mainland coastal targets to facilitate operations by penetrating platforms and standoff munitions. These efforts would collectively seek to prevent Beijing from securing an early victory and allow the United States to "seize the initiative" through the degrading of PLAN and PLAAF assets and the retention of air superiority over Japan.[14]

Stage two would focus on efforts to support U.S. national goals "by creating options to resolve a prolonged conventional conflict on favorable terms."

This would include a "distant blockade" to disrupt the flow of trade to and from the PRC, including its energy supplies. Sustaining a prolonged campaign would also require securing lines of communication and accelerating munitions production. Stage one efforts would continue in support.[15]

The CSBA report also highlighted the importance of joint operations. Notably, this included the U.S. Navy and USAF providing mutual support, including through the blinding of PLA space-based sensors to prevent the targeting of surface ships and the use of Aegis-equipped warships to protect forward air bases, Navy fighter suppression of PLAAF airborne assets to facilitate USAF tanker and wider support-aircraft operations, USAF strikes against sensors and weapon launch sites on the mainland that could target naval vessels, and USAF support of minelaying and distant blockade operations.[16]

The official reasoning behind ASB emerged slowly. The joint operational-access concept (JOAC)—a wider effort directed by the 2012 DSG to ensure theater access that included ASB under its umbrella—was published in January 2012. This document carefully noted that operational access was not an end in itself but provided the ability to achieve broader strategic goals.[17]

In May 2013 the ASB Office published *Air-Sea Battle: Service Collaboration to Address Anti-Access & Area Denial Challenges*. It noted, "While ASB is not a strategy, it is an important component of DoD's strategic mission to project power and sustain operations in the global commons during peacetime or crisis." Although the publication did highlight that the model was also applicable on the "low end of the conflict spectrum," a nod to the idea that it was not exclusively for high-intensity warfare, it described ASB as based on the assumption of an opponent commencing activities with little warning, the prewar presence of forward friendly forces in the A2/AD zone, direct attacks on U.S. and allied territory, and a contest across domains—essentially the same assumptions as the CSBA model. The core thrust was given a topline definition of "disrupt, destroy, defeat"—D3—with the lines of effort being to disrupt C4ISR networks to gain the decision advantage, destroy enemy capabilities to regain freedom of action, and defeat enemy-employed weapons to sustain offensive operations.[18]

Those outside the DOD voiced alternatives to ASB. The least aggressive was the distant blockade used in isolation.[19] This model would see the interdiction of routes at chokepoints like the Strait of Malacca targeting China's economic lifelines—while staying beyond the range of most PLA A2/AD systems—including imported energy and raw materials and exported manufactured goods. Furthermore, it avoided strikes on the Chinese mainland and exploited Beijing's limited ability to defend distant sea lanes. But a distant blockade could lead to a protracted conflict that the authoritarian PRC system is better placed to handle than those in the West and an implicit U.S. withdrawal from the western Pacific that left allies exposed. It is also unlikely that such an operation would be airtight enough to produce critical disruption. This is to say nothing of the fact that most of the PRC capabilities required to capture Taiwan would be left alone.[20]

"Offshore control"—also referred to as the "war at sea" or "maritime denial" option—is a more aggressive variant of the blockade model.[21] In addition to interdicting commercial shipping at a distance from the PRC, it would also seek to deny China the use of all of the maritime space, including within the first island chain, through deterrence and direct force. This would, in theory, deny Beijing any objective that required the use of sea power (including a landing on Taiwan). U.S. and allied A2/AD capabilities would exploit favorable geography to contribute to both the sea-denial effort and territorial defense, avoiding strikes on the Chinese mainland. Ideally, facing major economic damage and with no hope of accomplishing its military objectives, Beijing would see little point in continuing the war. But the question of China's ability to weather a protracted conflict remains.

A final model is "deterrence by denial."[22] This would seek to focus on preventing China from obtaining its objectives—in this case, obtaining a *fait accompli* with regard to Taiwan—chiefly through the use of an allied A2/AD approach. It would capitalize on the inherent difficulty of seizing and retaining (including through the supply of the invasion force) island territory. This would also allow for the avoidance of significant strikes on the mainland as well as a complex distant blockade. Regional allies would also be able to contribute a greater proportion of the effort than would be the case were the mission set broader. A more aggressive version of this is the "archipelagic defense" operational concept—the first island chain being the archipelago in question—an approach put forward by Andrew Krepinevich in February 2015 and elaborated on in an August 2017 study, later updated in September 2023 by the same author.[23] This incorporates not only denial but also a blockade element and if necessary limited strikes against the Chinese mainland.

In January 2015 it was announced that the ASB concept was to be evolved based on lessons learned to become the joint concept for access and maneuver in the global commons (JAM-GC), which was formally signed off in October 2016, also in support of JOAC.[24] This model involved the entire joint force. An overview published in early 2017 outlined that the joint force would have to be distributable in its positioning, resilient to recover from early setbacks, tailorable to accomplish the assigned mission, of sufficient scale, and have the "staying power" required, including a resilient logistics system and an ability to weather attrition. The idea of the direct and systematic dismantling of the opponent's A2/AD capabilities was replaced by defeating "an adversary's plan and intent," with "operations in contested environments that does not rely on overcoming a potential adversary's A2/AD military capabilities" being the goal.[25]

THE THIRD OFFSET

The 2014 *QDR* billed itself as a shift from the post-9/11 wars to the future, including by aligning with the Pacific rebalance outlined in the 2012 DSG. While China was not directly named, it again raised concerns about the reasons behind the PRC's military buildup, including A2/AD capabilities (with a similar approach taken to Russia). The nation-states directly identified as the leading threats were the established opponents North Korea and Iran.[26]

The scenarios that validated the 2014 *QDR* were not presented, but analysis suggested that a stepped version of the two-war concept was at the core, with the intention to be able to defeat one adversary outright in a "large-scale multi-phase campaign" and either prevent another adversary's victory "or impose an unacceptable cost" on them.[27]

A need to counter the emerging threat at speed and the budget constraints after the 2008 financial crisis spurred the "Third Offset," an initiative led by Deputy Secretary of Defense Robert O. Work. This focused on technology, process change, and facilitating a general policy shift toward adapting to great power competition—including acquiring counter-A2/AD capabilities. It was also an exercise in exploiting the "myth" of the first two offsets, much as ASB had sought to do with AirLand Battle.[28]

A notable callback to AirLand Battle was the DARPA-led "Assault Breaker II" project. Like its predecessor, it sought to develop new warfighting constructs built around existing and in-development weapon, sensor, and network technology—this time to prevent a rapid victory by China or Russia by engaging assets in an A2/AD environment via joint action.[29] Budget documents from 2024 indicate that the program is now complete, with U.S. military leadership indicating that the "Hellscape" operational concept—it is examined later in the chapter—was one of the outputs.[30]

The Third Offset only survived a short time past the Obama administration. In large part this was because the central concept of the challenges of great power competition was on its way to being fully adopted. The 2016 NSS and NMS remained restrained on the matter, albeit with the latter highlighting the need to "pay greater attention to challenges posed by state actors," further stating that "the probability of U.S. involvement in interstate war with a major power is assessed to be low but growing."[31] Yet this competition was clearly reflected in 2016's FY2017 defense budget request. The proposal stated that the DOD had prioritized "ongoing or possible future aggression from China, Russia, Iran, and North Korea" in addition to continuing counterterrorism efforts.[32]

THE CURRENT ERA

The 2017 NSS placed the Indo-Pacific first in order of priority in the listed regional strategies, and this designation was reinforced by renaming USPACOM as USINDOPACOM in May 2018. The security strategy stated that the United States faced "three main sets of challengers—the revisionist powers of China and Russia, the rogue states of Iran and North Korea, and transnational threat organizations, particularly jihadist terrorist groups," and it also noted the anti-access challenge from Beijing.[33]

More specific initiatives were provided in the summary of the 2018 NDS. Strategic competition with states, as opposed to terrorism, was identified as the leading challenge. Force-planning aims were noted as the joint force "defeating aggression by a major power; deterring opportunistic aggression elsewhere; and disrupting imminent terrorist and WMD threats," an indication of a shift to fighting only one major war with a great power as opposed to two wars with regional powers simultaneously. The prioritization of efforts toward resilience in space, cyberspace, logistics, and command, control, communications, computers, and intelligence networks speaks to the threat of attack from a highly capable opponent. This is underscored by recommendations for "transitioning from large, centralized, unhardened infrastructure to smaller, dispersed, resilient, adaptive basing that include active and passive defenses" and launching strikes against "mobile power projection platforms" in the face of advanced air- and missile-defense systems.[34]

The most notable feature of the 2018 NDS was its perceived departure from the two-war model.[35] But also outlined is the provision of two new operational approaches. The first is dynamic force employment (DFE), designed to break free of traditional force-deployment models and instead institute more flexibility. The second, the global operating model (GOM), outlines future force posture as made up of four "layers":

- *Contact*: the force element charged with favorably shaping the theater in times below the threshold of war, including in the gray zone
- *Blunt*: the in-theater and elsewhere-based force element that would seek to "delay, degrade, or deny adversary aggression"[36]
- *Surge*: additional units brought in from outside theater to manage escalation and secure victory
- *Homeland*: elements deterring and defeating attacks on the homeland in support of forward operations[37]

GOM has remained absent from recent documents amid claims that it and similar such terms are "buzzwords" rather than practical paths to problem solving.[38] Nevertheless, while the GOM was not explicitly mentioned in the 2022 NSS, NDS summary, or NMS summary, it was noted in the fiscal year 2024 budget request, indicating that it remains active.[39]

At the end of the first Trump administration, the 2018 strategic framework for the Indo-Pacific was declassified—a step originally not due until 2043. While a broad strategy, it presented several assumptions of relevance to a Taiwan scenario, including, "China will take increasingly assertive steps to compel unification with Taiwan." One objective to counter this was to "enable Taiwan to develop an effective asymmetric defense strategy and capabilities that will help ensure its security, freedom from coercion, resilience, and ability to engage China on its own terms." The wider U.S. approach was presented as the following:

- *Objective*: Deter China from using military force against the United States and U.S. allies and partners, and develop the capabilities and concepts to defeat Chinese action across the spectrum of conflict.

- *Actions*: Enhance combat-credible U.S. military presence and posture in the Indo-Pacific region to uphold U.S. interests and security commitments.
- Devise and implement a defensive strategy capable of, but not limited to: (1) *denying* China sustained air and sea dominance inside the "first island chain" in a conflict; (2) *defending* the first-island-chain nations, including Taiwan; and (3) *dominating* all domains outside the first island chain. [*additional text redacted*][40]

The Biden administration's 2022 NSS stuck to the same themes while further focusing on China. It explicitly referenced the Taiwan issue, noting the U.S. interest in maintaining peace and stability across the strait. The NSS framed China as the "pacing challenge."[41]

These themes were also carried over to the 2022 NDS. The document noted opponents' A2/AD (a term absent in the 2018 NDS) as a threat to the "American Way of War" and the ability to embark on rapid interventions. "Integrated deterrence" was to be executed in the form of deterrence by denial via preventing an opponent obtaining its goals early in a conflict, including through developing "concepts and capabilities that improve our ability to reliably hold at risk those military forces and assets that are essential to adversary operational success"; deterrence by resilience via continuing operations despite disruption; and deterrence by direct and collective cost imposition, which could include everything from bombardment to economic sanctions. There was also a pointed reference to supporting Taiwan's asymmetric defense capabilities. Campaigning was another major theme, with the aim to shape the strategic environment in conditions short of war.[42]

The summary of the 2022 NMS noted the joint force strategic objectives as

- Defend the U.S. Homeland against all-domain threats, prioritizing the PRC
- Deter strategic attacks and other aggression against the United States, allies, and partners
- Ensure the Joint Force possesses the combat-credible capabilities necessary to prevail in conflict against the PRC in the Indo-Pacific, then Russia in Europe
- Focus technical and non-technical modernization into a resilient Joint Force and maintain the ability to respond to crises[43]

The most recent development was the *Joint Warfighting Concept 3.0* capstone document, released in August 2023 as *Joint Warfighting* (Joint Publication 1, volume 1). In the words of former CJCS Gen. Mark Milley, the paper was designed to present a "threat-informed, operational concept that provides an overarching approach to how the Joint Force should fight in a future conflict."[44] While a broad document, it specifically addresses the anti-access challenge, noting that an enemy's capabilities can both hinder the ability of the joint force to take offensive action and interdict forces attempting to enter the areas of operations.[45] In an article accompanying the document's release, General Milley highlighted the central tenets as

- Integrated, Combined Joint Force: comprehensive cross-service operations in all domains
- Expanded Maneuver: innovative use of the domains across space and time
- Pulsed Operations: joint operations to create or exploit an advantage over an opponent
- Integrated Command, Agile Control: creation and maintenance of unified cross-domain C2 to facilitate awareness and decision making
- Global Fires: delivery of lethal and nonlethal fires across the globe in a manner spanning services, geography, and domains
- Information Advantage: utilizing advanced information collection and processing technology to facilitate rapid decision making and actions
- Resilient Logistics: logistics chain that is survivable in a high-threat environment[46]

At the time of writing, the publication of the NSS, NDS, and NMS of the second Trump administration is still awaited. But early guidance given to the DOD states that deterring China from taking Taiwan is to be the lead planning contingency aside from homeland defense.[47]

U.S. FORCE POSTURE

Guam is the central hub of U.S. military activity in its western Pacific territories. Andersen Air Force Base handles most aviation, while Naval Base Guam hosts an SSN squadron and a pair of submarine-repair ships and is large enough to accommodate an aircraft carrier. Camp Blaz hosts around five thousand Marines. Guam's importance has—unlike in the buildup to

A Standard Missile-3 Block IIA is launched from Andersen Air Force Base, Guam—a test of a component of the multilayered Guam Defense System. *Missile Defense Agency, photo by Nancy Jones-Bonbrest, December 10, 2024, DVIDS*

World War II—led to extensive investment in its defense, with the Enhanced Integrated Air and Missile Defense System incorporating systems including Aegis Guam System, THAAD, Patriot and Enduring Shield.[48]

The nearby Northern Mariana Islands—also U.S. territory—are currently seeing additional investment, with North Field on Tinian being reactivated and the civilian Tinian International Airport being expanded to host military deployments, including with additional aircraft parking and fuel storage.[49] Wake Island has also seen its facilities improved.[50]

In addition to its own territory, the United States is responsible for the defense of the states of the Republic of the Marshall Islands, Federated States of Micronesia, and Republic of Palau under the Compact of Free Association (COFA), which was recently renewed until 2043.[51] It also has the right to use the territory of these states for military purposes. For example, the United States has deployed an OTH radar on Palau to provide long-range situational awareness.[52] Military aircraft and Patriot missiles have also been deployed on exercise to Palau's main international airport and the renovated Angaur Airstrip.[53] And a missile-defense test site operates on Kwajalein Atoll in the

Republic of Marshall Islands. All three states would likely provide basing for military assets in the event of a conflict with China.

Japan hosts the largest U.S. military presence in the region. Fleet Activities Yokosuka hosts the headquarters of the U.S. Navy Seventh Fleet, an aircraft carrier, a destroyer squadron, and a command ship. Naval Air Facility Atsugi is home to the helicopter element of the carrier air wing, while the fixed-wing component is based at Marine Corps Air Station Iwakuni. Additionally, Iwakuni houses elements of the 1st Marine Air Wing including a pair of F-35B Lightning II squadrons. U.S. Fleet Activities Sasebo hosts amphibious and MCM vessels. USAF hub Misawa Air Base is set to host two F-35A squadrons by 2029.[54] Kadena Air Base on Okinawa is home to a pair of F-15EX Eagle II squadrons, an E-3G Sentry squadron, and a KC-135 Stratotanker squadron as well as a significant presence of intelligence and special forces, with RC-135 Rivet Joint and CV-22B Ospreys flying in support from Yokota Air Base. The U.S. Army provides Patriot batteries for air and missile defense.

U.S. forces are also present in South Korea. For the purposes of this analysis, we are assuming the ROK will stay out of the conflict due to its preference and need to contain North Korea should it attempt to take advantage of the situation with ROK-based U.S. forces following their lead.

Following a contentious period of relations, the United States has reinvigorated its relationship with the Philippines. While no U.S. forces are based there permanently, nine sites are now accessible for periodic deployments under the Enhanced Defense Cooperation Agreement (EDCA).

Around 2,500 Marines are based at the Robertson Barracks as part of Marine Rotational Force Darwin, Australia. Royal Australian Air Force (RAAF) Tindal has been upgraded using U.S. funds to be able to handle up to six heavy bombers, and RAAF Darwin has also received a new U.S.-funded fuel system.[55] As part of the Australia–United Kingdom–United States (AUKUS) agreement, up to four *Virginia*-class submarines will be forward deployed to HMAS Stirling near Perth.[56]

While located in the Indian Ocean rather than the Pacific, Diego Garcia could provide secure air and naval facilities to enforce sea control in the region. As such, it would be important in any enforcement of a blockade on China, particularly with regards to energy imports from the Middle East.

The Pacific Deterrence Initiative was created under the 2021 NDAA and has sought to provide a dedicated prioritization mechanism to support defense operations in the Indo-Pacific. Funding has been assigned to projects such as equipment prepositioning, wider infrastructure improvements and exercises, and generally supporting allies and partners.[57]

OPERATIONAL CONCEPTS

In 2015 the sea services published an updated version of its previous strategy, *Forward, Engaged Ready: A Cooperative Strategy for 21st Century Sea Power,* shifting the focus to warfighting, including the A2/AD challenges, and cross-domain synergy. It replaced the 2007 edition's "forward presence" with "all domain access" as one of the core sea-services functions alongside deterrence, power projection, sea control, and maritime security.[58]

The latest maritime strategy document was December 2020's *Advantage at Sea: Prevailing with Integrated All-Domain Naval Power,* which zeroed in on China and Russia, prioritizing "competition with the PRC over other challengers" and noting that threats below that sub–great power are to be dealt with by forces designed for the priority mission.[59] While emphasizing day-to-day competition, the mission in conflict was aggressively outlined. Descriptions of using sea denial in a way that "impedes a *fait accompli*" and block the intentions of opponents who need to cross the open sea clearly referred to a Taiwan scenario. The intention to use naval air power in conjunction with USAF assets to deliver "mass overwhelming anti-surface and land-attack fires" was more broadly applicable but reflected both ASB and related concepts directed at China.[60]

Advantage at Sea also highlighted key operating concepts, led by distributed maritime operations (DMO). DMO aims to reduce vulnerability, broaden offensive options including through revitalizing the fleet's ASuW capabilities, and complicate enemy targeting by disaggregating units while keeping them networked to unify effort in massing firepower.[61] Project Overmatch, the U.S. Navy component of the joint all-domain command and control (JADC2) initiative, supports this networking of the joint force.[62]

DMO is supported by littoral operations in a contested environment (LOCE)—a U.S. Navy/USMC model to meld operations in coastal regions—and the USMC expeditionary advanced-base operations (EABO). The latter seeks to avoid reliance on fixed infrastructure and specialist shipping and instead depend on field reconnaissance, defense, and strike assets

An F-35B Lighting II of VMX-1 undergoes ordinance loading during an Obsidian Iceberg EABO exercise. *U.S. Marine Corps photo by Cpl. Jade K. Venegas, July 31, 2023, DVIDS*

with a limited detection signature at austere locations that can be frequently changed. One of the most high-profile elements of EABO is the provision of forward-base facilities for F-35B aircraft—reminiscent of Harrier operations during the Falklands War.[63]

As part of *Force Design 2030,* the USMC has undergone a dramatic shift away from tanks and towed artillery toward missile systems for land attack, antiship strikes, and air defense, along with ISR, electronic warfare, and long-range, long-endurance UAVs.[64] These are designed to facilitate the LOCE and EABO, creating a force designed to operate in littoral zones.

The EABO concept supports the Stand-In Force of the USMC. These units will operate in the forward area and generate both situational awareness and options to defeat an opponent's counterintervention strategy by supporting joint operations alongside allies and partners, including at sea. While intended to "operate across the competition continuum" supporting peacetime campaigning and countering subthreshold threats, including as part of the GOM "contact layer," among other roles, in wartime they are designed to support the "blunt layer" of the GOM, disrupting enemy operations while remaining survivable and with minimal logistics requirements. Critical goals include countering an opponent's reconnaissance assets and performing sea-denial operations, particularly at maritime chokepoints.[65]

To support this, three Marine regiments in the Pacific will have been transformed into Marine littoral regiments by 2029—one each in Hawaii, Okinawa, and Guam. Each includes a littoral combat team for infantry and antiship operations, a littoral antiair battalion for air defense and support at EABO sites, and a littoral logistics battalion.[66]

The Navy's "Hellscape" concept envisages thousands of UAVs (including loitering munitions), uncrewed undersea vessels (UUVs), and USVs being deployed to target PLA assets such as landing craft in or near the Taiwan Strait to buy time for the main force to deploy. Details remain sparse, but much of this will come via the Replicator program to rapidly purchase large numbers of uncrewed systems.[67] The September 2024 CNO Navigation Plan gives 2027 as the deadline for these systems to be fielded, as that is the year "the Chairman of the People's Republic of China (PRC) has told his forces to be ready for war."[68]

While not quite a return to the Fleet Problems exercises of the War Plan Orange era, in 2021 the U.S. Navy and USMC began testing warfighting concepts worldwide under the auspice of the Large Scale Exercise. Repeated in 2023, this sees both actual and simulated units test the practicalities of fighting a major war at a global scale.[69]

The USAF's Future Operating Concept (AFFOC) was published in March 2023. It is built around five core functions: air superiority, global strike, global mobility, ISR, and integrated C2. At its heart are what it defines as the "six fights" to generate pulsed airpower—"concentrating of airpower in time and space to create windows of opportunity for the rest of the force." These are the "fight to compete with and deter," the "fight to get into the theater," the "fight to get airborne," the "fight for air superiority," the "fight to deny adversary objectives," and the "fight to sustain."[70]

The AFFOC is most readily embodied in the agile combat employment (ACE) operating model. Functionally, it is designed to reduce the vulnerability of aircraft and their supporting elements to being destroyed on the ground by missile or air attacks. In wartime it manifests as dispersing force elements away from large "enduring locations" and to several smaller "contingency locations" with minimal support in an unpredictable and difficult-to-track manner. While established bases remain a critical part of the overall basing mix as the central hub of "base clusters," they are no longer the exclusive ideal.[71]

Central to the contemporary U.S. Army vision of operations in the Pacific and beyond is the concept of multidomain operations (MDO). The Army plans to use positions and capabilities on land to support operations at sea and in the air. Central to this will be the multidomain task force (MDTF), identified as "theater-level maneuver elements designed to synchronize precision effects and precision fires in all domains against adversary anti-access/area denial (A2/AD) networks in all domains, enabling joint forces to execute their operational plan (OPLAN)-directed roles." Three are to be focused on the Indo-Pacific region.[72]

The JADC2 concept supports all this. It is designed to synchronize the services C2 systems, share data across domains and with partners to provide battlefield awareness, and enhance decision making. Critical missions will include the ability of sensors from one service to provide targeting data to the weapon systems of another. Predictive analysis, AI, and machine learning will support the processing of data.[73]

ENABLERS

U.S. carrier groups and other maritime assets will be targeted by PLA submarine-launched torpedoes and cruise missiles, ALCMs, and ASBMs. Naval efforts to counter the aerospace threats center on the Aegis Combat System which incorporates SM-2, SM-3 and SM-3 missiles. The fielding of the AN/SPY-6(v)1 radar on Flight III *Arleigh Burke*–class destroyers and the backfitting of smaller variants of the radar on earlier destroyers and other ships will drastically increase threat detection and engagement capabilities. These are augmented by air- and space-based sensors able to detect missile launches and track their flight paths. The deployment of the SEWIP Block III electronic-warfare system will enhance that layer of defense against air and missile attacks.[74]

Further development of cooperative engagement capability (CEC) in the form of the Naval Integrated Fire Control–Counter Air has facilitated the creation of a distributed kill chain required to persist in an A2/AD environment.[75] For example, it is now possible for platforms such as the E-2D Advanced Hawkeye or F-35C to provide targeting information for an SM-6 missile launched from an Aegis ship even when the target is not within view of the launching vessel.

By late in the 2020s, it is anticipated that one squadron of F-35C aircraft will serve alongside three squadrons of F/A-18E/F Super Hornets in most carrier air groups, together with one of EA-18 Growlers, one of E-2D (now with in-flight refueling capability), and one each of MH-60R and MH-60S Seahawks. The new F/A-18E/F-carried AIM-174 missile—it has a probable range in excess of 320 kilometers and is likely capable of striking not only targets in the air but also at sea and on land—made its debut in 2024.[76] The AIM-260, with a range of over 200 kilometers, will supplement the AMRAAM. The long-range antiship missile (LRASM) and joint air-to-surface standoff missile (JASSM) variants and the advanced anti-radiation guided missile–extended range (AARGM-ER) will also be available.

The US Navy's land-based aviation is led by the P-8A Poseidon. Not only is it more capable than its P-3C Orion predecessor, but it can also be refueled in flight, a critical capability given Pacific distances. The MQ-4C Triton long-range UAV augments this.

The U.S. Navy's SSN force of *Virginia-*, *Seawolf-*, and *Los Angeles*–class vessels will remain far superior to that of the PLAN's equivalents through 2030. These highly survivable submarines provide critical ASW, antiship, land attack, and ISR capability, moving quickly and operating independently of refueling. In addition to the Mk.48 torpedoes and Tomahawk land-attack missiles (TLAMs), Harpoon ASMs have returned to service after a post–Cold War hiatus. By 2029, Block V *Virginia*-class submarines should also be able to launch a hypersonic Intermediate Range Conventional Prompt Strike (IRCPS) land-attack missile with a range of at least 2,800 kilometers. Exercises with submarine-launched mobile mines have been stepped up. By the end of the 2020s, the MEDUSA system, a torpedo-launched UAV capable of deploying clandestine-delivered mines, will provide additional options.[77] U.S. Navy F/A-18/E/Fs and B-52H Stratofortresses can deploy the Quickstrike mine family, a type being upgraded with JDAM guidance systems and wings to give standoff range. The Hammerhead mine will be used to target submarines via Orca extra-large UUVs.[78]

Nevertheless, the naval services have several challenges. A major issue is the platforms the U.S. Navy will lose by 2029. The four cruise-missile-launching submarines (SSGNs) of the *Ohio* class—each capable of carrying up to 154

USS *Mississippi* (SSN 782) departs Joint Base Pearl Harbor–Hickam. The U.S. Navy's submarines will be one of the few platforms able to operate within China's A2/AD zone from early in a conflict. *U.S. Navy photo by Mass Communication Specialist 1st Class Scott Barnes, March 20, 2023, DVIDS*

Tomahawk missiles— will be retired by that year, and their effective replacements in the form of Block V and Block VI *Virginia*-class submarines will not have entered service in sufficient numbers to replace the lost vertical-launch cells. The last of the *Ticonderoga*-class cruisers will decommission in 2029. The current plan is to refit the three *Zumwalt*-class destroyers with twelve IRCPS missiles each, with test launches due in 2027 or 2028, but the overall capability this will provide is limited.[79] U.S. Navy munitions procurement is accelerating but remains largely inadequate for prolonged high-intensity warfare.

The numerical challenge facing the U.S. Navy is also significant. In 2029 the primary conventional combat element of the force is anticipated to be eleven carriers—a mix of *Nimitz*-class and *Gerald R. Ford*–class vessels—eighty-three *Arleigh Burke*–class destroyers, twenty-nine "small surface combatants" (the majority the limited-capability *Independence* class), and forty-nine *Los Angeles*–, *Seawolf*-, and *Virginia*-class SSNs.[80] In comparison, the PLAN is already numerically larger, although it falls short of the U.S. Navy in ship tonnage due to American ships and submarines being larger on average. The PLAN also does not face the strains of U.S. global commitments. In 2024 the PLAN is listed as possessing two STOBAR carriers, with a CATOBAR carrier undergoing trials; eight cruisers; forty-two destroyers; forty-nine frigates; over 142 patrol and coastal combatants; six SSNs; and forty-six SSKs, with a large-scale build program ongoing.[81] Unlike the situation prior to World War II with respect to the IJN, the rapid PLAN build program has no U.S. equivalent.

The growing naval threat has prompted an expansion in U.S. antiship weapons stockpiles. The acquisition of Block VA Tomahawks with an antishipping capability, LRASMs; the Naval Strike Missile (NSM); and the repurposing of the SM-6 for antiship taskings has broadened U.S. options for strikes against PLA maritime assets. The USMC has acquired the NMESIS system to launch NSMs from land to strike ships at sea. The Marines will be able to launch precision strike missile (PrSM) missiles with an antishipping capability from their HIMARS units. In a Taiwan scenario, this would translate into implementing sea denial within the first island chain to deny the PLA the ability to obtain their objectives.[82]

Sealift is also a major issue, with fuel being the single greatest challenge.[83] Military Sealift Command (MSC) notionally (there are crew shortages causing ship layups) runs approximately twenty *Henry J. Kaiser*– and *John Lewis*–class replenishment oilers supporting the U.S. Navy, plus two fast-replenishment ships with mixed fuel and dry stores. These are augmented by a small number of government-controlled oil-product tankers and up to ten vessels that would be made available in an emergency under the Tanker Security Program (TSP) and vessels from the Voluntary Tanker Agreement (VTA).[84] CONSOL is being revived to support underway-replenishment capabilities using nonmilitary tankers.[85] Yet in 2016 U.S. Transportation Command (USTRANSCOM) stated that in planning scenarios eighty-six petroleum tankers would be required beyond replenishment oilers (and also possibly not including CONSOL ships) even without attrition.[86] Several dozen U.S.–flagged tankers are classed as "militarily useful," but these are not guaranteed to be available.[87]

Sealift for dry cargo has similar challenges. The NDRF (and within it the RRF) is small, aging, and suffers from poor readiness and a shortfall in available mariners. Its recapitalization is proving prolonged.[88] The Maritime Security Program (MSP) provides additional sealift capacity sourced from the civilian market. The Voluntary Intermodal Sealift Agreement and VTA provide incentive to providers to make capacity available in crisis through preferential access to peacetime contracts.

Beyond the limitations in ship and submarine construction, there is also a lack of repair and refit capacity. Given the time it would require to build such

Military Sealift Command replenishment oiler USNS *Yukon* (*right*) conducts a consolidated loading with commercial tanker MT *Empire State*. Conflict in the western Pacific would necessitate pressing civilian shipping into service. *U.S. Navy photo by Mass Communication Specialist 1st Class Patrick W. Menah Jr., October 28, 2019, DVIDS*

infrastructure, the Navy will likely need to utilize allied capacity to perform such work during wartime.

The current goal is for seventy-five U.S. Navy surface ships to be combat ready at any one time. Maximizing fleet availability at the outbreak of a conflict is the task of the Global Maritime Response Plan, with efforts directed at identifying how to bring the roughly one-third of the fleet that is neither underway nor in deep maintenance to war readiness.[89]

Despite the USAF focus on ACE, the bomber force will act as the first responder and part of the "blunt layer" in a Taiwan scenario. In 2029 four types will be available: the B-52H, the B-1B Lancer, the B-2 Spirit, and the B-21 Raider. Caution will likely dictate that most early sorties are conducted from the CONUS, Hawaii, or Australia. By the time of our conflict scenario, all types are likely to be cleared to carry land-attack JASSM and JASSM-ER cruise missiles, the latter with a range of over 925 kilometers. Additionally, the B-1B is cleared to carry the LRASM. The USAF has developed the Rapid Dragon program to enhance the volume of munitions that can be deployed, enabling C-130J and C-17 aircraft to launch JASSMs using an airdropped pallet. Since 2025 the REFORPAC (Resolute Force Pacific) exercise series

A B-2 bomber is refueled in flight by a KC-46A Pegasus aerial-refueling tanker. A Taiwan contingency would see U.S. strategic bombers and other types being heavily dependent on such support. *U.S. Air Force photo by Christian Turner, April 23, 2019, Edwards Air Force Base*

will biennially test the rapid deployment of USAF units to the western Pacific region, mirroring the Cold War–era REFORGER (Return of Forces to Germany) exercise series in which U.S. forces were shipped across the Atlantic to rehearse fighting as part of a NATO operation in Europe against the Warsaw Pact.[90]

Beyond direct combat power, the major contribution of the USAF to a Pacific contingency will be logistical. Strategic bombers will rely on in-flight refueling to operate from secure bases, and platforms such as the P-8 maritime patrol aircraft are likely to be in a similar position. There will also be an extensive need to support carrier aircraft. This may cumulatively create a need for Falklands War–type aerial-tanker relays stretching as far as from Hawaii, Alaska, and the U.S. West Coast to the Japanese coast. By 2029, 179 KC-46 Pegasus tankers—capable of being refueled midair themselves—will enhance operations, up to 15 KC-46s flown by Japan. Test flights have already occurred, with aircraft having flown sorties of up to thirty-six hours in the air.[91] Heavy-lift transport aircraft like the C-17 Globemaster III and C-5M Super Galaxy would lead the transoceanic airlift, and the Civil

A JASSM is prepared for loading onto a B-52H at Andersen Air Force Base, Guam. This family of missiles would be central to U.S. strikes in a western Pacific conflict. *U.S. Air Force photo by Airman 1st Class Spencer Perkins, April 24, 2023, DVIDS*

Reserve Air Fleet and other commercial providers would supply additional capacity.

The U.S. Space Force (USSF), established in 2019 under the Department of the Air Force, organizes, trains, and equips forces that mostly fall under the jurisdiction of the U.S. Space Command. Their key assets include spacecraft tasked with monitoring the vehicles of other nations in space, such as the Space-Based Space Surveillance system in low orbit and the Geosynchronous Space Situational-Awareness Program covering geostationary orbit (the National Reconnaissance Office runs its own Silent Barker space-surveillance effort). Early warning of missile launches is provided through the Space-Based Infrared System. The threat to space-based assets has led to the development of proliferated satellite networks. The USSF's Space Development Agency is building a network of small, low-cost satellites to facilitate communication (transport layer), navigation (navigation layer), assist C2 and data processing (battle management layer), track missiles (tracking layer), track targets on the ground (custody layer, although this will not be a specific satellite type), and provide space situational awareness (deterrence layer).[92]

A PrSM is test-launched from a HIMARS. This system has land-attack and antiship roles and could operate from locations including the Ryukyu Islands. *Program Executive Office Missiles and Space, photo by White Sands Missile Range, October 12, 2019, DVIDS*

With the INF Treaty in abeyance since 2019, the U.S. Army is now acquiring three missiles that will reach beyond the 499-kilometer limit of that agreement. The MLRS and HIMARS-fired PrSM is the replacement for the ATACM, originally with a range capped at 499 kilometers but with a development program in train to extend it to 1,000 kilometers and provide a capability to attack ships as well as land targets. The MDTF's Mid-Range Capability

Typhon batteries will launch Tomahawk (as well as the SM-6 missiles) in the land-attack and antiship roles. Finally, the Army's long-range hypersonic weapon, Dark Eagle, is a ballistic missile fitted with a hypersonic guide body designed to hit land targets at over a 2,800-kilometer distance.[93]

Given the maritime nature of the theater, the U.S. Army will employ its force of watercraft, including landing ships and craft. To support operations in the Pacific, the Army formed a new watercraft unit in Japan in February 2024.[94]

ALLIES

The five leading U.S. regional allies are Japan, Australia, the Philippines, the Republic of Korea, and Thailand. For our purposes, we assume that the latter two states will not take an active role in hostilities during a Taiwan contingency and so will not examine them further here. The 1960 Treaty of Mutual Cooperation and Security between the United States and Japan covers the defense relationship between Washington and Tokyo. The United States has had a mutual defense treaty with the Philippines since 1951, and the 2014 Enhanced Defense Cooperation Agreement (EDCA) has given U.S. forces additional access rights. The Australia, New Zealand, and United States Security Treaty (ANZUS) was signed in 1951, although the United States partially ended its treaty links with New Zealand in 1986. Although somewhat overshadowed by the 2021 AUKUS agreement, which focuses on defense technology, particularly a joint Australia–United Kingdom–United States SSN program, it still provides the basis for military cooperation between Washington and Canberra. The United States, Canada, Australia, and New Zealand (along with the United Kingdom) also share intelligence under the Five Eyes agreement.

Japan

Japan's current policy notes the importance of supporting "peace and stability in the Taiwan Strait."[95] Tokyo does not recognize Taiwan as a separate state but maintains strong unofficial economic and cultural links. Geography also dictates the importance of Taiwan to Japan, as the former sits astride SLOC critical to the latter. While traditionally not keen to articulate a view of security matters, this has recently changed, with then–Deputy Defense Minister Nakayama Yasuhide stating in December 2020 that the security of the island was a "red line" for Tokyo.[96]

In December 2022 the Japanese government released a trio of documents that plotted the way ahead. The 2022 NSS provided an overview of Japan's challenge, mirroring a similar U.S. analysis about shifts in the global balance of power toward the Indo-Pacific and the actors attempting to "revise the existing international order." China's efforts to "unilaterally change the status quo" were explicitly called out, as were its intrusions into the waters and airspace around the Senkaku Islands, a territory controlled by Japan but claimed by China (and the ROC). It also noted that "concerns are mounting rapidly" about the situation around the Taiwan Strait, continuing, "Taiwan is an extremely important partner and a precious friend of Japan, with whom Japan shares fundamental values, including democracy, and has close economic and personal ties." Strengthening Japan's defensive capabilities was presented as a central part of countering such threats, with the development of cross-domain capabilities that mirror those of various U.S. initiatives. It emphasized standoff capabilities, along with stockpiling fuel and ammunition, hardening base facilities, and mobility. A counterstrike capability was presented as vital (and constitutional) given that Japan's ABM system was inadequate to manage that threat through purely defensive measures. The NSS stated that by 2027, defense spending would rise to 2 percent of GDP, roughly a 60-percent increase, and Tokyo would take primary responsibility for defeating an attempted invasion of the home islands. By approximately 2032, the JSDF would be able to defeat such an attack at a significant distance.[97]

The NDS reflected the NSS while providing additional detail regarding the technical aspects of the challenges faced, including China's A2/AD efforts and Japan's program to build a "Multi-Domain Defense Force" and a standoff defense capability as well as further enhance its ABM defenses and its force resilience. These include the establishment of a permanent joint headquarters to support cross-domain operations. Major programs listed include improvements to standoff defense capabilities; integrated air and missile defense capabilities; unmanned defense capabilities; cross-domain operation capabilities, covering air, land, sea, cyber, space and the electromagnetic spectrum, C2, and intelligence functions; mobile deployment capabilities and civil protection; and sustainability and resiliency.[98] The defense buildup plan provided a list of actions to take in support of these policies.[99]

In July 2024 Tokyo and Washington jointly announced that the United States Forces Japan headquarters would be upgraded to a joint force headquarters reporting to USINDOPACOM. This will allow it to operate in conjunction with the new JSDF Joint Operations Command.[100] The formulation of a joint U.S.–Japan contingency plan for defending Taiwan is also thought to have recently taken place, but there is no official confirmation.[101]

Assuming Tokyo made the political decision to support the defense of Taiwan, in wartime the JSDF would assume a role similar to that of a "shield to the U.S. spear" as envisaged during the Cold War, albeit acting in a more closely integrated fashion with American forces. Critical tasks would include air and missile defense, ASW, maintaining the SLOC to areas east of Japan, MCM, and controlling strategic maritime chokepoints on the country's periphery. To facilitate these, the JMSDF fields Aegis destroyers, general-purpose destroyers and frigates, advanced SSKs (some with air-independent propulsion), and MCM vessels. The JASDF operates upgraded F-15Js, F-35A and F-35B—the latter of which can operate from two JMSDF light aircraft carriers—and F-2 aircraft as well as an array of SAM/ABM systems, including the Patriot. The JGSDF operate land-based ASMs. The JSDF is also taking delivery of offensive systems, including TLAM and JASSM.

Australia

Australia has been torn over Taiwan, given its increasing economic dependence on China—particularly since the signing of a bilateral trade agreement in 2015. On the one hand, Canberra officially recognizes the government in Beijing being "the sole legal Government of China." Still, it remains ambiguous on Taiwan's status and maintains unofficial economic and cultural relations with Taipei, and only "acknowledges" China's view that Taiwan is a province of the PRC.[102] Yet there have been hawkish statements recently, with former Minister for Defense Peter Dutton stating in November 2021 that it would be "inconceivable" that Australia would not support the United States in the event of war over Taiwan.[103]

The 2023 *Defense Strategic Review* followed the U.S. and Japanese analysis of the growing threat environment. But it peddled relatively softly against Beijing despite noting, "China's military build-up is now the largest and most ambitious of any country since the end of the Second World War," and advising that it was no longer possible to be confident there would be ten years' warning of a major war. The main orientation was on a strategy of denial designed to prevent Australia's coercion, including a domestic A2/AD capability.

The country's strategy pivoted from a "balanced force" to a "focused force." Undersea warfare, long-range targeting and strikes, amphibious operations, sea denial, and air and missile defense are all priorities that have moved the Australian Defence Force (ADF) from the type of lower-level threats engaged over the last thirty years. The domestic manufacturing of munitions was also given prominence, along with the need to harden its northern facilities and to make provisions for force dispersal.[104] With a limited power-projection capability (the delivery of SSNs for the Royal Australian Navy falls outside our period of analysis), the ADF's wartime tasks would largely focus on territorial and SLOC defense to provide a secure base of operations for U.S.-led forces.

Philippines

As might be expected, the Philippines has adopted a One China policy that "fully understands and respects" Beijing's belief that Taiwan is part of China. Nevertheless, it has maintained unofficial links with the island.[105] The Batanes island group is only two hundred kilometers from Taiwan.[106]

The Mutual Defense Treaty between the Philippines and the United States was signed in 1951 and provides the bedrock of their defense relationship. While the United States withdrew permanently based forces from the country following the end of the Cold War, Manila's territorial conflicts with Beijing—most notably over Scarborough Shoal—have led to intensified collaboration.

Importantly, the Philippines is under no obligation to host U.S. forces in the event of a conflict. But Manila would be aware that PRC success in Taiwan would almost certainly lead to the pressing of its remaining territorial claims in the South China Sea and at least partial U.S. disengagement from the region.

The Philippines only possesses limited maritime and air capability and would be dependent on the United States for its defense against a major power in these realms. As such, its primary role in wartime would be to provide domestic security to allow the United States to counter the external threat.

Canada

Canada has a One China policy that simultaneously recognizes the Beijing government as the legitimate representative of China but only takes note of the government's belief that Taiwan is part of China. Located outside the main theater of operations, Canada would play a peripheral role in any conflict over Taiwan. Nevertheless, its commitment to the defense of North America, both bilaterally with the United States—including via the North American Aerospace Defense Command (NORAD)—and through NATO, would contribute to securing the U.S. homeland.

Canada's recent purchase of military equipment has given insight into the support Ottawa could provide. The F-35A aircraft on order will facilitate a major improvement in air-defense capability over their CF-18A/B predecessors. P-8 maritime patrol aircraft will likewise enhance both ASW and wider maritime awareness along the North American Pacific coast—critical capabilities given the potential threat from PLA submarines and the risk of missile and drone attack from merchant vessels controlled from Beijing. Both of these aircraft types can be aerially refueled by CC-330 Husky aircraft, which are far more capable than their predecessors, allowing them to operate at greater range.

SETTING THE BOARD

The United States maintained a solid understanding of the western Pacific threat as the early twenty-first century progressed but initially suffered significant shortcomings in translating this to practical planning and action. A number of similarities can be identified with the period immediately prior to World War II.

While far from an exact parallel, the U.S. approach to countering China's A2/AD has evolved similarly to War Plan Orange and the broader situation of the period. The Orange planners were torn between a "thrusters" rapid advance across the Pacific and a "cautionary" methodical march. While not a war plan as was Orange, the initial incarnation of ASB may be seen as the modern-day version of the thrusters approach: it correctly identified the challenges, but the notion that there was a head-on solution—for Orange, a rapid dash west; for ASB, its blinding and dismantling of the PLA's A2/AD system to facilitate a campaign—was unrealistic. Instead, a more plausible approach—for Orange, a steady advance; for ASB, the shift to JAM-GC's model of conducting operations that did not require the comprehensive defeat of the opponent's A2/AD system—has been adopted.

There are also parallels between the role of regional forces and the criticality of reinforcements in the run up to World War II to contemporary U.S. plans. The Asiatic Fleet and local ground forces in the Philippines were no match for their Japanese counterparts, and the planners' eventual conclusion was that wartime reinforcement was not realistic before defeat. Contemporary plans also rely on U.S. regional forces and local allies to lead efforts to prevent the enemy accomplishing its goals. Yet while as in 1941 they cannot do this alone, support from outside the region is now more plausible in an age of intercontinental air power and nuclear-powered submarines.

It is also possible to identify some similarities with treaty restrictions. The 1922 Washington Naval Treaty prevented the United States from establishing fortified bases in the Philippines or Guam, a stipulation that did not expire until 1937. Such facilities could have provided enhanced defensive options in the face of overwhelming local IJN superiority (although admittedly such facilities in Singapore did not save the British). The treaty also restricted gun calibers but failed to cover torpedoes—the IJN exploited this gap with the Long Lance torpedo, which could match or outrange even 16-inch guns and required only a cruiser or destroyer for launching. The 1988 INF Treaty prevented the United States from possessing ground-launched cruise and ballistic missiles of the type suitable for defensive options that mirrored the missile-based component of the PLA's anti-intervention system. When the United States withdrew from the INF Treaty in 2019, it opened up new avenues of capability, but realizing them at scale will take time and resources.

Finally, there is the issue of comparative preparation for potential hostilities. The IJN built up to, and in some instances surreptitiously beyond, treaty limitations throughout the lifetime of the Washington Naval Treaty. In contrast, only in the mid-1930s did the United States accelerate its efforts. Today, China is not subject to any legal constraints, but its military buildup has, among other achievements, resulted in the PLAN now being the largest navy in the world by ship numbers. The United States has accelerated its preparatory efforts over the last decade, yet major weaknesses remain.

CHAPTER 13

OPLAN 5077

If one day, China should change color and turn into a superpower,
if it should play the tyrant in the world, subject others to its bullying,
aggression, and exploitation, the people of the world should identify
it as social-imperialism, expose it, oppose it and work together
with the Chinese people to overthrow it.

—*Deng Xiaoping, April 10, 1974*

OPLAN 5077 is the "hook" of this book, but wider U.S. contingency plans for a Taiwan conflict are global in nature. Additionally, a regional successor or supplements to 5077 may be in place: as noted, a new joint U.S.–Japan plan for Taiwan—OPLAN number unknown—has allegedly already been drafted. Regardless, the main theater of such a conflict would center on the USINDOPACOM region, making a CCMD-level approach useful to outline a phased model for this area:

- Campaigning: *Pre-crisis status quo*—activities to shape the operational area in line with the wider GCP for China, including via the contact force layer, as well as intelligence gathering
- Phase I: *Crisis, Transition, and Initial PRC Attack*—initiate regional-force preparation and buildup to enhance deterrence and improve survivability, followed by transition to war and initial PLA-instigated hostilities
- Phase II: *Initial Retaliation and Recovery*—limited immediate counterattack by blunt-layer force, restore lost operational capability, blunt force prepares to facilitate the arrival of surge force

- Phase III: *Seize the Initiative*—comprehensive attack targeting PLA amphibious and air landing assets, defeat of any PLA ground force on Taiwan, impose a blockade on PRC, transition to sustained operations led by surge force
- Phase IV: *Prolonged Warfighting*—surge force leads efforts to degrade general PLA warfighting capability, secure air and sea control beyond the first island chain, and establish tentative lines of communication with Taiwan and secure favorable war termination

This scenario is just one possibility, but it is among the most plausible. The likely protracted nature of fighting is a critical concept. *Joint Warfighting* identifies three strategies available to belligerents: annihilation—destruction of the means to fight; attrition—the gradual reduction of the ability to fight; and exhaustion—the erosion of the will to continue.[1] As regards a Taiwan scenario, neither side can win outright through either annihilation or attrition. Vertical-escalation paths to annihilation are limited by the risk of mutual nuclear destruction. If the U.S.-led coalition defeats a landing attempt through denial and in the process inflicts attrition, the war would not automatically end. Early termination by Beijing is made less plausible by sunk costs and a likely unwillingness to abandon war goals even as they recede out of reach. This could mean that horizontal escalation to a broader array of targets, including the PLA's wider forces, regeneration capacity, and a blockade, could follow, meaning that exhaustion—or at least the inflicting of cost imposition, a strategy highlighted in the 2022 NDS alongside denial—may represent the most viable path to U.S. success and favorable war termination.[2]

To make this more accessible, I will forgo the standard OPLAN format sampled at the beginning of this book and use a simpler approach focusing on a few key areas. There is also some bending of the rules, as the forces envisaged would be available in 2029, breaking the norm of only planning with the resources to hand—something General MacArthur did in the Philippines to his detriment.

A conflict with China, a true peer competitor to the United States, carries immense risks. War Plan Orange and Rainbow 5 could depend on U.S. economic, manufacturing, and demographic strength to produce success. Cold War plans relied first on U.S. postwar industrial superiority and nuclear monopoly, then on nuclear supremacy, and subsequently on broader U.S. conventional technological superiority. The wars against Iraq saw initial rapid victory through full-spectrum dominance. A conflict with China would not replicate any of these. The United States lacks industrial—and in select areas technological—superiority and faces quantitative disadvantages, setting the stage for a long, bloody struggle with no guarantee of success.[3]

POSSIBLE CHINESE COURSES OF ACTION

Before examining a plausible U.S. response, the first question is what a likely PRC course of action could be in the late 2020s. Beijing itself realizes that gray-zone pressure will almost certainly not achieve the ultimate goal: irreversible control over ROC territories. Operations short of a full invasion, such as a blockade or bombardment, would also be unlikely to secure the desired end state. Therefore, the most credible military option is the most extreme: a full invasion. Strategically, this would require the defeat of ROC forces and assimilation of the territory while preventing the successful intervention of a U.S.-led coalition. Operationally, this would necessitate the suppression of ROC and in-theater U.S.-led coalition forces and an anti-access campaign to prevent resupply and reinforcement; air and sea landing operations to secure Taiwan and its outlying islands; and the garrisoning of this territory to facilitate assimilation into the PRC.

The PLA's general CONOPS are clear, but a key question remains: would Beijing target U.S. forces in an opening strike? If attacking Taiwan while avoiding war with the United States seems impossible for China, an early strike may be the least bad option—even if the price is a Pearl Harbor–style galvanizing of U.S. resolve. We will assume here they take this option.

There is also the question of the overall sequencing of the timeline. An opening attack against Taiwan, the United States, and their allies would have the greatest chance of achieving surprise if done before major Chinese mobilization. Yet weeks and likely months of PRC preparation required for a follow-up amphibious and air landing operation would give Beijing's opponents time to recover. The alternative—full mobilization by China before the opening action—would offer Taiwan, the United States, and their allies more warning but less recovery time before the decisive engagement.

ASSUMPTIONS

Planning assumptions are things we cannot know for certain in advance but are required to identify courses of action at the price of a degree of risk.[4] Contingency planning in advance of a crisis requires their extensive use, as the exact nature of the potential crisis will be uncertain.[5] I propose the following as the central assumptions.

The first assumption is that the PRC will be the objective instigator of the conflict. While there is a risk the ROC will take transparently provocative action such as unilaterally declaring independence, it does not seem likely given the probable consequences. An unprovoked U.S. attack on China is also not plausible.

The second assumption is sustained active resistance from the ROC. If the military and government were to collapse or surrender after the opening attacks, there would be no realistic hope of halting an invasion attempt. To borrow a quote from the Iraq War, the U.S. approach, by necessity, would have to be "we can't want this more than you do."[6]

Certain strategic and operational indications and warning measures providing notice of an upcoming attack—likely emerging weeks, if not months, in advance—is the third assumption. These would include PLA joint force exercises demonstrating capability on the scale required. While, as noted, the potential sequencing of an attack is unclear, a clear warning of some kind would also likely follow an execute decision by Beijing. With the Taiwan Strait and surrounding area under constant surveillance by the ROC, the United States, and allies, hiding major posture changes is effectively impossible. The PRC may attempt to use exercises to desensitize observers to such changes, so care must be taken in assessment. Early signs of hostilities may include ramped-up ammunition production, stockpiling, and the diversion of civilian assets—including shipping and land transport—for military purposes. Missile launchers and command posts would be dispersed from their peacetime locations, and equipment maintenance would be intensified. Political rhetoric directed toward the domestic population, Taiwan, and the wider world would likely intensify.[7]

Limited operational and tactical surprise is likely to be more obtainable. In this sense, events would resemble the Russian invasion of Ukraine in that the reality of a likely attack is clear, but the exact timing and form are opaque.[8]

The fourth major assumption is centered on prepositioning and regional basing. The United States would be seriously constrained by having to operate solely from its territory (plus the COFA states it has military use of), and any major attempt to reinforce Taiwan directly will likely be interdicted. Instead, it would rely on its regional treaty allies. Japanese bases are assumed to be accessible, with the JASDF defending its home territory. Australian cooperation is also expected. The participation of the Philippines would be desirable but not essential—it is included here. Meanwhile, we will assume that the ROK and the U.S. forces based there would not become directly involved.

Fifth, it is unlikely that there will be any safe domains, including in the U.S. homeland. Distance will still provide a degree of sanctuary from kinetic attacks, but the war will be like nothing resembling anything experienced by the United States since at least World War II, probably since the War of 1812. Still, both sides are likely to avoid all-out attacks in the space and cyber realms.

Sixth, nuclear weapons are unlikely to be used unless there is a drastic and improbable miscalculation. Their regional use by China would have only a limited operational effect on the PLA's chances of success as it would invite U.S. nuclear retaliation devastating to an amphibious operation. The loss of Taiwan would not carry the same weight as the loss of Western Europe to the USSR for the United States, meaning that the initiation of a nuclear exchange by Washington is unlikely.

The seventh assumption—U.S. leadership would authorize conventional strikes on mainland China—is less certain.[9] U.S. officials may deem such action out of bounds due to escalation risks. The unwillingness of Washington to bomb China during the Korean War superficially bolsters this claim, but a JCS memo from January 1951 recommended that attacks on the PRC occur only "at such time as the Chinese Communists attack any of our forces outside of Korea." The United States saw such restraint as providing it with a disproportionate advantage.[10] Given the likelihood of PLA strikes on U.S. assets outside the ROC, similar conditions are unlikely to be replicated. This does not mean strikes within the PRC in a contemporary conflict would be unlimited—for instance, conventional attacks on nuclear sites would be provocative. Strikes on dual-use capabilities, including early warning and C2 systems, would still require careful navigation.

The eighth and final assumption, as noted, is that such a conflict would be protracted. This goes against the interests of all parties, who desire a short war to minimize economic, political, and social disruption. Nevertheless, as outlined below, identifying a path to war termination is extremely challenging.[11]

CENTERS OF GRAVITY

The DOD defines the center of gravity as "the source of power that provides moral or physical strength, freedom of action, or will to act."[12] The PRC's strategic center of gravity is the CCP's domestic control of the state, rooted in party unity, loyalty of the party armed forces and security forces, and to a lesser extent its legitimacy among the population. This gives the CCP control of vast material and human resources, which form China's greatest strategic strength and from which critical military capabilities are generated.

In a Taiwan conflict, the PRC's operational centers of gravity will be assets to transport and sustain ground forces across the Taiwan Strait and the A2/AD capabilities—platforms, munitions, C4ISR systems, and so forth—needed to counter regional U.S. and allied forces while also interdicting reinforcements.

U.S. strategic centers of gravity are the policy preferences of the senior leadership, public opinion, mobilization capacity and its network of allies. Beijing likely sees U.S. public opinion as a weak point, especially in a drawn-out conflict—an issue that also concerned the War Plan Orange planners.

Operationally, the U.S. center of gravity is its ability to deploy and operate forces around the PRC's periphery including C4ISR. This is primarily centered on its ability to bring platforms—aircraft, ships, submarines, and land-based systems—into range of key Chinese assets and sustain C4ISR. The second center is the U.S. ability to suppress and defend against similar PLA systems.

Taiwan's strategic center of gravity is its ability to maintain functional governance when under attack in order to resist a PLA invasion through the mobilization of the population and material national assets. Operationally, this means maintaining C4ISR and communication links with the outside world, safeguarding the offensive and defensive systems required to inflict attrition on the PLA, and sustaining the material needs and morale of its forces and population.

U.S. CONCEPT OF OPERATIONS

In the event of hostilities, the U.S. strategic objectives will likely be a return to something akin to the status quo ante bellum regarding Taiwan. The central operational objectives will be to deny the PLA control of Taiwan, defending U.S. and allied territories, and restoring links between the ROC and the outside world to facilitate defense and resupply. The desired end state will be upholding representative government in Taiwan, severely degrading the PLA's ability to project meaningful aerospace and maritime power, and suppressing the PRC's force-regeneration capabilities.

In our model the U.S. approach will be based on a concept of defense, denial, disruption, and degrading. The opening and subsequent attacks by Beijing will require the defense of U.S. and allied assets. The denial of the PLA's objective of a successful invasion will be facilitated through an interdiction campaign against military and requisitioned transport shipping and air-transport assets stationed near the mainland coast opposite Taiwan. This and other lines of effort will require a campaign of disruption against PLA A2/AD systems to allow blunt-layer forces to recover and regenerate from the initial exchange and to facilitate the deployment of surge-layer forces to the region with the aim of facilitating wider action. This will be accomplished through the kinetic and nonkinetic targeting of sensor and relay nodes in all domains as a first line of offense and defense, with secondary efforts targeting launch platforms and munitions. Once the initiative has been seized, a (likely protracted) campaign to degrade wider PLA assets and their supporting networks and infrastructure will be undertaken as part of efforts to end the war on favorable terms.

WAR GAMES

The various attempts to simulate a conflict over Taiwan have been widely reported, so we will not examine them individually in depth.[13] But it is worthwhile studying a sample. Probably the most notorious is a 2019 claim by RAND analyst David Ochmanek that the United States gets its "ass handed to it" during war games featuring China and Russia, with aircraft on the ground and C3 capabilities being key points of vulnerability.[14] Classified war games reportedly point to defeat, but the little detail available from these suggests that they were using warfighting methods already known to be outmoded.[15]

Other games have been more optimistic while still emphasizing the daunting nature of the task at hand, and it is from these that this chapter takes the lead. The *Dangerous Straits* report of June 2022 outlines that while the United States could prevent a successful invasion (although a PLA lodgment was still established), China was unwilling to give up its efforts, pointing toward a protracted conflict.[16] A 2023 effort tested twenty-four different scenario variations assuming U.S. intervention and found that while the U.S.-led coalition defeated a PLA invasion, it came at a high price in casualties and material, with two carriers, ten to twenty large surface combatants, and dozens to hundreds of aircraft typically lost in the base scenario, with lighter but still substantial losses in the optimistic scenario. Pessimistic scenarios generally ended in stalemates and with even heavier U.S. aircraft losses.[17]

"TELL ME HOW THIS ENDS"

This was the essential question asked by Gen. David Petraeus during the buildup to the Iraq War.[18] The war with Imperial Japan ended with unconditional surrender. The envisaged end state of a war with the USSR evolved from Soviet defeat to the communist block's obliteration, to mutual destruction, then to a hope that war termination could be brought about by a diplomatic settlement. Before outlining the potential course of any conflict, it is important to have a broad understanding of how it might end—the "theory of victory."[19]

As noted, exhaustion is likely to be a critical component of ending the war. Analysis by the RAND Corporation identifies that a total victory that leaves the other side unable to fight—or dominance—is implausible for either side owing to the presence of nuclear weapons. Indeed, both sides can prevent their opponent achieving their maximalist goals—defined here as unchallenged control of Taiwan. There are, therefore, two basic requirements from the U.S. perspective: prevention of a PRC limited victory through denying them a successful invasion and securing of Taiwan by destroying the means for an invasion, and convincing China's leadership to end the conflict on terms acceptable to Taiwan and the U.S.-led coalition as part of the latter's limited victory. Denial may be accomplished without the buy-in of the PRC, but conflict termination cannot, as there is no prospect of the type of dominance this would require. While China might stop if its goals become unachievable, sunk costs make this unlikely early on. Thus, the denial element of the campaign may need to be supported by cost imposition despite the risk of escalation.[20]

A major challenge for a U.S.-led coalition is that Beijing could choose to continue to attempt to blockade and bombard Taiwan even if the invasion an invasion attempt fails, hoping to exhaust the ROC and its allies. Taiwan's proximity to the mainland allows China to rely on shore-launched missiles and UAVs alone, even if wider power-projection capabilities were destroyed. The United States could seek to suppress such efforts by disrupting the kill chain, intercepting missiles, and striking missile launch sites and production facilities. But while the ISTAR capabilities required to strike targets such as ballistic- and cruise-missile capable TELs have evolved since the Gulf War, running a comprehensive campaign to destroy them in the teeth of PLA air and missile defenses would be a tall order. An alternative path to conflict termination is likely to be to inflict costs sufficient to influence Beijing toward judging it not worthwhile to continue hostilities without triggering unacceptable escalation—including nuclear use. The above referenced RAND analysis refers to the implementation of this approach as the "Goldilocks Challenge."[21]

The chief material issue for the United States in a prolonged war would be industrial capacity. While the World War II U.S. Pacific Fleet and wider forces were at an initial disadvantage, America's overwhelming industrial power allowed it to defeat Imperial Japan within a few years. No such advantage exists over the PRC—if anything, it is the United States that is now dependent on the war being short to prevent its weaknesses from becoming manifest.[22] While the two nations' economic power remains broadly comparable, and the United States retains an edge in many areas, China vastly excels in industrial production.[23]

Beijing faces fewer political hurdles in sustaining a long war. The population would support a unification effort, and dissidents would be silenced. Severe economic strain, especially among elites, could pose challenges, but short-to-medium-term security would likely hold. Any decision to end the war would reside with the CCP leadership.

THE WAR OF 2029

Campaigning

Our scenario opens with USINDOPACOM in campaigning mode, as is always the case even in the absence of a crisis. The campaigning concept was introduced to remove the peace/war binary in an age of competition and seeks to shape the environment. Assets deployed in this role—including the contact-layer force—would help with intelligence gathering and early warning. These and other joint force elements would provide notice of potentially threatening PLA activity. The subsequent phased effort response to a crisis would not run purely sequentially but overlap as the weight of emphasis changes.

Phase I: Crisis, Transition, and Initial PRC Attack

An alert of unusual developments would prompt the repositioning of ISTAR assets and the reprioritization of analytical capability to confirm indications and gather additional information. At this time, the situation in the Taiwan Strait is likely to remain unclear, but decisions to enhance deterrence efforts and prepare for escalation will be required.

Forward-based forces would need an early decision to move to their wartime positions, to recall personnel from leave and exercises, and to step up equipment maintenance, among other activities. Should the order be given, U.S. Navy vessels forward deployed to locations including Japan and Guam would sail to positions away from their vulnerable ports and the coverage area of shorter-ranged PLA systems. USAF tactical and support aircraft in Japan would disperse to locations including civilian airports while mobile equipment is moved off base. USMC aircraft would move to safer fixed sites or prepare for further transit to undertake EABO in concert with Marine littoral regiments. Other U.S. geographical and functional commands would prepare to mitigate attacks from PRC conventional and unconventional forces and execute their element of the ICP while preparing to detach assets to USINDOPACOM.

In the United States, ships on exercise would be recalled, maintenance expedited, and leave canceled. The priority would be to bring additional SSNs into the theater to provide a survivable forward force to strike targets within the first island chain. Homeland-based bombers would load out with relevant munitions and remain on alert with their supporting tanker force ready to be called upon to conduct missile strikes directly from the continental United States (CONUS). A rapidly established air bridge to Japan and the Philippines would enable the deployment of extra ground and air assets to bolster the blunt-force layer. Reserve component mobilization would also commence.

Additionally, measures would be taken to defend ports, air bases, munitions storage sites, and other critical locations in CONUS using the

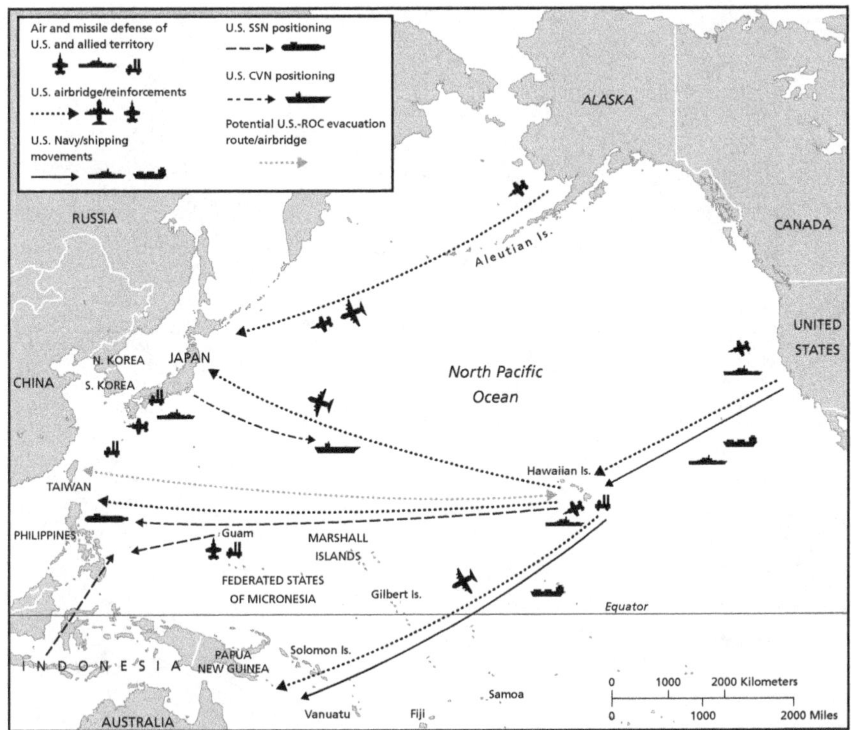

Phase I(a)—Crisis and Transition

homeland-force-layer assets, including those of the National Guard and Coast Guard under USNORTHCOM. U.S. Navy assets on the Atlantic coast would be alerted for a potential transfer to the Pacific. Mobilization of the RRF and wider NDRF and U.S. merchant fleet would also begin to facilitate transpacific resupply.

In parallel to this, the ROC would be implementing the force-protection and mobilization elements of the Gu'an OPLAN. Dispersion and concealment of assets would be a priority, as would the establishment of decentralized command arrangements and preparations for damage repair.

The initial attack from the PRC would seek to eliminate Taiwan's leadership, destroy force elements and cut off surviving assets from their supporting networks, and support the imposition of a blockade on the ROC as part of the JFSC and JBC. For the United States, kinetic attacks against main operating bases and identified dispersal sites in Japan, the Philippines, Guam, and

Phase I(b)—Initial PRC Attack

other Pacific islands, as well as strikes targeting U.S. Navy ships, are likely to account for the majority of losses, launched by the PLA as an active defense element of its JAAC. If the PRC decides to strike JSDF targets as part of the initial effort against U.S. forces stationed in Japan, those elements would likely be included in these initial strikes.

A limited kinetic attack on the U.S. mainland is possible. More comprehensive efforts by China would be challenging owing to the PLA's transpacific power-projection constraints. The limited probability of success of such activity would render it a supporting rather than a central component of the offensive. Cyberattacks against military assets in the CONUS and globally are highly probable with U.S. Cyber Command leading the U.S. countermeasures.

While offensive activities would span all domains, cyberattacks against U.S. civilian infrastructure and kinetic operations against space-based assets would likely be restrained owing to the risk of escalation and disproportionately negative consequences. There would, however, be activity in both realms. Some have proposed that options facing the PLA would include a "Space Pearl Harbor," with a massive strike against U.S. assets using direct-assent, directed-energy, coorbital, cyber, and electronic-warfare attacks or, alternatively, to take a "Counterspace in Being" approach, with such attacks held back less the counterattack cause damage that puts the instigator at a greater disadvantage at a critical moment in the campaign.[24]

Here, we assume that at least the kinetic element of counterspace operations takes the latter path. The proliferation of small, low-cost satellites and rapid launch systems and the risk of creating space debris that renders certain orbits unusable to anyone (including to states the PRC wishes to be supportive of or neutral to its campaign) makes such attacks less practical and appealing.

Phase II: Initial Retaliation and Recovery

The PLA's opening attack, likely its best chance of success, will significantly degrade Taiwanese, U.S., and allied regional forces across the spectrum—particularly fixed infrastructure and surface vessels. Defensive systems, passive measures, and reconstitution capabilities would only mitigate the damage caused.

U.S. retaliation would begin immediately, although it would be limited by available forces and supply challenges. ROC forces would also deploy their surviving strike systems. The JSDF may also retaliate with "defensive" strikes against PLA platforms responsible for attacks on Japanese territory. China's offensive and defensive efforts in this phase primarily would both be part of the PLA's JAAC.

U.S. recovery efforts would seek to rectify damage to the extent necessary to allow for blunt-force-layer operations using units both in theater and distantly based—the latter chiefly the strategic bomber force—and the reception of surge-force-layer units transiting China's now-active anti-access defenses

Phase II—Initial Retaliation and Recovery

into theater. Initial external support for recovery will be limited, with short-term reconstitution being dependent on local military stockpiles and requisitioned civilian resources. Initial relief efforts would primarily launch from the United States and limited-to-high-risk airlift operations. Surface maritime operations west of Hawaii would be conditional on the opening degree of success in countering the PLA missile strikes.

The homeland-force-layer would have a significant role in theater recovery efforts in the longer term. For example, seriously damaged vessels would need to withdraw to the United States for repair. Departure and reception points in the CONUS for material and personnel would need protection. Space-launch assets would replace satellites disabled by the PLA. Canada would also provide bilateral defensive support through NORAD. NATO may deploy forces, including fighters, tankers, and AEW&C aircraft from Europe, given the alliance's treaty obligations to help defend the mainland United States and Canada from attack.

Phase III: Seize the Initiative

Seizing the initiative hinges on denying the PLA's primary goal: invading and occupying Taiwan via its JILC. We are assuming that the ROC-controlled islands offshore of China, including the Kinmen and Matsu groups, would be lost either to invasion or irreversible isolation, with the Pescadores Islands also likely in PLA hands but kept under ROC and allied bombardment to limit their use as a forward base. If initial PLA strikes destroy most of the ROC Air Force and Navy, only ground-based forces on Taiwan would be functional. These might include air- and missile-defense systems and missiles capable of striking the mainland and enemy ships in Taiwan's littoral. But most of these resources would likely be conserved for the "critical moment" of a PLA landing attempt.

The United States would likely focus on halting a landing by targeting transport ships loading in port, at anchor, or loitering in coastal waters. These would include strikes against PLAN landing ships, a wide array of landing craft, hovercraft, and requisitioned merchant vessels. Aircraft and submarines would lay naval mines. As PLA forces approached the coast, the ROC would engage with ground-launched ASMs and other assets.

Interdicting airborne landing attempts would also be essential. Striking strategic transport aircraft based inland would be challenging, but helicopters would be required to operate along the mainland coast opposite Taiwan to make the round trip.

Cyber operations could be launched to disrupt PLA C4ISR as part of the counterlanding effort including Beijing's satellite coverage of Taiwan at the instance of landing. While the distributed nature of contemporary spaced-based surveillance assets would not make such disruption sustainable, employing such a capability at a critical moment could prove decisive.

The PLA will inevitably establish a ground-force presence in Taiwan of some type, ranging from relatively small special-forces units to a substantial conventional-force lodgment. Isolating them from reinforcements

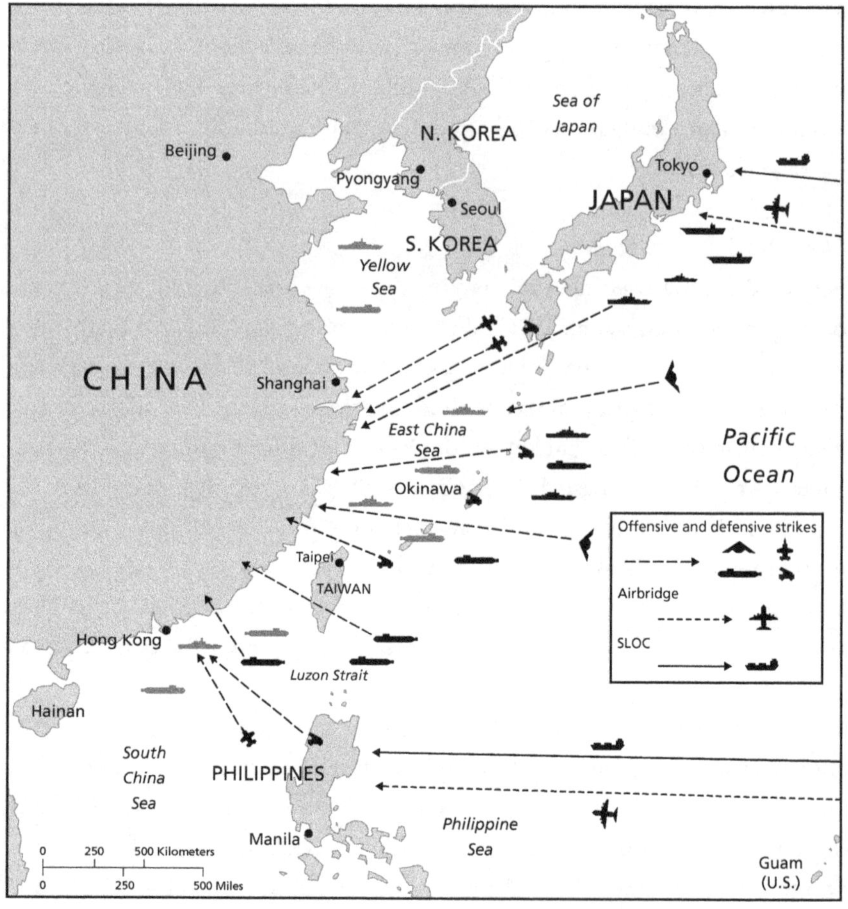

Phase III(a)—Seize the Initiative (Regional)

and resupply would be critical. They would then need to be contained and defeated—chiefly by the ROC's ground forces.

Turning the short-term defeat of a landing into wider success would require the degrading of PLA forces to the point where the ROC and its allies could secure sea and air links to the second island chain, even if accessing territory within it was initially limited to relatively brief windows in time, space, and circumstances. This would require the disruption of PLA C4ISR and network capabilities to the extent that the kill chain beyond these islands is severely disrupted while keeping U.S. systems functional enough to operate effectively.

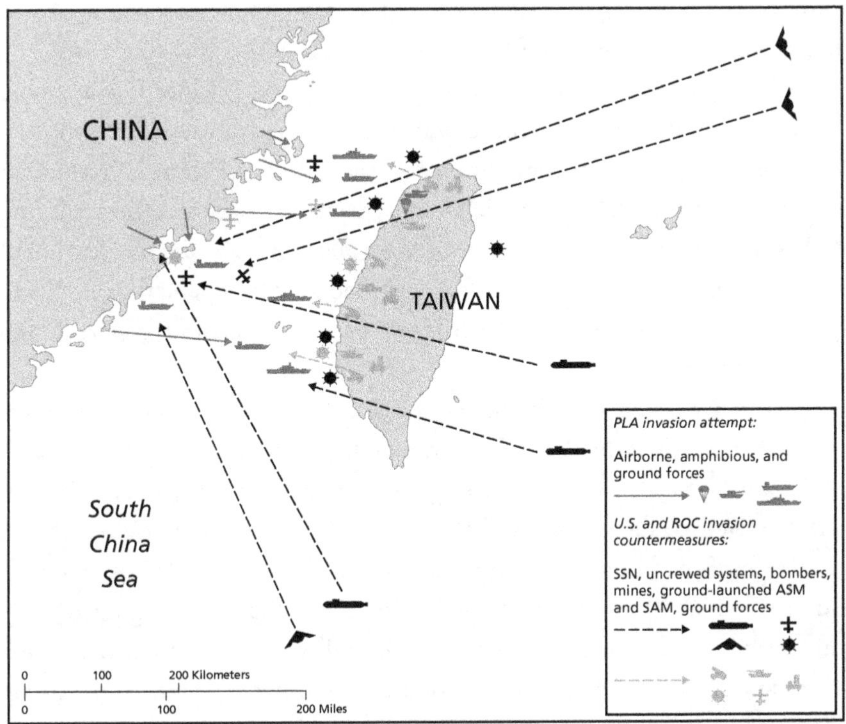

Phase III(b)—Seize the Initiative (Republic of China)

At this stage, the U.S. surface force, including carrier groups, can play a pivotal role. U.S. and JSDF aircraft and missile batteries at dispersed sites within Japan and the Philippines could provide a partial defensive "shield" to surface vessels, including carrier groups operating near the countries' coasts. This would allow surface vessels to be within 1,600 kilometers of the Chinese mainland, sufficient for TLAM strikes, carrier-based bomber escort, and potentially carrier-based mainland strikes using standoff munitions. Simultaneously, the USAF would accelerate the deployment of tactical aircraft to military and civilian airfields in Japan to bolster forces in theater to ensure air superiority over the Ryukyu Islands and augment bomber strikes on PLA coastal facilities, with offensive and defensive missile systems fielded in support. Similar assets would be deployed to the Philippines.

A blockade of the PRC will also be critical, coupled with an effort to "roll up" global PLA and wider military and intelligence-gathering assets through military and nonmilitary means. Allied forces unwilling or unequipped to engage near the Chinese mainland may find a role in this cluster of tasks.

While military mobilization begins during phase I, wider U.S. national resources would be a critical component of regaining and retaining the initiative. Using various emergency authorities, including the Defense Production Act, munitions production would rapidly increase as part of a wider surging and expansion of the defense industrial base and reconfiguration of disrupted supply chains. Additional forces would be generated to expand the joint force base, provide for force rotation and casualty replacements, and prepare for the postconflict environment.

Logistics requirements for activities east of Hawaii and many of the transits farther west will be dependent on mobilized civilian assets such as U.S. Merchant Marine shipping, including vessels under the MSP, TSP, VTA, and VISA, as well as allied vessels and chartered U.S. and foreign vessels. Notably, civilian tankers would be hastily modified to provide CONSOL support. Limited availability of escort vessels would mean that "bottling up" PLAN submarines and bombers within the first island chain would be critical. Such adversary assets that penetrate beyond this perimeter would be primarily engaged by aircraft flying from Hawaii, Alaska, the U.S. West Coast, and—once reasonably secure—Guam and other Pacific islands.

Phase IV: Prolonged Warfighting

Once the initiative is secured, the conflict will likely shift to a prolonged phase of warfare of variable intensity. The U.S.-led coalition would expand its maritime presence, aiming to neutralize the PLAN as an offensive fighting force and confine it to within the first island chain. A modicum of air and sea control will be obtained up to the edge of most of these islands, although Taiwan would remain too close to the mainland for all but the most limited access.

Allied operations will need to be "pulsed," with intense action during windows of temporary degradation of PLA defenses balanced with lulls in activity to prevent allied forces reaching a culmination point—that is, no longer having the capability to continue the mission due to issues such as attrition, exhaustion, and supply shortfalls. The U.S. Navy will have to rotate ships on station rather than risk burnout with an all-out surge. Estimates suggest that after an initial opening surge, only five or six U.S. SSNs forward at

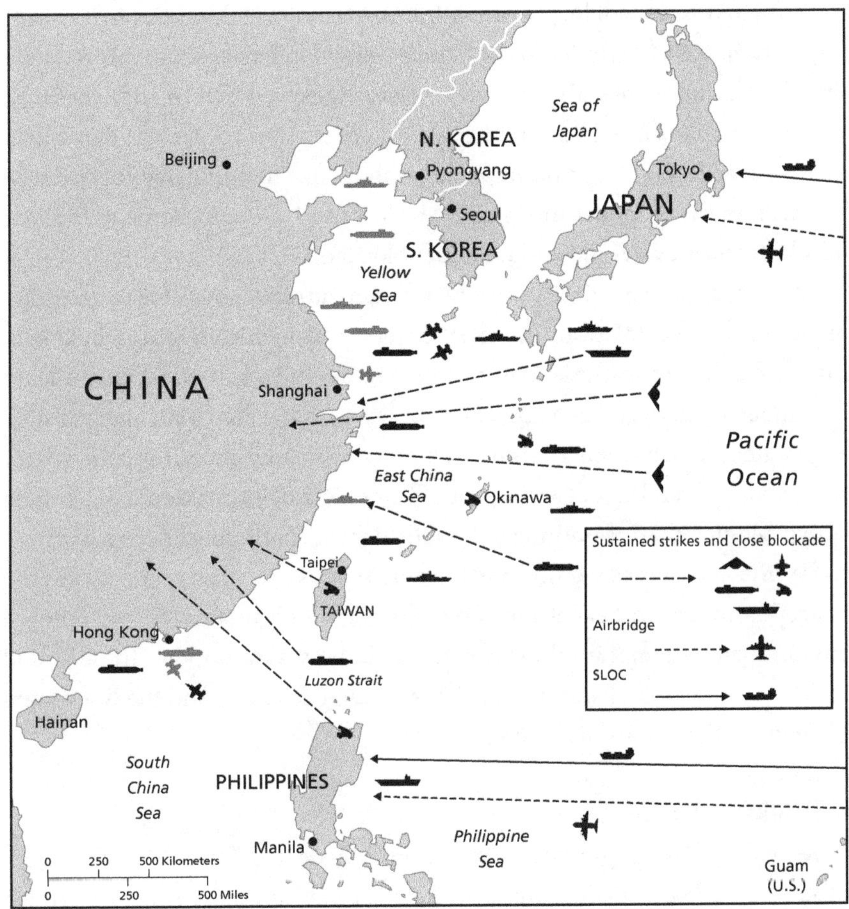

Phase IV—Prolonged Warfighting

any one time would be sustainable.[25] Given maintenance and repair requirements, it is also likely that only two or three carrier groups could be sustained forward at any one time, even assuming no attrition. After the defeat of the initial invasion attempt, a key question would be what targets to follow up with. A broad effort to strike target sets such as offensive military forces in southeast China or to suppress the PLA's regeneration capability by striking shipyards and defense-production sites would present an overwhelming challenge regarding the need to penetrate PLA defenses and the effort's munitions requirements.[26] A more selective approach is likely to be unavoidable unless the conflict continues for years.

A further issue will be providing life-sustaining commodities to Taiwan's population, as its proximity to the Chinese mainland makes resupply in quantity almost impossible. This is a major challenge given that in 2022 the ROC was over 97-percent reliant on imports for energy and 70-percent dependent on imported food.[27] Despite stockpiles—about one hundred days of crude oil and six months of food—much could be lost to PLA bombardment, limiting how long the island could endure under blockade.[28]

As noted, neither side is positioned to win outright, and there is a requirement to contain escalation. The exact criteria under which Beijing would consider a cessation of hostilities is uncertain. The desired result would be similar to that aimed for in the 1980s Maritime Strategy, with the PRC's strategy defeated and its global reach amputated but the mainland broadly intact, the ruling party still in control (and so not acting out of fear of loss of its position), and Beijing convinced that there is nothing to be gained from continuing operations.[29]

While U.S. forces would have to remain active to shape and sustain the peace—a return to peacetime campaigning, albeit in a drastically altered environment—demobilization efforts would be set in motion. These would include the transfer of assets back to the civilian economy and the drawdown of temporarily mobilized personnel.

ALTERNATIVE PATHWAYS

Several alternative pathways could significantly deviate from the above structure. While there is inadequate space here to examine them in detail, a sample is worthwhile.

The first and most apparent way reality might diverge from the OPLAN outlined is that the United States may take a strategic political decision not to intervene in a PRC attempt to conquer the ROC. What motivates this decision—isolationism, preoccupation with another crisis, or a simple assessment that it is either impossible or the risk does not justify the reward—hardly matters. Delayed decisions by the U.S. leadership—particularly with regard to regional forces making war preparations—could alter the course of the conflict but not halt it entirely.

There could also be a broader Chinese attempt to strike the CONUS including through capabilities they have not yet been proven to have deployed. This could include using conventionally armed ICBMs, missiles and UAVs launched from ostensibly commercial ships, and the extensive use of sabotage teams within the CONUS. Targets could include naval ships in port on both coasts, bomber and tanker bases, munitions-production facilities, and aircraft factories. The potential for such action is considerably higher than it was during the war against Imperial Japan.

The most urgent issue in the minds of many will be the risk of nuclear escalation as a policy decision. It is highly unlikely that the United States would use nuclear weapons first to prevent a successful invasion of Taiwan, but it is not an impossible scenario. Similarly, it is unlikely that the PRC would respond to U.S. conventional success with nuclear use, but this, too, is not out of the question.

It is also unclear what role China's allies would wish to take in such a conflict. Russia would likely offer political and economic support and intelligence collaboration at least. North Korea is a mixed picture: objectively, it would stand to gain by largely remaining aloof aside from minor provocative acts to distract the United States. Yet the development of the Korean Peninsula as an additional theater—in a perverse reversal of the position the two had in 1950—remains a possibility.

EPILOGUE

TOMORROW'S END

If we do our jobs right, the Lord willing,
history will never know our names.
—*Adm. Samuel John Paparo Jr.,*
USINDOPACOM commander,
February 14, 2024

Hector Charles Bywater died on August 17, 1940, living long enough to see tensions between the United States and Imperial Japan build to a near-crescendo but not bearing witness to the conflict he foresaw in his books.[1] The final paragraph of his 1921 volume asked whether Tokyo would have the acumen to avoid "a militarist gamble more reckless even than that which caused the ruin of the German Empire."[2] They did not.

Yet there is nothing inevitable about a twenty-first-century great power war in the Pacific. As we have seen, neither the possibility of aggression nor contingency plans to counter it make war a foregone conclusion. This has certainly so far been the case with Taiwan, with U.S. plans for the island's defense having been in place in some form since 1950—far longer than even the earliest drafts of War Plan Orange reached back before World War II—without a need for enacting them. We also have the knowledge that fractures between great powers can be managed over a multidecade timescale in the nuclear era. The United States and its allies never had to face the USSR in a strategic nuclear exchange, a battle over Western Europe, or counter a Soviet attack on Japan. The early war plans of the 1940s and 1950s, the SIOP, and the various OPLANs for general and regional war with the communist-ruled Soviet Union are now (partially) declassified historical documents rather than potentially the last thing someone with the required security clearance would ever read.

The ROC's dominion over Taiwan had inauspicious beginnings, starting with its only attraction to the United States being its anticommunist stance. This relationship would eventually evolve into a productive partnership serving the interest of both parties. Beijing's brief security marriage of convenience with the United States led to Washington abandoning joint defensive plans with Taipei and placing unilateral contingency options for preventing an invasion of Taiwan on the back burner. ROC liberalization from the late 1980s, the collapse of the USSR, and the PRC's growing power and actions in Tiananmen Square provided moral and practical motivation to steadily rebuild links between the United States and Taiwan. This process has only accelerated since the rise to power of Chairman Xi and the deepening of PRC authoritarianism and aggression in the South China Sea, Hong Kong, and beyond. In 2026 the ROC, while not a treaty ally of the United States, has a critical role to play in the containment of the threat from the PRC.

Technological shifts of the last century in weaponry, countermeasures, and strategy have been a mix of continuity and change. One constant has been the search for range and precision. From battleship gun elevation to ballistic missiles, the ability to strike an opponent at ever-increasing distance has been a persistent ambition. For those who have opposed the United States and possess the required resources, this has often been combined with a form of A2/AD warfare—chiefly in the maritime realm. Imperial Japan failed, and we will never know how the Soviets would have fared. It would be glib to talk about the "rise and fall" of nuclear weapons, but there were less than three decades between their appearance and the beginning of the success of a microchip-powered drive to create conventional weapons that could substitute for them in any type of warfare that would be rational to fight. Aircraft carriers, submarines, and strategic bombers—all came of age before the nuclear era then became essential components of it—have not only survived but also found new relevance with the brief "unipolar moment" of uncontested U.S. access to the global common coming to an end. The relatively new realms of space and cyber have emerged as important factors, but they remain facilitating, rather than decisive, areas of operation.

The United States is now back into the rhythm of great power competition and all that goes with it—including military planning. As we have seen, many challenges exist today in the Pacific that can benefit from lessons pulled directly from the last century of war planning. Yet while planning is essential, bad planning can portend disaster, be it of a theoretical nature, as was the case in the early versions of War Plan Orange and the OPLANs to defend Iran from the USSR, or actual fact, as seen in the aftermath of the invasion of Iraq. Furthermore, the challenges China presents are unlike those of the twentieth century, with the United States having neither the option of industrially steamrollering its opponent nor the desire to return to threatening a war of mutual suicide to sustain something resembling peace.

All periods of tension and war end. The Entente Cordiale marked the conclusion of a millennium of periodic conflict between Britain and France. Germany and Japan were brought into the liberal international system following World War II. Russia has not yet followed this trend, but its latest incarnation as a vicious nationalist dictatorship has seen it reduced to fighting for scraps of its former empire rather than continental hegemony, and the background specter of a potential Third World War that threatened for much of the USSR's existence never manifested. There is no reason to believe that China is locked into a course of inevitable conflict or destined to maintain its belligerent stance in perpetuity. Ironically, the presence of an alternative Chinese governance model on an island Beijing covets may be part of the formula for a resolution to tensions.

NOTES

INTRODUCTION

1. See, for example, Helen Davidson, "China Could Invade Taiwan in Next Six Years, Top U.S. Admiral Warns," *The Guardian*, Mar. 10, 2021, https://www.theguardian.com/world/2021/mar/10/china-could-invade-taiwan-in-next-six-years-top-us-admiral-warns (accessed Jan. 21, 2025); and Roxana Tiron, "China on Track to Be Ready to Invade Taiwan by 2027, U.S. Says," Bloomberg, Mar. 20, 2024, https://www.bloomberg.com/news/articles/2024-03-20/china-on-track-to-be-ready-for-taiwan-invasion-by-2027-us-says (accessed Jan. 21, 2025). For context over the timetable debate, see Noah Robertson, "How DC Became Obsessed with a Potential 2027 Chinese Invasion of Taiwan," *Defense News*, May 7, 2024, https://www.defensenews.com/pentagon/2024/05/07/how-dc-became-obsessed-with-a-potential-2027-chinese-invasion-of-taiwan/ (accessed Jan. 15, 2025).
2. See U.S. CNO, *Navigation Plan for America's Warfighting Navy 2024* (Washington, DC: Department of the Navy, 2024), https://s3.documentcloud.org/documents/25150208/770319356-cno-navigation-plan-2024.pdf (accessed Jan. 20, 2025).
3. U.S. DOD, *2022 National Defense Strategy of the United States of America* (Washington, DC: Office of the Secretary of Defense, 2022), 1, https://apps.dtic.mil/sti/trecms/pdf/AD1183514.pdf (accessed Jan. 21, 2025); Ely Ratner, statement before the U.S. Senate Committee on Foreign Relations, 117th Cong., Dec. 8, 2021, 3, https://www.foreign.senate.gov/imo/media/doc/120821_Ratner_Testimony.pdf (accessed Jan. 21, 2025).
4. U.S. DOD, *DOD Dictionary of Military and Associated Terms* (Washington, DC: JCS, November 2021), 17–18, https://irp.fas.org/doddir/dod/dictionary.pdf (accessed Jan. 23, 2025).
5. See Keith Burkepile, ed., *Campaign Planning Handbook, Academic Year 2024* (Carlisle Barracks, PA: U.S. Army War College, 2024), https://usawc-ssi-media.s3.us-east-1.amazonaws.com/misc/AY24-Campaign-Planning-Handbook.pdf (accessed May 23, 2025); U.S. JCS, *Joint Planning, Joint Publication 5-0* (Washington, DC: JCS, 2021), https://irp.fas.org/doddir/dod/jp5_0.pdf (accessed Jan. 21, 2025); U.S. JCS, *Joint Strategic Planning System* (Washington, DC: JCS, 2024), https://www.jcs.mil/Portals/36/Documents/Library/Instructions/CJCSI3100.01F.pdf (accessed Jan. 21, 2025); and U.S. JCS, *Management and Review of Campaign and Contingency Planning* (Washington, DC: JCS, 2019) https://www.jcs.mil/Portals/36/Documents/Library/Instructions/CJCSI3141.01F.pdf (accessed Jan. 21, 2025). For a history of the process, see Christopher D. Holmes and Francis J. Park, *History of Joint Staff Strategic Planning, 1949–2020*, Special Historical Study 14 (Washington, DC: Joint History and Research Office, Office of the CJCS, 2021). For practical reflections on the process, see Chad Pillai, "Developing a Combatant Command Campaign Plan: Lessons Learned at US Central Command," Modern War Institute at West Point, June 16, 2021, https://mwi

.westpoint.edu/developing-a-combatant-command-campaign-plan-lessons-learned-at-us-central-command/ (accessed Jan. 21, 2025).

6. Burkepile, *Campaign Planning Handbook*, 3–5, 7–11; U.S. JCS, *Joint Planning*, I-2, II-3–7.
7. Burkepile, *Campaign Planning Handbook.*, 5–7; U.S. JCS, *Joint Planning*, xvii, I-10, II-4–5.
8. Burkepile, *Campaign Planning Handbook*, 4, 14–16; U.S. JCS, *Joint Planning*, II-8, I-10, III-15.
9. Burkepile, *Campaign Planning Handbook*, 11–13. For full details, see U.S. JCS, *Joint Strategic Planning System*.
10. Burkepile, *Campaign Planning Handbook*, 1, 11–13; U.S. JCS, *Joint Strategic Planning System*, A-2–3, D-1. See also "Global Military Integration—Executive Summary for Fellows," Jan. 9, 2024, National Military University, https://capstone.ndu.edu/Portals/83/(U)CAPGIO20240109ExecutiveOverview.pdf (accessed Jan. 21, 2025); and Brandon J. Archuleta and Jonathan I. Gerson, "Fight Tonight Reenergizing the Pentagon for Great Power Competition," *Joint Forces Quarterly* 100 (1st Quarter 2020): 82–87, https://ndupress.ndu.edu/Portals/68/Documents/jfq/jfq-100/jfq-100_81-87_Archuleta-Gerson.pdf (accessed Jan. 27, 2025).
11. U.S. JCS, *Management and Review of Campaign and Contingency Planning*, A3.
12. Burkepile, *Campaign Planning Handbook*, 48–50; See also U.S. JCS, *Joint Planning*, V-1–17.
13. U.S. JCS, *Joint Planning* I-9.
14. Burkepile, *Campaign Planning Handbook*, 22–24.
15. Burkepile, 24–25; U.S. JCS, *Joint Planning*, xxvi, I-9.
16. U.S. JCS, *Joint Planning*, I-9–10.
17. Archuleta and Gerson, "Fight Tonight," 82.
18 U.S. JCS, *Joint Planning*, I-12–14.
19. Michael J. Mazarr et al., *The U.S. DOD's Planning Process: Components and Challenges* (Santa Monica, CA: RAND Corp., 2019), 30, https://www.rand.org/content/dam/rand/pubs/research_reports/RR2100/RR2173z2/RAND_RR2173z2.pdf (accessed Jan. 21, 2025); Anna Mulrine, "In His Memoir, Donald Rumsfeld Admits Five Mistakes, Sort Of," *Christian Science Monitor*, Feb. 9, 2011, https://www.csmonitor.com/USA/Military/2011/0209/In-his-memoir-Donald-Rumsfeld-admits-five-mistakes-sort-of/The-Army-you-have (accessed May 23, 2025).
20. Burkepile, *Campaign Planning Handbook*, 50.
21. Burkepile, 26, 184–85; U.S. JCS, *Joint Planning*, I-23.
22. U.S. JCS, *Joint Strategic Planning System*, D-4–5.
23. Burkepile, *Campaign Planning Handbook*, 51–53; U.S. JCS, *Joint Planning*, I-11–12.
24. U.S. JCS, *Joint Planning*, GL-12.
25. U.S. JCS, I-1; U.S. DOD, *DOD Dictionary*, 176.
26. The original article was part of William M. Arkin, "America's New China War Plan," *Early Warning* (blog), *Washington Post*, May 24, 2006 (blog discontinued). For extracts from Arkin, see Russell Hsiao, "Fortnightly Review," *Global Taiwan Brief* 5, no. 15 (July 29, 2020), https://globaltaiwan.org/2020/07/fortnightly-review-8/ (accessed Jan. 21, 2025).
27. U.S. DOD, Inspector General, *Follow up Audit: Basic Expeditionary Airfield Resources Support and Repair Spare Kits* (Redacted), DODIG-2018-029 (Washington, DC, 2017), https://media.defense.gov/2017/Nov/20/2001846115/-1/-1/1/DODIG-2018-029.PDF (accessed May 23, 2025).

28. The templates vary in exact layout detail. See Burkepile, *Campaign Planning Handbook*, 223–27; U.S. JCS, *Joint Planning*, app. A, A-1–10.
29. U.S. JCS, *Joint Planning*, IV-37–38.
30. Annexes typically include A (Task Organization), B (Intelligence), C (Operations), D (Logistics), J (Command Relationships), K (Command, Control, Communications, and Computer Systems), S (Special Technical Operations), V (Interagency Interorganizational Coordination), and Z (Distribution).
31. For a partially declassified (June 2015) real-world example, see Headquarters, U.S. Central Command, "USCENTCOM, OPLAN 1003V—Change 1," Feb. 27, 2023, MacDill Air Force Base, FL, 22, 25, 28, 32, U.S. Army Heritage and Education Center, https://ahec.armywarcollege.edu/CENTCOM-IRAQ-papers/0987.%201003V27Feb03.pdf (accessed Jan. 21, 2025). See the entire document for a draft of the main body of OPLAN 1003V.
32. Nora Bensahel, Olga Oliker, Keith Crane, Richard R. Brennan Jr., Heather S. Gregg, Thomas Sullivan, and Andrew Rathmell, *After Saddam: Prewar Planning and the Occupation of Iraq* (Santa Monica, CA: RAND Corp., 2008), 10–11, https://www.rand.org/content/dam/rand/pubs/monographs/2008/RAND_MG642.sum.pdf (accessed Jan. 21, 2025).
33. Walter Perry, "Planning the War and the Transition to Peace," in *Operation Iraqi Freedom: Decisive War, Elusive Peace*, ed. Walter L. Perry, Richard E. Darilek, Laurinda L. Rohn, and Jerry M. Sollinger (Santa Monica, CA: RAND Corp., 2016), 40, https://www.rand.org/pubs/research_reports/RR1214.html (accessed Jan. 21, 2025).

CHAPTER 1. FROM ORANGE TO RAINBOW

1. Michael L. Green, *By More Than Providence: Grand Strategy and American Power in the Asia Pacific since 1783* (New York: Columbia University Press, 2017), 46, 48; Michael Turton, "America, Taiwan, and the Inevitability of History," *American Citizens for Taiwan*, June 16, 2018, https://medium.com/american-citizens-for-taiwan/america-taiwan-and-the-inevitability-of-history-9b5f8eba2f09 (accessed Jan. 21, 2025). See also Thomas R. Cox, "Harbingers of Change: American Merchants and the Formosa Annexation Scheme," *Pacific Historical Review* 42, no. 2 (May 1973): 163–84, https://doi.org/10.2307/3638465 (accessed Jan. 21, 2025).
2. Louis Morton, "War Plan Orange: Evolution of a Strategy," *World Politics* 11, no. 2 (Jan. 1959): 221–22, https://www.jstor.org/stable/2009529 (accessed Jan. 21, 2025). See also Michael K. Doyle, "The U.S. Navy and War Plan Orange, 1933–1940: Making Necessity a Virtue," *Naval War College Review* 33, no. 3 (May–June 1980): 49–63, https://www.jstor.org/stable/44642633 (accessed Jan. 21, 2025).
3. For an overview of the Naval War College's role, see Michael Vlahos, "The Naval War College and the Origins of War-Planning against Japan," *Naval War College Review* 33, no. 4 (July–Aug. 1980): 23–41, https://www.jstor.org/stable/44642074 (accessed Jan. 21, 2025). For an overview of the Army War College's role, see Henry G. Gole, *The Road to Rainbow: Army Planning for Global War, 1934–1940* (Annapolis, MD: Naval Institute Press, 2003).
4. Edward S. Miller, *War Plan Orange: The U.S. Strategy to Defeat Japan, 1897–1945* (Annapolis, MD: Naval Institute Press, 1991), 88–91, 98–99.
5. Miller, 36, 75.

6. Miller, 32–36, 54, 79, 93-94, 103, 111, 119, 151, 159–61, 190. For a broader analysis, see Miller, chaps. 7, 9, 10.
7. See Miller, 29–30, 35–36, 77–79, 203–5. For more detail, see Miller, chaps. 8, 10–11, 22.
8. Miller, 28, 33.
9. See Miller, chap. 26.
10. Ian Easton, *Invasion Plans: Operation Causeway and Taiwan's Defense in World War II*, China Maritime Report 42 (Newport, RI: U.S. Naval War College, 2024), 4, U.S. Naval War College Digital Commons, https://digital-commons.usnwc.edu/cgi/viewcontent.cgi?article=1042&context=cmsi-maritime-reports (accessed Jan. 15, 2025); Miller, *War Plan Orange*, 154–57.
11. Miller, *War Plan Orange*, 362.
12. Miller, 4–5, 203–5, and chap. 14.
13. See Gole, *Road to Rainbow*, chap. 5.
14. Steven T. Ross, *American War Plans, 1941–1945: The Test of Battle* (London: Frank Cass, 1997), 4–6, 16–17; Ross, *American War Plans, 1919–1941* (New York: Garland, 1992), 70–72, 79–81. For an overview of the development process, see Mark E. Grotelueschen, "Joint Planning for Global Warfare: The Development of the Rainbow Plans in the United States, 1938–1941," *Army History* 97 (Fall 2015): 8–27, https://www.jstor.org/stable/26300432 (accessed Jan. 21, 2025); and Col. Brit K. Erslev, "U.S. Joint War Planning for Twentieth-Century Large-Scale Combat Operations: Case Studies and Implications for Current Joint Planners" (master's thesis, School of Advanced Military Studies, U.S. Army Command and General Staff College, 2020), 18–19, https://apps.dtic.mil/sti/citations/trecms/AD1160006 (accessed Jan. 21, 2025).
15. Adm. Harold Stark, "'Memorandum for the Secretary,' Navy Department, Office for the Chief of Naval Operations," Nov. 12, 1940, FDR Presidential Library and Museum, http://docs.fdrlibrary.marist.edu/psf/box4/a48b01.html (and subsequent links to the remaining twenty-five pages) (accessed Jan. 21, 2025).
16. Ross, *American War Plans, 1941–1945*, 8, 16–17.
17. Exhibit 4, "Rainbow 5," in *Hearings before the Joint Committee on the Investigation of the Pearl Harbor Attack*, 79th Cong., 1st sess., pt. 33 (Washington, DC: Government Printing Office, 1946), 926–85, http://www.ibiblio.org/pha/pha/misc/rainbow5.html (accessed Jan. 21, 2025).
18. Miller, *War Plan Orange*, 274. For the full document, see Exhibit 16, "From: Commander-in-Chief, U.S. Pacific Fleet; Subject: WPPac-46," July 25, 1941, in *Hearings before the Joint Committee on the Investigation of the Pearl Harbor Attack*, 500–501, https://www.ibiblio.org/pha/timeline/410725apac.html (accessed Jan. 21, 2025).
19. Exhibit 16, "WPPac-46," 499–500.
20. List taken from Exhibit 16, 500.
21. Adapted from Exhibit 16, 500–502.
22. Exhibit 16, 518–20.
23. Exhibit 4, "Rainbow 5," 964.
24. U.S. War Department, *War Department Operations Plan, Rainbow No. 5* (1941), 10, Ike Skelton Combined Arms Research Library Digital Library, https://cgsc.contentdm.oclc.org/digital/collection/p4013coll8/id/4282/ (accessed Jan. 21, 2025).

25. Miller, *War Plan Orange*, 60–62.
26. Account of reinforcements and planning from Louis Morton, *The Fall of the Philippines*, United States Army in World War Two: The War in the Pacific (1953; repr., Washington, DC: Center of Military History U.S. Army, 1993), 31–50, 61–71, https://history.army.mil/Portals/143/Images/Publications/PublicationByTitleImages/FPdf/CMH_Pub_5-2-1.pdf (accessed May. 21, 2025); Morton, *Strategy and Command: The First Two Years*, United States Army in World War Two: The War in the Pacific (1962; repr., Washington, DC: Center of Military History U.S. Army, 2000), 98–100, https://history.army.mil/Portals/143/Images/Publications/PublicationByTitleImages/SPDF/CMH_Pub_5-1.pdf (accessed May 21, 2025); and Miller, *War Plan Orange*, 60–62.
27. Morton, *Fall of the Philippines*, 21–22, 25–31.
28. Cdr. Malcolm A. LeCompte, "Radar and the Air Battles of Midway," *Naval History Magazine* 6, no. 2 (June 1992), https://www.usni.org/magazines/naval-history-magazine/1992/june/radar-and-air-battles-midway (accessed Jan. 21, 2025). Battleship modernization data from John J. Kuehn, *Agents of Innovation: The General Board and the Design of the Fleet That Defeated the Japanese Navy* (Annapolis, MD: Naval Institute Press, 2008), 63–87, Kindle; and Norman Friedman, "Armaments and Innovations—The Launch of Navy Radar," *Naval History Magazine* 27, no. 4 (July 2013), https://www.usni.org/magazines/naval-history-magazine/2013/july/armaments-and-innovations-launch-navy-radar (accessed Jan. 21, 2025).
29. For an overview, see Albert A. Nofi, *To Train the Fleet for War: The U.S. Navy Fleet Problems, 1923–1940*, Historical Monographs 18 (Newport, RI: U.S. Naval War College, 2020), https://permanent.fdlp.gov/gpo150777/HM_18_To_Train_the_Fleet_for_War_The_U.S._Navy_Fleet_Problems.pdf (accessed Jan. 21, 2025). For their applicability to modern A2/AD scenarios, see Daniel Kostecka, "Fleet Problem IX and the Enduring Lessons for the Anti-Access Dilemma," CIMSEC, Aug. 5, 2021, https://cimsec.org/fleet-problem-ix-and-enduring-lessons-for-the-anti-access-dilemma (accessed Jan. 21, 2025).
30. See Kuehn, *Agents of Innovation*, 125–31, 132–43; and U.S. Marine Corps, *Advanced Base Operations in Micronesia* (1921; rev. ed., Washington DC: Department of Navy, 1992), Black Vault, https://www.theblackvault.com/documents/wwii/marine1/1246.pdf (accessed Jan. 21, 2025).
31. Gole, *Road to Rainbow*, xvi. For further analysis of industrial mobilization, see Lt. Col. Thomas D. Morgan, "The Industrial Mobilization of World War II: America Goes to War," *Army History* 30 (Spring 1994): 31–35, https://www.jstor.org/stable/26304207 (accessed Jan. 21, 2025).
32. Michael D. Hull, "FDR & His Mighty Navy," U.S. Naval Institute *Proceedings* 33, no. 1 (Feb. 2019), https://www.usni.org/magazines/naval-history-magazine/2019/february/fdr-his-mighty-navy.
33. Kiyoshi Aizawa, "Japanese Strategy in the First Phase of the Pacific War," research paper presented at the Ninth NIDS International Forum on War History (2010), 33–37 https://www.nids.mod.go.jp/english/event/forum/pdf/2009/04.pdf (accessed Jan. 21, 2025).
34. Tomoyuki Wada, "Japanese Perspective Total War," research paper presented at the Tenth NIDS International Forum on War History (2011), 143, https://www.nids.mod.go.jp/english/event/forum/pdf/2011/17.pdf (accessed Jan. 21, 2025).

35. Phase model taken from David C. Evans and Mark R. Peattie, *Kaigun: Strategy, Tactics, and Technology in the Imperial Japanese Navy, 1887–1941* (Barnsley, Eng.: Seaforth, 2012), 464. For slight variations on this model, see Himadri Bose, "Influence of Alfred Thayer Mahan on Japanese Maritime Strategy," *Journal of Defence Studies* 14, no. 1–2 (Jan.–June 2020): 60–61, https://www.idsa.in/system/files/jds/14-2-2020-influence-of-alfred-thayer-mahan-hbose.pdf (accessed May 21, 2025). Bose assumes the destruction of local units before the operation and identifies the first phase as "Scouting." Phase III would have opened up with a night attack by torpedo-armed cruisers and destroyers. See also Capt. Yoji Koda, "A Commander's Dilemma: Admiral Yamamoto and the 'Gradual Attrition' Strategy," *Naval War College Review* 46, no. 4 (Autumn 1993): 66–69, https://www.jstor.org/stable/44642525 (accessed Jan. 21, 2025).
36. For the plan's development, see Evans and Peattie, *Kaigun*, 471–77.
37. See Evans and Peattie, 238–49, 295, 334, 357–60.
38. See Evans and Peattie, 250–63, 293–95; and Yôichi Hirama, "Japanese Naval Preparations for World War II," *Naval War College Review* 44, no. 2 (Spring 1991): 72, https://www.jstor.org/stable/44638027 (accessed Jan. 24, 2025).
39. See Evans and Peattie, *Kaigun*, 266–72; and Bob Poling, "A2/AD and the Long-Lance Torpedo," CIMSEC, Aug. 15, 2017, https://cimsec.org/long-lance-anti-access-area-denial/ (accessed Jan. 24, 2025).
40. See Evans and Peattie, *Kaigun*, 308–12.
41. See Evans and Peattie, 307, 312; and Hirama, "Japanese Naval Preparations," 72.
42. For details of the development of the fleet, see Carl Boyd and Akihiko Yoshida, *The Japanese Submarine Force in World War II* (Annapolis, MD: Naval Institute Press, 1995), 8–35. For prewar planning for their use, see Evans and Peattie, *Kaigun*, 428–34.
43. See Evans and Peattie, *Kaigun*, 395–398.
44. George H. Kerr, *Formosa Betrayed*, 2nd ed. (Irvine, CA: Taiwan Publishing, 1992), 7. For a 1943 analysis, see James K. Eyre Jr., "Formosa, Japan's Southern Naval Bastion," U.S. Naval Institute *Proceedings* 69/3/481 (Mar. 1943), https://www.usni.org/magazines/proceedings/1943/march/formosa-japans-southern-naval-bastion (accessed Jan. 27, 2025).
45. For an account, see Morton, *Fall of the Philippines*, 81–88.
46. John J. Domalgalski, "Disaster at Cavite," *Naval History Magazine* 32, no. 6 (Dec. 2018), https://www.usni.org/magazines/naval-history-magazine/2018/december/disaster-cavite (accessed Jan. 21, 2025).
47. Morton, *Fall of the Philippines*, 156.
48. Morton, 161, 163–64.
49. Brian Lane Herder, *Early Pacific Raids 1942: The American Carriers Strike Back* (Oxford: Bloomsbury, 2023), 8, 24, 35–56, 66–75, 78–89. For a contemporary account of these operations, see Office of Naval Intelligence, *Early Raids in the Pacific Ocean, February 1 to March 10, 1942: Marshall and Gilbert Islands, Rabaul, Wake and Marcus, Lae, and Salamaua* (1943; repr., Washington, DC: Office of Naval Intelligence, 2017), https://www.history.navy.mil/content/dam/nhhc/browse-by-topic/WarandConflict/WWII/Early-Raids-170407.pdf (accessed Jan. 21, 2025).
50. Adapted from OPNAV Support Section, *Richmond Kelly Turner: Planning the Pacific War* (Washington, DC: Naval History and Heritage Command, 2021), 32, https://www

.govinfo.gov/content/pkg/GOVPUB-D221-PURL-gpo171981/pdf/GOVPUB-D221-PURL-gpo171981.pdf (accessed May. 21, 2025).

51. LeCompte, "Radar and the Air Battles of Midway."

52. Walter G. Berl, "Annotated Bumblebee Initial Report February 1945," John Hopkins Applied Physics Laboratory *Technical Digest* 3, no. 2 (1982): 172, https://secwww.jhuapl.edu/techdigest/Content/techdigest/pdf/V03-N02/03-02-Berl.pdf (accessed Jan. 21, 2025).

53. See Lt. Col. Mark E. Kipphut, *Crossbow and Gulf War Counter-Scud Efforts: Lessons from History*, USAF Counterproliferation Center Future War Series 15 (Maxwell Air Force Base, AL: Air University Press, 2003), 6–10, https://media.defense.gov/2019/Apr/11/2002115481/-1/-1/0/15crossbow.pdf (accessed Jan. 21, 2025).

54. Steven J. Zaloga, *Kamikaze: Japanese Special Attack Weapons, 1944–45* (London: Osprey, 2011), 46–47, Kindle.

55. Shawn R. Woodford, '"The Most Difficult Antiaircraft Problem Yet Faced by the Fleet": U.S. Navy vs. Kamikazes at Okinawa," Naval History and Heritage Command, June 18, 2020, https://www.history.navy.mil/browse-by-topic/wars-conflicts-and-operations/world-war-ii/1945/battle-of-okinawa/antiaircraft-problem.html (accessed Jan. 21, 2025); Trent Hone, "Countering the Kamikaze," *Naval History Magazine* 34, no. 5 (Oct. 2020), https://www.usni.org/magazines/naval-history-magazine/2020/october/countering-kamikaze (accessed Jan. 27, 2025).

56. Hone, "Countering the Kamikaze"; Norman Friedman, *Fighters over the Fleet: Naval Air Defense from Biplanes to the Cold War* (Barnsley, Eng.: Seaforth, 2016), 474–75, 479–86, Kindle.

57. Walter O'Neill, "Operation Gi: The Japanese Attack on Yontan Airbase Okinawa," Medium, Feb. 6, 2022, https://wjon3117.medium.com/operation-gi-the-japanese-attack-on-yontan-airbase-okinawa-d1fa340b0e3d; Osamu Tagaya, *Mitsubishi Type 1 Rikko "Betty" Units of World War 2* (London: Osprey, 2013), 189–93, Kindle.

58. Wesley Frank Craven and James Lea Cate, *The Army Air Forces in World War II: The Pacific: Matterhorn to Nagasaki, June 1944 to August 1945* (Washington, DC: Office of Air Force History, 1948), xviii, https://www.ibiblio.org/hyperwar/AAF/V/index.html (accessed Jan. 21, 2025).

59. Alvin D. Coox, "Air War against Japan," in *Case Studies in the Achievement of Air Superiority*, ed. Benjamin Franklin Cooling (Washington, DC: Center for Air Force History, 1994), 410–12, https://media.defense.gov/2010/Oct/12/2001330116/-1/-1/0/AFD-101012-038.pdf (accessed Jan. 21, 2025).

60. Hector C. Bywater, *The Great Pacific War: A History of the American-Japanese Campaign of 1931–33* (Boston: Houghton Mifflin, 1925), 21–25, https://babel.hathitrust.org/cgi/pt?id=uc1.31822013308325&seq=9 (accessed Jan. 21, 2025).

61. See Fredrick M. Sallagar, *Lessons from an Aerial Mining Campaign (Operation "Starvation")* (Santa Monica, CA: RAND Corp., 1974), https://www.rand.org/content/dam/rand/pubs/reports/2006/R1322.pdf (accessed Jan. 21, 2025).

62. James M. Scott, "America's Undersea War on Shipping," *Naval History Magazine* 28, no.6 (Dec. 2014), https://www.usni.org/magazines/naval-history-magazine/2014/december/americas-undersea-war-shipping (accessed Jan. 21, 2025); Cdr. Stanley A. Wheeler, "The Lost Merchant Fleet of Japan," U.S. Naval Institute *Proceedings* 82/12/646 (Dec. 1956),

https://www.usni.org/magazines/proceedings/1956/december/lost-merchant-fleet-japan (accessed Jan. 21, 2025).

63. See Brian Lane Herder, *The Naval Siege of Japan: War Plan Orange Triumphant* (Oxford: Bloomsbury, 2020).
64. For a full account of Pacific War naval logistics, see Worrall Reed Carter, *Beans, Bullets, and Black Oil: The Story of Fleet Logistics Afloat in the Pacific during World War Two* (1953; repr., San Francisco: Verdun, 2015), Kindle. For a study of Service Squadron Ten, see W. R. Carter, "Seron Ten," U.S. Naval Institute *Proceedings* 74/2/540 (Feb. 1948), https://www.usni.org/magazines/proceedings/1948/february/seron-ten (accessed Jan. 21, 2025).
65. For the occupation preparations, see Leonard Gordon, "American Planning for Taiwan, 1942–1945," *Pacific Historical Review* 37, no. 2 (May 1968): 205–8.
66. Kerr, *Formosa Betrayed*, 26.
67. Robert Ross Smith, *Triumph in the Philippines*, United States Army in World War Two: The Pacific War (1963; repr., Washington, DC: Center for Military History, 1993), 4; "Causeway Joint Staff Study," U.S. Pacific Fleet, 1944, 2–4, https://apps.dtic.mil/sti/pdfs/ADA606376.pdf (accessed Jan. 21, 2025); Kerr, *Formosa Betrayed*, 28–33.
68. For a detailed analysis of Operation Causeway, see Easton, *Invasion Plans*.
69. Adapted from "Causeway Joint Staff Study," 4, 12–14.
70. "Causeway Joint Staff Study," 7, 9.
71. For accounts of the debate over the invasion of Formosa, see Kerr, *Formosa Betrayed*, 28–33, 35; Smith, *Triumph in the Philippines*, 4–17; and Gordon, "American Planning for Taiwan," 221–25.
72. See VAdm. Shigeru Fukudome, "Strategic Aspects of the Battle off Formosa," U.S. Naval Institute *Proceedings* 78/21/598 (Dec. 1952), https://www.usni.org/magazines/proceedings/1952/december/strategic-aspects-battle-formosa (accessed Jan. 21, 2025).

CHAPTER 2. AFTERMATH

1. Office of the Supreme Commander for the Allied Powers, "General Order No. 1," Sept. 2, 1945, 2, https://www.mofa.go.jp/mofaj/files/000097066.pdf (accessed Jan. 21, 2025).
2. Xiaobing Li, *The History of Taiwan* (Santa Barbara, CA: Greenwood, 2019), 116.
3. Michael Forsythe, "Taiwan Turns Light on 1947 Slaughter by Chiang Kai-shek's Troops," *New York Times*, July 14, 2015, https://www.nytimes.com/2015/07/15/world/asia/taiwan-turns-light-on-1947-slaughter-by-chiang-kai-sheks-troops.html (accessed Jan. 21, 2025).
4. Martial law was in place from February 28 to March 2; from March 9 to May 16, 1947; then from May 20, 1949, to July 15, 1987.
5. U.S Central Intelligence Agency, "Prospects for a Negotiated Peace in China," e-Asia Digital Library, Oregon Digital, Aug. 3, 1948, 5, https://oregondigital.org/concern/documents/df72ds73n?locale=en#page/1/mode/1up (accessed Jan. 21, 2025).
6. Hsiao-Ting Lin, *Accidental State: Chiang Kei-Shek, the United States, and the Making of Taiwan* (Cambridge, MA: Harvard University Press, 2016), 77, 83, 85.
7. Han Cheung, "Taiwan in Time: The Great Retreat," *Taipei Times*, Dec. 4, 2016, https://www.taipeitimes.com/News/feat/archives/2016/12/04/2003660529 (accessed Jan. 21, 2025).
8. U.S. DOS, OOTH, *FRUS, 1949, The Far East: China, Volume IX*, ed. Francis C. Prescott, Herbert A. Fine, and Velma Hastings Cassidy (Washington, DC: Government Printing

Office, 1974), Document 291, https://history.state.gov/historicaldocuments/frus1949v09/d291 (accessed Jan. 21, 2025).

9. U.S. DOS, Document 291.
10. U.S. DOS, Document 408, https://history.state.gov/historicaldocuments/frus1949v09/d408 (accessed Jan. 21, 2025).
11. U.S. DOS, Document 298, https://history.state.gov/historicaldocuments/frus1949v09/d298 (accessed Jan. 21, 2025).
12. U.S. DOS, Document 310, https://history.state.gov/historicaldocuments/frus1949v09/d310 (accessed Feb. 14, 2025).
13. U.S. DOS, Document 314, https://history.state.gov/historicaldocuments/frus1949v09/d314 (accessed Jan. 21, 2025).
14. U.S. DOS, Document 320, https://history.state.gov/historicaldocuments/frus1949v09/d320 (accessed Jan. 21, 2025).
15. U.S. DOS, Document 320.
16. U.S. DOS, Document 408.
17. U.S. DOS, Document 414, https://history.state.gov/historicaldocuments/frus1949v09/d414 (accessed May. 21, 2025).
18. U.S. DOS, Document 431, https://history.state.gov/historicaldocuments/frus1949v09/d431 (accessed Jan. 21, 2025).
19. U.S. DOS, Document 488, https://history.state.gov/historicaldocuments/frus1949v09/d488 (accessed May 21, 2025); U.S. DOS, OOTH, *FRUS, 1949, The Far East and Australasia, Volume VII, Part 2*, ed. John G. Reid John P. Glennon (Washington, DC: Government Printing Office, 1976), Document 387, https://history.state.gov/historicaldocuments/frus1949v07p2/d387 (accessed Jan. 21, 2025).
20. John W. Garver, *The Sino-American Alliance: Nationalist China and American Cold War Strategy in Asia* (1997; repr., London: Routledge, 2015),
21. "The President's News Conference," Harry S. Truman Library and Museum, Jan. 5, 1950, https://www.trumanlibrary.gov/library/public-papers/3/presidents-news conference (accessed Jan. 21, 2025).
22. Dean Acheson, "Speech on the Far East," Jan. 20, 1950, Teaching American History, https://teachingamericanhistory.org/document/speech-on-the-far-east/ (accessed May 18, 2025).
23. He Di, "'The Last Campaign to Unify China': The CCP's Unmaterialized Plan to Liberate Taiwan, 1949–1950," *Chinese Historians* 5, no.1 (1992): 4. For additional accounts of the plans and buildup to the aborted invasion of Taiwan, see Ian Easton, *The Chinese Invasion Threat Taiwan's Defense and America's Strategy in Asia* (Arlington, VA: Project 2049 Institute, 2017), 37–57; and Jon W. Huebner, "The Abortive Liberation of Taiwan," *China Quarterly* 110 (June 1987): 256–75, https://www.jstor.org/stable/653999 (accessed Jan. 21, 2025).
24. Di, "'Last Campaign to Unify China,'" 1–5.
25. Toshi Yoshihara, *Mao's Army Goes to Sea: The Island Campaign and the Founding of China's Navy* (Washington DC: Georgetown University Press, 2022), 123–30, Kindle; Maochun Miles Yu, "The Battle of Quemoy: The Amphibious Assault That Held the Postwar Military Balance in the Taiwan Strait," *Naval War College Review* 69, no. 2 (Spring 2016): 94–96, https://www.jstor.org/stable/26397935 (accessed Jan. 21, 2025).
26. Di, "'Last Campaign to Unify China,'" 6–7.

27. Di, 8–10.
28. Di, 10. Exact figures vary by source.
29. Easton, *Chinese Invasion Threat,* 45.
30. Di, "'Last Campaign to Unify China,'" 11.
31. Di, 12.
32. U.S. DOS, OOTH, *FRUS, 1950, Korea, Volume VII,* ed. John P. Glennon (Washington, DC: Government Printing Office, 1974), Document 86, https://history.state.gov/historicaldocuments/frus1950v07/d86 (accessed Jan. 21, 2025).

CHAPTER 3. THE PLURAL OF APOCALYPSE

1. Steven T. Ross, *American War Plans, 1945–1950* (London: Routledge, 1996), 3–4, Kindle. Contrary to initial reports (such as the one in the epigraph), B-47s could be fitted with conventional-bomb racks in about ten hours, but SAC was unhappy with such a move. See M. H. Halperin, *The 1958 Taiwan Straits Crisis: A Documented History* (Santa Monica, CA: RAND Corp., 1966), 149, https://archive.org/details/The1958TaiwanStraitsCrisisADocumentedHistory_201712/page/n52/mode/1up (accessed Jan. 22, 2025).
2. James R Schnabel, *The Joint Chiefs of Staff and National Policy,* vol. 1, *1945–1947,* History of the Joint Chiefs of Staff (Washington, DC: Office of Joint History, Office of the CJCS, 1996), 70–74, https://apps.dtic.mil/sti/tr/pdf/ADA323795.pdf (accessed May 21, 2025); Ross, *American War Plans, 1945–1950,* 25, 31–33.
3. Ross, *American War Plans, 1945–1950,* 24, 27, 31.
4. Sean M. Maloney, *Emergency War Plan: The American Doomsday Machine, 1945–1960* (Lincoln: University of Nebraska Press, 2021), 28, Kindle.
5. For a full overview, see Ross, *American War Plans, 1945–1950.*
6. For an overview of late–World War II and early postwar naval planning, see Clare Scammell, "Anglo-American Strategic Cooperation: The Role of Carrier Aviation in Western Strategy, 1945–1955" (PhD diss., King's College London, 2002), 80–93, 98–100, 189–90, https://kclpure.kcl.ac.uk/ws/portalfiles/portal/2933044/272027.pdf (accessed Jan. 22, 2025).
7. Samuel P. Huntington, "National Policy and the Transoceanic Navy," U.S. Naval Institute *Proceedings* 80/5/615 (May 1954), https://www.usni.org/magazines/proceedings/1954/may/national-policy-and-transoceanic-navy (accessed Jan. 22, 2025).
8. Michael A. Palmer, *Origins of the Maritime Strategy: American Naval Strategy in the First Postwar Decade* (Washington, DC: Naval Historical Center, 1988), 12–13.
9. See Robert E. Fisher, "The U.S. Navy's Search for a Strategy, 1945–1947," *Naval War College Review* 48, no. 3 (Summer 1995): 79–84, https://www.jstor.org/stable/44642808 (accessed Jan. 22, 2025).
10. Fleet. Adm. Chester W. Nimitz, "The Future Employment of Naval Forces," in *The Legacy of American Naval Power: Reinvigorating Maritime Strategic Thought—an Anthology,* ed. Paul Westermeyer (Quantico, VA: USMC History Division, 2019), 136, https://www.govinfo.gov/content/pkg/GOVPUB-D214-PURL-gpo119074/pdf/GOVPUB-D214-PURL-gpo119074.pdf (accessed Jan. 24, 2025).
11. Palmer, *Origins of the Maritime Strategy,* 74.

12. Adm. Forrest Sherman, "Top Secret Presentation to the President, Senate and House," no. 26, box 8, Sherman Papers, quoted in Palmer, 30, 88.
13. Palmer, 29, 88.
14. Lester J. Foltos, "The New Pacific Barrier: America's Search for Security in the Pacific, 1945–47," *Diplomatic History* 13, no. 3 (Summer 1989): 319–22, https://www.jstor.org/stable/24911748 (accessed Jan. 22, 2025).
15. Friedman, *Fighters over the Fleet*, 831–32.
16. "Nuclear Weapons at Sea—Heavy Attack," *Naval Gazing* (blog), May 13, 2020, https://www.navalgazing.net/Nuclear-Weapons-at-Sea-Heavy-Attack.
17. Jeffry G. Barlow, *Revolt of the Admirals: The Fight for Naval Aviation, 1945–1950* (Washington, DC: National Historic Center, Dept. of Navy, 1995), 137, Kindle.
18. Maloney, *Emergency War Plan*, 303–4.
19. "Strategic Estimates and Deployments in the Pacific," Apr. 2, 1947, JSC1259/36, p. 286, cited in Palmer, *Origins of the Maritime Strategy*, 29, 102.
20. Roger Dingman, "Strategic Planning and the Policy Process: American Plans for War in East Asia, 1945–1950," *Naval War College Review* 34, no. 7 (Nov.–Dec. 1979): 11–12, 15, https://digital-commons.usnwc.edu/nwc-review/vol32/iss7/3/ (accessed May 21, 2025). See also Ross, *American War Plans, 1945–1950*, 43–46.
21. Carl A. Posey, "How the Korean War Almost Went Nuclear," *Smithsonian Magazine*, July 2015, https://www.smithsonianmag.com/air-space-magazine/how-korean-war-almost-went-nuclear-180955324/ (accessed Jan. 22, 2025).
22. Bernard Gwertzman, "US Paper Tells of '53 Policy to Use A-Bomb in Korea," *New York Times*, June 8, 1984, https://www.nytimes.com/1984/06/08/world/us-papers-tell-of-53-policy-to-use-a-bomb-in-korea.html (accessed Jan. 22, 2025); Steven L. Rearden, *Council of War: A History of the Joint Chiefs of Staff, 1942–1992* (Washington, DC: Joint History Office, Office of the Director, JCS, 2012), 138–40, https://www.jcs.mil/Portals/36/Documents/History/Institutional/Council_of_War.pdf (accessed Jan. 22, 2025).
23. Matthew Jones, "Targeting China: U.S. Nuclear Planning and 'Massive Retaliation' in East Asia, 1953–1955," *Journal of Cold War Studies*, 10, no. 4 (Fall 2008): 39–41, 48–51, https://www.jstor.org/stable/26922983?read-now=1&seq=12#page_scan_tab_contents.
24. Jones, 54–55.
25. Jones, 56–58.
26. U.S. DOS, OOTH, *FRUS, 1952–1954, National Security Affairs, Volume II, Part 1*, ed. Lisle A. Rose and Neal H. Petersen (Washington, DC: Government Printing Office, 1984), 577–97, (Document 101) https://history.state.gov/historicaldocuments/frus1952-54v02p1/pg_577 (accessed Jan. 22, 202).
27. For an overview, see Peter Grier, "The First Offset," *Air & Space Force Magazine*, June 2016, 56–60, https://www.airandspaceforces.com/PDF/MagazineArchive/MagazineDocuments/2016/June 2016/0616offset.pdf (accessed Jan. 22, 2025).
28. Jacob Van Staaveren, *Air Operations in the Taiwan Crisis of 1958* (Washington, DC: USAF Historical Division Liaison Office, November 1962), 5–6, https://nsarchive.gwu.edu/document/21083-doc-10-taiwan-1958 (accessed Jan. 22, 2025). The document styles "OPLAN" as "OPS PLAN."

29. U.S. DOS, OOTH, *FRUS, 1955–1957, China, Volume II*, ed. Harriet D. Schwar (Washington, DC: Government Printing Office, 1986), Document 142, https://history.state.gov/historicaldocuments/frus1955-57v02/d142 (accessed Jan. 24, 2025).
30. Halperin, *1958 Taiwan Strait Crisis*, 15–16.
31. Halperin, 49.
32. Adapted from Halperin, 49.
33. Staaveren, *Air Operations in the Taiwan Crisis of 1958*, 15–16.
34. Halperin, *1958 Taiwan Strait Crisis*, 49–50, 55.
35. Halperin, 50–55.
36. Halperin, 55–56.
37. Halperin, 126–27.
38. Staaveren, *Air Operations in the Taiwan Crisis of 1958*, 16; See also Halperin, *1958 Taiwan Strait Crisis*, 84–85.
39. Staaveren, *Air Operations in the Taiwan Crisis of 1958*, 23–24.
40. Hans M. Kristensen, "Nukes in the Taiwan Crisis," FAS, May 13, 2008, https://fas.org/publication/nukes-in-the-taiwan-crisis (accessed Jan. 22, 2025).
41. John T. Farquhar, "Better a Footnote Than a Blast: Airpower Shapes the Second Taiwan Strait Crisis, 1958," *Journal of the Air Force Historical Foundation* 70, no. 4 (Winter 2023) 11, https://www.afhistory.org/wp-content/uploads/2023/11/Winter2023-Issue_all.pdf (accessed Jan. 22, 2025).
42. Halperin, *1958 Taiwan Strait Crisis*, 142.
43. U.S. DOS, OOTH, *FRUS, 1958–1960, China, Volume XIX*, Document 62, https://history.state.gov/historicaldocuments/frus1958-60v19/d62 (accessed Jan. 22, 2025).
44. Halperin, *1958 Taiwan Strait Crisis*, 197, 285–87.
45. Halperin, 77–78.
46. Halperin, 128–29, 379–87, 534.
47. Halperin, 126–28, 144.
48. Adapted from Staaveren, *Air Operations in the Taiwan Crisis of 1958*, 30–31; and Halperin, *1958 Taiwan Strait Crisis*, 381–87.
49. Staaveren, *Air Operations in the Taiwan Crisis of 1958*, 29.
50. Halperin, *1958 Taiwan Strait Crisis*, 292.
51. Halperin, 112–13.
52. Halperin, 115–16.
53. Halperin, 378.
54. For further insight, see Scott D. Sagan, "SIOP-62: The Nuclear War Plan Briefing to President Kennedy," *International Security* 12, no. 1 (Summer 1987): 22–51, https://www.jstor.org/stable/2538916 (accessed May 20, 2025).
55. Hans M. Kristensen, "The Awakening Asian Tiger: China in U.S. Nuclear War Planning," working paper, Nautilus Institute, Nov. 2000, https://www.nautilus.org/wp-content/uploads/2015/07/ChinaNuke.pdf (accessed Jan. 22, 2025).
56. The White House, "Strategic Air Planning and Berlin: Memorandum for General Lemnitzer," Sept. 6, 1961, Annex B, p. 3, https://nsarchive2.gwu.edu/NSAEBB/NSAEBB56/BerlinC1.pdf (accessed Jan. 22, 2025).
57. Hans M. Kristensen, Robert S. Norris, and Matthew G. McKinzie, *Chinese Nuclear Forces and U.S. Nuclear War Planning* (Washington, DC: FAS and Natural Resources Defense

Council, 2006), 132–33, https://nuke.fas.org/guide/china/Book2006.pdf (accessed Jan. 22, 2025); William Burr, "The Nixon Administration, the SIOP, and the Search for Limited Nuclear Options, 1969–1974," National Security Archive, Nov. 23, 2005, https://nsarchive2.gwu.edu/NSAEBB/NSAEBB173/index.htm (accessed Jan. 22, 2025).

58. Kristensen, Norris, and McKinzie, *Chinese Nuclear Forces*, 141–44.
59. Kristensen, Norris, and McKinzie, 152.
60. U.S. DOS, OOTH, *FRUS, 1948, General: The United Nations, Volume I, Part 2*, ed. Neal H. Petersen, Ralph R. Goodwin, Marvin W. Kranz, and William Z. Slany (Washington, DC: Government Printing Office, 1996), Document 60, https://history.state.gov/historicaldocuments/frus1948v01p2/d60 (accessed Jan. 22, 2025).
61. Adapted from Ross, *American War Plans, 1945–1950*, 114–18.
62. NET Evaluation Subcommittee of the NSC, *The Management and Termination of War with the Soviet Union*, Nov. 4, 1963, 4–13, 22–29, 30–35, https://www.cia.gov/readingroom/docs/CIA-RDP80B01676R002900110001-0.pdf (accessed Jan. 22, 2025).

CHAPTER 4. ALIGNMENT

1. "An Unsinkable Aircraft Carrier," *Time*, Sept. 4, 1950, https://content.time.com/time/subscriber/article/0,33009,856644,00.html (accessed Jan. 24, 2025).
2. "Message to General MacArthur Regarding the Withdrawal of the General's Message to the Veterans of Foreign Wars," Aug. 29, 1950, Harry S. Truman Library and Museum, https://www.trumanlibrary.gov/library/public-papers/226/message-general-macarthur-regarding-withdrawal-generals-message-veterans (accessed Jan. 22, 2025).
3. Lin, *Accidental State*, 171.
4. U.S. DOS, OOTH, *FRUS, 1950, East Asia and the Pacific: Volume VI*, ed. Neal H. Petersen, William Z. Slany, Charles S. Sampson, John P. Glennon, and David W. Mabon (Washington, DC: Government Printing Office, 1974), Document 224, https://history.state.gov/historicaldocuments/frus1950v06/d224 (accessed Jan. 22, 2025).
5. ComCruDivONE Operation Order No. 7-50, Oct. 7, 1950, Post-1946 Operation Plans, Task Force 72, NHHC, cited in Bruce A. Elleman, *Taiwan's Offshore Islands: Pathway or Barrier?*, Naval War College Newport Papers 44 (Newport, RI: Naval War College Press, 2019), 21, U.S. Naval War College Digital Commons, https://digital-commons.usnwc.edu/cgi/viewcontent.cgi?article=1042&context=usnwc-newport-papers (accessed Jan. 22, 2025).
6. It was initially named the Formosa Patrol, then from March 7, 1953, the Formosa Patrol Force; in late 1955 the Taiwan Patrol Surface Force; the U.S. Taiwan Straits Patrol in 1958; and finally, from November 1958, the Taiwan Patrol Force. Bruce A. Elleman, *High Seas Buffer: The Taiwan Patrol Force, 1950–1979*, Naval War College Newport Papers 38 (Newport, RI: Naval War College Press, 2012), 2, U.S. Naval War College Digital Commons, https://digital-commons.usnwc.edu/cgi/viewcontent.cgi?article=1037&context=newport-papers.
7. Elleman, 31–34, 39.
8. U.S. DOS, OOTH, *FRUS, 1952–1954, China and Japan, Volume XIV, Part 1*, ed. David W. Mabon and Harriet D. Schwar (Washington, DC: Government Printing Office, 1985), Document 249, https://history.state.gov/historicaldocuments/frus1952-54v14p1/d249 (accessed Jan. 22, 2025).

9. Walter S. Poole, *The Joint Chiefs of Staff and National Policy*, vol. 4, *1950–1952*, History of the Joint Chiefs of Staff (Washington, DC: Historical Office, Office of the Secretary of Defense, 1998), 202, https://www.jcs.mil/Portals/36/Documents/History/Policy/Policy_V004.pdf (accessed Jan., 2025). See also CIA National Intelligence Estimate, *Consequences of Early Employment of Chinese Nationalists in Korea*, Dec. 27 1950, https://www.cia.gov/readingroom/docs/DOC_0001356472.pdf (accessed Jan. 22, 2025).
10. Steven M. Goldstein, "The United States and the Republic of China, 1949–1978: Suspicious Allies," paper, Feb. 2000, 34, https://fsi-live.s3.us-west-1.amazonaws.com/s3fs-public/Goldstein.pdf (accessed Jan. 25, 2025).
11. Lin, *Accidental State*, 203–6; Steve Tsang, *In the Shadow of China: Political Developments in Taiwan since 1949* (Honolulu: University of Hawai'i Press, 1993), 50, 52.
12. Goldstein, "United States and the Republic of China," 13; U.S. DOS, OOTH, *FRUS, 1942–1954, China and Japan, Volume XIV, Part 1*, ed. David W. Mabon and Harriet D. Schwar (Washington, DC: Government Printing Office, 1985), Document 75, https://history.state.gov/historicaldocuments/frus1952-54v14p1/d75 (accessed Jan. 22, 2025).
13. Lin, *Accidental State*, 217–18.
14. U.S. DOS, OOTH, *FRUS, 1951, East Asia and the Pacific, Volume VI*, Document 362, https://history.state.gov/historicaldocuments/frus1950v06/d362 (accessed Jan. 22, 2025).
15. Lin, *Accidental State*, 168, 188.
16. Lin, 189–91; Eric Setzekorn, *The Rise and Fall of an Officer Corps: The Republic of China Military, 1942–1955* (Norman: University of Oklahoma Press, 2018), 129, Kindle.
17. Eric Setzekorn, *Arming East Asia: Deterring China in the Early Cold War* (Annapolis, MD: Naval Institute Press, 2023), 76–78.
18. Setzekorn, 90.
19. Lin, *Accidental State*, 192.
20. Setzekorn, *Rise and Fall of an Officer Corps*, 121.
21. Elleman, *High Seas Buffer*, 79–81. For a breakdown of larger vessels by type and year of delivery from 1952 to 1978, see Garver, *Sino-American Alliance*, 69.
22. For a breakdown of aircraft by type and year of deliver from 1953 to 1973 by type, see Garver, *Sino-American Alliance*, 67.
23. Elleman, *Taiwan's Offshore Islands*, 72; U.S. DOS, OOTH, *FRUS, 1952–1954, China and Japan, Volume XIV, Part 1*, Document 150, https://history.state.gov/historicaldocuments/frus1952-54v14p1/d150 (accessed Jan. 22, 2025).
24. U.S. DOS, Document 177, https://history.state.gov/historicaldocuments/frus1952-54v14p1/d177 (accessed Jan. 15, 2025). See also Setzekorn, *Arming East Asia*, 77.
25. U.S. DOS, Document 150.
26. Elleman, *Taiwan's Offshore Islands*, 39.
27. Goldstein, "United States and the Republic of China," 7.
28. Goldstein, 7.
29. Gregory Kulacki, "Nuclear Weapons in the Taiwan Strait Part I," *Journal for Peace and Nuclear Disarmament* 3, no. 2 (2020): 321, 323, https://doi.org/10.1080/25751654.2020.1834963 (accessed Jan. 22, 2025).
30. Elleman, *High Seas Buffer*, 59.
31. Elleman, 65.

32. Elleman, *Taiwan's Offshore Islands*, 53–54.

33. Staaveren, *Air Operations in the Taiwan Strait Crisis of 1958*, 5; Kenneth W. Condit, *The Joint Chiefs of Staff and National Policy*, vol. 6, *1955–1956*, History of the Joint Chiefs of Staff (Washington, DC: Historical Office, Office of the Secretary of Defense), 207, https://www.govinfo.gov/content/pkg/GOVPUB-D5-PURL-gpo57192/pdf/GOVPUB-D5-PURL-gpo57192.pdf (accessed Jan. 22, 2025).

34. "Mutual Defense Treaty between the United States and the Republic of China, December 2, 1954," Avalon Project, Yale Law School, https://avalon.law.yale.edu/20th_century/chin001.asp#art1 (accessed Jan. 22, 2025); "Exchange of Notes Constituting an Agreement between the United States of America and the Republic of China Relating to the Mutual Defense Treaty of 2 December 1954," Dec. 10, 1954, Taiwan Document Project, http://www.taiwandocuments.org/mutual02.htm (accessed Jan. 22, 2025). For the note, see U.S. DOS, OOTH, *FRUS, 1952–1954, China and Japan, Volume XIV, Part 1*, Document 401, https://history.state.gov/historicaldocuments/frus1952-54v14p1/d401 (accessed Jan. 22, 2025).

35. U.S. DOS, OOTH, *FRUS, 1955–1957, China, Volume II*, ed. Harriet D. Schwar (Washington, DC: Government Printing Office, 1986), Document 56, https://history.state.gov/historicaldocuments/frus1955-57v02/d56 (accessed Jan. 22, 2025).

36. U.S. DOS, OOTH, "U.S.-China Ambassadorial Talks, 1955–1970," Milestones: 1953–1969, https://history.state.gov/milestones/1953-1960/china-talks (accessed Jan. 22, 2025).

37. Initially known as the Formosa Liaison Center, it was reorganized as USTDC in November 1955.

38. U.S. DOS, OOTH, *FRUS, 1955–1957, China, Volume II*, Document 240, https://history.state.gov/historicaldocuments/frus1955-57v02/d240 (accessed Jan. 22, 2025). See also Project 2049 Institute, "Memorandum," 18; and "Memorandum to the Next President of the United States—The Inheritance in the Indo-Pacific and the Challenges and Opportunities for Your Presidency," Project 2049 Institute, Dec. 2020, 18–19, https://project2049.net/wp-content/uploads/2020/12/Memo-to-the-Next-President_Schriver_P2049_201201.pdf (accessed Jan. 22, 2025).

39. U.S. DOS, OOTH, *FRUS, 1955–1957, China, Volume II*, Document 240. "Chinese" in this instance refers to the ROC.

40. John A. Froebe Jr., NSC, "Memorandum for Major General John A. Wickham—Subject: Significant Military Exercise FOOD CHAIN VI," Mar. 28, 1975, CIA Reading Room https://www.cia.gov/readingroom/docs/LOC-HAK-65-4-15-9.pdf (accessed Jan. 22, 2025).

41. Kristensen, "Nukes in the Taiwan Crisis."

42. Matsu was only briefly shelled with leaflets.

43. Laurence S. Kuter, "The Meaning of the Taiwan Strait Crisis," *Air & Space Forces Magazine*, Mar. 1, 1959, https://www.airandspaceforces.com/article/0359meaning (accessed Jan. 22, 2025).

44. Excerpt from *Ike's Bluff*, by Evan Thomas, NBC News, Sept. 27, 2012, https://www.nbcnews.com/news/world/excerpt-evan-thomas-ikes-bluff-flna6143046 (accessed Jan. 22, 2025).

45. For a full overview, see Garver, *Sino-American Alliance*, 148–66.

46. Lin, *Accidental State*, 137–38.

47. Lin, 210–11.
48. Garver, *Sino-American Alliance*, 169.
49. Philip J. Barton, "Tibet and China: History, Insurgency, and Beyond" (thesis, Naval Postgraduate School, 2003), 40, https://core.ac.uk/download/pdf/36694767.pdf (accessed Jan. 22, 2025).
50. Garver, *Sino-American Alliance*, 188.
51. ROC Air Force, "The Black Cat Squadron," last updated Mar. 9, 2023, https://air.mnd.gov.tw/EN/Unit/Activity_Detail.aspx?CID=174&ID=114 (accessed Jan. 22, 2025).
52. ROC Air Force, "The Black Bat Squadron," last updated Mar. 9, 2023, https://air.mnd.gov.tw/EN/Unit/Activity_Detail.aspx?CID=173&ID=113 (accessed Jan. 22, 2025)
53. Li Wang and Art Winn, "Heavy Tea, Black Bats, and the CIA," Museum of Flight, YouTube, Sept. 1, 2018, video, 44:40–53:04, https://www.youtube.com/watch?v=dKC2vqScC94 (accessed Jan. 24, 2025) (private video unavailable).

CHAPTER 5. DEALIGNMENT

1. Lin, *Accidental State*, 199–200.
2. Lin, 200–207.
3. Lin, 221–22; Garver, *Sino-American Alliance*, 76.
4. Lin, *Accidental State*, 223.
5. Lin, 224.
6. Garver, *Sino-American Alliance*, 82–83.
7. U.S. DOS, OOTH, *FRUS, 1958–1960, China, Volume XIX*, ed. Harriet Dashiell Schwar (Washington, DC: Government Printing Office, 1986), Document 209, https://history.state.gov/historicaldocuments/frus1958-60v19/d209 (accessed Jan. 22, 2025).
8. Garver, *Sino-American Alliance*, 88–89.
9. Isabelle Cheng, "Saving the Nation by Sacrificing Your Life: Authoritarianism and Chiang Kai-shek's War for the Retaking of China," *Journal of Current Chinese Affairs* 47, no. 2 (2018): 70.
10. Cheng, 71.
11. Cheng, 72.
12. Cheng, 72.
13. Garver, *Sino-American Alliance*, 90.
14. Garver, 91.
15. Cindy Sui, "Taiwan's Plan to Take Back Mainland," BBC News, Sept. 7, 2009, http://news.bbc.co.uk/1/hi/world/asia-pacific/8183412.stm (accessed Jan. 22, 2025).
16. Takayuki Igarashi, "When Did the ROC Abandon 'Retaking the Mainland'?: The Transformation of Military Strategy in Taiwan," Saving the Nation, *Journal of Contemporary East Asia Studies* 10, no. 1 (2021): 138.
17. CIA, "Intelligence Memorandum: Probable Effects in China and Taiwan of a GRC Attack on the Mainland," Aug. 18, 1965, cover page, https://www.cia.gov/readingroom/docs/DOC_0000475036.pdf (accessed Jan. 22, 2025).
18. Igarashi, "When Did the ROC Abandon 'Retaking the Mainland'?," 139.
19. Igarashi, 139–40.
20. Igarashi, 140.

21. Commission on Presidential Debates, "October 7, 1960 Debate Transcript: Kennedy-Nixon Presidential Debate," www.debates.org/index.php?page=october-7-1960-debate-transcript (accessed Jan. 22, 2025).
22. Charles J. Pellegrin, "'There Are Bigger Issues at Stake': The Administration of John F. Kennedy and United States–Republic of China Relations," in *John F. Kennedy: History, Memory, and Legacy—An Interdisciplinary Inquiry*, ed. John Delane Williams, Robert G. Waite, and Gregory S. Gordon (Grand Fork: University of North Dakota, 2010), 100–102.
23. Nancy Bernkopf Tucker, *Strait Talk: United States–Taiwan Relations and the Crisis with China* (Cambridge, MA: Harvard University Press, 2009), 19–20.
24. U.S. DOS, OOTH, *FRUS, 1964–1968, Volume XXX*, China, ed. Harriet Dashiell Schwar, (Washington, DC: Government Printing Office, 1998), foreword, https://history.state.gov/historicaldocuments/frus1964-68v30/summary (accessed Jan. 22, 2025).
25. For an overview of the conflict, see Michael S. Gerson, *The Sino-Soviet Border Conflict: Deterrence, Escalation, and the Threat of Nuclear War in 1969* (CNA, 2010), https://www.cna.org/archive/CNA_Files/pdf/d0022974.a2.pdf (accessed Jan. 22, 2025).
26. Tucker, *Strait Talk*, 36.
27. U.S. DOS, OOTH, *FRUS, 1969–1976, Volume XVII, China, 1969–1972*, ed. Steven E. Phillips (Washington, DC: Government Printing Office, 1998), Document 3, https://history.state.gov/historicaldocuments/frus1969-76v17/d3 (accessed Jan. 27, 2025).
28. Tucker, *Strait Talk*, 38–39, 42.
29. U.S. JCS, "Memorandum for the Secretary of Defense: Implications of Removal of US Military Presence in Taiwan," Aug. 30, 1971, in *Documentary Supplement*, of *Melvin Laird and the Foundation of the Post-Vietnam Military, 1969–1973*, ed., Richard A. Hunt, Secretaries of Defense Historical Series 7 (Washington, DC: Historical Office, Office of the Secretary of Defense, 2016), 340–41, https://history.defense.gov/Portals/70/Documents/secretaryofdefense/Laird Document Supplement.pdf (accessed Jan. 22, 2025).
30. Robert S. Norris, William M. Arkin, and William Burr, "Where They Were," *Bulletin of Atomic Science* (Nov.–Dec. 1999), 34, https://www.archives.gov/files/declassification/pidb/meetings/where-they-were.pdf (accessed Jan. 24, 2025).
31. "Joint Communique between the United States and China," Feb. 27, 1972, Wilson Center Digital Archive, https://digitalarchive.wilsoncenter.org/document/joint-communique-between-united-states-and-china (accessed Jan. 22, 2025).
32. Dave Makichuk, "Taiwan Can Wait 100 Years, Mao Told Nixon," China Factor, Nov. 22, 2021, https://chinafactor.news/2021/11/22/taiwan-can-wait-100-years-mao-told-nixon (accessed Jan. 22, 2025).
33. "Memorandum of Conversation between Mao Zedong and Henry A. Kissinger," Oct. 21, 1975, Wilson Center Digital Archive, https://digitalarchive.wilsoncenter.org/document/memorandum-conversation-between-mao-zedong-and-henry-kissinger-0 (accessed Jan. 22, 2025).
34. Secretary of Defense, "Memorandum for the Assistant to the President for National Security Affairs: U.S. Security Assistance to the Republic of China," Apr. 12, 1976, National Security Archive, George Washington University, 1–2, Annex C I–II, https://nsarchive2.gwu.edu/NSAEBB/NSAEBB19/docs/doc07.pdf (accessed May 24, 2025).

35. Bernard Gwertzman, "U.S. Modifies Taiwan's Request for Advanced Planes," *New York Times*, Nov 7, 1978, https://www.nytimes.com/1978/11/07/archives/us-modifies-taiwans-request-for-advanced-planes-taiwan-sought.htm.l (accessed Jan. 22, 2025).
36. Command History Branch, Office of the Joint Secretary, *Commander in Chief Pacific Command History 1979* (Camp H. M. Smith, HI: Headquarters CINPAC, 1980), app. 1, "Taiwan Wrap-Up," pt. 2, chap. 1, sec. 1, p. 71, https://nautilus.org/wp-content/uploads/2015/07/Taiwan79c.pdf (accessed Jan. 22, 2025).
37. Command History Branch, x.
38. For the full text, see Taiwan Relations Act, Pub. L. No. 96-8, 93 Stat. 14 (1979), https://www.congress.gov/96/statute/STATUTE-93/STATUTE-93-Pg14.pdf (accessed Jan. 22, 2025).
39. Tucker, *Strait Talk*, 131.
40. Tucker, 142.
41. "U.S.-PRC Joint Communique ([Aug. 17], 1982)," American Institute in Taiwan, Mar. 31, 2022, https://www.ait.org.tw/u-s-prc-joint-communique-1982/ (accessed May. 24, 2025).
42. "Declassified Cables: Taiwan Arms Sales and the Six Assurances (1982)," American Institute in Taiwan, Mar. 30, 2022, https://www.ait.org.tw/declassified-cables-taiwan-arms-sales-six-assurances-1982 (accessed Jan. 22, 2025).
43. "Declassified Cables."
44. "Declassified Cables."
45. "U.S.-PRC Joint Communique ([Aug. 17], 1982)."
46. Tucker, *Strait Talk*, 155–57.
47. For a complete overview of the ROC's efforts to develop nuclear weapons, see David Albright and Andrea Strickler, *Taiwan's Former Nuclear Weapons Program: Nuclear Weapons on Demand* (Washington, DC: Institute for Science and International Security, 2018), https://web.archive.org/web/20220116043944/https://isis-online.org/uploads/isis-reports/documents/TaiwansFormerNuclearWeaponsProgram_POD_color_withCover.pdf (accessed Jan. 22, 2025).
48. Albright and Strickler, 4–5.
49. Albright and Strickler, 6, 9–13, 16.
50. Albright and Strickler, 65–70, 72–76, 81–84.
51. Albright and Strickler, 121–28, 143–44, 146–48, 179–85.
52. Albright and Strickler, 171–74.

CHAPTER 6. APOCALYPSE LATER

1. Walter S. Poole, *The Joint Chiefs of Staff and National Policy*, vol. 8, *1961–1964*, History of the Joint Chiefs of Staff (Washington DC: Office of Joint History, Office of the CJCS, 2011), 61, https://www.jcs.mil/Portals/36/Documents/History/Policy/Policy_V008.pdf (accessed Jan. 22, 2025).
2. D. A. Paolucci, "Draft Summary Report of The Long Range Research and Development Planning Program," Lulejian & Associates, Feb. 7, 1975, iii, http://albertwohlstetter.com/writings/19750207-PaolucciEtAl-Draft-LRRDPP.pdf (accessed Jan. 22, 2025).
3. Rebecca Grant, "The Second Offset," *Air and Space Forces Magazine*, June 24, 2016, https://www.airandspaceforces.com/article/the-second-offset (accessed Jan. 22, 2025).

4. Robert O. Work and Greg Grant, *Beating the Americans at Their Own Game: An Offset Strategy with Chinese Characteristics* (Washington, DC: CNAS, 2019), 2, 3, https://s3.us-east-1.amazonaws.com/files.cnas.org/hero/documents/CNAS-Report-Work-Offset-final-B.pdf (accessed Jan. 22, 2025).
5. For a study of the path from Active Defense to AirLand Battle, see John L. Romjue, *From Active Defense to AirLand Battle: The Development of Army Doctrine, 1973–1982* (Washington, DC: Historical Office, U.S. Army Training and Doctrine Command, 1984), https://www.tradoc.army.mil/wp-content/uploads/2020/10/From-Active-Defense-to-AirLand-Battle.pdf (accessed Jan. 22, 2025). See also R. Kent Laughbaum, *Synchronizing Airpower and Firepower in the Deep Battle* (Montgomery, AL: Air University Press, 1999), 7–23, https://www.jstor.org/stable/resrep13949.7 (accessed Jan. 22, 2025).
6. Robert Tomes, "The Cold War Offset Strategy: Assault Breaker and the Beginning of the RSTA Revolution," *War on the Rocks*, Nov. 20, 2014, https://warontherocks.com/2014/11/the-cold-war-offset-strategy-assault-breaker-and-the-beginning-of-the-rsta-revolution (accessed Jan. 22, 2025); Donn Starry, "Extending the Battlefield," *Military Review*, Mar. 1981, 31–50, https://www.armyupress.army.mil/Portals/7/online-publications/documents/1981-mr-donn-starry-extending-the-battlefield.pdf.
7. Jim Tegnelia and Rich Wagner, "Technology-Strategy Seminar: NATO's AirLand Battle Strategy and Future Extended Deterrence," CSIS, YouTube, Sept. 13, 2013, educational video, 2:01.37, https://www.youtube.com/watch?v=rSukv1CcORk (accessed Jan. 22, 2025).
8. Taken from Historical Branch, Office of the Joint Secretary, *Commander in Chief Pacific Command History 1972*, vol. 1 (Camp H. M. Smith, HI: Headquarters CINPAC, 1973), 99, https://nautilus.org/wp-content/uploads/2012/01/c_seventytwo.pdf (accessed Jan. 22, 2025).
9. See Joseph M. Ha and Laura Heard, "The Buildup of the Soviet Pacific Fleet: An Indication of Foreign Policy in Northeast," *Asian Perspective* 7, no. 2 (Fall–Winter 1983): 275–316, https://www.jstor.org/stable/43738012 (accessed Jan. 22, 2025).
10. See Derek da Cunha, "Soviet Strike Warfare in the Pacific," U.S. Naval Institute *Proceedings*, 115/2/1,032 (Feb. 1989), https://www.usni.org/magazines/proceedings/1989/february/soviet-strike-warfare-pacific (accessed Jan. 22, 2025).
11. For an analysis of Soviet Cold War A2/AD efforts in the Pacific and how they can be applied to China, see Narushige Michishita, Peter M. Swartz, and David F. Winkler, *Lessons of the Cold War in the Pacific: U.S. Maritime Strategy, Crisis Prevention, and Japan's Role* (Washington, DC: Wilson Center and the Sasakawa Peace Foundation, 2016), https://www.wilsoncenter.org/sites/default/files/media/documents/publication/lessons_of_the_cold_war_in_the_pacific_one_page.pdf (accessed Jan. 22, 2025).
12. Command History Branch, Office of the Joint Secretary, *Commander in Chief Pacific Command History 1978*, vol. 1 (Camp H. M. Smith, HI: Headquarters CINCPAC, 1979), 159, https://nautilus.org/wp-content/uploads/2011/12/c_seventyeight.pdf (accessed Jan. 22, 2025).
13. John B. Hattendorf and Peter M. Swartz, eds., *U.S. Naval Strategy in the 1980s—Selected Documents*, Newport Papers 33 (Newport, RI: Naval War College Press, December 2008), 29, U.S. Naval War College Digital Commons, https://digital-commons.usnwc.edu/cgi/viewcontent.cgi?article=1032&context=newport-papers (accessed Jan. 22, 2025).

14. John B. Hattendorf, ed., *U.S. Naval Strategy in the 1970s: Selected Documents*, Newport Papers 30 (Newport, RI: Naval War College Press, 2007), 12, U.S. Naval War College Digital Commons, https://digital-commons.usnwc.edu/cgi/viewcontent.cgi?article=1029&context=newport-papers (accessed Jan. 24, 2025).
15. Adm. James L. Holloway III, *Aircraft Carriers at War: A Personal Retrospective of Korea, Vietnam, and the Soviet Confrontation* (Annapolis, MD: Naval Institute Press, 2007), 759, Kindle.
16. Capt. James Matthew Patton, "Air Raid Petropavlovsk—the Drill That Became a Strategy," *Submarine Review* (Apr. 2013): 52–57, https://archive.navalsubleague.org/2013/air-raid-petropavlovsk-the-drill-that-became-a-strategy (accessed Jan. 22, 2025); Hattendorf, *U.S. Naval Strategy in the 1970s*, 18; Hattendorf, *The Evolution of the U.S. Navy's Maritime Strategy, 1977–1986*, Newport Papers 19 (Newport, RI: Naval War College Press, 2004), 15–16, U.S. Naval War College Digital Commons, https://digital-commons.usnwc.edu/cgi/viewcontent.cgi?article=1019&context=usnwc-newport-papers (accessed Jan. 22, 2025). For a contemporary (1984) assessment of the offensive strategy's development and implantation, see William M. Arkin and David Chappell, "Forward Offensive Strategy: Raising the Stakes in the Pacific," *World Policy Journal* 2, no. 3 (Summer 1985): 481–500, https://www.jstor.org/stable/40208995 (accessed Jan. 22, 2025).
17. Hattendorf, *Evolution of the U.S. Navy's Maritime Strategy*, 15–16, 19–20.
18. Arkin and Chappell, "Forward Offensive Strategy," 483.
19. Norman Polmar, "The U.S. Navy: Toward a 600-Ship Fleet," U.S. Naval Institute *Proceedings* 108/2/948 (Feb. 1982), https://www.usni.org/magazines/proceedings/1982/february/u-s-navy-toward-600-ship-fleet (accessed Jan. 22, 2025).
20. Adapted from Hattendorf and Swartz, *U.S. Naval Strategy in the 1980s*, 163–91.
21. Sarah Fallon, "The Secret History of the First Microprocessor, the F-14, and Me," *Wired*, Dec. 23, 2020, https://www.wired.com/story/secret-history-of-the-first-microprocessor-f-14 (accessed Jan. 22, 2025).
22. Friedman, *Fighters over the Fleet*, 1166.
23. Hattendorf and Swartz, *U.S. Naval Strategy in the 1980s*, 77, 158, 177, 207, 241.
24. Hattendorf and Swartz, 174.
25. "US-A," *Encyclopedia Astronautica*, http://www.astronautix.com/u/us-a.html; "US-P," *Encyclopedia Astronautica*, http://www.astronautix.com/u/us-p.html (accessed Jan. 22, 2025).
26. Maksim Y. Tokarev, "Kamikazes: The Soviet Legacy," *Naval War College Review* 67, no.1 (Winter 2014): 78–79, https://digital-commons.usnwc.edu/cgi/viewcontent.cgi?article=1247&context=nwc-review (accessed Jan. 22, 2025).
27. Command History Division, Office of the Joint Secretary, *Commander in Chief U.S. Pacific Command History 1984*, vol. 1 (Camp H. M. Smith, HI: Headquarters USCINCPAC, 1985), 46, https://nautilus.org/wp-content/uploads/2012/01/c_eightyfour.pdf (accessed May 18, 2025).
28. Garren Mulloy, *Defenders of Japan* (London: Hurst, 2021), 80–83.
29. For a then-contemporary overview of the Soviet conventional threat to northern Japan, see G. Keith Jacobs, "A Soviet War for Northern Japan," *Asian Defense Journal* 1, no. 83 (1983): 6–17, https://www.academia.edu/39907894/A_Soviet_War_for_Northern_Japan (accessed Jan. 22, 2025).

30. Jacobs, 14.
31. Mulloy, *Defenders of Japan,* 58–59.
32. Command History Division, *Commander in Chief U.S. Pacific Command History 1984,* 1:60.
33. Hattendorf and Swartz, *U.S. Naval Strategy in the 1980s,* 184–86, 190–91, 198.
34. Hattendorf, and Swartz, 191.
35. Gerry Doyle and Blake Heringer, *Carrier Killers: China's Anti-Ship Ballistic Missiles and Theater of Operations in the Early 21st Century* (Warwick, Eng.: Helion, 2022), 3, 27; "R-27 Submarine Ballistic Missile (4K10, RSM-25)," Missilery.info, https://en.missilery.info/missile/r27 (accessed Jan. 22, 2025).
36. Friedman, *Fighters over the Fleet,* 1154–55.
37. Friedman, 1172–73.
38. "Standard Missile-2 Block IV," Missile Threat, last updated Feb. 27, 2023, https://missilethreat.csis.org/defsys/standard-missile-2-block-iv (accessed Jan. 22, 2025).
39. U.S. Senate, Committee on Appropriations, 95th Congress, *Department of Defense Appropriations for Fiscal Year 1974,* pt. 5, *Research, Development, Test, and Evaluation* (Washington, DC: Government Printing Office, 1978), 101, https://books.google.co.uk/books?id=TxAULaOoC98C&pg=PA101&lpg=PA101&dq (accessed Jan. 22, 2025).
40. Thomas P. Ehrhard, *Air Force UAVs: The Secret History* (Arlington, VA: Mitchell Institute for Airpower Studies, 2010), 1–17, https://apps.dtic.mil/sti/pdfs/ADA525674.pdf (accessed Jan. 22, 2025).
41. Richard H. Van Atta et al., *Transformation and Transition: DARPA's Role in Fostering an Emerging Revolution in Military Affairs,* vol. 1, *Overall Assessment* (Alexandria, VA: Institute for Defense Analyses, 2003), S-4–5, 23–24, https://irp.fas.org/agency/dod/idarma.pdf (accessed Jan. 22, 2025).

CHAPTER 7. THE SOUTH ATLANTIC AND SOUTHWEST ASIA

1. Committee of Privy Counsellors (Chair: Lord Franks), *Falkland Islands Review* (London: HM Stationery Office, Jan. 1983), paragraphs 139, 293, https://archive.margaretthatcher.org/doc02/E415E0802DAA482297D889B9B43B70DE.pdf (accessed May 19, 2025) (hereafter cited as Franks, *Falkland Islands Review*).
2. Lawrence Freedman, *The Official History of the Falklands Campaign,* 2 vols. (London: Routledge, 2005), 1:69–70, Kindle; Franks, *Falkland Islands Review,* paragraphs 46–47.
3. Freedman, *Official History of the Falklands Campaign,* 1:63.
4. Franks, *Falkland Islands Review,* paragraphs 47, 64.
5. Franks, paragraph 112.
6. Franks, paragraphs 109, 113.
7. Martin Middlebrook, *Argentina's Fight for the Falklands* (Barnsley, Eng.: Pen & Sword, 2009), 14, Kindle; Francis X. Kinney, "The Malvinas Conflict: Argentine Practice of the Operational Art" (monograph, School of Advanced Military Studies, U.S. Army Command and General Staff College, 1990), 10, https://apps.dtic.mil/sti/tr/pdf/ADA234161.pdf (accessed Jan. 22, 2025). While the planning officially began in January 1982, there had long been war college–level studies of the mission. See Middlebrook, *Argentina's Fight for the Falklands,* 15.
8. Middlebrook, *Argentina's Fight for the Falklands,* 15; Kinney, "Malvinas Conflict," 1990, 10.
9. Kinney, "Malvinas Conflict," 11.

10. Kinney, 19–21, 28–30.
11. Franks, *Falkland Islands Review*, paragraph 149.
12. Kinney, "Malvinas Conflict," 12–13.
13. Franks, *Falkland Islands Review*, paragraphs 233, 235.
14. Freedman, *Official History of the Falklands Campaign*, 2:48, 50, 52–53.
15. Freedman, 2:55.
16. Adapted from Freedman, 2:445–46.
17. Middlebrook, *Argentina's Fight for the Falklands*, 18.
18. Middlebrook, 93–95; Freedman, *Official History of the Falklands Campaign*, 2:257–558.
19. Freedman, *Official History of the Falklands Campaign*, 2:77, 257–58.
20. Mariano Sciaroni, *Carrier at Risk: Argentine Aircraft Carrier and Anti-Submarine Operations against the Royal Navy's Attack Submarines during the Falklands War* (Warwick, Eng.: Helion, 2019), 8–9.
21. UK MOD, *Narrative of RAF Operations during the Falklands Conflict 1982* (London: MOD Air Historical Branch, 1988), paragraphs 2.27–2.33, https://www.raf.mod.uk/what-we-do/our-history/air-historical-branch/regional-studies-post-coldwar-narratives/raf-operations-during-the-falklands-conflict-1982/(accessed Jan. 22, 2025).
22. UK MOD, paragraphs 3.66, 6.29.
23. Doug Gordon, "Harrier GR.3 Frontline RAF Germany Cold War Operations," *Aviation News Magazine*, Jan. 19, 2017, https://www.key.aero/article/harrier-gr3s-frontline-raf-germany-cold-war-ops (accessed Jan. 22, 2025).
24. See UK MOD, *Narrative of RAF Operations during the Falklands Conflict*, paragraphs 754–61; and "The San Carlos FOB (Forward Operating Base)," *Think Defence* (blog), updated June 2024, https://www.thinkdefence.co.uk/2024/06/the-san-carlos-fob-forward-operating-base (accessed Jan. 22, 2025).
25. Dario Leone, "Black Buck 6 and ACME Missions: A Quick Look at British Operations on Latin American Soil during the Falklands War," Aviation Geek Club, July 17, 2019, https://theaviationgeekclub.com/black-buck-6-and-acme-missions-a-quick-look-at-british-operations-on-latin-american-soil-during-the-falklands-war (accessed Jan. 22, 2025).
26. Dave Cassan, "Target Gibraltar: Operation Algeciras," in *Falklands: Untold Stories of the War in the South Atlantic: An Invaluable Reference in Words and Pictures*, ed. Martin Mace and John Grehan (Stamford, Eng.: Key, 2012), 68–74.
27. Richard Clements, "'Operation Mikado': A One-Way Mission to Wipe Out Argentine Exocet Missiles during the Falklands War," Aviationist, July 21, 2012, https://theaviationist.com/2012/07/21/operation-mikado (accessed Jan. 22, 2025).
28. See Roger Villar, *Merchant Ships at War: The Falklands Experience* (London: Conway Maritime and Lloyd's of London, 1984), chap. 3.
29. Villar, chap. 5.
30. See Villar, chap. 12.
31. See Villar, chaps. 6, 11.
32. See Villar, chap. 10.
33. Kenneth L. Privratsky, *Logistics in the Falklands War: A Case Study in Expeditionary Warfare* (Barnsley, Eng.: Pen and Sword Books, 2014), 84.

34. Villar, *Merchant Ships at War*, chap. 4.
35. See Villar, chap. 8.
36. U.S. Dept. of the Navy, *Lessons of the Falklands: Summary Report* (Washington, DC: Office of Program Appraisal, Dept. of the Navy, 1983), https://apps.dtic.mil/sti/pdfs/ADA133333.pdf (accessed Jan. 22, 2025).
37. U.S. Dept. of the Navy, 1–2, 51–53.
38. John Lehman Jr., address to "The Falklands at 40: Reflections on Maritime Strategy and Anti-Ship Cruise Missiles," transcript, CSIS, May 4, 2022, https://www.csis.org/analysis/falklands-40 (accessed Jan. 22, 2025).
39. U.S. Dept. of the Navy, *Lessons of the Falklands*, 2–3, 27, 31–34.
40. U.S. Dept. of the Navy, 7–8, 34, 36.
41. U.S. Dept. of the Navy, 46.
42. U.S. Dept. of the Navy, 34, 36.
43. U.S. Dept. of the Navy, 11.
44. Lyle Goldstein, "China's Falklands Lessons," *Survival* 50, no. 3 (2008): 66–67, https://doi.org/10.1080/00396330802173214 (accessed Jan. 22, 2025).
45. Goldstein, 67–71.
46. Goldstein, 70–73.
47. Goldstein, 75.
48. Goldstein, 77–78.
49. Christopher D. Yung, "Sincia Rules the Waves?: The People's Liberation Army Navy's Power Projection and Anti-Access/Area Denial Lessons from the Falklands/Malvinas Conflict," in *Chinese Lessons from Other People's Wars*, ed. Andrew Scobell, Davids Lai, and Roy Kamphausen (Carlisle Barracks, PA: Strategic Studies Institute, 2011), 83, 86.
50. Roland White, *Vulcan 607* (London: Transworld, 2007; repr., London: Corgi, 2012), 5770, Kindle.
51. Jimmy Carter, "Presidential Directive NSC-18," Aug. 24, 1977, 4, https://irp.fas.org/offdocs/pd/pd18.pdf (accessed Jan. 22, 2025).
52. David B. Crist, *The Twilight War: The Secret History of America's Thirty-Year Conflict with Iran* (New York: Penguin, 2013), 38, Kindle.
53. Crist, 39–41.
54. David B. Crist, "US Central Command Campaign Planning against the Soviet Union, 1979–1987," offsite presentation for U.S. CENTCOM, Sept. 18, 2020, slide 4, https://www.jcs.mil/Portals/36/Documents/History/Dec21/Crist%20CENTCOM%20offsite%2018%20Sep%2020_complete.pdf (accessed Jan. 22, 2025).
55. Walter K. Andersen, "Soviets in the Indian Ocean: Much Ado about Something—But What?," *Asian Survey* 24, no. 9 (Sept. 1984): 919, https://www.jstor.org/stable/2644076 (accessed Jan. 22, 2025).
56. Samuel J. Cox, "H-061-3: Desert Storm—Sealift, Seabees, Navy Medicine," Naval History and Heritage Command, May 2021, https://www.history.navy.mil/about-us/leadership/director/directors-corner/h-grams/h-gram-061/h-061-3.html (accessed Jan. 22, 2025).
57. U.S. Dept. of Transportation, Maritime Administration, "History of the Ready Reserve Force (RRF)," updated July 12, 2022, https://www.maritime.dot.gov/outreach/history/history-ready-reserve-force-rrf (accessed Jan. 24, 2025); and "History of the National

Defense Reserve Fleet (NDRF)," updated Oct. 4, 2021, https://www.maritime.dot.gov/outreach/history/history-national-defense-reserve-fleet-ndrf (accessed Jan. 22, 2025).

58. Crist, *Twilight War*, 584.
59. Elliot A. Cohen et al., *Gulf War Air Power Survey*, vol. 3, *Logistics and Support* (Washington, DC, 1993), 58, https://apps.dtic.mil/sti/tr/pdf/ADA279743.pdf (accessed Jan. 22, 2025).
60. Crist, *Twilight War*, 58–59.
61. Crist, "US Central Command Campaign Planning," slide 9.
62. Crist, slides 5–6.
63. Norman Schwarzkopf and Peter Petre, *It Doesn't Take a Hero: The Autobiography of General Norman Schwarzkopf* (New York: Bantam, 1992), 454–55, Kindle.
64. Jacob L. Heim, Zachary Burdette, and Nathan Beauchamp-Mustafaga, *U.S. Military Theories of Victory for a War with the People's Republic of China* (Santa Monica, CA: RAND Corp., Feb. 21, 2024), 20, https://www.rand.org/pubs/perspectives/PEA1743-1.html (accessed Jan. 22, 2025).
65. Joshua M. Epstein, "Soviet Vulnerabilities in Iran and the RDF Deterrent," *International Security* 6, no. 2 (Fall 1981): 130–32, 139–41, https://www.jstor.org/stable/2538649 (accessed Jan. 22, 2025).
66. Crist, *Twilight War*, 81.
67. Schwarzkopf and Petre, *It Doesn't Take a Hero*, 456.
68. Eliot A. Cohen et al., *Gulf War Air Power Survey*, vol. 1, *Planning and Command and Control* (Washington, DC: 1993), 20–21, https://media.defense.gov/2010/Sep/27/2001329802/-1/-1/0/AFD-100927-062.pdf (accessed Jan. 22, 2025).
69. Cohen et al., 1:26.
70. Cohen et al., 1:27–29. This description is reformatted to match other overviews.
71. Diane T. Putney, *Airpower Advantage: Planning the Gulf War Air Campaign, 1989–1991*. The USAF in the Persian Gulf War (Washington, DC: Air Force History and Museums Program, 2004), 17–18, https://media.defense.gov/2010/May/25/2001330265/-1/-1/0/AFD-100525-065.pdf (accessed Jan. 22, 2025).
72. Putney, 17.
73. Kevin M. Woods, *The Mother of All Battles: Saddam Hussain's Strategic Plan for the Persian Gulf War* (Annapolis, MD: Naval Institute Press, 2008), 63, 72.
74. Schwarzkopf and Petre, *It Doesn't Take a Hero*, 467.
75. See E. R. Hooton and Tom Cooper, *Desert Storm Volume 1: The Iraqi Invasion of Kuwait and Operation Desert Shield, 1990–1991* (Warwick, Eng.: Helion, 2019), 46–60.
76. Putney, *Airpower Advantage*, 28–29.
77. U.S. DOD, *Conduct of the Persian Gulf War: Final Report to Congress* (Washington, DC: DOD, 1992), 23, https://apps.dtic.mil/sti/pdfs/ADA249270.pdf (accessed Jan. 22, 2025).
78. Cohen et al., *Gulf War Air Power Survey*, 1:108–13.
79. Cohen et al., 1:136–40.
80. CCMD was known as commander in chief (CINC) until October 2002.
81. U.S. DOD, *Conduct of the Persian Gulf War*, 97.
82. U.S. DOD, 98.
83. U.S. DOD, 96–97.

84. Col. Mandeep Singh, "Looking Back at Iraqi Air Defences during Operation Desert Storm," From Balloons to Drones, Oct. 19, 2022, https://balloonstodrones.com/2022/10/19/looking-back-at-iraqi-air-defences-during-operation-desert-storm/ (accessed May 29, 2025).
85. Kipphut, *Crossbow and Gulf War Counter-Scud Efforts*, 11–15.
86. Kipphut, 16–18.
87. Van Atta et al., *Transformation and Transition*, S-4, 23–245; "AGM-129 Advanced Cruise Missile [ACM]," Global Security, https://www.globalsecurity.org/wmd/systems/acm.htm (accessed Jan. 22, 2025).
88. See Robert H. Scales Jr., *The United States Army in the Gulf War: Certain Victory* (Washington, DC: Office of the Chief of Staff of the U.S. Army, 1993), 71–73, https://apps.dtic.mil/sti/pdfs/ADA361975.pdf (accessed Jan. 22, 2025).
89. U.S. General Accounting Office, "Operation Desert Storm: Data Does Not Exist to Conclusively Say How Well Patriot Performed," report to Congress, Sept. 2002, 2–3, https://www.gao.gov/assets/nsiad-92-340.pdf (accessed Jan. 22, 2025).
90. Paul W. Westermeyer, *U.S. Marines in the Gulf War, 1990–1991: Liberating Kuwait* (Quantico, VA: History Division, USMC, 2014), 147, https://www.usmcu.edu/Portals/218/LiberatingKuwait.pdf (accessed Jan. 22, 2024); Adam B. Siegel, "Scuds Against Al Jubayl?," U.S. Naval Institute *Proceedings* 128/12/1,198 (Dec. 2002), https://www.usni.org/magazines/proceedings/2002/december/scuds-against-al-jubayl (accessed Jan. 22, 2025).
91. Eliot A. Cohen et al., *Gulf War Air Power Survey*, vol. 2, *Operations and Effects and Effectiveness* (Washington, DC, 1993), 337, https://apps.dtic.mil/sti/pdfs/ADA279742.pdf (accessed Jan. 22, 2025).
92. Stephen C. LeSueur, "To Halt Raids by Fast Patrol Boats: Navy Laid Mines in River Bordering Iraq and Kuwait during Persian Gulf War," *Inside the Pentagon* 8, no. 17 (Apr. 23, 1992): 1, 9–19, https://www.jstor.org/stable/43987962 (accessed Jan. 22, 2025).
93. U.S. DOD, *Conduct of the Persian Gulf War*, 273–74.
94. Andrew F. Krepinevich Jr., *The Military-Technical Revolution: A Preliminary Assessment* (Washington, DC: Office of Net Assessment, U.S. DOD, 1992; repr., Washington, DC: CSBA, 2022), 39, https://csbaonline.org/uploads/documents/2002.10.02-Military-Technical-Revolution.pdf (accessed Jan. 22, 2025).
95. Krepinevich, 44.
96. Andrew F. Krepinevich Jr., "The Military Revolution," Nov. 1993, unpublished draft, 60–62, cited in *Why AirSea Battle?*, by Andrew F. Krepinevich Jr. (Washington, DC: CSBA, 2010), 8–9, https://csbaonline.org/uploads/documents/2010.02.19-Why-AirSea-Battle.pdf (accessed Jan. 22, 2025).
97. U.S. DOD, *Conduct of the Persian Gulf War*, vii–viii.
98. See Dean Cheng, "Chinese Lessons from the Gulf Wars," in *Chinese Lessons from Other People's Wars*, ed. Andrew Scobell, David Lai, and Roy Kamphausen (Carlisle, PA: U.S. Army Strategic Studies Institute, 2011), 153–91.
99. M. Taylor Fravel, *Active Defense: China's Military Strategy since 1949* (Princeton, NJ: Princeton University Press, 2019), 187.
100. Harlan W. Jenks, "Chinese Evaluation of 'Desert Storm': Implications for PRC Security," *Journal of East Asian Affairs* 6, no. 2 (Summer/Fall 1992): 462, 464–66.

101. Fravel, *Active Defense*, 139, 141–43, 149–51, 187–91.
102. Fravel, 191.
103. Walter L. Perry, "Planning the War and the Transition to Peace," in *Operation Iraqi Freedom*, ed. Walter L. Perry, Richard E. Darilek, Laurinda L. Rohn, and Jerry M. Sollinger (Santa Monica, CA: RAND Corp., 2015), 31, https://www.rand.org/pubs/research_reports/RR1214.html (accessed Jan. 22, 2025); Michael Gordon and Bernard Trainor, *Cobra II: The Inside Story of the Invasion and Occupation of Iraq* (London: Atlantic Books, 2007), 29–30.
104. Roger Strother, "Post-Saddam Iraq: The War Game," National Security Archives, George Washington University, Nov. 4, 2006, https://nsarchive2.gwu.edu/NSAEBB/NSAEBB207/index.htm (accessed Jan. 22, 2025).
105. Gordon and Trainor, *Cobra II*, 32.
106. Gordon and Trainor, 33, 41; Tommy Franks with Malcolm McConnel, *American Soldier* (New York: Harper Collins, 2004), 562, Kindle. In his book the USCENTCOM commander notes that by the third week of March, total Coalition personnel numbered 292,000, of whom 170,000 were soldiers and Marines.
107. Perry et al., *Operation Iraqi Freedom*, 31, 34–35, 37.
108. Headquarters, USCENTCOM, "USCENTCOM OPLAN 1003V Change 1," Feb. 27, 2003, MacDill Air Force Base, FL, 22.
109. Perry et al., *Operation Iraqi Freedom*, 48–50.
110. Greg Myre and Steve Inskeep, "Jim Mattis: 'Nations with Allies Thrive, Nations without Allies Wither,'" *Morning Edition*, NPR, Sept. 2, 2019, https://www.npr.org/2019/09/02/756681750/jim-mattis-nations-with-allies-thrive-nations-without-allies-wither (accessed May 24, 2024).

CHAPTER 8. REALIGNMENT

1. Li, *History of Taiwan*, 161–63.
2. Li, 167–70. For a study of the early stages of the democratization process, see Hung-Mao Tien and Chyuan-Jeng Shiau, "Taiwan's Democratization: A Summary," *World Affairs* 155, no. 2 (Fall 1992): 58–61, https://www.jstor.org/stable/20672340 (accessed Jan. 22, 2025).
3. Tucker, *Strait Talk*, 181–92.
4. Li, *History of Taiwan*, 158–59; Tucker, *Strait Talk*, 166; Ryan Hass, Bonnie Glaser, and Richard Bush, *U.S.-Taiwan Relations: Will China's Challenge Lead to a Crisis* (Washington, DC: Brookings Institute Press, 2023), 41–42.
5. Hass et al., *U.S.-Taiwan Relations*, 55. For the legal context of the 1992 consensus, see Yu-Jie Chen and Jerome A. Cohen, "China-Taiwan Relations Re-examined: The '1992 Consensus' and Cross-Strait Agreements," *University of Pennsylvania Asian Law Review* 14, no. 1 (2019): 1–40, https://scholarship.law.upenn.edu/cgi/viewcontent.cgi?article=1039&context=alr (accessed Jan. 22, 2025).
6. Shao-Chuan Leng and Cheng-yi Lin, "Political Change on Taiwan: Transition to Democracy?," Special Issue: Greater China, *China Quarterly* no. 136 (Dec. 1993): 813–17, https://www.jstor.org/stable/655592 (accessed Jan. 22, 2025).
7. Tucker, *Strait Talk*, 198–99, 203–5.
8. John W. Garver, *Face Off: China, the United States, and Taiwan's Democratization* (Seattle: University of Washington Press, 2000), 4, 22–23.

9. Tucker, *Strait Talk*, 214; Garver, *Face Off*, 29–31.
10. Robert S. Ross, "The 1995–96 Taiwan Strait Confrontation: Coercion, Credibility, and the Use of Force," *International Security* 25, no. 2 (Fall 2000): 94–95, https://www.jstor.org/stable/2626754 (accessed Jan. 22, 2025).
11. Tucker, *Strait Talk*, 217–18; Ross, "1995–96 Taiwan Strait Confrontation," 97.
12. Ross, "1995–96 Taiwan Strait Confrontation," 102.
13. Ross, 102–3.
14. Tucker, *Strait Talk*, 218–19; Ross, "1995–96 Taiwan Strait Confrontation," 104–5.
15. For an analysis of the March 1996 PLA exercises, see "Chinese Exercise Strait 961: 8–25 March 1996," Office of Naval Intelligence, National Security Archives, Georgetown University, https://nsarchive2.gwu.edu/NSAEBB/NSAEBB19/docs/doc14.pdf (accessed Jan. 22, 2025).
16. Ross, "1995–96 Taiwan Strait Confrontation," 108; Li, *History of Taiwan*, 182–83; Tucker, *Strait Talk*, 219–21; Garver, *Face Off*, 105–6.
17. Ross, "1995–96 Taiwan Strait Confrontation," 109.
18. Ross, 110.
19. Kristen Gunness and Phillip C. Saunders, *Averting Escalation and Avoiding War: Lessons from the 1995–1996 Taiwan Strait Crisis*, China Strategic Perspectives 17 (Washington, DC: Institute for National Strategic Studies, National Defense University Press, 2023), 27–33, 42, https://ndupress.ndu.edu/Portals/68/Documents/stratperspective/china/china-perspectives-17.pdf (accessed Jan. 22, 2025); Hass et al., *U.S.-Taiwan Relations*, 61. For an analysis of U.S. engagement that emerged from the crisis, see Michael Pillsbury, "The U.S. Role in Taiwan's Defense Reforms," remarks to ITDSS Conference, Taipei, Feb. 2004, https://www.uscc.gov/sites/default/files/Research/The US Role in Taiwan's Defense.pdf (accessed Jan. 22, 2025).
20. Bonnie S. Glaser, Richard C. Bush, and Michael J. Green, *Toward a Stronger U.S.-Taiwan Relationship* (Washington, DC: CSIS, 2020), app. 3, 46, https://csis-website-prod.s3.amazonaws.com/s3fs-public/publication/201021_Glaser_TaskForce_Toward_A_Stronger_USTaiwan_Relationship_0.pdf (accessed Jan. 22, 2025).
21. Jim Mann, "Clinton 1st to OK China, Taiwan '3 No's,'" *Los Angeles Times*, July 8 1998, https://www.latimes.com/archives/la-xpm-1998-jul-08-mn-1834-story.html (accessed Jan. 22, 2025).
22. Spencer Ackerman, "Taiwan's Massive, Mega-Powerful Radar Is Finally Operational," *Wired*, Mar. 8, 2018, https://www.wired.com/2013/03/taiwan-radar/ (accessed Jan. 22, 2025).
23. Wendell Minnick, "Spook Mountain: How the US Spies on China from Taiwan," *China in Arms*, May 6, 2023, https://chinainarms.substack.com/p/spook-mountain-how-the-us-spies-on (accessed Jan. 22, 2025).
24. Hass et al., *U.S.-Taiwan Relations*, 67; Li, *History of Taiwan*, 189.
25. See Bonnie Glaser, "China's Taiwan Policy in the Wake of 'One Country on Each Side,'" *American Foreign Policy Interests* 24, no. 6 (2006): 515–24, https://doi.org/10.1080/10803920216379 (accessed May 25, 2025).
26. Martin Kettle and John Hooper, "Military Force an Option to Defend Taiwan, Warns Bush," *The Guardian*, Apr. 26, 2001, https://www.theguardian.com/world/2001/apr/26/china.usa (accessed Jan. 22, 2025).

27. "President Bush and Premier Wen Jiabao Remarks to the Press," White House Press Conference (Office of the Press Secretary), Dec. 9, 2003, https://georgewbush-whitehouse.archives.gov/news/releases/2003/12/text/20031209-2.html (accessed Jan. 22, 2025).
28. It may have at some point been known as, or existed in parallel to, a non-numbered special access plan for Taiwan reportedly referred to as Project 19. William M. Arkin, *Code Names, Deciphering U.S. Military Plans, Programs, and Operations in a Post 9/11 World* (Hanover, NH: Steerforth, 2005), 54, https://archive.org/details/codenamesdecipheooarki/mode/2up?view=theater (accessed Jan. 22, 2025).
29. "Fortnightly Review," Global Taiwan Institute, July 29, 2020, https://globaltaiwan.org/2020/07/fortnightly-review-8 (accessed Jan. 22, 2025).
30. Tucker, *Strait Talk*, 262.
31. "Talking to Taiwan's New President," *Time*, Aug. 11, 2008, https://web.archive.org/web/20090917183803/http://www.time.com/time/world/article/0,8599,1831748,00.html (accessed Jan. 22, 2025); Ralph Jennings, "Taiwan and China Sign Flight, Cargo Agreements," Reuters, Nov. 4, 2008, https://www.reuters.com/article/us-taiwan-china-idUSTRE4A30E420081104 (accessed Jan. 22, 2025).
32. "Taiwan Talks End amid Clashes," Radio Free Asia, Nov. 7, 2008, https://www.rfa.org/english/news/china/taiwan-11072008104420.html (accessed Jan. 22, 2025).
33. "Taiwan and China Sign Landmark Trade Agreement," BBC News, June 29, 2019, https://www.bbc.co.uk/news/10442557 (accessed Jan. 22, 2025); Hass et al., *U.S.-Taiwan Relations*, 78–81.
34. Helen Davidson, "How the Sunflower Movement Birthed a Generation Determined to Protect Taiwan," *The Guardian*, Mar. 21, 2024, https://www.theguardian.com/world/2024/mar/21/what-is-taiwan-sunflower-movement-china.
35. Hass et al., *U.S.-Taiwan Relations*, 82, 279–80.
36. Hass et al., 95.
37. Josh Rogin, "When Trump Caved to Xi and Threw Taiwan under the Bus," *Daily Beast*, Mar. 8, 2021, https://www.thedailybeast.com/when-trump-caved-to-xi-and-threw-taiwan-under-the-bus (accessed Jan. 22, 2025).
38. Hass et al., *U.S.-Taiwan Relations*, 123, 280–81.
39. Nick Wadhams, "U.S. Eases Limits on Taiwan Contacts as Taiwan Tensions Climb," Bloomberg, Apr. 9, 2021, https://www.bloomberg.com/news/articles/2021-04-09/u-s-eases-limits-on-taiwan-meetings-as-china-tensions-climb?leadSource=uverifywall (accessed Jan. 22, 2025).
40. Hass et al., *U.S.-Taiwan Relations*, 102, 163–64; Ying Yu Lin, "The Fourth Taiwan Strait Crisis: What Did the August Exercises around Taiwan Accomplish?," *China Brief* 22, no. 18, Jamestown Foundation, Oct. 4, 2022, https://jamestown.org/program/the-fourth-taiwan-strait-crisis-what-did-the-august-exercises-around-taiwan-accomplish/ (accessed Jan. 22, 2025).
41. Ralph Jennings, "US State Department Walks Back Biden's Unusually Strong Comments on Taiwan," VOA, May 24, 2022, https://www.voanews.com/a/us-state-department-walks-back-biden-s-unusually-strong-comments-on-taiwan-/6588234.html (accessed Jan. 22, 2025).
42. Joseph Trevithick, "Army Releases Ultra Rare Video Showing Green Berets Training in Taiwan," *War Zone*, June 29, 2020, https://www.twz.com/34474/army-releases-ultra-rare-video-showing-green-berets-training-in-taiwan (accessed Jan. 22, 2025).

43. Keoni Everington, "200 US Military Trainers Now in Taiwan," *Taiwan News*, Apr. 17, 2023, https://www.taiwannews.com.tw/en/news/4866003 (accessed Jan. 22, 2025).
44. Yuko Mukai, Masatsugu Sonoda, and Yomiuri Shimbun, "U.S. Plans to Expand Scale of Training of Taiwan Military; Defense against Potential Invasion to Be Strengthened," *Japan News*, Sept. 17, 2023, https://japannews.yomiuri.co.jp/politics/politics-government/20230917-137027/ (accessed Jan. 22, 2025).
45. Keoni Everington, "Taiwan Confirms the Presence of U.S. Green Berets on Outer Islands," *Taiwan News*, Mar. 14, 2024, https://www.taiwannews.com.tw/news/5115290 (accessed Jan. 26, 2025).
46. National Defense Authorization Act for Fiscal Year 2023, Pub. L. No. 117-263, 136 Stat. 2395 (2023), secs. 5502 (3293), 5504 (3298), and 5506 (3299), https://www.congress.gov/117/plaws/publ263/PLAW-117publ263.pdf (accessed May 25, 2025).
47. National Defense Authorization Act for Fiscal Year 2024, Pub. L. No. 118-31, 137 Stat. 136 (2023), sec 1518 (549–50), https://www.congress.gov/118/plaws/publ31/PLAW-118publ31.pdf (accessed May 25, 2025).
48. Further Consolidated Appropriations Act 2024, Pub. L. No. 118-47, 138 Stat. 460 (2024), sec. 7043 (814–15), https://www.congress.gov/118/plaws/publ47/PLAW-118publ47.pdf (accessed May 25, 2025).
49. [Further Consolidated Appropriations Act 2024], Pub. L. No. 118-50, 138 Stat. 895 (2024), div. C (925), https://www.congress.gov/118/plaws/publ50/PLAW-118publ50.pdf (accessed May 25, 2025); Noah Robertson, "US Close to Sending $2 Billion in Security Aid across the Indo-Pacific," *Defense News*, July 19, 2024, https://www.defensenews.com/pentagon/2024/07/19/us-close-to-sending-2-billion-in-security-aid-across-the-indo-pacific (accessed Jan. 22, 2025).
50. Noah Robertson, "Money, Weapons, and Secret Meetings: What the Pentagon Is Doing to Arm Taiwan," *Defense News*, May 30, 2024, https://www.defensenews.com/pentagon/2024/05/30/money-weapons-and-secret-meetings-what-the-pentagon-is-doing-to-arm-taiwan (accessed Jan. 22, 2025).
51. National Defense Authorization Act for Fiscal Year 2025, Pub. L. No. 118-159, 138 Stat. 1773 (2024), secs. 1323 (2116), 5121 (2428), https://www.congress.gov/118/plaws/publ159/PLAW-118publ159.pdf (accessed May 29, 2024).
52. Mark F. Cancian and Bonny Lin, "A New Mechanism for an Old Policy: The United States Uses Drawdown Authority to Support Taiwan," CSIS, Aug. 3, 2023, https://www.csis.org/analysis/new-mechanism-old-policy-united-states-uses-drawdown-authority-support-taiwan (accessed Jan. 22, 2025).
53. Reuters, "Biden Approves US$571m Taiwan Aid," *Taipei Times*, Dec. 22, 2024, https://www.taipeitimes.com/News/front/archives/2024/12/22/2003828894 (accessed Jan. 15, 2025).
54. Helen Davidson and Chi Hui Lin, "China Launches 'Punishment' Drills around Taiwan after Inauguration of New President," *The Guardian*, May 23, 2024, https://www.theguardian.com/world/article/2024/may/23/china-taiwan-punishment-military-drills-president-inauguration (accessed Jan. 22, 2025).
55. "The Donald Trump Interview Transcript," Bloomberg Businessweek, July 14, 2024, https://www.bloomberg.com/features/2024-trump-interview-transcript (accessed Jan. 22, 2025).

56. "Read the Full Transcript: President-elect Donald Trump Interviewed by 'Meet the Press' Moderator Kristen We," NBC News, Dec. 8, 2024, https://www.nbcnews.com/politics/donald-trump/trump-interview-meet-press-kristen-welker-election-president-rcna182857 (accessed Jan. 15, 2025).
57. Demetri Sevastopulo and Kathrin Hille, "Taiwan Considers Big US Defence Purchases as Overture to Donald Trump," *Financial Times*, Nov. 10, 2024, https://www.ft.com/content/7b218d0f-31dc-4b74-b993-797388767b85 (accessed Jan. 22, 2025).

CHAPTER 9. THE OTHER SIDE OF THE HILL

1. U.S. DOD, *Military and Security Developments involving the People's Republic of China, 2024* (Washington, DC: DOD, 2024), 127, https://media.defense.gov/2024/Dec/18/2003615520/-1/-1/0/military-and-security-developments-involving-the-peoples-republic-of-china-2024.PDF (accessed Jan. 22, 2025).
2. U.S. DOD, 2.
3. Taiwan Affairs Office of the State Council, *The Taiwan Question and China's Reunification in the New Era* (English translation), White Paper, Aug. 2022, 1, download link available at "China Releases White Paper on Taiwan Question, Reunification in New Era," State Council, People's Republic of China, updated Aug. 10, 2022, https://english.www.gov.cn/archive/whitepaper/202208/10/content_WS62f34f46c6d02e533532f0ac.html (accessed Jan. 22, 2025); Xi Jinping, "Achieving Rejuvenation Is the Dream of the Chinese People," speech presented at The Road to Rejuvenation exhibition, Nov. 29, 2012, NEAC, https://www.neac.gov.cn/seac/c103372/202201/1156514.shtml (accessed Jan. 22, 2025).
4. Taiwan Affairs Office of the State Council, *Taiwan Question and China's Reunification*, 8–9, 17–19, 20.
5. Third Session of the 10th National People's Congress, Anti-Succession Law, Mar. 14, 2005 (English translation), European Parliament, 2, https://www.europarl.europa.eu/meetdocs/2004_2009/documents/fd/d-cn2005042601/d-cn20050426 01en.pdf (accessed Jan. 22, 2025).
6. U.S. DOD, *Military and Security Developments Involving the People's Republic of China*, 31.
7. Robertson, "How DC Became Obsessed with a Potential 2027 Chinese Invasion of Taiwan." For further sources, see Andrew S. Erickson, "PRC Pursuit of Xi's 2027 'Centennial Military Building Goal' (建军一百年奋斗目标): Sources & Analysis," Dec. 19, 2021, updated Apr. 18, 2023, https://www.andrewerickson.com/2021/12/prc-pursuit-of-2027-centennial-military-building-goal-sources-analysis/ (accessed Jan. 18, 2025).
8. Laurence Karacsony, "Chinese President Xi Jinping Claimed United States Is Trying to Goad Beijing into a Military Conflict with Taiwan: Report," *Sky News*, June 17, 2024, https://www.skynews.com.au/world-news/china/chinese-president-xi-jinping-claimed-united-states-is-trying-to-goad-beijing-into-a-military-conflict-with-taiwan-report/news-story/f7aa51cfee0f70695b3290d38e66dca8 (accessed Jan. 22, 2025).
9. "China Lacks the Ability to Invade, but Has Options," *Taipei Times*, Aug. 31, 2024, https://www.taipeitimes.com/News/taiwan/archives/2024/08/31/2003823049 (accessed Jan. 22, 2025).
10. John Grady, "China Expanding Pacific Operations, Taiwan Invasion 'Not Possible' by 2027, Say DoD Officials," *USNI News*, Dec. 19, 2024, https://news.usni.org/2024/12/19

/china-expanding-pacific-operations-taiwan-invasion-not-possible-by-2027-say-dod-officials (accessed Jan. 15, 2025).

11. Fravel, *Active Defense*, 27.
12. Junshi kexue yuan, ed., 中国人民解放军军语 (Military Terminology of the Chinese People's Liberation Army) (Beijing: Junshi kexue chubanshe, 2011), 50, cited in M. Taylor Fravel, "Testimony before the U.S.-China Economic and Security Review Commission, Hearing on 'A "World-Class" Military: Assessing China's Global Military Ambitions,'" June 20, 2019, 7, https://www.uscc.gov/sites/default/files/Fravel_USCC Testimony_FINAL.pdf (accessed Jan. 22, 2025); Guo Xiangjie, ed., *Biography of Zhang Wannian, Part Two* (Beijing: PLA Press, 2011), 60, cited in Joel Wuthnow and M. Taylor Fravel, "China's Military Strategy for a 'New Era': Some Change, More Continuity, and Tantalizing Hints," *Journal of Strategic Studies* 46, nos. 6–7 (Mar. 2023): 4, https://doi.org/10.1080/01402390.2022.2043850 (accessed May 19, 2025).
13. For an overview of table of the 1956–2014 reforms, see Fravel, *Active Defense*, 25. For an analysis of the 2019 shift, see Wuthnow and Fravel, "China's Military Strategy for a 'New Era,'" 1-36.
14. Fravel, *Active Defense*, 28. For further analysis of PLA strategy, operating concepts, and doctrine, see Edmund J. Burke et al., *People's Liberation Army Operational Concepts* (Santa Monica, CA: RAND Corp., 2020), https://www.rand.org/content/dam/rand/pubs/research_reports/RRA300/RRA394-1/RAND_RRA394-1.pdf (accessed Jan. 22, 2025).
15. For a full analysis of this MSG, see Fravel, *Active Defense*, 182–216.
16. Jiang Zemin, *Jiang Zemin's Selected Works, Vol. 1* (Beijing: Renmin chubanshe, 2006), 285, cited in Fravel, *Active Defense*, 184.
17. Zhang Zhen, *Zhang Zhen's Memoirs* (Beijing: Jiefangjun chubanshe, 2003), 361, cited in Fravel, *Active Defense*, 201.
18. For a full analysis of this MSG, see Fravel, *Active Defense*, 218–30.
19. Fravel, 219–21.
20. Jeffrey Engstrom, *Systems Confrontation and System Destruction Warfare: How the Chinese People's Liberation Army Seeks to Wage Modern Warfare* (Santa Monica, CA: RAND Corp., 2018), 9–11, https://www.rand.org/pubs/research_reports/RR1708.html (accessed Jan. 22, 2025).
21. For a full analysis of this MSG, see Fravel, *Active Defense*, 230–35.
22. Wuthnow and Fravel, "China's Military Strategy for a 'New Era,'" 7.
23. Wuthnow and Fravel, 8.
24. Wuthnow and Fravel, 12, 14.
25. For a full analysis of this MSG, see Wuthnow and Fravel, 1–36.
26. Wuthnow and Fravel, 14–15, 17–18.
27. Fravel, *Active Defense*, 236–37.
28. Liping Xia, "China's Nuclear Doctrine: Debates and Evolution," Carnegie Endowment for International Peace, June 6, 2016, https://carnegieendowment.org/2016/06/30/china-s-nuclear-doctrine-debates-and-evolution-pub-63967 (accessed Jan. 22, 2025).
29. Joel Wuthnow and Phillip C. Saunders, "Chairman Xi Remakes the PLA," in *Chairman Xi Remakes the PLA: Assessing Chinese Military Reforms*, ed. Phillip C. Saunders et al. (Washington, DC: National Defense University Press, 2019), 1–2, 6, 8, https://ndupress

.ndu.edu/Portals/68/Documents/Books/Chairman-Xi/Chairman-Xi.pdf (accessed Jan. 22, 2025). The primary Chinese command the United States would face would vary. For example, Southern Theater Command would likely lead the effort against USINDOPACOM in the South China Sea.

30. Cristina L. Garafola, "People's Liberation Army Reforms and Their Ramifications," RAND Corp., Sept. 23, 2016, https://www.rand.org/pubs/commentary/2016/09/pla-reforms-and-their-ramifications.html (accessed Jan. 22, 2025).
31. Gordon Arthur, "China Dissolves Strategic Support Force, Focused on Cyber and Space," *Defense News*, Apr. 23, 2024, https://www.defensenews.com/global/asia-pacific/2024/04/23/china-dissolves-strategic-support-force-focused-on-cyber-and-space (accessed Jan. 22, 2025).
32. IISS, *The Military Balance 2024* (London: IISS, 2024), 254–55.
33. Ian Easton, *China's Evolving Reconnaissance Strike Capabilities: Implications for the U.S.-Japan Alliance* (Washington DC: Project 2049 Institute; Tokyo: Japan Institute for International Affairs, 2014), 10, https://www2.jiia.or.jp/pdf/fellow_report/140219_JIIA-Project2049_Ian_Easton_report.pdf (accessed Jan. 22, 2025).
34. China Aerospace Studies Institute, Air University, "China Aerospace Studies Institute: Commander's Toolkit for China—PLA Space," PPT, 6–7, 11, https://www.airuniversity.af.edu/Portals/10/CASI/documents/Toolkit presentations/8 Commanders Toolkit-PLA Space.pdf (accessed Jan. 22, 2025).
35. China Aerospace Studies Institute, 8. See entire presentation for an overview of cyber and related capabilities.
36. Meia Nouwens, "China's New Information Support Force," IISS, May 24, 2024, https://www.iiss.org/online-analysis/online-analysis/2024/05/chinas-new-information-support-force (accessed Jan. 22, 2025).
37. U.S. DOD, *Military and Security Developments involving the People's Republic of China*, 72.
38. U.S. DOD, 24–26.
39. U.S.-China Economic and Security Review Commission, "[Chapter 4], Section 2: Weapons, Technology, and Export Controls," *2023 Annual Report to Congress* (Washington, DC), 444, https://www.uscc.gov/sites/default/files/2023-11/Chapter_4_Section_2--Weapons_Technology_and_Export_Controls.pdf (accessed Jan. 24, 2025).
40. See M. Taylor Fravel and Christopher P. Twomey, "Projecting Strategy: The Myth of Chinese Counter-Intervention," *Washington Quarterly* 37, no. 4 (2014): 171–87, https://doi.org/10.1080/0163660X.2014.1002164 (accessed Jan. 24, 2025); Timothy Heath and Andrew S. Erickson, "Is China Pursuing Counter-Intervention?," *Washington Quarterly* 38, no. 3 (2015): 143–56, https://doi.org/10.1080/0163660X.2015.1099029 (accessed Jan. 15, 2024); Tom Shugart, "Deterring the Powerful Enemy: China's Counter-Intervention Capability in a Regional Conflict," Mar. 26, 2024, CNAS, https://www.cnas.org/publications/congressional-testimony/deterring-the-powerful-enemy (accessed Jan. 15, 2025).
41. SIPRI Military Expenditure Database, SPIRI, https://milex.sipri.org/sipri (accessed Jan. 24, 2025).
42. IISS, *Military Balance 2024*, 253.
43. Li Weichao, ed., "China's Defense Budget Transparent and Moderate: Defense Spokesperson," China Military Online, Mar. 9, 2024, http://eng.mod.gov.cn/xb/News_213114/TopStories/16292566.html (accessed Jan. 24, 2025).

44. M. Taylor Fravel, George J. Gilboy, and Eric Heginbotham, "Estimating China's Defense Spending: How to Get It Wrong (and Right)," *Texas National Security Review* 7, no. 3 (Summer 2024), https://tnsr.org/2024/06/estimating-chinas-defense-spending-how-to-get-it-wrong-and-right/ (accessed Jan. 24, 2025).
45. Fravel, Gilboy, and Heginbotham.
46. References to specific equipment are largely from IISS, *Military Balance 2024*, 253–64.
47. Carlo Kopp, "PLA-AF and PLA-N Flanker Variants," Australia Air Power, Jan. 27, 2014, https://www.ausairpower.net/APA-PLA-Flanker-Variants.html (accessed Jan. 24, 2025).
48. Thomas Newdick, "A Guide to China's Increasingly Impressive Air-to-Air Missile Inventory," *War Zone*, Sept. 1, 2022, https://www.thedrive.com/the-war-zone/a-guide-to-chinas-increasingly-impressive-air-to-air-missile-inventory (accessed Jan. 24, 2025).
49. Thomas Newdick and Tyler Rogoway, "China Stuns with Heavy Stealth Tactical Jet's Sudden Appearance (Updated)," *War Zone*, Dec. 26, 2024, https://www.twz.com/air/china-stuns-with-heavy-stealth-tactical-jets-sudden-appearance (accessed Jan. 15, 2025).
50. "Changjian-20 (CJ-20)," Missile Threat, MDAA, Jan. 2023, https://missiledefenseadvocacy.org/missile-threat-and-proliferation/todays-missile-threat/china/changjian-20-cj-20 (accessed Jan. 24, 2025); "Chinese H-6N Bomber Aircraft Seen Carrying Hypersonic Missile," *Army Recognition*, Apr. 21, 2022, https://www.armyrecognition.com/news/navy-news/2022/chinese-h-6n-bomber-aircraft-seen-carrying-hypersonic-missile (accessed Jan. 24, 2025); Thomas Newdick, "This Is Our Best Look Yet at China's Air-Launched 'Carrier Killer' Missile," *War Zone*, Apr. 19, 2022, https://www.thedrive.com/the-war-zone/this-is-our-best-look-yet-at-chinas-air-launched-carrier-killer-missile (accessed Jan. 24, 2025).
51. For an analysis of China's air defenses, see Justin Bronk, *Modern Russian and Chinese Integrated Air Defence Systems The Nature of the Threat, Growth Trajectory and Western Options* (London: Royal United Services Institute, 2020), 15–23, https://static.rusi.org/20191118_iads_bronk_web_final.pdf (accessed Jan. 24, 2025).
52. "HQ-15," Missile Threat, MDAA, June 20, 2018, https://missiledefenseadvocacy.org/missile-threat-and-proliferation/todays-missile-threat/china/china-anti-access-area-denial/hq-15/ (accessed Jan. 24, 2025); "HQ-18," Missile Threat, MDAA, June 2018, https://missiledefenseadvocacy.org/missile-threat-and-proliferation/todays-missile-threat/china/china-anti-access-area-denial/hq-18 (accessed Jan. 24, 2025).
53. "Russia Completes Delivery of Second S-400 Missile System Regimental Set to China—Source," TASS, Jan. 27, 2020, https://tass.com/world/1113113 (accessed Jan. 24, 2025).
54. Emma Helfrich, "China Conducts Midcourse Missile Defense Test One Year after Last," *War Zone*, June 21, 2022, https://www.thedrive.com/the-war-zone/china-conducts-sixth-missile-defense-test-one-year-after-the-last-one (accessed Jan. 24, 2025).
55. "Project 2319 Tianbo [Sky Wave] Over-the-Horizon Backscatter Radar [OTH-B]," Global Security, https://www.globalsecurity.org/wmd/world/china/oth-b.htm (accessed Jan. 24, 2025).
56. Joseph Trevithick, "China's New Domestically Developed Y-20 Airborne Early Warning Jet Spotted," *War Zone*, Dec. 27, 2024, https://www.twz.com/air/chinas-new-domestically-developed-y-20-airborne-early-warning-jet-spotted (accessed Jan. 15, 2025).

57. For an analysis of the role of the Airborne Corps in an invasion of Taiwan, see Cristina L. Garafola, *The PLA Airborne Corps in a Joint Island Landing Campaign*, China Maritime Report 19 (Newport, RI: China Maritime Studies Institute, U.S. Naval War College, 2022), U.S. Naval War College Digital Commons, https://digital-commons.usnwc.edu/cmsi-maritime-reports/19 (accessed Jan. 24, 2025).
58. Dylan Malyasov, "China Places Massive Order for Kamikaze Drone," *Defense Blog*, Dec. 22, 2024, https://defence-blog.com/china-places-massive-order-for-kamikaze-drones/?amp (accessed Jan. 15, 2025).
59. "China Modifies Its H-6 Strategic Bombers into Potent Electronic Warfare Platforms," *Military Watch Magazine*, Jan. 27, 2018, https://militarywatchmagazine.com/article/china-modifies-its-h-6-strategic-bombers-into-potent-electronic-warfare-platforms (accessed Jan. 24, 2025).
60. Bates Gill and Taeho Kim, *China's Arms Acquisitions from Abroad—A Quest for "Superb and Secret Weapons"* (Oxford: Oxford University Press, 1995), 38–40, https://www.sipri.org/sites/default/files/files/RR/SIPRIRR11.pdf (accessed Jan. 24, 2025).
61. Thomas Newdick, "China's New Nuclear Submarine Sank during Mysterious Incident in Wuhan: Report," *War Zone*, Sept. 26, 2024, https://www.twz.com/sea/chinas-new-nuclear-submarine-sank-during-mysterious-incident-in-wuhan-report (accessed Jan. 24, 2025).
62. For an overview of the submarine force, see J. Michael Dahm and Alison Zhao, *Bitterness Ends, Sweetness Begins: Organizational Changes to the PLAN Submarine Force since 2015*, China Maritime Report 28 (Newport, RI: China Maritime Studies Institute, U.S. Naval War College, 2022), U.S. Naval War College Digital Commons, https://digital-commons.usnwc.edu/cmsi-maritime-reports/28/ (accessed Jan. 24, 2025).
63. Rick Joe, "The Future of China's Amphibious Assault Fleet," *The Diplomat*, July 17, 2019, https://thediplomat.com/2019/07/the-future-of-chinas-amphibious-assault-fleet (accessed Jan. 24, 2025).
64. Dennis J. Blasko and Roderick Lee, "The Chinese Navy's Marine Corps, Part 1: Expansion and Reorganization," *China Brief* 19, no. 3, Jamestown Foundation, Feb. 1, 2019, https://jamestown.org/program/the-chinese-navys-marine-corps-part-1-expansion-and-reorganization (accessed Jan. 24, 2025). For a full analysis of the PLANMC and its role in a war over Taiwan, see Conor Kennedy, *The New Chinese Marine Corps: A "Strategic Dagger" in a Cross-Strait Invasion*, China Maritime Report 15 (Newport, RI: China Maritime Studies Institute, U.S. Naval War College, 2021), U.S. Naval War College Digital Commons, https://digital-commons.usnwc.edu/cmsi-maritime-reports/15/ (accessed Jan. 24, 2025).
65. For information on the potential role of China's merchant ships in amphibious operations, see Thomas Shugart, "Mind the Gap: How China's Civilian Shipping Could Enable a Taiwan Invasion," *War on the Rocks*, Aug. 16, 2021, https://warontherocks.com/2021/08/mind-the-gap-how-chinas-civilian-shipping-could-enable-a-taiwan-invasion (accessed Jan. 24, 2025); Shugart, "Mind the Gap, Part II: The Cross-Strait Potential of China's Civilian Shipping Fleet has Grown," *War on the Rocks*, Oct. 12, 2022, https://warontherocks.com/2022/10/mind-the-gap-part-2-the-cross-strait-potential-of-chinas-civilian-shipping-has-grown (accessed Jan. 24, 2025); H. I. Sutton, "Chinese Launch

Assault Craft from Civilian Car Ferries in Mass Amphibious Invasion Drill, Satellite Photos Show," *USNI News*, Sept. 28, 2022, https://news.usni.org/2022/09/28/chinese-launch-assault-craft-from-civilian-car-ferries-in-mass-amphibious-invasion-drill-satellite-photos-show (accessed Jan. 24, 2025).

66. H. I. Sutton, "China Suddenly Building Fleet of Special Barges Suitable for Taiwan Landings," *Naval News*, Jan. 10, 2025, https://www.navalnews.com/naval-news/2025/01/china-suddenly-building-fleet-of-special-barges-suitable-for-taiwan-landings/ (accessed Jan. 16, 2025).
67. Brian Waidelich and George Pollitt, *PLAN Mine Countermeasures: Platforms, Training, and Civil-Military Integration*, China Maritime Report 29 (Newport, RI: China Maritime Studies Institute, U.S. Naval War College, 2023), 5, 13–14, U.S. Naval War College Digital Commons, https://digital-commons.usnwc.edu/cgi/viewcontent.cgi?article=1028&context=cmsi-maritime-reports (accessed Jan. 24, 2025). See all of Waidelich and Pollitt for an analysis of PLA MCM approach.
68. Rod Lee, "PLA Naval Aviation Reorganization 2023," China Aerospace Studies Institute, Air University, July 31, 2023, https://www.airuniversity.af.edu/CASI/Display/Article/3475163/pla-naval-aviation-reorganization-2023 (accessed Jan. 24, 2025).
69. Elsa Kania, *The PLA's Unmanned Aerial Systems: New Capabilities for a "New Era" of Chinese Military Power* (Montgomery, AL: China Aerospace Studies Institute, Air University, 2018), 15–17, https://www.airuniversity.af.edu/Portals/10/CASI/documents/Research/PLAAF/2018-08-29 PLAs_Unmanned_Aerial_Systems.pdf (accessed Jan. 24, 2025).
70. For analysis, see Lonnie D. Henley, *Civilian Shipping and Maritime Militia: The Logistics Backbone of a Taiwan Invasion*, China Maritime Report 21 (Newport, RI: China Maritime Studies Institute, U.S. Naval War College, 2022), U.S. Naval War College Digital Commons, https://digital-commons.usnwc.edu/cgi/viewcontent.cgi?article=1020&context=cmsi-maritime-reports (accessed Jan. 24, 2025).
71. Details on the PLAGF can be found in *People's Liberation Army "Ground Forces": Quick Reference Guide* (Newport News, RI: U.S. Army Training and Doctrine Command, 2021), https://rdl.train.army.mil/catalog-ws/view/100.ATSC/D9915B53-207D-4EB8-9305-D5D01541842D-1640033052890/gta20_10_002.pdf (accessed Jan. 24, 2025).
72. U.S. DOD, *Military and Security Developments Involving the People's Republic of China*, 45.
73. For details of the PHL-16's potential role in a Taiwan contingency, see Joshua Arostegui, *The PCH191 Modular Long-Range Rocket Launcher: Reshaping the PLA Army's Role in a Cross-Strait Campaign*, China Maritime Report 32 (Newport, RI: China Maritime Studies Institute, U.S. Naval War College, 2023), U.S. Naval War College Digital Commons, https://digital-commons.usnwc.edu/cmsi-maritime-reports/32/ (accessed Jan. 24, 2025).
74. Kania, *PLA's Unmanned Aerial Systems*, 12–14.
75. For a full analysis of the PLAGF amphibious brigades and their role, see Dennis J. Blasko, *The PLA Army Amphibious Force*, China Maritime Report 20 (Newport, RI: China Maritime Studies Institute, U.S. Naval War College, 2022), U.S. Naval War College Digital Commons, https://digital-commons.usnwc.edu/cmsi-maritime-reports/20/ (accessed May 25, 2025).
76. For a full analysis of PLA special forces in the event of an invasion of Taiwan, see John Chen and Joel Wuthnow, *Chinese Special Operations in a Large-Scale Island Landing*,

China Maritime Report 18 (Newport, RI: China Maritime Studies Institute, U.S. Naval War College, 2022), U.S. Naval War College Digital Commons, https://digital-commons.usnwc.edu/cgi/viewcontent.cgi?article=1017&context=cmsi-maritime-reports (accessed Jan. 24, 2025).

77. See Anthony H. Cordesman, with Joseph Kendall, *Chinese Strategy and Military Modernization in 2016: A Comparative Analysis* (Washington, DC: CSIS, 2016), 377–426, https://www.jstor.org/stable/resrep23376.14 (accessed Jan. 24, 2025).

78. Christopher J. Mihal, "Understanding the People's Liberation Army Rocket Force: Strategy, Armament, and Disposition," *Military Review* (July–Aug. 2021): 223–25, https://www.armyupress.army.mil/Portals/7/military-review/Archives/English/SE-S21/SES21-Mihal-PLA-Rocket-Force.pdf (accessed Jan. 24, 2025); Zuzanna Gwadera, "Intelligence Leak Reveals China's Successful Test of a New Hypersonic Missile," IISS, May 18, 2023, https://www.iiss.org/online-analysis/online-analysis/2023/05/intelligence-leak-reveals-chinas-successful-test-of-a-new-hypersonic-missile/ (accessed Jan. 20, 2025).

79. For analysis, see Andrew S. Erickson, *Chinese Anti-Ship Ballistic Missile (ASBM) Development: Drivers, Trajectories, and Strategic Implications* (Washington, DC: Brookings Institute Press, 2013); and Doyle and Herzinger, *Carrier Killers.*

80. U.S. DOD, *Military and Security Developments involving the People's Republic of China,* 64–65.

81. Newdick, "Our Best Look Yet at China's Air-Launched 'Carrier Killer' Missile."

82. Mihal, "Understanding the People's Liberation Army Rocket Force," 223–334.

83. Mihal, 225–26.

84. Matt Korda and Hans Kristensen, "China Is Building a Second Nuclear Missile Silo Field," FAS, July 26, 2021, https://fas.org/publication/china-is-building-a-second-nuclear-missile-silo-field (accessed Jan. 24, 2025).

85. Hans M. Kristensen, Matt Korda, and Eliana Johns, "Nuclear Notebook: Chinese Nuclear Weapons, 2023," *Bulletin of the Atomic Scientists* 79, no. 2 (2023): 108, https://doi.org/10.1080/00963402.2023.2178713 (accessed Jan. 24, 2025); U.S. DOD, *Military and Security Developments involving the People's Republic of China,* 108–9.

86. Mathieu Duchâtel, "An Assessment of China's Options for Military Coercion of Taiwan," in *Crossing the Strait: China's Military Prepares for War with Taiwan,* ed. Joel Wuthnow et al. (Washington, DC: National Defense University Press, 2022), 103, https://ndupress.ndu.edu/Portals/68/Documents/Books/crossing-the-strait/crossing-the-strait.pdf (accessed Jan. 24, 2025).

87. Dmitri Alperovitch, "A Chinese Economic Blockade of Taiwan Would Fail or Launch a War," *War on the Rocks,* June 5, 2024, https://warontherocks.com/2024/06/a-chinese-economic-blockade-of-taiwan-would-fail-or-launch-a-war (accessed Jan. 24, 2025).

88. Mark Cozad, "The PLA and Contingency Planning," in *The People's Liberation Army and Contingency Planning in China,* ed. Andrew Scobell et al. (Washington, DC: National Defense University Press, 2015), 18–19, 21–24, https://ndupress.ndu.edu/Portals/68/Documents/Books/PLA-contingency/PLA-Contingency-Planning-China.pdf (accessed Jan. 24, 2025).

89. See Joel Wuthnow, "What I Learned from the PLA's Latest Strategy Textbook," *China Brief* 21, no. 11, Jamestown Foundation, May 25, 2021, https://jamestown.org/program

/what-i-learned-from-the-plas-latest-strategy-textbook (accessed Jan. 24, 2025). For English translations of core texts, see *In Their Own Words: Foreign Military Thought—Science of Campaigns (2006)* (Montgomery, AL: China Aerospace Studies Institute, Air Force University, [2020]), translation of *Science of Campaigns*, ed. Zhang Yuliang (Beijing: National Defense University Press, 2006), https://www.airuniversity.af.edu/Portals/10/CASI/documents/Translations/2020-12-02 (accessed Jan. 24, 2025); and *In Their Own Words: Science of Military Strategy 2020* (Montgomery, AL: China Aerospace Studies Institute, Air Force University, 2022), translation of *Science of Military Strategy*, ed. Xiao Tianliang (Beijing: National Defense University Press, 2020), https://www.airuniversity.af.edu/Portals/10/CASI/documents/Translations/2022-01-26%202020%20Science%20of%20Military%20Strategy.pdf (accessed Jan. 24, 2025).

90. Michael Casey, "Firepower Strike, Blockade, Landing: PLA Campaigns for a Cross-Strait Conflict," in *Crossing the Strait: China's Military Prepares for War with Taiwan*, ed. Joel Wuthnow et al. (Washington, DC: National Defense University Press, 2022), 114, 117, https://ndupress.ndu.edu/Portals/68/Documents/Books/crossing-the-strait/crossing-the-strait.pdf (accessed Jan. 24, 2025).
91. Casey, 116–17.
92. Casey, 115.
93. The PLA defines campaigns as how to employ particular types of forces to achieve narrow objectives, which means that a conflict may require several campaigns: Cozad, "PLA and Contingency Planning," 12. For a more comprehensive overview of PLA Taiwan war plans, see Easton, *Chinese Invasion Threat*, 93–142.
94. See *In Their Own Words: Foreign Military Thought—Science of Campaigns (2006)*, 329–50; and Casey, "Firepower Strike, Blockade, Landing," 123–28. Ian Easton translates the original Chinese as "Joint Blockade Operations against Taiwan" because, while the literal translation of the last word is "large island or islands," supporting literature makes it clear that this is a reference to Taiwan. Ian Easton, *China's Top Five War Plans* (Arlington, VA: Project 2049 Institute, 2019), 2, https://project2049.net/wp-content/uploads/2019/01/Chinas-Top-Five-War-Plans_Ian_Easton_Project2049.pdf (accessed Jan. 24, 2025).
95. Casey, "Firepower Strike, Blockade, Landing," 118–23. Ian Easton translates this as "Joint Firepower Strike Operations against Taiwan." Easton, *China's Top Five War Plans*, 2.
96. See *In Their Own Words: Foreign Military Thought—Science of Campaigns (2006)*, 351–73; and Casey, "Firepower Strike, Blockade, Landing," 128–32. Ian Easton translates this as "Joint Attack Operations against Taiwan." Easton, *China's Top Five War Plans*, 2.
97. See *In Their Own Words: Foreign Military Thought—Science of Campaigns (2006)*, 375–93. Ian Easton translates this as "Joint Anti-Air Raid Operations." Easton, *China's Top Five War Plans*, 2.
98. Casey, "Firepower Strike, Blockade, Landing," 124.
99. See Bradley Martin, Kristen Gunness, Paul DeLuca, and Melissa Shostak, *Implications of a Coercive Quarantine of Taiwan by the People's Republic of China* (Santa Monica, CA: RAND Corp., 2023), https://www.rand.org/pubs/research_reports/RRA1279-1.html (accessed Jan. 24, 2025).
100. Easton, *China's Top Five War Plans*, 4; Easton, *Chinese Invasion Threat*, 98; Casey, "Firepower Strike, Blockade, Landing," 123–24.
101. Easton, *Chinese Invasion Threat*, 99–105.

102. Casey, "Firepower Strike, Blockade, Landing," 118–20; Easton, *China's Top Five War Plans*, 3–5. Ian Easton also analyses the two campaigns as one integrated action. See Easton, *Chinese Invasion Threat*, 97–113.
103. Casey, "Firepower Strike, Blockade, Landing," 121–22; Easton, *Chinese Invasion Threat*, 100, 107–11.
104. Casey, "Firepower Strike, Blockade, Landing," 128.
105. Easton, *Chinese Invasion Threat*, 119–21; Keoni Everington, "Leaked Map Shows China Plans to Invade S. Taiwan after Taking Kinmen, Penghu," *Taiwan News*, Jan. 20, 2020, https://www.taiwannews.com.tw/en/news/3861097 (accessed Jan. 24, 2025).
106. Chen and Wuthnow, *Chinese Special Operations*, 3–4.
107. Garafola, *PLA Airborne Corps in a Joint Island Landing*, 5–6. For additional analysis, see Roderick Lee, "The PLA Airborne Corps in a Taiwan Scenario," in Wuthnow et al., *Crossing the Strait*, 195–222.
108. Kennedy, *New Chinese Marine Corps*, 12, 19–20.
109. Blasko, *PLA Army Amphibious Force*, 3–5.
110. Easton, *Chinese Invasion Threat*, 151–53.
111. Easton, 147–64.
112. See Easton, 132–42; Sale Lilly, "Killing Rats in a Porcelain Shop: PLA Urban Warfare in a Taiwan Campaign" in *Crossing the Strait: China's Military Prepares for War with Taiwan*, ed. Joel Wuthnow et al., 139–57.
113. Easton, *China's Top Five War Plans*, 5–6.

CHAPTER 10. ISLAND DEFENSE

1. For a slightly different chronology to the one outlined in this section, though conforming to the same trend, see ROC MND, *2019 National Defense Report* (Taipei: MND, 2019), 68–69, https://www.ustaiwandefense.com/wp-content/uploads/2025/02/Taiwan-National-Defense-Report-2009.pdf (accessed Jan. 24, 2025).
2. York W. Chen, "The Evolution of Taiwan's Military Strategy: Convergence and Dissonance," *China Brief*, 9, no. 23, Jamestown Foundation, Nov. 19, 2009, https://jamestown.org/program/the-evolution-of-taiwans-military-strategy-convergence-and-dissonance (accessed Jan. 24, 2025). See also Arthur S. Ding and Paul A. Huang, "Taiwan's Paradoxical Perceptions of the Chinese Military," *China Perspective* 2011, no. 4 (Dec. 30, 2024): 46–47, https://doi.org/10.4000/chinaperspectives.5742 (accessed Jan. 24, 2025).
3. Chen, "Evolution of Taiwan's Military Strategy"; Ding and Huang, "Taiwan's Paradoxical Perceptions," 47–48.
4. Ian Easton, Eric Lee, Grace Price, Colby Ferland, Cathy Fang, Mark Stokes, and Alice Cho, *Before Zero Day: Taiwan's Evolving Defense Strategy and the Struggle for Peace* (Arlington, VA: Project 2049 Institute, Sept. 2023), 33–34, https://project2049.net/2023/09/27/before-zero-day-taiwans-evolving-defense-strategy-and-the-struggle-for-peace/ (accessed Jan. 24, 2025).
5. ROC MND, *Quadrennial Defense Review 2009* (Taipei: MND, 2009), 74, https://www.ustaiwandefense.com/wp-content/uploads/2025/02/2009-Taiwan-Quadrennial-Defense-Review-QDR.pdf (accessed Jan. 24, 2025).
6. ROC MND, *2021 Quadrennial Defense Review* (Taipei: MND, 2021), 19, https://www.ustaiwandefense.com/wp-content/uploads/2025/02/2021-Taiwan-Quadrennial-Defense-Review-QDR.pdf (accessed Jan. 24, 2025).

7. ROC MND, *2025 Quadrennial Defense Review* (Taipei: MND, 2025), 27–29, https://www.ustaiwandefense.com/wp-content/uploads/2023/09/2025-Taiwan-Quadrennial-Defense-Review-QDR.pdf (accessed May 25, 2025).
8. For two of many examples, see William S. Murray, "Revisiting Taiwan's Defense Strategy," *Naval War College Review* 63, no. 3 (Summer 2008), https://digital-commons.usnwc.edu/cgi/viewcontent.cgi?article=1814&context=nwc-review (accessed Jan. 24, 2025); and James Timbie and James O. Ellis Jr., "A Large Number of Small Things: A Porcupine Strategy for Taiwan," *Texas National Security Review* 5, no. 1 (Winter 2021–22): 83–93, https://tnsr.org/2021/12/a-large-number-of-small-things-a-porcupine-strategy-for-taiwan (accessed Jan. 24, 2025).
9. Lee Hsi-min, "Taiwan's Overall Defense Concept: Theory and the Practice," draft of remarks to the Hoover Institute, Sept. 27, 2021, 2–3, https://www.hoover.org/sites/default/files/210927_adm_lee_hoover_remarks_draft4.pdf (accessed Jan. 24, 2025). For descriptions of the ODC, see ROC MND, *2019 National Defense Report*, 75–76; Lee Hsi-min and Eric Lee, "Taiwan's Overall Defense Concept, Explained," *The Diplomat*, Nov. 3, 2020, https://thediplomat.com/2020/11/taiwans-overall-defense-concept-explained (accessed Jan. 24, 2025); Drew Thompson, "Hope on the Horizon: Taiwan's Radical New Defense Policy," *War on the Rocks*, Oct. 2, 2018, https://warontherocks.com/2018/10/hope-on-the-horizon-taiwans-radical-new-defense-concept (accessed Jan. 24, 2025); Alexander Chieh-cheng Huang, "A Net Assessment of Taiwan's Overall Defense Policy," in Wuthnow et al., *Crossing the Straits*, 321–44.
10. Hsi-min and Lee, "Taiwan's Overall Defense Concept, Explained."
11. Thomas Newdick, "Taiwan Disguises Armored Vehicles as Cranes and Scrapheaps during Urban Warfare Maneuvers," *War Zone*, Oct. 29, 2020, https://www.thedrive.com/the-war-zone/37349/taiwan-disguises-armored-vehicles-as-cranes-and-scrapheaps-during-urban-warfare-maneuvers (accessed Jan. 24, 2025); Gabriel Dominguez, "US State Department Approves Potential USD280 Million FMS to Taiwan of Field Information Communication System," *Janes*, Dec. 8, 2020, https://www.janes.com/osint-insights/defence-news/us-state-department-approves-potential-usd280-million-fms-to-taiwan-of-field-information-communication-system (accessed May 19, 2025); Kelvin Chen, "Taiwan Military's Hangar Construction Project in Kaohsiung Faces Budgetary Issues," *Taiwan News*, Mar. 28, 2022, https://www.taiwannews.com.tw/en/news/4488021 (accessed Jan. 24, 2025).
12. Timbie and Ellis, "Large Number of Small Things."
13. ROC MND, *2019 National Defense Report*, 75–76; Timbie and Ellis, "Large Number of Small Things"; Yimou Lee, "Taiwan's Special Defence Budget to Go Mostly on Anti-Ship Capabilities," Reuters, Oct. 5, 2021, https://www.reuters.com/world/asia-pacific/taiwans-special-defence-budget-go-mostly-anti-ship-capabilities-2021-10-05/ (accessed Jan. 24, 2025).
14. Joseph Trevithick, "Sale of Over 1,000 Kamikaze Drones to Taiwan Points to Grand 'Hellscape' Counter-China Plans," *War Zone*, June 19, 2024, https://www.twz.com/air/sales-of-over-1000-kamikaze-drones-to-taiwan-point-to-grand-hellscape-counter-china-plans (accessed Jan. 24, 2025).
15. Michael A. Hunzeker, "Taiwan's Defense Plans Are Going off the Rails," *War on the Rocks*, Nov. 18, 2021, https://warontherocks.com/2021/11/taiwans-defense-plans-are-going-off-the-rails/; Tim Fish, "Taiwan's Navy Caught between Two Strategies to Counter Chinese

Threat," *Defense News,* June 7, 2023, https://news.usni.org/2023/06/07/taiwans-navy-caught-between-two-strategies-to-counter-chinese-threat (accessed Jan. 24, 2025).

16. Kelvin Chen, "Taiwan's Plan to Purchase Seahawk Helicopters Hits Roadblock," *Taiwan News,* Feb. 22, 2022, https://www.taiwannews.com.tw/en/news/4451502 (accessed Jan. 24, 2025); "US Accused of Undermining Taiwan Defences by Focusing on 'D-Day' Scenario," *Financial Times,* May 17, 2022, https://www.ft.com/content/dd0a987e-d2d3-4f8c-be65-bf897645dbf0 (accessed Jan. 24, 2025).
17. ROC MND, *1993–1994 Defense Report,* trans. Yang Lien-ching, Le Chang-hao, and Hsieh Yung-t'ien (Taipei: Li Ming Cultural Enterprises for MND, 1994), 102, https://china.usc.edu/sites/default/files/article/attachments/taiwan-1993-1994-national-defense-report.pdf (accessed Jan. 24, 2025).
18. John Dotson, "Taiwan's 'Military Force Restructuring Plan' and the Extension of Conscripted Military Service," *Global Taiwan Brief* 8, no. 3, Global Taiwan Institute, Feb. 8, 2023, https://globaltaiwan.org/2023/02/taiwan-military-force-restructuring-plan-and-the-extension-of-conscripted-military-service (accessed Jan. 24, 2025).
19. IISS, *Military Balance 2024,* 315.
20. Aaron Tu and Jonathan Chin, "Armed Forces at 80% Strength, Report Says," *Taipei Times,* May 29, 2024, https://www.taipeitimes.com/News/taiwan/archives/2024/05/29/2003818561 (accessed Jan. 24, 2025).
21. Gordon Arthur, "Taiwan Boosts Defense Spending in Face of Chinese Military Prodding," *Defense News,* Aug. 23, 2024, https://www.defensenews.com/global/asia-pacific/2024/08/23/taiwan-boosts-defense-spending-in-face-of-chinese-military-prodding/?utm_source=twitter&utm_medium=social&utm_campaign=tw_dfn (accessed Jan. 24, 2025).
22. See Paul Huang, "Taiwan's Military Is a Hollow Shell," *Foreign Policy,* Feb. 15, 2020, https://foreignpolicy.com/2020/02/15/china-threat-invasion-conscription-taiwans-military-is-a-hollow-shell (accessed Jan. 24, 2025); Klaus Bardenhagen, "Taiwan's Army 'Ill-Prepared' for Attack," *DW,* May 4, 2021, https://www.dw.com/en/taiwans-army-ill-prepared-for-potential-chinese-attack/a-57102659 (accessed Jan. 24, 2025); Bernard D. Cole, "The Growing Urgency of Taiwan Military Personnel Reforms," *Global Taiwan Brief* 6, no. 18, Global Taiwan Institute, Sept. 8, 2021, https://globaltaiwan.org/2021/09/the-growing-urgency-of-taiwan-military-personnel-reforms (accessed Jan. 24, 2025).
23. "MND Shares 2029 Conscript Target," *Taipei Times,* Mar. 6, 2023, https://www.taipeitimes.com/News/front/archives/2023/03/06/2003795558 (accessed Jan. 24, 2025).
24. "Han Kuang Drills to Switch Focus," *Taipei Times,* June 24, 2024, https://www.taipeitimes.com/News/front/archives/2024/06/24/2003819800 (accessed Jan. 24, 2025).
25. Dotson, "Taiwan's 'Military Force Restructuring Plan'"; ROC MND, *National Defense Report 2023,* 94–96; ROC MND, "Force Structure Adjustment of All-Out Defense," 6. https://www.mnd.gov.tw/NewUpload/202303/Force Structure Adjustment of All-out Defense_404109.pdf (accessed Jan. 24, 2025).
26. Contemporary force data is largely taken from IISS, *Military Balance 2024,* 314–19.
27. Roy Choo and Peter Ho, *Modern Taiwanese Air Power: The Republic of China Air Force Today* (Wien, Aust.: Harpia, 2021), 24. See also Ian Easton, *Able Archers: Taiwan's Defense Strategy in an Age of Precision Strike* (Arlington, VA: Project 2049 Institute, 2014), 26–30,

https://project2049.net/wp-content/uploads/2018/06/Easton_Able_Archers_Taiwan_Defense_Strategy.pdf (accessed Jan. 24, 2025); and Mark Stokes and Eric Lee, *Early Warning in the Taiwan Strait* (Arlington, VA: Project 2049 Institute, 2022), https://project2049.net/wp-content/uploads/2022/04/Stokes-and-Lee-Early-Warning-in-the-Taiwan-Strait-Project-2049.pdf (accessed Jan. 24, 2025).

28. See Choo and Ho, *Modern Taiwanese Air Power,* 62–67; and Thomas Newdick, "Air-Launched Supersonic Anti-Ship Missile Being Tested by Taiwan," *War Zone,* Feb. 24, 2025, https://www.twz.com/air/taiwan-is-testing-an-air-launched-supersonic-anti-ship-missile (assessed May 25, 2025).
29. See Choo and Ho, *Modern Taiwanese Air Power,* 58–62.
30. Choo and Ho, 52–53, 55.
31. See Choo and Ho, 50–57, 79–80.
32. Choo and Ho, 29–30.
33. Keoni Everington, "Taiwan to Buy 4 NASAMS Systems from U.S. to Defend Capital, Key Air Bases," *Taiwan News,* July 22, 2023, https://www.taiwannews.com.tw/en/news/5024226 (accessed Jan. 24, 2025).
34. Choo and Ho, *Modern Taiwanese Air Power,* 25–28.
35. Choo and Ho, 82–83. Other sources refer to the SkyGuardian rather than SeaGuardian variant.
36. Choo and Ho, 31.
37. Rowan Allport, "Long-Range Conventional Precision Strike: Taiwan's Post-Nuclear Deterrent?," *The Diplomat,* Aug. 13, 2021, https://thediplomat.com/2021/08/long-range-conventional-precision-strike-taiwans-post-nuclear-deterrent (accessed Jan. 24, 2025).
38. Emma Helfrich, "Taiwan's Coast Guard Tests Its Ability to Turn Cutters into Ship Killers," *War Zone,* May 27, 2022, https://www.twz.com/taiwans-coast-guard-test-its-ability-to-turn-cutters-into-ship-killers (accessed Jan. 24, 2025).
39. Tso-Juei Hsu, "Taiwan Starts Construction of New Light ASW Frigate," *Naval News,* Jan. 22, 2024, https://www.navalnews.com/naval-news/2024/01/taiwan-starts-construction-of-new-light-asw-frigate (accessed Jan. 24, 2025).
40. Rowan Allport, "Taiwan's New Submarines Will Be a Mixed Blessing," *The Diplomat,* Sept. 30, 2023, https://thediplomat.com/2023/09/taiwans-new-submarines-will-be-a-mixed-blessing (accessed Jan. 24, 2025).
41. Lo Tien-pin and Jake Chung, "New Navy Command to Operate Harpoon Missiles," *Taipei Times,* Aug. 24, 2024, https://www.taipeitimes.com/News/taiwan/archives/2024/08/24/2003822696 (accessed Jan. 24, 2025).
42. For a discussion of their role in the ODC, see Yu-Tai Chang, "The ROC Marine Corps Future Role in Overall Defense Concept (ODC)" (master's paper, USMC Command and Staff College, 2021), https://apps.dtic.mil/sti/trecms/pdf/AD1177947.pdf (accessed Jan. 24, 2025).
43. Mike Yeo, "Taiwan Unveils Army Restructure Aimed at Decentralizing Military," *Defense News,* May 17, 2021, https://www.defensenews.com/global/asia-pacific/2021/05/17/taiwan-unveils-army-restructure-aimed-at-decentralizing-military (accessed Jan. 24, 2025); Easton et al., *Before Zero Day,* 6.
44. IISS, *Military Balance* 2024, 315.

45. ROC MND, "All-Out Defense Mobilization, Armed Forces Reserve Command, All-Out Defense Mobilization Agency," updated June 21, 2024, https://afrc.mnd.gov.tw/afrcweb/Content_en.aspx?MenuID=6305&MP=2 (accessed Jan. 24, 2025). For a reserve force overview, see Ian Easton, Mark Stokes, Cortez A. Cooper, and Arthur Chan, *Transformation of Taiwan's Reserve Force* (Santa Monica, CA: RAND Corp., 2017), https://www.rand.org/content/dam/rand/pubs/research_reports/RR1700/RR1757/RAND_RR1757.pdf (accessed Jan. 24, 2025).
46. Easton et al., *Before Zero Day*, 64. IISS, *Military Balance 2024*, 315.
47. ROC MND, *National Defense Report 2023*, 94–96.
48. Wu Huizhong, "Army Reserves Worry Taiwan as China Looms," *Taipei Times*, Sept. 12, 2022, https://www.taipeitimes.com/News/taiwan/archives/2022/12/07/2003790274 (accessed Jan. 24, 2025). One commentator has suggested that 20,000 combat-ready reservists would be the maximum possible. See Paul Huang (@PaulHuangReport), "Mark Milley said Taiwan has a million-strong reserve," X, Apr. 2, 2023, https://x.com/PaulHuangReport/status/1642502629745123328 (accessed Jan. 24, 2025).
49. Ben Blanchard, "Ukraine War Gives Taiwan's Military Reservist Reform New Impetus," Reuters, Mar. 12, 2022, https://www.reuters.com/world/asia-pacific/ukraine-war-gives-taiwans-military-reservist-reform-new-impetus-2022-03-12 (accessed Jan. 24, 2025); ROC MND, *National Defense Report 2023*, 106–8.
50. ROC Ministry of Foreign Affairs, "Ministry of National Defense Launches New Cybersecurity Command," Mar. 7, 2017, https://nspp.mofa.gov.tw/nsppe/content_tt.php?unit=2&post=117794 (accessed Jan. 24, 2025).
51. Valentin Weber, "Taiwan's Offensive Cyber Capabilities and Ramifications for a Taiwan-China Conflict," Council on Foreign Relations, Dec. 7, 2022, https://www.cfr.org/blog/taiwans-offensive-cyber-capabilities-and-ramifications-taiwan-china-conflict (accessed Jan. 24, 2025); Hsini Huang, "A Collaborative Battle in Cybersecurity?: Threats and Opportunities for Taiwan," *Asia Policy* 15, no. 2 (Apr. 2020): 103–4.
52. Mark Stokes, Yang Kuang-shun, and Eric Lee, *Preparing for the Nightmare: Readiness and Ad hoc Coalition Operations in the Taiwan Strait* (Arlington, VA: Project 2049 Institute, 2020), 27–28, https://project2049.net/wp-content/uploads/2020/09/Preparing-for-the-Nightmare_Readiness-and-Ad-hoc-Coalition-Operations-in-the-Taiwan-Strait_Stokes_Yang_Lee_P2049_200901.pdf (accessed Jan. 21, 2025). See also Easton, *Chinese Invasion Threat*, 197–201.
53. ROC MND, *2021 Quadrennial Defense Review*, 19; ROC MND, *National Defense Report 2023*, 63–64.
54. For analysis on the change, see Kitsch Liao, "Taiwan Focuses on Societal Resilience and U.S. Cooperation in New Defense Review," Jamestown Foundation, Apr. 28, 2025, https://jamestown.org/program/taiwan-focuses-on-societal-resilience-and-u-s-cooperation-defense-review/ (accessed June 1, 2025).
55. ROC MND, *2025 Quadrennial Defense Review*, 28.
56. ROC MND, 28.
57. Ian Easton, "Taiwan, Asia's Secret Air Power," *The Diplomat*, Sept. 25, 2014, https://thediplomat.com/2014/09/taiwan-asias-secret-air-power (accessed Jan. 24, 2025); Emma Helfrich, "Extremely Rare Photos inside Taiwan's Underground Fighter Jet Caves," *War Zone*, July 26, 2022, https://www.thedrive.com/the-war-zone/extremely-rare-photos

-inside-taiwans-underground-fighter-jet-caves (accessed Jan. 24, 2025); Easton, *Able Archers*, 50–52.

58. Easton, *Able Archers*, 47–50.
59. ROC MND, *National Defense Report 2023*, 64.
60. ROC MND, *2019 National Defense Report*, 68–69; ROC MND, *National Defense Report 2023*, 64.
61. Easton, *Chinese Invasion Threat*, 205–9.
62. Easton, 231–32.
63. For comment from China to this effect, see "Envoy's 'Re-Education' of Taiwanese Remark Draws Ire," *Taipei Times*, Aug. 6, 2022, https://www.taipeitimes.com/News/front/archives/2022/08/06/2003783061 (accessed Jan. 24, 2025).

CHAPTER 11. PRIMACY

1. Dick Cheney, *Defense Strategy for the 1990s: The Regional Defense Strategy* (Washington, DC: DOD, 1993), 16–18, https://apps.dtic.mil/sti/tr/pdf/ADA268979.pdf (accessed Jan. 24, 2025).
2. For an overview of the process, see Lorna S. Jaffe, *The Development of the Base Force, 1989–1992* (Washington, DC: Joint History Office, Office of the CJCS), https://www.airandspaceforces.com/PDF/DocumentFile/Documents/2005/baseforce_Jaffe_070193.pdf (accessed May 24, 2025).
3. Eric V. Larson, *Force Planning Scenarios, 1945–2016: Their Origins and Use in Defense Strategic Planning* (Santa Monica, CA: RAND Corp., 2019), 127, 131–32, https://www.rand.org/pubs/research_reports/RR2173z1.html (accessed Jan. 24, 2025).
4. Larson, 139–42.
5. For an overview of the Bottom-Up Review and its scenario planning process, see Larson, 145–73.
6. U.S. DOD, *Report of the Quadrennial Defense Review* (Washington DC: Office if the Secretary of Defense, May 1997), 5, https://history.defense.gov/Portals/70/Documents/quadrennial/QDR1997.pdf (accessed Jan. 24, 2025).
7. National Defense Panel, *Transforming Defense: National Security in the 21st Century* (Arlington, VA, 1997), 11–13, 33–34, Homeland Security Digital Library, https://www.hsdl.org/c/abstract/?docid=438820 (accessed Jan. 24, 2025).
8. U.S. DOD, *Report of the Quadrennial Defense Review*, 15–16, 24; Larson, *Force Planning Scenarios*, 174, 186.
9. Adm. Walter F. Doran, "Pacific Fleet Focuses on War Fighting," U.S. Naval Institute *Proceedings* 129/8/1,206 (Aug. 2003), https://www.usni.org/magazines/proceedings/2003/august/pacific-fleet-focuses-war-fighting (accessed Jan. 21, 2025).
10. Stokes, Yang, and Lee, *Preparing for the Nightmare*, 46–47.
11. Bryan Clark, "How to Keep War with China from Being a Pick-Up Game," Defense One, Hudson Institute, Nov. 22, 2022, https://www.hudson.org/how-keep-war-china-being-pick-game-bryan-clark (accessed Jan. 24, 2025).
12. Kristensen, Norris, and McKinzie, *Chinese Nuclear Forces and U.S. Nuclear War Planning*, 160–64; Hans M. Kristensen, "US Nuclear War Plan Updated amidst Nuclear Policy Review," FAS, Apr. 4, 2013, https://fas.org/publication/oplan8010-12/.
13. For an overview of U.S. Navy strategies and concepts during the 1990s, see Peter M. Swartz with Karin Duggan, *U.S. Navy Capstone Strategies and Concepts (1991–2000): Strategy, Policy,*

Concept, and Vision Documents (Alexandria, VA: CNA Corp., 2012), https://www.history.navy.mil/research/library/online-reading-room/title-list-alphabetically/u/us-navy-capstone-strategies-concepts-1991-2000.html (accessed Jan. 24, 2025). For an analysis of post–Cold War policy, see Amund Lundesgaard, *US Navy Strategy and Force Structure after the Cold War* (Oslo: IFS Insights, 2011), https://fhs.brage.unit.no/fhs-xmlui/bitstream/handle/11250/99587/Insight2011_nov.pdf?sequence=1&isAllowed=y (accessed Jan. 24, 2025).

14. H. Lawrence Garrett III, Adm. Frank B. Kelso II, and Gen. A. M. Gray, "The Way Ahead," U.S. Naval Institute *Proceedings* 117/4/1,058 (Apr. 1991), https://www.usni.org/magazines/proceedings/1991/april/way-ahead (accessed Jan. 24, 2025).
15. U.S. Dept. of the Navy, *From the Sea: Preparing the Naval Service for the 21st Century* (Washington, DC: Dept. of the Navy, 1992), https://apps.dtic.mil/sti/pdfs/ADA338570.pdf (accessed Jan. 24, 2025); U.S. Dept. of the Navy, *Forward . . . From the Sea* (Washington, DC: Dept. of the Navy, 1994), https://apps.dtic.mil/sti/pdfs/ADA338561.pdf (accessed Jan. 24, 2025).
16. Adm. Jay Johnson, "Anytime, Anywhere: A Navy for the 21st Century," U.S. Naval Institute *Proceedings* 123/11/1,137 (Nov. 1997), https://www.usni.org/magazines/proceedings/1997/november/anytime-anywhere-navy-21st-century (accessed Jan. 24, 2025). See also VAdm. A. K. Cebrowski and Capt. Wayne P. Hughes Jr. (Ret.), "Rebalancing the Fleet," U.S. Naval Institute *Proceedings* 125/11/1,161 (Nov. 1999), https://www.usni.org/magazines/proceedings/1999/november/rebalancing-fleet (accessed Jan. 24, 2025).
17. Lundesgaard, *US Navy Strategy and Force Structure after the Cold War*, 17.
18. Adm. Vern Clark, "Sea Power 21: Projecting Decisive Joint Capabilities," U.S. Naval Institute *Proceedings*, 128/10/1,196 (Oct. 2002), https://www.usni.org/magazines/proceedings/2002/october/sea-power-21-projecting-decisive-joint-capabilities (accessed Jan. 24, 2025); Lundesgaard, *US Navy Strategy and Force Structure after the Cold War*, 18–19.
19. Burton L. Streicher, *Navy Shore Surge Requirements Support* (Alexandria, VA: CNA, 2005), 2, 9 https://apps.dtic.mil/sti/tr/pdf/AD1014544.pdf (accessed Jan. 24, 2025).
20. U.S. Dept. of the Navy, *A Cooperative Strategy for 21st Century Seapower* (Washington DC: Dept. of the Navy, 2007), 3–5, 10, https://permanent.fdlp.gov/gp010908/Maritime strategy.pdf (accessed May 20, 2025); Lundesgaard, *US Navy Strategy and Force Structure after the Cold War*, 21, 22.
21. For additional analysis of the concepts in this paragraph, see Andrew Krepinevich, Barry Watts, and Robert Work, *Meeting the Anti-Access and Area-Denial Challenge* (Washington, DC: CSBA, 2003).
22. Clark, "Sea Power 21."
23. John J. Jumper, "Global Strike Task Force: A Transforming Concept, Forged by Experience," *Aerospace Power Journal* (Spring 2001): 29–33, https://apps.dtic.mil/sti/pdfs/ADA518979.pdf (accessed Jan. 24, 2025).
24. U.S. Army, *Concepts for the Objective Force*, White Paper, Army Chief of Staff, Nov. 2001, https://apps.dtic.mil/sti/pdfs/ADA578581.pdf (accessed Jan. 24, 2025).
25. "US Ship Force Levels, 1886–Present," Naval History and Heritage Command, Nov. 17, 2017, https://www.history.navy.mil/research/histories/ship-histories/us-ship-force-levels.html (accessed Jan. 24, 2025).

26. Benjamin S. Lambeth, *Air Power against Terror: America's Conduct of Operation Enduring Freedom* (Santa Monica, CA: RAND Corp., 2005), 48–49, https://www.rand.org/pubs/monographs/MG166-1.html (accessed Jan. 24, 2025). For contemporary coverage of the QDR, see Thom Shanker, "The Pentagon: New Blueprint for Military Shifts Priority to U.S. Soil, Revising 2-War Strategy," *New York Times*, Oct. 2, 2001, https://www.nytimes.com/2001/10/02/us/nation-challenged-pentagon-new-blueprint-for-military-shifts-priority-us-soil.html (accessed Jan. 24, 2025).
27. U.S. DOD, *Quadrennial Defense Review Report* (Washington, DC: Office of the Secretary of Defense, 2001), 14, https://history.defense.gov/Portals/70/Documents/quadrennial/QDR2001.pdf (accessed Jan. 24, 2025).
28. U.S. DOD, iv, 4, 17, 30, 43–44.
29. Nina Silove, "The Pivot before the Pivot: U.S. Strategy to Preserve the Power Balance in Asia," *International Security* 40, no. 4 (Spring 2016): 53–58, https://www.jstor.org/stable/43828314?read-now=1&seq=2#page_scan_tab_contents (accessed Jan. 25, 2025); Michael R. Gordon, "Pentagon Review Puts Emphasis on Long-Range Arms in the Pacific," *New York Times*, May 17, 2021, https://www.nytimes.com/2001/05/17/world/pentagon-review-puts-emphasis-on-long-range-arms-in-pacific.html (accessed Jan. 25, 2025).
30. Silove, "Pivot before the Pivot," 57–58.
31. Silove, 58–61, 67–69.
32. U.S. DOD, *Quadrennial Defense Review Report* (Washington, DC: Office of the Secretary of Defense, 2006), 9, 29–30, https://history.defense.gov/Portals/70/Documents/quadrennial/QDR2006.pdf.
33. Krepinevich, Watts, and Work, *Meeting the Anti-Access Challenge*, iii, 7.

CHAPTER 12. GREAT POWER COMPETITION

1. U.S. DOD, *Quadrennial Defense Review Report* (Washington, DC: Office of the Secretary of Defense, 2010), v–vii, 11–16, https://history.defense.gov/Portals/70/Documents/quadrennial/QDR2010.pdf (accessed May 20, 2025).
2. Larson, *Force Planning Scenarios*, 238–39; U.S. DOD, *Quadrennial Defense Review Report*, v–vii, 42–43.
3. U.S. DOD, *Quadrennial Defense Review Report*, 9, 15, 17, 31.
4. U.S. DOD, 31.
5. U.S. DOD, *Sustaining U.S. Global Leadership: Priorities for 21st Century Defense* (Washington, DC: DOD, 2012), 2, 4, 5, https://apps.dtic.mil/sti/pdfs/ADA554328.pdf (accessed Jan. 25, 2025).
6. U.S. DOD, *Quadrennial Defense Review Report*, 32. Use of the term "AirSea Battle" can be traced back to 1992. See Cdr. James Stavridis, "A New Air Sea Battle Concept: Integrated Strike Forces" (report, National War College, 1992), https://apps.dtic.mil/sti/tr/pdf/ADA436862.pdf (accessed Jan. 24, 2025).
7. U.S. DOD, *National Defense Strategy* (Washington, DC: Office of the Secretary of Defense, 2008), 3, 4, 16, https://www.oas.org/csh/spanish/documentos/2008NationalDefenseStrategy.pdf (accessed Jan. 24, 2025).
8. Richard Halloran, "PACAF's 'Vision' Thing," *Air Force Magazine*, Jan. 2009, 54–56, https://www.airandspaceforces.com/PDF/MagazineArchive/Documents/2009/January2009/0109vision.pdf (accessed Jan. 24, 2025).

9. Richard Halloran, "War Game Prepares U.S. Forces for Next Threat," *Taipei Times*, Oct. 25, 2008, https://www.taipeitimes.com/News/editorials/archives/2008/10/25/2003426904 (accessed Jan. 24, 2025).
10. Krepinevich, *Why AirSea Battle?*, 1.
11. Krepinevich, 5–7, 13–25.
12. Jan van Tol, Mark Gunzinger, Andrew Krepinevich, and Jim Thomas, *AirSea Battle: A Point of Departure Operational Concept* (Washington, DC: CSBA, 2010), https://csbaonline.org/uploads/documents/2010.05.18-AirSea-Battle.pdf (accessed Jan. 24, 2025). Even if we put the DOD concept's not mentioning China down to diplomacy, the concept also included broader forms that the PLA was unlikely to utilize. For further discussion of the differentiation, see Cdr. David Forman, "The First Rule of Air-Sea Battle," U.S. Naval Institute *Proceedings* 140/4/1,334 (Apr. 2014), https://www.usni.org/magazines/proceedings/2014/april/first-rule-air-sea-battle (accessed Jan. 24, 2025). See also Greg Jaffe, "U.S. Model for a Future War Fans Tensions with China and inside Pentagon," *Washington Post*, Aug. 1, 2012, https://www.washingtonpost.com/world/national-security/us-model-for-a-future-war-fans-tensions-with-china-and-inside-pentagon/2012/08/01/gJQAC6F8PX_story.html (accessed Jan. 24, 2025).
13. Van Tol et al., *AirSea Battle*, xi–xii, 50–52.
14. Van Tol et al., 52–74.
15. Van Tol et al., 73–79.
16. Van Tol et al., 66–67, 95–96.
17. U.S. DOD, *Joint Operational Access Concept (JOAC) Version 1.0* (Washington, DC: JCS, 2012), 4, https://apps.dtic.mil/sti/citations/ADA555385 (accessed Jan. 24, 2025). For a JSOC overview, see Gregory Kreuder, "Lead Turning the Fight: The Joint Operational Access Concept and Joint Doctrine," *Joint Force Quarterly* 69 (2nd Quarter 2013): 103–8, https://ndupress.ndu.edu/Portals/68/Documents/jfq/jfq-69/JFQ-69_103-108_Kreuder.pdf (accessed Jan. 24, 2025).
18. U.S. DOD, ASB Office, *Air-Sea Battle: Service Collaboration to Address Anti-Access & Area Denial Challenges* (Washington, DC: DOD, 2013), i, 3–7, https://apps.dtic.mil/sti/pdfs/ADA584067.pdf (accessed May 25, 2025).
19. The following overview is derived from Aaron L. Friedberg, *Beyond Air-Sea Battle: The Debate over U.S. Military Strategy in Asia* (London: IISS, 2014), 105–16.
20. For further analysis, see Sean Mirski, "Consequences of an American Naval Blockade of China," *Journal of Strategic Studies*, Feb. 12, 2013, https://carnegieendowment.org/2013/02/12/stranglehold-context-conduct-and-consequences-of-american-naval-blockade-of-china-pub-51135 (accessed Jan. 24, 2025); and Douglas C. Peifer, "China, the German Analogy, and the New AirSea Operational Concept," *Orbis* 55, no. 1 (2011): 114–31, https://www.sciencedirect.com/science/article/abs/pii/S0030438710000694 (accessed Jan. 24, 2025).
21. See T. X. Hammes, *Offshore Control: A Proposed Strategy for an Unlikely Conflict*, Strategic Forum 278 (Washington, DC: INSS National Defense University, 2012), https://ndupress.ndu.edu/Portals/68/Documents/stratforum/SF-278.pdf (accessed Jan. 24, 2025); Friedberg, *Beyond Air-Sea Battle*, 116–28; Eirik Torsvoll, "Deterring Conflict with China: A Comparison of the Air-Sea Battle Concept, Offshore Control, and Deterrence by Denial," *Fletcher Forum of World Affairs* 39, no. 1 (Winter 2015): 44–48, https://

www.jstor.org/stable/45290097 (accessed Jan. 24, 2025); Jeffrey E. Kline and Wayne P. Hughes Jr., "Between Peace and the Air-Sea Battle: A War at Sea Strategy," *Naval War College Review* 65, no. 4 (Autumn 2012): 35–40, https://digital-commons.usnwc.edu/cgi/viewcontent.cgi?article=1490&context=nwc-review (accessed Jan., 2025).

22. See Andrew S. Erickson, "Deterrence by Denial: How to Prevent China from Using Force," *National Interest*, Dec. 16, 2013, https://nationalinterest.org/commentary/war-china-two-can-play-the-area-denial-game-9564 (accessed Jan. 24, 2025); Torsvoll, "Deterring Conflict with China," 48–54; Mike Gallagher, "State of (Deterrence by) Denial," *Washington Quarterly* 42, no. 2 (Summer 2019): 31–45, https://www.mca-marines.org/wp-content/uploads/Rep.-Gallagher-State-of-Deterrence-by-Denial.pdf (accessed Jan. 24, 2025).
23. See Andrew F. Krepinevich Jr., *Archipelagic Defense: The Japan–U.S. Alliance and Preserving Peace and Stability in the Western Pacific* (Washington, DC: Sasakawa Peace Foundation, 2017), https://www.spf.org/en/jpus/publications/20170810_1.html (accessed Jan. 24, 2025); Krepinevich, *Archipelagic Defense 2.0* (Washington, DC: Hudson Institute, 2023), https://www.hudson.org/archipelagic-defense-2-taiwan-china-japan-australia-deterrence-us-navy-andrew-krepinevich-jr (accessed Jan. 24, 2025).
24. Sam Lagrone, "Pentagon Drops Air Sea Battle Name, Concept Lives On," *USNI News*, Jan. 20, 2015, updated Apr. 27, 2017, https://news.usni.org/2015/01/20/pentagon-drops-air-sea-battle-name-concept-lives (accessed Jan. 26, 2025).
25. Capt. Michael E. Hutchens, Col. William D. Dries, Lt. Col. Jason C. Perdew, Col. Vincent D. Bryant, and Col. Kerry E. Moores, "Joint Concept for Access and Maneuver in the Global Commons: A New Joint Operational Concept," *Joint Forces Quarterly* 84 (1st Quarter 2017): 134–39, https://ndupress.ndu.edu/Portals/68/Documents/jfq/jfq-84/jfq-84_134-139_Hutchens-et-al.pdf (accessed Jan. 24, 2025).
26. U.S. DOD, *Quadrennial Defense Review 2014* (Washington, DC: Office of the Secretary of Defense, 2014), iii, vii–viii, 4, 7, 20, 21, https://history.defense.gov/Portals/70/Documents/quadrennial/QDR2014.pdf (accessed Jan. 24, 2025).
27. U.S. DOD, "Fact Sheet: Highlights of the NDAA," May 2014, cited in Larson, *Force Planning Scenarios*, 255–56.
28. Gian Gentile, Michael Shurkin, Alexandra T. Evans, Michelle Grisé, Mark Hvizda, and Rebecca Jensen, *The History of the Third Offset, 2014–2018* (Santa Monica, CA: RAND Corp., 2021), 2–3, 8, https://www.rand.org/pubs/research_reports/RRA454-1.html (accessed Jan. 24, 2025). See also Richard A. Bitzinger, *Third Offset Strategy and Chinese A2/AD Capabilities* (Washington, DC: CNAS, 2016), https://www.jstor.org/stable/resrep06122 (accessed Jan. 24, 2025).
29. U.S. DOD, Defense Science Board, *2017 Summer Study: Long-Range Effects—Executive Summary* (Washington, DC: Defense Science Board, 2018), 1–4, https://dsb.cto.mil/wp-content/uploads/reports/2010s/LRE Executive Summary__Final.pdf (accessed Jan. 24, 2025); Undersecretary for Defense Engineering Hedi Shuy, "Outpacing China: Expediting Innovation to the Warfighter," Feb. 15, 2024, statement to U.S. House Armed Services Committee, 6–7, https://docs.house.gov/meetings/AS/AS00/20240215/116887/HHRG-118-AS00-Wstate-ShyuH-20240215.pdf (accessed Jan. 24, 2025).
30. U.S. DOD, *Fiscal Year (FY) 2025 Budget Estimates: DARPA, Defense-Wide Justification Book*, vol. 1, *Research, Development, Test & Evaluation, Defense-Wide* (Washington, DC: DOD), 200, https://comptroller.defense.gov/Portals/45/Documents/defbudget

/FY2025/budget_justification/pdfs/03_RDT_and_E/RDTE_Vol1_DARPA_MasterJustificationBook_PB_2025.pdf (accessed Jan. 24, 2025); Patrick Tucker, "'Hellscape': DOD Launches Massive Drone Swarm Program to Counter China," *Defense News*, Aug. 28, 2023, https://www.defenseone.com/technology/2023/08/hellscape-dod-launches-massive-drone-swarm-program-counter-china/389797 (accessed Jan. 24, 2025).

31. U.S. JCS, *The National Military Strategy of the United States* (Washington, DC: CJCS, 2025), 3–4, https://www.jcs.mil/portals/36/documents/publications/2015_national_military_strategy.pdf (accessed Jan. 25, 2025).
32. U.S. DOD, Chief Financial Officer, *Defense Budget Overview: United States Department of Defense Fiscal Year 2017 Budget Request* (Washington, DC: Office of the Undersecretary of Defense [Comptroller], 2016), 2-2, https://comptroller.defense.gov/portals/45/documents/defbudget/fy2017/fy2017_budget_request_overview_book.pdf (accessed Jan. 24, 2025).
33. President of the United States, *National Security Strategy of the United States of America* (Washington, DC: White House, 2017), 25, 46, https://trumpwhitehouse.archives.gov/wp-content/uploads/2017/12/NSS-Final-12-18-2017-0905.pdf (accessed Jan. 24, 2025).
34. U.S. DOD, *Summary of the 2018 National Defense Strategy of the United States of America: Sharpening the American Military's Competitive Edge* (Washington, DC: CJCS), S-2, 6–7, https://media.defense.gov/2020/May/18/2002302061/-1/-1/1/2018-national-defense-strategy-summary.pdf (accessed Jan. 24, 2025).
35. Ken Moriyasu, "U.S. Faces 4 Threats but Only Equipped for 1 War, Experts Say," *Nikkei Asia*, Feb. 23, 2024, https://asia.nikkei.com/Politics/Defense/U.S.-faces-4-threats-but-only-equipped-for-1-war-experts-say (accessed Jan. 24, 2025).
36. For example, U.S.-based bombers could be counted as part of the blunt layer as they would be able to respond rapidly despite not being in the theater.
37. U.S. DOD, *Summary of the 2018 National Defense Strategy*, 7. See also U.S. JCS, *Description of the National Military Strategy 2018* (Washington, DC: CJCS, 2018), 2, 3, https://www.jcs.mil/Portals/36/Documents/Publications/UNCLASS_2018_National_Military_Strategy_Description.pdf (accessed Jan. 24, 2025).
38. Michael J. Mazarr, *Defending without Dominance: Accelerating the Transition to a New U.S. Defense Strategy* (Santa Monica, CA: RAND Corp., 2023), 20, https://www.rand.org/content/dam/rand/pubs/perspectives/PEA2500/PEA2555-1/RAND_PEA2555-1.pdf (accessed Jan. 24, 2025).
39. U.S. DOD, Chief Financial Officer, *Defense Budget Overview: United States Department of Defense Fiscal Year 2024 Budget Request* (Washington, DC: Office of the Undersecretary of Defense [Comptroller] 2023), 3–8, https://comptroller.defense.gov/Portals/45/Documents/defbudget/FY2024/FY2024_Budget_Request_Overview_Book.pdf (accessed Jan. 24, 2025).
40. NSC, "U.S. Strategic Framework for the Indo-Pacific," 2021, 2, 5, 7, https://trumpwhitehouse.archives.gov/wp-content/uploads/2021/01/IPS-Final-Declass.pdf (accessed Jan. 24, 2025). See also Rory Medcalf, "Declassification of Secret Document Reveals U.S. Strategy in the Indo-Pacific," *The Strategist*, Jan. 13, 2021, https://www.aspistrategist.org.au/declassification-of-secret-document-reveals-real-us-strategy-in-the-indo-pacific (accessed Jan. 24, 2025).

41. White House, *National Security Strategy* (Washington, DC, 2022), 11, 12, 20–22, 23–24, https://www.documentcloud.org/documents/23165487-biden-harris-administrations-national-security-strategy-102022-1/ (accessed Feb. 16, 2025).
42. U.S. DOD, *2022 National Defense Strategy of the United States of America*, 4, 8–9, 12–13, 15, 17.
43. U.S. JCS, *National Military Strategy 2022: Strategic Discipline* (Washington, DC: CJCS, 2022), 6, https://www.jcs.mil/Portals/36/NMS 2022_Signed.pdf (accessed Jan. 24, 2025).
44. Gen. Mark A. Milley, "Strategic Inflection Point," *Joint Forces Quarterly* 110 (3rd Quarter 2023): 9, https://ndupress.ndu.edu/Portals/68/Documents/jfq/jfq-110/jfq-110_6-15_Milley.pdf (accessed Jan. 24, 2025).
45. U.S. DOD, *Joint Warfighting*, Joint Publication 1, vol. 1, https://keystone.ndu.edu/Portals/86/Joint Warfighting.pdf.
46. Adapted from Milley, "Strategic Inflection Point," 12.
47. Alex Horton and Hannah Natanson, "Secret Pentagon Memo on China, Homeland Has Heritage Fingerprints," *Washington Post*, Mar. 25, 2025, https://www.washingtonpost.com/national-security/2025/03/29/secret-pentagon-memo-hegseth-heritage-foundation-china/.
48. Andrew Tilghman, "Guam: Defense Infrastructure Readiness," Congressional Research Service, Aug. 3, 2023, 9, 11, 18–19, 25–26, https://crsreports.congress.gov/product/pdf/R/R47643 (accessed Jan. 24, 2025); Joseph Trevithick, "Guam's Airspace Set to Be Most Defended on Earth in New Plans," *War Zone*, Aug. 11, 2013, https://www.thedrive.com/the-war-zone/guams-airspace-set-to-be-most-defended-on-earth-in-new-plans (accessed Jan. 24, 2025).
49. Joseph Trevithick, "Construction of Airbase on Tinian Island in Case Guam Gets Knocked Out Has Begun," *War Zone*, June 15, 2022, https://www.thedrive.com/the-war-zone/construction-of-airbase-on-tinian-island-in-case-guam-gets-knocked-out-has-begun (accessed Jan. 24, 2025).
50. Tylor Rogoway, "Major Airfield Expansion on Wake Island Seen by Satellite as U.S. Preps for Pacific Fight," *War Zone*, July 3, 2022, https://www.thedrive.com/the-war-zone/34404/big-airfield-expansion-on-wake-island-seen-by-satellite-as-u-s-preps-for-pacific-fight (accessed Jan. 24, 2025).
51. For details of the political arrangement, see Thomas Lum, "The Compacts of Free Association," Congressional Research Service, Nov. 13, 2023, updated Apr. 25, 2024, https://crsreports.congress.gov/product/pdf/IF/IF12194 (accessed Jan., 2025). For the utility of access to these states in a Taiwan scenario, see Angela Smith, "U.S. Compacts of Free Association Are Key to Deterring a Taiwan Contingency," *The Diplomat*, Aug. 9, 2022, https://thediplomat.com/2022/08/us-compacts-of-free-association-are-key-to-deterring-a-taiwan-contingency (accessed Jan., 2025).
52. Emma Helfrich and Tylor Rogoway, "U.S. Building Advanced Over-the-Horizon Radar on Palau," *War Zone*, Dec. 30, 2022, https://www.thedrive.com/the-war-zone/u-s-building-advanced-over-the-horizon-radar-on-palau (accessed Jan. 24, 2025).
53. Thomas Newdick, "Australian Airbase Gets Upgrades for American Bomber Deployments," *War Zone*, Oct. 31, 2022, https://www.thedrive.com/the-war-zone/australian-airbase-gets-upgrades-for-american-bomber-deployments (accessed Jan. 24, 2025); Akhil Kadidal, "US-Funded Fuel Facility Built at RAAF Base Darwin," *Janes Defence*,

Oct. 31, 2023, https://www.janes.com/osint-insights/defence-news/air/us-funded-fuel-facility-built-at-raaf-base-darwin (accessed Jan. 24, 2025).

54. Greg Hadley, "Air Force Will Swap in F-15EX and F-35 Fighters on Japan," *Air & Space Force Magazine*, July 3, 2024, https://www.airandspaceforces.com/air-force-f-15ex-f-35-japan-kadena-misawa (accessed Jan. 24, 2025).
55. Newdick, "Australian Airbase Gets Upgrades"; Kadidal, "US-Funded Fuel Facility."
56. U.S. DOD, "Joint Statement—Submarine Tendered Maintenance Period," Aug. 23, 2024, https://www.defense.gov/News/Releases/Release/Article/3882302 (accessed Jan. 24, 2025).
57. Luke A. Nicastro, "The Pacific Deterrence Initiative: A Budgetary Overview," Congressional Research Service, Jan. 9, 2023, updated Nov. 25, 2024, https://crsreports.congress.gov/product/pdf/IF/IF12303 (accessed Jan. 24, 2025).
58. U.S. Dept. of the Navy, *Forward, Engaged Ready: A Cooperative Strategy for 21st Century Sea Power* (Washington, DC: Dept. of the Navy, 2015), 8, 11, 13, 19–21, 33–34, https://apps.dtic.mil/sti/pdfs/ADA615292.pdf (accessed Jan. 24, 2025).
59. U.S. Dept. of the Navy, *Advantage at Sea: Prevailing with Integrated All-Domain Naval Power* (Washington, DC: Office of the Secretary of the Navy, 2020), 1, 5, 9, https://media.defense.gov/2020/Dec/16/2002553074/-1/-1/0/triservicestrategy.pdf (accessed Jan. 24, 2025).
60. U.S. Dept. of the Navy, 13, 14.
61. See Ronald O'Rourke, "Defense Primer: Navy Distributed Maritime Operations (DMO) Concept," Congressional Research Service, June 26, 2024, updated Nov. 20, 2024, https://sgp.fas.org/crs/natsec/IF12599.pdf (accessed Jan. 24, 2025).
62. Megan Eckstein and Colin Demarest, "Project Overmatch: U.S. Navy Preps to Deploy Secretive Multidomain Tech," *Defense News*, Dec. 8, 2022, https://www.defensenews.com/outlook/2022/12/05/project-overmatch-us-navy-preps-to-deploy-secretive-multidomain-tech (accessed Jan. 24, 2025).
63. See U.S. Dept. of the Navy, *Tentative Manual for Expeditionary Advanced Base Operations*, 2nd ed. (Washington, DC: Headquarters of the USMC, May 2023), https://www.marines.mil/Portals/1/Docs/230509-Tentative-Manual-For-Expeditionary-Advanced-Base-Operations-2nd-Edition.pdf (accessed Jan. 24, 2025).
64. See Headquarters, USMC, *Force Design 2030* (Washington, DC: Dept. of the Navy, 2020), https://www.hqmc.marines.mil/Portals/142/Docs/CMC38%20Force%20Design%202030%20Report%20Phase%20I%20and%20II.pdf(accessed Jan. 24, 2025).
65. Headquarters, USMC, *A Concept for Stand-In Forces* (Washington, DC: Dept. of the Navy, 2021), 1–2, 4, 5, 7, 14, https://www.hqmc.marines.mil/Portals/142/Users/183/35/4535/211201_A%20Concept%20for%20Stand-In%20Forces.pdf (accessed Jan. 24, 2025). See also David H. Berger, "A Concept for Stand-In Forces," U.S. Naval Institute *Proceedings* 147/11/1,425 (Nov. 2021), https://www.usni.org/magazines/proceedings/2021/november/concept-stand-forces (accessed Jan. 24, 2025); Gen. Eric Smith, "Stand-In Forces: Adapt or Perish," U.S. Naval Institute *Proceedings* 148 (Apr. 2022), https://www.usni.org/magazines/proceedings/2022/april/stand-forces-adapt-or-perish (accessed Jan. 24, 2025).
66. Andrew Feickert, "The U.S. Marine Corps Marine Littoral Regiment (MLR)," Congressional Research Service, Aug. 17, 2023, https://crsreports.congress.gov/product/pdf/IF/IF12200/5 (accessed June 1, 2025).
67. John Grady, "'Hellscape' Swarms Could Be a Cost-Effective Taiwan Defense, Says Report," *USNI News*, July 1, 2024, https://news.usni.org/2024/07/01/hellscape-swarms

-could-be-as-cost-effective-taiwan-defense-says-report (accessed Jan. 24, 2025); Carter Johnston, "Breaking Down the U.S. Navy's 'Hellscape' in Detail," *Naval News*, June 16, 2024, https://www.navalnews.com/naval-news/2024/06/breaking-down-the-u-s-navys-hellscape-in-detail/ (accessed Jan. 24, 2025).

68. U.S. CNO, *Navigation Plan*, 6.
69. Aaron-Matthew Lariosa, "U.S. and Philippine Forces Defend Island Chain near Taiwan in Balikatan 2024 Exercise," *USNI News*, May 9, 2024, https://news.usni.org/2023/08/16/large-scale-exercise-2023-was-custom-built-to-push-fleet-to-the-limit-say-planners (accessed Jan. 24, 2025).
70. U.S. DOD, "Air Force Future Operating Concept Executive Summary," Dept. of the Air Force, Mar. 6, 2023, 1–2, https://www.af.mil/Portals/1/documents/2023SAF/Air_Force_Future_Operating_Concept_exsum_final.pdf (accessed Jan. 24, 2025).
71. USAF, *Air Force Doctrine Note 1-21: Agile Combat Employment* (Washington, DC: Dept. of the Air Force, 2022), 1–4, https://www.doctrine.af.mil/Portals/61/documents/AFDN_1-21/AFDN 1-21 ACE.pdf (accessed Jan. 24, 2025).
72. Andrew Feickert, "The Army's Multi-Domain Task Force (MDTF)," Congressional Research Service, Dec. 26, 2022, 1–2, https://crsreports.congress.gov/product/pdf/IF/IF11797 (accessed June 1, 2025).
73. U.S. DOD, *Summary of the Joint All-Domain Command and Control (JADC2) Strategy*, Mar. 2022, https://media.defense.gov/2022/Mar/17/2002958406/-1/-1/1/summary-of-the-joint-all-domain-command-and-control-strategy.pdf (accessed Jan. 24, 2025). See also Timothy Marler, Carra S. Sims, Mark Toukan, Ajay K. Kochhar, Shawn Cochran, Christine Kistler Lacoste, and Matt Strawn, *Assessment of Joint All Domain Command and Control Requirements and the Use of Live, Virtual, and Constructive Capabilities for Training* (Santa Monica, CA: RAND Corp., 2023), 15–19, https://www.rand.org/content/dam/rand/pubs/research_reports/RRA900/RRA985-2/RAND_RRA985-2.pdf (accessed Jan. 24, 2025).
74. Tyler Rogoway, "This Is What the Navy's New Shipboard Electronic Warfare System Can Actually Do," *War Zone*, Aug. 4, 2021, https://www.thedrive.com/the-war-zone/41829/this-is-what-the-navys-new-shipboard-electronic-warfare-system-can-actually-do (accessed Jan. 24, 2025).
75. For an overview, see Nicholas A. O'Donoughue, Samantha McBirney, and Brad Persons, *Distributed Kill Chains* (Santa Monica, CA: RAND Corp., 2021), 41–57, https://www.rand.org/content/dam/rand/pubs/research_reports/RRA500/RRA573-1/RAND_RRA573-1.pdf (accessed Jan. 24, 2025).
76. Thomas Newdick and Tyler Rogoway, "AIM-174 Super Hornet-Launched Variant of SM-6 Missile Breaks Cover in Hawaii," *War Zone*, July 3, 2024 https://www.twz.com/air/aim-174-super-hornet-launched-variant-of-sm-6-missile-breaks-cover-in-hawaii (accessed Jan. 24, 2025).
77. Zach Abdi, "US Navy Issues Updated Solicitation on MEDUSA UUV," *Naval News*, Oct. 18, 2023, https://www.navalnews.com/naval-news/2023/10/us-navy-issues-updated-solicitation-on-medusa-uuv/ (accessed May 21, 2025).
78. Ronald O'Rourke, "Navy Large Unmanned Surface and Undersea Vehicles: Background and Issues for Congress," Congressional Research Service, updated July 15, 2024, 12–13, https://sgp.fas.org/crs/weapons/R45757.pdf (accessed Jan. 24, 2025).

79. Mallory Shelbourne, "Navy Wants to Start Conventional Prompt Strike Tests aboard USS Zumwalt in 2027," *Defense News*, Nov. 14, 2024, https://news.usni.org/2024/11/14/navy-wants-to-start-conventional-prompt-strike-tests-aboard-uss-zumwalt-in-2027.
80. Office of the CNO, *Report to Congress on the Annual Long-Range Plan for Construction of Naval Vessels for Fiscal Year 2025* (Washington, DC: Office of the CNO, 2024), 20, https://subscriber.politicopro.com/f/?id=0000018e-5808-df63-a1fe-d8db12d10000 (accessed Jan. 24, 2025; subscription required).
81. IISS, *Military Balance 2024*, 256–57.
82. Dmitry Filipoff, "Fighting DMO, Pt. 1: Defining Distributed Maritime Operations and the Future of Naval Warfare," CIMSEC, Feb. 20, 2023, https://cimsec.org/fighting-dmo-pt-1-defining-distributed-maritime-operations-and-the-future-of-naval-warfare/ (accessed Jan. 24, 2025).
83. Stephen M. Carmel, "Tankers in the Pacific Fight: A Crisis in Capability," CIMSEC, Jan. 23, 2023, https://cimsec.org/tankers-for-the-pacific-fight-a-crisis-in-capability (accessed Jan. 24, 2025).
84. U.S. Dept. of Transportation Maritime Administration, "Tanker Security Program," July 25, 2023, https://www.maritime.dot.gov/national-security/strategic-sealift/tanker-security-program (accessed Jan. 24, 2025).
85. Sarah Cannon, "MSC Conducts Underway Replenishment Operations with Tanker Ship off the Coast of Southern California," DVIDS, June 15, 2021, https://www.dvidshub.net/news/398973/msc-conducts-underway-replenishment-operations-with-tanker-ship-off-coast-southern-california (accessed Jan. 24, 2025); Edward Lundquist, "Navy Develops Modular "CONSOL" Capability to Refuel Oilers at Sea," National Defense Transportation Association, Sept. 7, 2021, https://www.ndtahq.com/navy-develops-modular-consol-capability-to-refuel-oilers-at-sea (accessed Jan. 24, 2025).
86. Timothy A. Walton, Ryan Boone, and Harrison Schramm, *Sustaining the Fight: Resilient Maritime Logistics for a New Era* (Washington DC: CSBA, 2019), 12, 77–78, https://csbaonline.org/uploads/documents/Resilient_Maritime_Logistics.pdf (accessed Jan. 24, 2025).
87. U.S. Dept. of Transportation, "United States–Flag Privately Owned Merchant Fleet Report, Oceangoing, Self-Propelled Vessels of 1,000 Gross Tons and above That Carry Cargo from Port to Port," Maritime Administration, 2023, 6, https://www.maritime.dot.gov/sites/marad.dot.gov/files/2023-02/DS_USFlag-Fleet_2023_01_24Bundle(1).pdf (accessed Jan. 24, 2025).
88. John Grady, "MARAD Head 'Not at All Confident' Ready Reserve Fleet Could Be Crewed in a Crisis," *USNI News*, Nov. 15, 2023, https://news.usni.org/2023/03/29/marad-head-not-at-all-confident-ready-reserve-fleet-could-be-crewed-in-a-crisis (accessed Jan. 24, 2025).
89. Megan Eckstein, "Seeking 75 Ships Ready for Combat, Navy Turns to New Readiness Orgs," *Defense News*, Jan. 6, 2024, https://www.defensenews.com/naval/2024/01/09/seeking-75-ready-ships-navy-turns-to-new-readiness-orgs (accessed Jan. 24, 2025); Sam Lagrone, "Fleet Forces Working on New Navy War Plan, Learning Lessons from Red Sea Deployments," *Defense News*, Jan. 6, 2024, https://news.usni.org/2024/01/09/fleet-forces-working-on-new-navy-war-plan-learning-lessons-from-red-sea-deployments (accessed Jan. 24, 2025).

90. Joseph Trevithick, "Air Force Units Will Flood the Western Pacific in Huge New Airpower Exercise Next Summer," *War Zone*, Aug. 19, 2024, https://www.twz.com/air/air-force-units-will-flood-the-western-pacific-in-huge-new-airpower-exercise-next-summer (accessed Jan. 24, 2025).
91. Courtney Mabeus-Brown, "McConnell-Based KC-46 Completes Around-the-World Flight in 45 Hours," *Air Force Times*, July 10, 2024, https://www.airforcetimes.com/news/your-air-force/2024/07/10/mcconnell-based-kc-46-completes-round-the-world-flight-in-45-hours (accessed Jan. 24, 2025). For further analysis, see Timothy A. Walton and Bryan Clark, *Resilient Aerial Refueling: Safeguarding the U.S. Military's Global Reach* (Washington, DC: Hudson Institute, Nov. 2021), https://s3.amazonaws.com/media.hudson.org/Walton Clark_Resilient Aerial Refueling.pdf (accessed Jan. 24, 2025).
92. Stew Magnuson, "Details of the Pentagon's New Space Architecture Revealed," *National Defense Magazine*, Sept. 19, 2019, https://www.nationaldefensemagazine.org/articles/2019/9/19/details-of-the-pentagon-new-space-architecture-revealed (accessed Jan. 24, 2025).
93. Andrew Feickert, "The U.S. Army's Long-Range Hypersonic Weapon (LRHW)," Congressional Research Service, Mar. 22, 2025, https://crsreports.congress.gov/product/pdf/IF/IF11991 (accessed May 25, 2025).
94. Aaron-Matthew Lariosa, "Army Activates New Watercraft Formation in Japan," *USNI News*, Feb. 9, 2024, https://news.usni.org/2024/02/09/army-activates-new-watercraft-formation-in-japan (accessed Jan. 25, 2025).
95. U.S.-Japan Joint Leaders' Statement, "U.S.-Japan Global Partnership for a New Era," statements and releases, The White House, Apr. 16, 2021, https://bidenwhitehouse.archives.gov/briefing-room/statements-releases/2021/04/16/u-s-japan-joint-leaders-statement-u-s-japan-global-partnership-for-a-new-era/ (accessed May 25, 2025).
96. Ju-Min Park, "Japan Official, Calling Taiwan 'Red Line,' Urges Biden to 'Be Strong,'" Reuters, Dec. 25, 2020, https://www.reuters.com/article/world/japan-official-calling-taiwan-red-line-urges-biden-to-be-strong-idUSKBN28Z0JQ/ (accessed Jan. 24, 2025). For further analysis of Japanese policy regarding Taiwan in the context of its relationship with the United States, see Jeffrey W. Hornung, Miranda Priebe, Bryan Rooney, Patrick Hulme, Nobuhiko Tamaki, and Yu Inagaki, *Like-Minded Allies?: Indo-Pacific Partners' Views on Possible Changes in the U.S. Relationship with Taiwan* (Santa Monica, CA: RAND Corp., July 20, 2023), 31–48, https://www.rand.org/content/dam/rand/pubs/research_reports/RRA700/RRA739-7/RAND_RRA739-7.pdf (accessed Jan. 24, 2025). For further analysis of the role of Japan in the event of a conflict over Taiwan, see Takashi Hosoda, "Japan and the Taiwan 'Contingency,'" Sinopsis, May 3, 2023, https://sinopsis.cz/en/japan-and-the-taiwan-contingency (accessed Jan. 24, 2025).
97. Government of Japan, "National Security Strategy of Japan," Dec. 2022, provisional translation, 1–2, 5–6, 8, 14, 18–20, 27, https://www.cas.go.jp/jp/siryou/221216anzenhoshou/nss-e.pdf (accessed Jan. 24, 2025).
98. Government of Japan, "National Defense Strategy," Dec. 16, 2022, provisional translation, 23–29, https://www.mod.go.jp/j/policy/agenda/guideline/strategy/pdf/strategy_en.pdf (accessed Jan. 25, 2025).
99. Government of Japan, "Defense Buildup Program," Dec. 16, 2022, provisional translation, Mar. 14, 2023, https://www.mod.go.jp/j/policy/agenda/guideline/plan/pdf/program_en.pdf (accessed Jan. 24, 2025).

100. U.S. DOD, "Joint Statement of the Security Consultative Committee ('2+2')," July 28, 2024, https://www.defense.gov/News/Releases/Release/Article/3852169/joint-statement-of-the-security-consultative-committee-22/ (accessed Jan. 24, 2025).
101. Geoff Ziezulewicz, "Marine HIMARS Deployment to Southern Japanese Islands during Taiwan Crisis Detailed in Report," *War Zone,* Nov. 26, 2024, https://www.twz.com/news-features/marine-himars-deployment-to-southern-japanese-islands-during-taiwan-crisis-detailed-in-report (accessed Jan. 18, 2025).
102. Australian Government, Department of Foreign Affairs and Trade, "Australia-Taiwan Relationship," n.d., https://www.dfat.gov.au/geo/taiwan/australia-taiwan-relationship (accessed Jan. 24, 2025).
103. "'Inconceivable' Australia Would Not Join U.S. to Defend Taiwan—Australian Defence Minister," Reuters, Nov. 13, 2021, https://www.reuters.com/world/asia-pacific/inconceivable-Australia-would-not-join-us-defend-Taiwan-australian-defence-2021-11-12 (accessed Jan. 24, 2025).
104. Australian Government, *National Defence: Defence Strategic Review, 2023* (Canberra: Commonwealth of Australia, 2023), 19, 23, 24–25, 28, 31, 49, 53–55, 60, 75–76, https://www.defence.gov.au/about/reviews-inquiries/defence-strategic-review (accessed Jan. 24, 2025).
105. For further analysis of Japanese policy regarding Taiwan in the context of its relationship with the United States, see Hornung et al., *Like-Minded Allies?,* 67–83.
106. Lariosa, "U.S. and Philippine Forces Defend Island Chain near Taiwan."

CHAPTER 13. OPLAN 5077

1. U.S. DOD, *Joint Warfighting,* I-4–5, III-15.
2. See Andrew Krepinevich Jr., *Protracted Great-Power War: A Preliminary Assessment* (Washington, DC: CNAS, 2020), 1–2, 10–12, 18–19, 21, 34–35, https://s3.us-east-1.amazonaws.com/files.cnas.org/backgrounds/documents/CNAS-Report_Defense-Great-Power-War-DoS-Proof-B.pdf (accessed Jan. 24, 2025). Krepinevich places an emphasis on economic warfare—for example, blockade operations—as a component of horizontal escalation rather than mainland strikes. See also U.S. JCS, *Joint Planning,* Joint Publication 5-0 (Washington, DC: JCS, 2021), IV-41–44, https://irp.fas.org/doddir/dod/jp5_0.pdf (accessed Jan. 22, 2025).
3. For examination of defeat as a concept and possible scenarios, see Edward Geist, "Defeat Is Possible," *War on the Rocks,* June 17, 2021, https://warontherocks.com/2021/06/defeat-is-possible/ (accessed Jan. 24, 2025); and Capt. Dale Rielage, "How We Lost the Great Pacific War," U.S. Naval Institute *Proceedings* 144/5/1,383 (May 2018), https://www.usni.org/magazines/proceedings/2018/may/how-we-lost-great-pacific-war (accessed Jan. 24, 2025).
4. U.S. JCS, *Joint Planning,* I-6.
5. U.S. JCS, I-14.
6. Gen. George W. Casey Jr., testimony, Sept. 29, 2005, in U.S. Senate Committee on the Armed Services, "US Military Operations and Stabilization Activities in Iraq and Afghanistan," 109th Cong., 1st. sess., 302, https://www.govinfo.gov/content/pkg/CHRG-109shrg27523/pdf/CHRG-109shrg27523.pdf (accessed Jan. 24, 2025).
7. John Culver, "How We Would Know When China Is Preparing to Invade Taiwan," Carnegie Endowment for International Peace, Oct. 3, 2022, https://carnegieendowment.org

/posts/2022/10/how-we-would-know-when-china-is-preparing-to-invade-taiwan?lang =en (accessed Jan. 24, 2025). See also Easton, *Chinese Invasion Threat*, 67–84.

8. Easton, *Chinese Invasion Threat*, 85–90.
9. For an analysis of the debate, see John Speed Meyers, "Mainland Strikes and U.S. Military Strategy towards China: Historical Cases, Interviews, and a Scenario-Based Survey of American National Security Elites" (PhD diss., RAND School of Public Policy, 2019), https://www.rand.org/pubs/rgs_dissertations/RGSD430.html (accessed Jan. 24, 2025).
10. Harry S. Truman Library, President's Secretary's File, Box 182, Meetings: 80: Jan. 17, 1951, NSC 101 A Report to the National Security Council, Jan. 12, 1951, cited in Meyers, "Mainland Strikes and U.S. Military Strategy towards China," 67–68.
11. Andrew F. Krepinevich defines "protracted" as in excess of eighteen months on the basis that this is "the point at which considerable strain is placed on a belligerent's morale, material resources, industrial base, and financial standing." Krepinevich, *Protracted Great-Power War*, 6, 10. For further discussion on protracted major wars in the modern era, see John Mauk, "Facts Are Stubborn Things: The Danger of Protracted War with China," *War Room*, Apr. 27, 2023, https://warroom.armywarcollege.edu/articles/stubborn-things/ (accessed Jan. 24, 2025); and Patrick Savage, "What If It Doesn't End Quickly?: Reconsidering U.S. Preparedness for Protracted Conventional War," Modern War Institute, July 23, 2020, https://mwi.westpoint.edu/what-if-it-doesnt-end-quickly-reconsidering-us -preparedness-for-protracted-conventional-war/ (accessed Jan. 24, 2025).
12. U.S. DOD, *DOD Dictionary*, 33.
13. For an overview of the game of recent years, see Robert Kitchen, "Red Dragon Rising?: Insights from a Decade of China Conflict Studies and Wargames," CIMSEC, Feb. 28, 2024, https://cimsec.org/red-dragon-rising-insights-from-a-decade-of-wargames/ (accessed Jan. 24, 2025).
14. Sydney J. Freedberg Jr., "US 'Gets Its Ass Handed to It' in Wargames: Here's a $24 Billion Fix," Breaking Defense, Mar. 7, 2019, https://breakingdefense.com/2019/03/us-gets-its -ass-handed-to-it-in-wargames-heres-a-24-billion-fix (accessed Jan. 24, 2025).
15. Brett Tingly, "Joint Chiefs Seek a New Warfighting Paradigm after Devastating Losses in Classified Wargames," *War Zone*, July 27, 2021, https://www.twz.com/41712/joint-chiefs -seek-a-new-warfighting-paradigm-after-devastating-losses-in-classified-wargames (accessed Jan. 24, 2025).
16. Stacie Pettyjohn, Becca Wasser, and Chris Dougherty, *Dangerous Straits: Wargaming a Future Conflict over Taiwan* (Washington, DC: CNAS, 2022), 106–15, https://s3 .amazonaws.com/files.cnas.org/CNAS+Report-Dangerous+Straits-Defense-Jun+2022 -FINAL-print.pdf (accessed Jan. 24, 2025).
17. Mark F. Cancian, Matthew Cancian, and Eric Heginbotham, *The First Battle of the Next War: Wargaming a Chinese Invasion of Taiwan* (Washington, DC: CSIS, 2023), 83, 87–94, https://www.naval.com.br/blog/wp-content/uploads/2023/01/Wargaming-a-chinese -invasion-of-Taiwan.pdf (accessed Jan. 24, 2025).
18. Katina Slavkova, "Tell Me How This Ends," Government Affairs Institute at Georgetown University, n.d., https://gai.georgetown.edu/tell-me-how-this-ends (accessed Jan. 24, 2025).
19. U.S. JCS, *Joint Planning*, IV-41–44.

20. U.S. DOD, 2022 *National Defense Strategy*, 9; Heim, Burdette, and Beauchamp-Mustafaga, *U.S. Military Theories of Victory*, 3–8, 13–16.
21. Heim, Burdette, and Beauchamp-Mustafaga, *U.S. Military Theories of Victory*, 10, 16–17, 26–28.
22. For an exploration of the IJN-U.S. analogy, see John T. Kuehn, "Lying to Ourselves: Has the U.S. Navy Become the Imperial Japanese Navy of 1941?," USMC University, May 4, 2023, https://www.usmcu.edu/Outreach/Marine-Corps-University-Press/Expeditions-with-MCUP-digital-journal/Lying-to-Ourselves (accessed Jan. 24, 2025).
23. Richard Baldwin, "China Is the World's Sole Manufacturing Superpower: A Line Sketch of the Rise," CEPR, Jan. 24, 2024, https://cepr.org/voxeu/columns/china-worlds-sole-manufacturing-superpower-line-sketch-rise (accessed Jan. 24, 2025).
24. Concept taken from Bleddyn E. Bowen, *War in Space: Strategy, Spacepower, and Geopolitics* (Edinburgh: Edinburgh University Press, 2020), chap.6.
25. Capt. William Toti (ret.), "You Can't Win without (More) Submarines," U.S. Naval Institute *Proceedings* 149/12/1,450 (Dec. 2023), https://www.usni.org/magazines/proceedings/2023/december/you-cant-win-without-more-submarines (accessed Jan. 24, 2025).
26. For an analysis of munitions requirements for various target packages, see Tyler Hacker, *Beyond Precision: Maintaining America's Strike Advantage in Great Power Conflict* (Washington, DC: CSBA, 2023), https://csbaonline.org/uploads/documents/Beyond_Precision_Report_CSBA8355_FINAL_web.pdf (accessed Jan. 24, 2025).
27. Jackson Rice, *The Resilience of Taiwan's Energy and Food Systems to Blockade* (San Diego: UC San Diego School of Global Policy and Strategy, 2023), 3, https://www.cfe-dmha.org/LinkClick.aspx?fileticket=sJ7hhDPJFl8%3D&portalid=0 (accessed Jan. 24, 2025).
28. Rice, 6, 14. See also Gustavo F. Ferreira and Jamie A. Critelli, "Taiwan's Food Resiliency—or Not—in a Conflict with China," *U.S. Army War College Quarterly: Parameters* 53, no. 2 (Summer 2023): 39–60, https://press.armywarcollege.edu/parameters/vol53/iss2/10/ (accessed Jan. 24, 2025).
29. Hattendorf and Swartz, *U.S. Naval Strategy in the 1980s*, 191.

EPILOGUE. TOMORROW'S END

1. Epigraph from Adm. Samuel John Paparo Jr., keynote address, Feb. 14, 2024, WEST 2024 Conference, YouTube, video, 16:28–16:37, https://www.youtube.com/watch?v=BJOb6SLT9rQ (accessed Jan. 24, 2025). At the time of this address, Admiral Paparo had been appointed the next USINDOPACOM commander, taking up that role on May 3, 2024.
2. Hector Charles Bywater, *Sea-Power in the Pacific: A Study of the American-Japanese Naval Problem* (London: Constable, 1921), 319, https://archive.org/details/cu31924023233822/page/n333/mode/2up (accessed Jan. 22, 2025).

SELECTED BIBLIOGRAPHY

PUBLISHED ITEMS (PRINT OR ONLINE)

Aizawa, Kiyoshi. "Japanese Strategy in the First Phase of the Pacific War." Research paper presented at the Ninth NIDS International Forum on War History, 2010. https://www.nids.mod.go.jp/english/event/forum/pdf/2009/04.pdf.

Arkin, William M. "America's New China War Plan." *Early Warning* (blog). *Washington Post*, May 24, 2006. (Blog discontinued).

Berl, Walter G. "Annotated Bumblebee Initial Report February 1945." John Hopkins Applied Physics Laboratory *Technical Digest* 3, no. 2 (1982): 171–79. https://secwww.jhuapl.edu/techdigest/Content/techdigest/pdf/V03-N02/03-02-Berl.pdf.

Blasko, Dennis J. *The PLA Army Amphibious Force*. China Maritime Report 20. Newport, RI: China Maritime Studies Institute, U.S. Naval War College, 2022. U.S. Naval War College Digital Commons. https://digital-commons.usnwc.edu/cgi/viewcontent.cgi?article=1019&context=cmsi-maritime-reports.

Blasko, Dennis J., and Roderick Lee. "The Chinese Navy's Marine Corps, Part 1: Expansion and Reorganization." *China Brief* 19, no. 3. Jamestown Foundation, February 1, 2019. https://jamestown.org/program/the-chinese-navys-marine-corps-part-1-expansion-and-reorganization.

Burke, Edmund J., Kristen Gunness, Cortez A. Cooper III, and Mark Cozad. *People's Liberation Army Operational Concepts*. Santa Monica, CA: RAND Corporation, 2020. https://www.rand.org/content/dam/rand/pubs/research_reports/RRA300/RRA394-1/RAND_RRA394-1.pdf.

Burkepile, Keith, ed. *Campaign Planning Handbook, Academic Year 2024*. Carlisle Barracks, PA: U.S. Army War College, 2024. https://usawc-ssi-media.s3.us-east-1.amazonaws.com/misc/AY24-Campaign-Planning-Handbook.pdf.

Bywater, Hector Charles. *The Great Pacific War: A History of the American-Japanese Campaign of 1931–33*. Boston: Houghton Mifflin, 1925. https://babel.hathitrust.org/cgi/pt?id=uc1.31822013308325&seq=9.

———. *Sea-Power in the Pacific: A Study of the American-Japanese Naval Problem*. London: Constable, 1921. https://archive.org/details/cu31924023233822/page/n7/mode/2up.

Carter, Worrall Reed, *Beans, Bullets, and Black Oil: The Story of Fleet Logistics Afloat in the Pacific during World War Two*. 1953. Reprint, San Francisco: Verdun, 2015. Kindle.

"Causeway Joint Staff Study." U.S. Pacific Fleet and Pacific Ocean Area, 1944. https://apps.dtic.mil/sti/pdfs/ADA606376.pdf.

Chen, John, and Joel Wuthnow. *Chinese Special Operations in a Large-Scale Island Landing*. China Maritime Report 18. Newport, RI: China Maritime Studies Institute, U.S. Naval War College, 2022. U.S. Naval War College Digital Commons. https://digital

-commons.usnwc.edu/cgi/viewcontent.cgi?article=1017&context=cmsi-maritime-reports.

Cheng, Dean. "Chinese Lessons from the Gulf Wars." In *Chinese Lessons from Other People's Wars*, edited by Andrew Scobell, David Lai, and Roy Kamphausen. Carlisle, PA: U.S. Army Strategic Studies Institute, 2011.

Cheng, Isabelle. "Saving the Nation by Sacrificing Your Life: Authoritarianism and Chiang Kai-shek's War for the Retaking of China." *Journal of Current Chinese Affairs* 47, no. 2 (August 2018): 55–86.

Choo, Roy, and Peter Ho. *Modern Taiwanese Air Power: The Republic of China Air Force Today*. Wien, Aust.: Harpia, 2021.

Cohen, Eliot A., et al. *Gulf War Air Power Survey*. Vol. 1, *Planning and Command and Control*. Washington, DC, 1993. https://media.defense.gov/2010/Sep/27/2001329802/-1/-1/0/AFD-100927-062.pdf.

———. *Gulf War Air Power Survey*. Vol. 2, *Operations and Effects and Effectiveness*. Washington, DC, 1993. https://apps.dtic.mil/sti/pdfs/ADA279742.pdf.

———. *Gulf War Air Power Survey*. Vol. 3, *Logistics and Support*. Washington, DC, 1993. https://apps.dtic.mil/sti/tr/pdf/ADA279743.pdf.

Command History Branch, Office of the Joint Secretary. *Commander in Chief Pacific Command History 1979*. Camp H. M. Smith, HI: Headquarters Commander in Chief Pacific Fleet, 1980. https://nautilus.org/wp-content/uploads/2011/12/c_seventynine.pdf.

Committee of Privy Counsellors (Chair: Lord Franks). *Falkland Islands Review*. London: HM Stationery Office, 1983. https://archive.margaretthatcher.org/doc02/E415E0802DAA482297D889B9B43B70DE.pdf.

Cozad, Mark. "The PLA and Contingency Planning." In *The People's Liberation Army and Contingency Planning in China*, edited by Andrew Scobell, Arthur S. Ding, Phillip C. Saunders, and Scott W. Harold. Washington, DC: National Defense University Press, 2015. https://ndupress.ndu.edu/Portals/68/Documents/Books/PLA-contingency/PLA-Contingency-Planning-China.pdf.

Crist, David B. *The Twilight War: The Secret History of America's Thirty-Year Conflict with Iran*. New York: Penguin, 2013. Kindle.

———. "US Central Command Campaign Planning against the Soviet Union, 1979–1987." Offsite presentation for U.S. CENTCOM, September 18, 2020. https://www.jcs.mil/Portals/36/Documents/History/Dec21/CristCENTCOMoffsite18Sep20_complete.pdf.

"Declassified Cables: Taiwan Arms Sales and the Six Assurances (1982)." American Institute in Taiwan, March 30, 2022. https://www.ait.org.tw/declassified-cables-taiwan-arms-sales-six-assurances-1982.

Di, He. "'The Last Campaign to Unify China': The CCP's Unmaterialized Plan to Liberate Taiwan, 1949–1950." *Chinese Historians* 5, no. 1 (1992): 1–16. https://doi.org/10.1080/1043643X.1992.11876883.

Doran, Walter F. "Pacific Fleet Focuses on War Fighting." U.S. Naval Institute *Proceedings* 129/8/1,206 (August 2003). https://www.usni.org/magazines/proceedings/2003/august/pacific-fleet-focuses-war-fighting.

Dotson, John. "Taiwan's 'Military Force Restructuring Plan' and the Extension of Conscripted Military Service." *Global Taiwan Brief* 8, no. 3 (February 8, 2023).

https://globaltaiwan.org/2023/02/taiwan-military-force-restructuring-plan-and-the-extension-of-conscripted-military-service.

Doyle, Gerry, and Blake Heringer. *Carrier Killers: China's Anti-Ship Ballistic Missiles and Theater of Operations in the Early 21st Century*. Warwick, Eng.: Helion, 2022.

Doyle, Michael K. "The U.S. Navy and War Plan Orange, 1933–1940: Making Necessity a Virtue." *Naval War College Review* 33, no. 3 (May–June 1980): 49–63. https://www.jstor.org/stable/44642633.

Easton, Ian. *Able Archers: Taiwan's Defense Strategy in an Age of Precision Strike*. Arlington, VA: Project 2049 Institute, 2014. https://project2049.net/wp-content/uploads/2018/06/Easton_Able_Archers_Taiwan_Defense_Strategy.pdf.

———. *China's Evolving Reconnaissance-Strike Capabilities: Implications for the U.S.–Japan Alliance*. Arlington, VA: Project 2049 Institute; Tokyo: Japan Institute for International Affairs, 2014. https://www2.jiia.or.jp/pdf/fellow_report/140219_JIIA-Project2049_Ian_Easton_report.pdf.

———. *China's Top Five War Plans*. Arlington, VA: Project 2049 Institute, 2019. https://project2049.net/wp-content/uploads/2019/01/Chinas-Top-Five-War-Plans_Ian_Easton_Project2049.pdf.

———. *The Chinese Invasion Threat: Taiwan's Defense and America's Strategy in Asia*. Arlington, VA: Project 2049 Institute, 2017.

Easton, Ian, Eric Lee, Grace Price, Colby Ferland, Cathy Fang, Mark Stokes, and Alice Cho. *Before Zero Day: Taiwan's Evolving Defense Strategy and the Struggle for Peace*. Arlington, VA: Project 2049 Institute, 2023. https://project2049.net/2023/09/27/before-zero-day-taiwans-evolving-defense-strategy-and-the-struggle-for-peace.

Elleman, Bruce A. *High Seas Buffer: The Taiwan Patrol Force, 1950–1979*. Naval War College Newport Papers 38. Newport, RI: Naval War College Press, 2012. U.S. Naval War College Digital Commons. https://digital-commons.usnwc.edu/cgi/viewcontent.cgi?article=1037&context=newport-papers.

———. *Taiwan's Offshore Islands: Pathway or Barrier?* Naval War College Newport Papers 44. Newport, RI: Naval War College Press, 2019. U.S. Naval War College Digital Commons. https://digital-commons.usnwc.edu/cgi/viewcontent.cgi?article=1042&context=usnwc-newport-papers.

Erickson, Andrew S. "Deterrence by Denial: How to Prevent China from Using Force." *National Interest*, December 16, 2013. https://nationalinterest.org/commentary/war-china-two-can-play-the-area-denial-game-9564.

Erslev, Brit K. "U.S. Joint War Planning for Twentieth-Century Large-Scale Combat Operations: Case Studies and Implications for Current Joint Planners." Master's thesis, School of Advanced Military Studies, U.S. Army Command and General Staff College, 2020. https://apps.dtic.mil/sti/citations/trecms/AD1160006.

Evans, David C., and Mark R. Peattie. *Kaigun: Strategy, Tactics, and Technology in the Imperial Japanese Navy, 1887–1941*. Barnsley, Eng.: Seaforth, 2012.

Exhibit 4, "Rainbow 5." In *Hearings before the Joint Committee on the Investigation of the Pearl Harbor Attack*, 79th Cong., 1st sess., pt. 33:926–85. Washington, DC: Government Printing Office, 1946. http://www.ibiblio.org/pha/pha/misc/rainbow5.html.

Feickert, Andrew. "The Army's Multi-Domain Task Force (MDTF)." Congressional Research Service, December 26, 2022. https://crsreports.congress.gov/product/pdf/IF/IF11797.

Fravel, M. Taylor. *Active Defense: China's Military Strategy since 1949*. Princeton, NJ: Princeton University Press, 2019.

Fravel, M. Taylor, George J. Gilboy, and Eric Heginbotham. "Estimating China's Defense Spending: How to Get It Wrong (and Right)." *Texas National Security Review* 7, no. 3 (Summer 2024). https://tnsr.org/2024/06/estimating-chinas-defense-spending-how-to-get-it-wrong-and-right.

Freedman, Lawrence. *The Official History of the Falklands Campaign*. 2 vols. London: Routledge, 2005.

Friedberg, Aaron L. *Beyond Air-Sea Battle: The Debate over U.S. Military Strategy in Asia*. London: IISS, 2014.

Friedman, Norman. *Fighters over the Fleet: Naval Air Defense from Biplanes to the Cold War*. Barnsley, Eng.: Seaforth, 2016. Kindle.

Garafola, Cristina L. *The PLA Airborne Corps in a Joint Island Landing Campaign*. China Maritime Report 19. Newport, RI: China Maritime Studies Institute, U.S. Naval War College, 2022. U.S. Naval War College Digital Commons. https://digital-commons.usnwc.edu/cmsi-maritime-reports/19.

Garrett, Lawrence, III, Frank B. Kelso II, and A. M. Gray. "The Way Ahead." U.S. Naval Institute *Proceedings* 117/4/1,058 (April 1991). https://www.usni.org/magazines/proceedings/1991/april/way-ahead.

Garver, John W. *Face Off: China, the United States, and Taiwan's Democratization*. Seattle: University of Washington Press, 2000.

———. *The Sino-American Alliance: Nationalist China and American Cold War Strategy in Asia*. 1997. Reprint, London: Routledge, 2015.

Goldstein, Lyle. "China's Falklands Lessons." *Survival* 50, no. 3 (2008): 65–82. https://doi.org/10.1080/00396330802173214.

Goldstein, Steven M. "The United States and the Republic of China, 1949–1978: Suspicious Allies." Paper, February 2000. https://fsi-live.s3.us-west-1.amazonaws.com/s3fs-public/Goldstein.pdf.

Grant, Rebecca. "The Second Offset." *Air and Space Forces Magazine*, June 24, 2016. https://www.airandspaceforces.com/article/the-second-offset.

Halloran, Richard. "PACAF's 'Vision' Thing." *Air Force Magazine*, January 2009, 54–56. https://www.airandspaceforces.com/PDF/MagazineArchive/Documents/2009/January 2009/0109vision.pdf.

Halperin, M. H. *The 1958 Taiwan Strait Crisis: A Documented History*. Santa Monica, CA: RAND Corporation, 1966. https://int.nyt.com/data/documenttools/quemoy-study-the-1958-taiwan-straits-crisis-partial-plus-total-redactions-december-1966/2a096c90d03e079a/full.pdf.

Hammes, T. X. *Offshore Control: A Proposed Strategy for an Unlikely Conflict*. Strategic Forum 278. Washington, DC: INSS National Defense University, 2012. https://ndupress.ndu.edu/Portals/68/Documents/stratforum/SF-278.pdf.

Hattendorf, John B. *The Evolution of the U.S. Navy's Maritime Strategy, 1977–1986*. Naval War College Newport Papers 19. Newport, RI: Naval War College Press, 2004. U.S. Naval War College Digital Commons. https://digital-commons.usnwc.edu/cgi/viewcontent.cgi?article=1019&context=usnwc-newport-papers.

———, ed. *U.S. Naval Strategy in the 1970s: Selected Documents*. Naval War College Newport Papers 30. Newport, RI: Naval War College Press, 2007. U.S. Naval War

College Digital Commons. https://www.ibiblio.org/anrs/docs/V/1101USNaval Strategyinthe1970s.pdf.

Hattendorf, John B., and Peter M. Swartz, eds. *U.S. Naval Strategy in the 1980s: Selected Documents*. Naval War College Newport Papers 33. Newport, RI: Naval War College Press, 2008. U.S. Naval War College Digital Commons. https://digital-commons.usnwc.edu/cgi/viewcontent.cgi?article=1032&context=newport-papers.

Headquarters, U.S. Central Command. "USCENTCOM OPLAN 1003V—Change 1." February 27, 2003. MacDill Air Force Base, FL. Declassified June 2015. U.S. Army Heritage and Education Center, https://ahec.armywarcollege.edu/centcom-iraq-papers/0987. 1003V27Feb03.pdf.

Headquarters, U.S. Marine Corps. *A Concept for Stand-In Forces*. Washington, DC: Department of Navy, 2021. https://www.hqmc.marines.mil/Portals/142/Users/183/35/4535/211201_A Concept for Stand-In Forces.pdf.

———. *Force Design 2030*. Washington, DC: Department of the Navy, 2020. https://www.hqmc.marines.mil/Portals/142/Docs/CMC38 Force Design 2030 Report Phase I and II.pdf.

Heim, Jacob L., Zachary Burdette, and Nathan Beauchamp-Mustafaga. *U.S. Military Theories of Victory for a War with the People's Republic of China*. Santa Monica, CA: RAND Corporation, 2024. https://www.rand.org/pubs/perspectives/PEA1743-1.html.

Henley, Lonnie D. *Civilian Shipping and Maritime Militia: The Logistics Backbone of a Taiwan Invasion*. China Maritime Report 21. Newport, RI: China Maritime Studies Institute, U.S. Naval War College, 2022. U.S. Naval War College Digital Commons. https://digital-commons.usnwc.edu/cgi/viewcontent.cgi?article=1020&context=cmsi-maritime-reports.

Herder, Brian Lane. *Early Pacific Raids 1942: The American Carriers Strike Back*. Oxford: Bloomsbury, 2023.

Holmes, Christopher D., and Francis J. Park. *History of Joint Staff Strategic Planning, 1949–2020*. Special Historical Study 14. Washington, DC: Joint History and Research Office, Office of the Chairman of the Joint Chiefs of Staff, 2021. https://www.jcs.mil/Portals/36/Documents/History/Dec21/SHS_14_History of Joint Staff Strategic Planning.pdf.

Hsiao, Russell. "Fortnightly Review." *Global Taiwan Brief* 5, no. 15 (July 29, 2020). https://globaltaiwan.org/2020/07/fortnightly-review-8/.

Hsi-min, Lee, and Eric Lee. "Taiwan's Overall Defense Concept, Explained." *The Diplomat*, November 3, 2020. https://thediplomat.com/2020/11/taiwans-overall-defense-concept-explained.

Hunzeker, Michael A. "Taiwan's Defense Plans Are Going off the Rails." *War on the Rocks*, November 18, 2021. https://warontherocks.com/2021/11/taiwans-defense-plans-are-going-off-the-rails/.

International Institute for Strategic Studies. *The Military Balance 2024*. London: IISS, 2024.

In Their Own Words: Foreign Military Thought—Science of Campaigns (2006). Montgomery, AL: China Aerospace Studies Institute, Air Force University, [2020]. Translation of *Science of Campaigns*, edited by Zhang Yuliang. Beijing: National Defense University Press, 2006. https://www.airuniversity.af.edu/Portals/10/CASI/documents/Translations/2020-12-02 In Their Own Words- Science of Campaigns (2006).pdf.

In Their Own Words: Science of Military Strategy, 2020. Montgomery, AL: China Aerospace Studies Institute, Air Force University, 2022. Translation of *Science of Military Strategy*, edited by Xiao Tianliang. Beijing: National Defense University Press, 2020. https://www.airuniversity.af.edu/Portals/10/CASI/documents/Translations/2022-01-26 2020 Science of Military Strategy.pdf.

Jacobs, G. Keith. "A Soviet War for Northern Japan." *Asian Defense Journal* 1, no. 83 (1983): 6–17. https://www.academia.edu/39907894/A_Soviet_War_for_Northern_Japan.

Jenks, Harlan W. "Chinese Evaluation of 'Desert Storm': Implications for PRC Security." *Journal of East Asian Affairs* 6, no. 2 (Summer/Fall 1992): 447–77.

Joe, Rick. "The Future of China's Amphibious Assault Fleet." *The Diplomat*, July 17, 2019. https://thediplomat.com/2019/07/the-future-of-chinas-amphibious-assault-fleet/.

Johnson, Jay. "Anytime, Anywhere: A Navy for the 21st Century." U.S. Naval Institute *Proceedings* 123/11/1,137 (November 1997). https://www.usni.org/magazines/proceedings/1997/november/anytime-anywhere-navy-21st-century.

Jones, Matthew. "Targeting China: U.S. Nuclear Planning and 'Massive Retaliation' in East Asia, 1953–1955." *Journal of Cold War Studies* 10, no. 4 (Fall 2008): 37–65. https://www.jstor.org/stable/26922983.

Kan, Shirley A. "China/Taiwan: Evolution of the 'One China' Policy—Key Statements from Washington, Beijing, and Taipei." Congressional Research Service, October 10, 2014. https://sgp.fas.org/crs/row/RL30341.pdf.

Kennedy, Conor. *The New Chinese Marine Corps: A "Strategic Dagger" in a Cross-Strait Invasion*. China Maritime Report 15. Newport, RI: China Maritime Studies Institute, U.S. Naval War College, 2021. U.S. Naval War College Digital Commons. https://digital-commons.usnwc.edu/cmsi-maritime-reports/15/.

Kerr, George. *Formosa Betrayed*. 2nd ed. Irvine, CA: Taiwan Publishing, 1992.

Kinney, Francis X. "The Malvinas Conflict: Argentine Practice of the Operational Art." Monograph, School of Advanced Military Studies, U.S. Army Command and General Staff College, 1990. https://apps.dtic.mil/sti/tr/pdf/ADA234161.pdf.

Kipphut, Mark E. *Crossbow and Gulf War Counter-Scud Efforts: Lessons from History*. USAF Counterproliferation Center Future War Series 15. Maxwell Air Force Base, AL: Air University Press, 2003. https://media.defense.gov/2019/Apr/11/2002115481/-1/-1/0/15crossbow.pdf.

Krepinevich, Andrew F., Jr. *Archipelagic Defense: The Japan–U.S. Alliance and Preserving Peace and Stability in the Western Pacific*. Washington, DC: Sasakawa Peace Foundation, 2017. https://www.spf.org/en/jpus/publications/20170810_1.html.

———. *Archipelagic Defense 2.0*. Washington, DC: Hudson Institute, 2023. https://www.hudson.org/archipelagic-defense-2-taiwan-china-japan-australia-deterrence-us-navy-andrew-krepinevich-jr.

———. *The Military-Technical Revolution: A Preliminary Assessment*. Washington, DC: Office of Net Assessment, U.S. Dept. of Defense, 1992. Reprint, Washington, DC: CSBA, 2022. https://csbaonline.org/uploads/documents/2002.10.02-Military-Technical-Revolution.pdf.

———. *Protracted Great-Power War: A Preliminary Assessment*. Washington, DC: CNAS, 2020. https://s3.us-east-1.amazonaws.com/files.cnas.org/backgrounds/documents/CNAS-Report_Defense-Great-Power-War-DoS-Proof-B.pdf.

———. *Why AirSea Battle?* Washington, DC: CSBA, 2010. https://csbaonline.org/uploads/documents/2010.02.19-Why-AirSea-Battle.pdf.

Krepinevich, Andrew F., Barry Watts, and Robert Work. *Meeting the Anti-Access and Area-Denial Challenge*. Washington, DC: CSBA, 2003.

Kristensen, Hans M. "The Awakening Asian Tiger: China in US Nuclear War Planning." Working paper, Nautilus Institute, November 2000. https://www.nautilus.org/wp-content/uploads/2015/07/ChinaNuke.pdf.

———. "Nukes in the Taiwan Crisis." FAS, May 13, 2008. https://fas.org/publication/nukes-in-the-taiwan-crisis.

Kristensen, Hans M., Robert S. Norris, and Matthew G. McKinzie. *Chinese Nuclear Forces and U.S. Nuclear War Planning*. Washington, DC: FAS and Natural Resources Defense Council, 2006. https://nuke.fas.org/guide/china/Book2006.pdf.

Kuehn, John J. *Agents of Innovation: The General Board and the Design of the Fleet That Defeated the Japanese Navy*. Annapolis, MD: Naval Institute Press, 2008. Kindle.

Kulacki, Gregory. "Nuclear Weapons in the Taiwan Strait Part I." *Journal for Peace and Nuclear Disarmament* 3, no. 2 (2020): 310–41. https://doi.org/10.1080/25751654.2020.1834963.

Larson, Eric V. *Force Planning Scenarios, 1945–2016: Their Origins and Use in Defense Strategic Planning*. Santa Monica, CA: RAND Corporation, 2019. https://www.rand.org/pubs/research_reports/RR2173z1.html.

Li, Xiaobing. *The History of Taiwan*. Santa Barbara, CA: Greenwood, 2019.

Lin, Hsiao-Ting. *Accidental State: Chiang Kei-Shek, the United States, and the Making of Taiwan*. Cambridge, MA: Harvard University Press, 2016.

Maloney, Sean M. *Emergency War Plan: The American Doomsday Machine, 1945–1960*. Lincoln: University of Nebraska Press, 2021. Kindle.

Mazarr, Michael J., Katharina Ley Best, Burgess Laird, Eric V. Larson, Michael E. Linick, and Dan Madden. *The U.S. DOD's Planning Process: Components and Challenges*. Santa Monica, CA: RAND Corporation, 2019. https://www.rand.org/content/dam/rand/pubs/research_reports/RR2100/RR2173z2/RAND_RR2173z2.pdf.

Meyers, John Speed. "Mainland Strikes and U.S. Military Strategy towards China: Historical Cases, Interviews, and a Scenario-Based Survey of American National Security Elites." PhD diss., RAND School of Public Policy, 2019. https://www.rand.org/pubs/rgs_dissertations/RGSD430.html.

Michishita, Narushige, Peter M. Swartz, and David F. Winkler. *Lessons of the Cold War in the Pacific: U.S. Maritime Strategy, Crisis Prevention, and Japan's Role*. Washington, DC: Wilson Center and the Sasakawa Peace Foundation, 2016. https://www.wilsoncenter.org/sites/default/files/media/documents/publication/lessons_of_the_cold_war_in_the_pacific_one_page.pdf.

Middlebrook, Martin. *Argentina's Fight for the Falklands*. Barnsley, Eng.: Pen & Sword, 2009. Kindle.

Miller, Edward S. *War Plan Orange: The U.S. Strategy to Defeat Japan, 1897–1945*. Annapolis, MD: Naval Institute Press, 1991.

Milley, Mark A. "Strategic Inflection Point." *Joint Forces Quarterly* 110 (3rd Quarter 2023): 6–15. https://ndupress.ndu.edu/Portals/68/Documents/jfq/jfq-110/jfq-110_6-15_Milley.pdf.

Morton, Louis. *The Fall of the Philippines*. United States Army in World War Two: The War in the Pacific. 1953. Reprint, Washington, DC: Center of Military History, U.S. Army, 1993. https://history.army.mil/Portals/143/Images/Publications/Publication By Title Images/F Pdf/CMH_Pub_5-2-1.pdf.

———. *Strategy and Command: The First Two Years*. United States Army in World War Two: The War in the Pacific. 1962. Reprint, Washington, DC: Center of Military History, U.S. Army, 2000. https://history.army.mil/Portals/143/Images/Publications/Publication By Title Images/S PDF/CMH_Pub_5-1.pdf.

———. "War Plan Orange: Evolution of a Strategy." *World Politics* 11, no. 2 (January 1959): 221–50. https://www.jstor.org/stable/2009529.

"Mutual Defense Treaty between the United States and the Republic of China, December 2, 1954." Avalon Project, Yale Law School. https://avalon.law.yale.edu/20th_century/chin001.asp#art1.

National Defense Panel. *Transforming Defense: National Security in the 21st Century*. Arlington, VA, 1997. Homeland Security Digital Library. https://www.hsdl.org/c/abstract/?docid=438820.

National Security Council. "U.S. Strategic Framework for the Indo-Pacific." 2021. https://trumpwhitehouse.archives.gov/wp-content/uploads/2021/01/IPS-Final-Declass.pdf.

OPNAV Support Section. *Richmond Kelly Turner: Planning the Pacific War*. Washington, DC: Naval History and Heritage Command, 2021. https://www.govinfo.gov/content/pkg/GOVPUB-D221-PURL-gpo171981/pdf/GOVPUB-D221-PURL-gpo171981.pdf.

Palmer, Michael A. *Origins of the Maritime Strategy: American Naval Strategy in the First Postwar Decade*. Washington, DC: Naval Historical Center, 1988.

Paolucci, D. A. "Draft Summary Report of the Long Range Research and Development Planning Program." Lulejian & Associates, February 7, 1975. http://albertwohlstetter.com/writings/19750207-PaolucciEtAl-Draft-LRRDPP.pdf.

Patton, James Matthew. "Air Raid Petropavlovsk—the Drill That Became a Strategy." *Submarine Review*, April 2013, 52–57. https://archive.navalsubleague.org/2013/air-raid-petropavlovsk-the-drill-that-became-a-strategy.

Privratsky, Kenneth L. *Logistics in the Falklands War: A Case Study in Expeditionary Warfare*. Barnsley, Eng.: Pen and Sword Books, 2014.

Putney, Diane T. *Airpower Advantage: Planning the Gulf War Air Campaign, 1989–1991*. The USAF in the Persian Gulf War. Washington, DC: Air Force History and Museums Program, 2004. https://media.defense.gov/2010/May/25/2001330265/-1/-1/0/AFD-100525-065.pdf.

Republic of China Ministry of National Defense. *2019 National Defense Report*. Taipei: Ministry of National Defense, 2019. https://www.ustaiwandefense.com/wp-content/uploads/2025/02/Taiwan-National-Defense-Report-2019.pdf.

———. *2021 Quadrennial Defense Review*. Taipei: Ministry of National Defense, 2021. https://www.ustaiwandefense.com/wp-content/uploads/2025/02/2021-Taiwan-Quadrennial-Defense-Review-QDR.pdf.

———. *2023 National Defense Report*. Taipei: Ministry of National Defense, 2023. https://www.ustaiwandefense.com/wp-content/uploads/2025/02/Taiwan-National-Defense-Report-2023.pdf.

———. *2025 Quadrennial Defense Review*. Taipei: Ministry of National Defense, 2025. https://www.ustaiwandefense.com/wp-content/uploads/2023/09/2025-Taiwan-Quadrennial-Defense-Review-QDR.pdf.

———. "Force Structure Adjustment of All-Out Defense." https://www.mnd.gov.tw/NewUpload/202303/Force Structure Adjustment of All-out Defense_404109.pdf.

———. *Quadrennial Defense Review 2009*. Taipei: Ministry of National Defense, 2009. https://www.ustaiwandefense.com/wp-content/uploads/2025/02/2009-Taiwan-Quadrennial-Defense-Review-QDR.pdf.

———. *ROC National Defense Report 2023*. Taipei: Ministry of National Defense, 2023. https://www.ustaiwandefense.com/wp-content/uploads/2025/02/Taiwan-National-Defense-Report-2023.pdf.

Ross, Robert S. "The 1995–96 Taiwan Strait Confrontation: Coercion, Credibility, and the Use of Force." *International Security* 25, no. 2 (Fall 2000): 87–123. https://www.jstor.org/stable/2626754.

Ross, Steven T. *American War Plans, 1919–1941*. New York: Garland, 1992.

———. *American War Plans, 1941–1945: The Test of Battle*. London: Frank Cass, 1997.

———. *American War Plans, 1945–1950*. London: Routledge, 1996. Kindle.

Scales, Robert H., Jr. T*he United States Army in the Gulf War: Certain Victory*. Washington, DC: Office of the Chief of Staff of the U.S. Army, 1993. https://apps.dtic.mil/sti/pdfs/ADA361975.pdf.

Setzekorn, Eric. *The Rise and Fall of an Officer Corps: The Republic of China Military, 1942–1955*. Norman: University of Oklahoma Press, 2018. Kindle.

Shugart, Thomas. "Mind the Gap: How China's Civilian Shipping Could Enable a Taiwan Invasion." *War on the Rocks*, August 16, 2021. https://warontherocks.com/2021/08/mind-the-gap-how-chinas-civilian-shipping-could-enable-a-taiwan-invasion.

———. "Mind the Gap, Part II: The Cross-Strait Potential of China's Civilian Shipping Fleet has Grown." *War on the Rocks*, October 12, 2022. https://warontherocks.com/2022/10/mind-the-gap-part-2-the-cross-strait-potential-of-chinas-civilian-shipping-has-grown.

Smith, Robert Ross. *Triumph in the Philippines*. United States Army in World War Two: The Pacific War. 1963. Reprint, Washington, DC: Center for Military History, 1993. https://history.army.mil/Portals/143/Images/Publications/Publication By Title Images/T PDF/CMH_Pub_5-10-1.pdf.

Staaveren, Jacob Van. *Air Operations in the Taiwan Crisis of 1958*. Washington, DC: USAF Historical Division Liaison Office, 1962. https://nsarchive.gwu.edu/document/21083-doc-10-taiwan-1958.

State Council of the People's Republic of China. "China's National Defense in the New Era," July 24, 2019. https://english.www.gov.cn/archive/whitepaper/201907/24/content_WS5d3941ddc6d08408f502283d.html.

Stokes, Mark, and Eric Lee. *Early Warning in the Taiwan Strait*. Arlington, VA: Project 2049 Institute, 2022. https://project2049.net/wp-content/uploads/2022/04/Stokes-and-Lee-Early-Warning-in-the-Taiwan-Strait-Project-2049.pdf.

Stokes, Mark, Yang Kuang-shun, and Eric Lee. *Preparing for the Nightmare: Readiness and Ad hoc Coalition Operations in the Taiwan Strait*. Arlington, VA: Project 2049 Institute, 2020. https://project2049.net/wp-content/uploads/2020/09/Preparing-for

-the-Nightmare_Readiness-and-Ad-hoc-Coalition-Operations-in-the-Taiwan-Strait_Stokes_Yang_Lee_P2049_200901.pdf.

Tangredi, Sam J. *Anti-Access Warfare: Countering A2/AD Strategies*. Annapolis, MD: Naval Institute Press, 2013.

Thompson, Drew. "Hope on the Horizon: Taiwan's Radical New Defense Policy." *War on the Rocks*, October 2, 2018. https://warontherocks.com/2018/10/hope-on-the-horizon-taiwans-radical-new-defense-concept.

Tucker, Nancy Bernkopf. *Strait Talk: United States–Taiwan Relations and the Crisis with China*. Cambridge, MA: Harvard University Press, 2009.

UK Ministry of Defense. *Narrative of RAF Operations during the Falklands Conflict 1982*. London: Ministry of Defense Air Historical Branch, 1988. https://www.raf.mod.uk/what-we-do/our-history/air-historical-branch/regional-studies-post-coldwar-narratives/raf-operations-during-the-falklands-conflict-1982/

U.S. Chief of Naval Operations. *The United States Navy in "Desert Shield" and "Desert Storm."* Washington, DC: Department of the Navy, 1991. https://www.google.co.uk/books/edition/The_United_States_Navy_in_Desert_Shield/bskt6MxocdsC?hl.

U.S. Department of Defense. *2022 National Defense Strategy of the United States of America*. Washington, DC: Office of the Secretary of Defense, 2022. https://apps.dtic.mil/sti/trecms/pdf/AD1183514.pdf.

———. "Air Force Future Operating Concept Executive Summary." U.S. Air Force, March 6, 2023. https://www.af.mil/Portals/1/documents/2023SAF/Air_Force_Future_Operating_Concept_exsum_final.pdf.

———. *Joint Operational Access Concept (JOAC) Version 1.0*. Washington, DC: Joint Chiefs of Staff, 2012. https://apps.dtic.mil/sti/pdfs/ADA555385.

———. *Military and Security Developments Involving the People's Republic of China 2024*. Washington, DC, 2024. https://media.defense.gov/2024/Dec/18/2003615520/-1/-1/0/military-and-security-developments-involving-the-peoples-republic-of-china-2024.pdf.

———. *Quadrennial Defense Review 2014*. Washington, DC: Office of the Secretary of Defense, 2014. https://history.defense.gov/Portals/70/Documents/quadrennial/QDR2014.pdf.

———. *Quadrennial Defense Review Report*. Washington, DC: Office of the Secretary of Defense, 2001. https://history.defense.gov/Portals/70/Documents/quadrennial/QDR2001.pdf.

———. *Quadrennial Defense Review Report*. Washington, DC: Office of the Secretary of Defense, 2006. https://history.defense.gov/Portals/70/Documents/quadrennial/QDR2006.pdf.

———. *Quadrennial Defense Review Report*. Washington, DC: Office of the Secretary of Defense, 2010. https://history.defense.gov/Portals/70/Documents/quadrennial/QDR2010.pdf.

———. *Report of the Quadrennial Defense Review*. Washington, DC: Office of the Secretary of Defense, 1997. https://history.defense.gov/Portals/70/Documents/quadrennial/QDR1997.pdf.

———. *Summary of the 2018 National Defense Strategy of the United States of America: Sharpening the American Military's Competitive Edge*, Washington, DC: Office of the Secretary of Defense, 2018. https://media.defense.gov/2020/May/18/2002302061/-1/-1/1/2018-national-defense-strategy-summary.pdf.

U.S. Department of Defense, Air-Sea Battle Office. *Air-Sea Battle: Service Collaboration to Address Anti-Access & Area Denial Challenges*. Washington, DC: Department of Defense, 2013. https://apps.dtic.mil/sti/pdfs/ADA584067.pdf.

U.S. Department of the Navy. *Advantage at Sea: Prevailing with Integrated All-Domain Naval Power*. Washington, DC: Department of the Navy, 2020. https://media.defense.gov/2020/Dec/16/2002553074/-1/-1/0/triservicestrategy.pdf.

———. *A Cooperative Strategy for 21st Century Seapower*, Washington, DC: Department of the Navy, 2007. https://permanent.fdlp.gov/gpo10908/Maritimestrategy.pdf.

———. *Forward . . . from the Sea*. Washington, DC: Department of the Navy, 1994. https://apps.dtic.mil/sti/pdfs/ADA338561.pdf.

———. *Forward, Engaged Ready: A Cooperative Strategy for 21st Century Sea Power*. Washington, DC: Department of the Navy, 2015. https://apps.dtic.mil/sti/pdfs/ADA615292.pdf.

———. *From the Sea: Preparing the Naval Service for the 21st Century*, Washington, DC: Department of the Navy, 1992. https://apps.dtic.mil/sti/pdfs/ADA338570.pdf.

———. *Lessons of the Falklands: Summary Report*. Washington, DC: Office of Program Appraisal, Department of the Navy, 1983. https://apps.dtic.mil/sti/pdfs/ADA133333.pdf.

U.S. Department of State, Office of the Historian. *Foreign Relations of the United States*. 1948–76. https://history.state.gov/historicaldocuments.

U.S. Joint Chiefs of Staff. *Description of the National Military Strategy 2018*. Washington, DC: Chairman of the Joint Chiefs of Staff, 2018. https://www.jcs.mil/Portals/36/Documents/Publications/UNCLASS_2018_National_Military_Strategy_Description.pdf.

———. *Joint Planning*. Joint Publication 5-0. Washington, DC: Joint Chiefs of Staff, 2021. https://irp.fas.org/doddir/dod/jp5_0.pdf.

———. *Joint Strategic Planning System*. Washington, DC: Joint Chiefs of Staff, 2024. https://www.jcs.mil/Portals/36/Documents/Library/Instructions/CJCSI3100.01F.pdf.

———. *Management and Review of Campaign and Contingency Planning*. Washington, DC: Joint Chiefs of Staff, 2019. https://www.jcs.mil/Portals/36/Documents/Library/Instructions/CJCSI3141.01F.pdf.

———. *National Military Strategy 2022: Strategic Discipline*. Washington, DC: Chairman of the Joint Chiefs of Staff, 2022. https://www.jcs.mil/Portals/36/NMS 2022 _ Signed.pdf.

"U.S.-PRC Joint Communique ([August 17], 1982)." American Institute in Taiwan, March 31, 2022. https://www.ait.org.tw/u-s-prc-joint-communique-1982.

Van Atta, Richard H., et al. *Transformation and Transition: DARPA's Role in Fostering an Emerging Revolution in Military Affairs*. Vol. 1, *Overall Assessment*. Alexandria, VA: Institute for Defense Analyses, 2003. https://irp.fas.org/agency/dod/idarma.pdf.

Van Tol, Jan, Mark Gunzinger, Andrew Krepinevich, and Jim Thomas. *AirSea Battle: A Point of Departure Operational Concept*. Washington, DC: CSBA, 2010. https://csbaonline.org/uploads/documents/2010.05.18-AirSea-Battle.pdf.

Villar, Roger. *Merchant Ships at War: The Falklands Experience*. London: Conway Maritime and Lloyd's of London, 1984.

Wada, Tomoyuki. "Japanese Perspective Total War." Research paper presented at the Tenth NIDS International Forum on War History, 2011. https://www.nids.mod.go.jp/english/event/forum/pdf/2011/17.pdf.

The White House. *National Security Strategy*. Washington, DC, 2022. https://www.documentcloud.org/documents/23165487-biden-harris-administrations-national-security-strategy-102022-1/.

———. *National Security Strategy of the United States of America*. Washington, DC, 2017. https://trumpwhitehouse.archives.gov/wp-content/uploads/2017/12/NSS-Final-12-18-2017-0905.pdf.

Wuthnow, Joel, and M. Taylor Fravel. "China's Military Strategy for a 'New Era': Some Change, More Continuity, and Tantalizing Hints." *Journal of Strategic Studies* 46, nos. 6–7 (Mar. 2023): 1149–84. https://doi.org/10.1080/01402390.2022.2043850.

Wuthnow, Joel, and Phillip C. Saunders. "Chairman Xi Remakes the PLA." In *Chairman Xi Remakes the PLA: Assessing Chinese Military Reforms*, edited by Phillip C. Saunders, Arthur S. Ding, Andrew Scobell, Andrew N. D. Yang, and Joel Wuthnow. Washington, DC: National Defense University Press, 2019. https://ndupress.ndu.edu/Portals/68/Documents/Books/Chairman-Xi/Chairman-Xi.pdf.

Wuthnow, Joel, Derek Grossman, Phillip C. Saunders, Andrew Scobell, and Andrew N. D. Yang. *Crossing the Strait: China's Military Prepares for War with Taiwan*. Washington, DC: National Defense University Press, 2022. https://ndupress.ndu.edu/Portals/68/Documents/Books/crossing-the-strait/crossing-the-strait.pdf.

Xi Jinping. "Achieving Rejuvenation Is the Dream of the Chinese People." Speech presented at The Road to Rejuvenation exhibition, November 29, 2012. NEAC. https://www.neac.gov.cn/seac/c103372/202201/1156514.shtml.

Yoshihara, Toshi. *Mao's Army Goes to Sea: The Island Campaign and the Founding of China's Navy*. Washington, DC: Georgetown University Press, 2022. Kindle.

Yung, Christopher D. "Sincia Rules the Waves?: The People's Liberation Army Navy's Power Projection and Anti-Access/Area Denial Lessons from the Falklands/Malvinas Conflict." In *Chinese Lessons from Other People's Wars*, edited by Andrew Scobell, David Lai, and Roy Kamphausen. Carlisle Barracks, PA: Strategic Studies Institute, 2011.

NEWSPAPERS, PERIODICALS, AND ONLINE MEDIA

Air & Space Force Magazine
Air Force Times
Aviation News Magazine
BBC News
Bloomberg
Defense News
Defense One
The Diplomat
DW
Financial Times
Focus Taiwan
Foreign Policy
The Guardian
Japan News
Los Angeles Times
National Defense Magazine
Naval News
New York Times
Politico
Radio Free Asia
Reuters
Sky News
Smithsonian Magazine
The Strategist
Taiwan News
Tapai Times
TASS
Time
USNI News
War on the Rocks
War Zone
Washington Post
Wired

INDEX

Note: page numbers in italics refer to figures.

ABOUT THE AUTHOR

ROWAN ALLPORT is a deputy director at the Human Security Centre, a London-based foreign-policy think tank. Previously a lobbyist in Westminster and a senior analyst for RAND Europe's Security, Defense, and Infrastructure Group, he has addressed audiences at NATO and Royal Navy events and given evidence on defense matters in front of UK parliamentary committees. His publications include *Fire and Ice: A New Maritime Strategy for NATO's Northern Flank* and articles in outlets including *Foreign Policy, The Diplomat,* and *Defense One*. He holds a PhD in politics from the University of York.

www.ingramcontent.com/pod-product-compliance
Lightning Source LLC
Jackson TN
JSHW030818050126
95819JS00001B/1

* 9 7 8 1 6 8 2 4 7 8 0 8 0 *